The Successful Softw Manager

The definitive guide to growing from developer to manager

Herman Fung

BIRMINGHAM - MUMBAI

The Successful Software Manager

Acquisition Editor: Andrew Waldron
Acquisition Editor - Peer Reviews: Suresh Jain
Project Editor: Tom Jacob
Development Editor: Alex Sorrentino
Copy Editor: Safis Editing
Technical Editor: Aniket Shetty
Proofreader: Safis Editing
Indexer: Tejal Daruwale Soni
Graphics: Sandip Tadge
Production Coordinator: Sandip Tadge

First published: June 2019

Production reference: 1270619

Published by Packt Publishing Ltd.
Livery Place
35 Livery Street
Birmingham
B3 2PB, UK.

ISBN 978-1-78961-553-1

www.packtpub.com

Specifications

	Elan S1 & S2	Elan S3
Engine	Four-cylinder in-line	Four-cylinder in-line
Bore & stroke	82.55 x 72.75 mm	82.55 x 72.75 mm
Cubic capacity	1558 cc	1558 cc
Valves	Twin ohc	Twin ohc
Compression ratio	9.5:1	9.5:1
Carburettors	Twin Weber 40DCOE	Twin Weber 40DCOE
Max power models)	105 bhp at 5500 rpm	105 bhp at 5500 rpm (115 bhp at 6000 rpm on SE)
Max torque	108 lb/ft at 4000 rpm	108 lb/ft at 4000 rpm
Transmission	Four-speed manual	Four-speed manual
Final drive	Hypoid bevel 3.9:1 (3.55:1 optional)	3.9:1 (3.77 on later models and 3.55 optional)
Brakes	Girling discs; front 9.5 in, rear 10 in	Girling discs; front 9.5 in, rear 10 in. Servo-assisted on SE
Front suspension	Independent; double wishbones, coil springs, telescopic dampers, anti-roll bar	Independent; double wishbones, coil springs, telescopic dampers, anti-roll bar
Rear suspension	Independent; lower wishbones, coil springs, telescopic dampers	Independent; lower wishbones, coil springs, telescopic dampers
Steering	Rack and pinion	Rack and pinion
Wheels	Bolt-on 4.5J pressed steel wheels (knock-off optional on S2)	Knock-off 4.5J steel wheels
Tyres	5.20 x 13 (later 145 x 13 radial on S1 and S2)	145 x 13 (155 x 13 on SE)
Body & chassis	GRP; steel box-section backbone chassis	GRP; steel box-section backbone chassis

Dimensions

	Elan S1 & S2	Elan S3
Length	12 ft 1 in	12 ft 1 in
Width	4 ft 8 in	4 ft 8 in
Height	3 ft 9.5 in	3 ft 9.5 in (3 ft 10 in on FHC)
Wheelbase	7 ft 0 in	7 ft 0 in
Weight	1410 lb (S2 1485 lb)	1530 lb

	Elan S4	**Elan Sprint**
Engine	Four-cylinder in-line	Four-cylinder in-line
Bore & stroke	82.55 x 72.75 mm	82.55 x 72.75 mm
Cubic capacity	1558 cc	1558 cc
Valves	Twin ohc	Twin ohc
Compression ratio	9.5:1	10.3:1
Carburettors	Twin Zenith-Stromberg 175CD	Twin Weber 40DCOE or twin Dell'Orto DHLA40
Max power	105 bhp at 5500 rpm (118 bhp at 6000 rpm on SE)	126 bhp at 6500 rpm
Max torque	108 lb/ft at 4000 rpm	113 lb/ft at 5500 rpm
Transmission	Four-speed manual	Four-speed manual (five-speed on a few later cars)
Final drive	3.77:1 (3.55 optional)	3.77:1 (3.55 optional)
Brakes	Girling discs; front 9.5 in, rear 10 in. Servo-assisted on SE	Girling discs; front 9.5 in, rear 10 in with servo assistance
Front suspension	Independent; double wishbones, coil springs, telescopic dampers, anti-roll bars	Independent; double wishbones, coil springs, telescopic dampers, anti-roll bars
Rear suspension	Independent; lower wishbones, coil springs, telescopic dampers	Independent; lower wishbones, coil springs, telescopic dampers
Steering	Rack and pinion	Rack and pinion
Wheels	Knock-off 4.5J steel wheels	Knock-off 4.5J steel wheels
Tyres	155 x 13	155 x 13
Body and chassis	GRP; steel box-section backbone chassis	GRP; steel box-section backbone chassis

Dimensions

Length	12 ft 1 in	12 ft 1 in
Width	4 ft 8 in	4 ft 8 in
Height	3 ft 9.5 in (3 ft 10.5 in on FHC)	3 ft 9.5 in (3 ft 10.5 in on FHC)
Wheelbase	7 ft 0 in	7 ft 0 in
Weight	1540 lb	1540 lb

	Elan Plus 2 & Plus 2S	Elan Plus 2S
Engine	Four-cylinder in-line	Four-cylinder in-line
Bore & stroke	82.55 x 72.75 mm	82.55 x 72.55 mm
Cubic capacity	1558 cc	1558 cc
Valves	Twin ohc	Twin ohc
Compression	9.5:1	10.3:1
Carburettors	Twin Weber 40DCOE (twin Zenith-Stromberg on some Plus 2s)	Twin Weber 40DCOE
Max power	115 bhp at 6250 rpm	126 bhp at 6500 rpm
Max torque	108 lb/ft at 4000 rpm	113 lb/ft at 5500 rpm
Transmission	Four-speed manual	Four-speed manual (five-speed on Plus 2S 150/5)
Final drive	3.77:1	3.77:1
Brakes	Girling discs; front/rear 10 in with vacuum servo-assistance	Girling discs; front/rear 10 in with vacuum servo-assistance
Front suspension	Independent; double wishbones, coil springs, telescopic dampers, anti-roll bar	Independent; double wishbones, coil springs, telescopic dampers, anti-roll bar
Rear suspension	Independent; lower wishbones, coil springs, telescopic dampers	Independent; lower wishbones, coil springs, telescopic dampers
Steering	Rack and pinion	Rack and pinion
Wheels	Knock-off 5.5J steel wheels	Knock-off 5.5J steel wheels
Tyres	165 x 13	165 x 13
Body and chassis	Glassfibre reinforced plastic; steel box-section backbone chassis	GRP; steel box-section backbone chassis
Dimensions		
Length	14 ft 0 in	14 ft 0 in
Width	5 ft 3.5 in	5 ft 3.5 in
Height	3 ft 11 in	3 ft 11 in
Wheelbase	8 ft 0 in	8 ft 0 in
Weight	1880 lb (Plus 2S 1970 lb)	1970 lb

The New Elan

Engine	Four-cylinder, in-line 'Isuzu-Lotus' 4XE1-MT (Turbo) or 4XE1-M (NA)
Bore & stroke	80.00 x 79.00 mm
Cubic capacity	1588 cc
Valves	Twin ohc, 16-valve
Compression	8.5:1 (Turbo), 9.8:1 (NA)
Fuel system	Rochester electronic multi-point injection
Max power (Turbo)	165 bhp at 6600 rpm
Max power (NA)	130 bhp at 7200 rpm
Max torque (Turbo)	148 lb/ft at 4200 rpm
Max torque (NA)	105 lb/ft at 4200 rpm
Transmission	Five-speed all-synchromesh manual, front-wheel-drive
Final drive (Turbo)	3.833:1
Final drive (NA)	4.117:1
Brakes	Ventilated 10.0 in disc brakes on front, solid 9.3 in discs on rear with vacuum servo-assistance
Front suspension	Independent; double wishbones, co-axial coil springs, telescopic dampers, anti-roll bar, longitudinal compliance by individual cast aluminium rafts
Rear suspension	Independent; upper link and wide-based lower wishbone, co-axal coil springs, telescopic dampers, anti-roll bar
Steering	Adwest rack and pinion; power assistance standard on Turbo, optional on NA
Wheels	Lotus 6.5J x 15 cast alloy (7J x 16 in US)
Tyres (Turbo)	Michelin MXX2 205/50 ZR 15
Tyres (NA)	Michelin MXV2 205/50 VR 15
Tyres (US)	Goodyear Eagle GS-D 205/45 ZR 16
Body and chassis	VARI-moulded glassfibre reinforced plastic composite; steel backbone chassis attached to front longeron/underframe sub-assembly
Dimensions	
Length	12 ft 9.7 in
Width	5 ft 8.3 in
Height	4 ft 0.4 in
Wheelbase	7 ft 8.6 in
Weight (Turbo)	2392 lb
Weight (NA)	2276 lb
Weight (US spec)	2451 lb

Launch dates of Lotus Elan models

S1 convertible 1500	October 1962	Elan Plus 2S	October 1968
S1 convertible 1600	May 1963	Sprint	October 1970
S2 convertible	November 1964	Elan Plus 2S 130	December 1970
S3 Fixed Head Coupe	September 1965	Elan Plus 2S 130/5	October 1972
S2 convertible, SE	January 1966	Elan production ceased	August 1973
S3 convertible	June 1966	Elan Plus 2 production ceased	December 1974
S3 Fixed Head Coupe, SE	July 1966	New Elan launched	October 1988
Elan Plus 2	June 1966	New Elan production ceased	June 1992
S4	March 1968		

The front number plate partially obscures the 'Lotus mouth' for the radiator intake – a subtle homage to the design of the original Elan by stylist Peter Stevens. Pop-up headlights were de rigueur, all cars from chassis number 6300 having the 'single-pivot' mechanism common to the Esprit and Excel. One turn on the switch behind the right-hand column stalk activates the sidelights, a second turn raises the headlight pods and illuminates dipped beam, while a pull operates the interior lights. The sharply raked front windscreen contributes to the car's slippery aerodynamics

Packt.com

Subscribe to our online digital library for full access to over 7,000 books and videos, as well as industry leading tools to help you plan your personal development and advance your career. For more information, please visit our website.

Why subscribe?

- Spend less time learning and more time coding with practical eBooks and Videos from over 4,000 industry professionals

- Improve your learning with Skill Plans built especially for you

- Get a free eBook or video every month

- Fully searchable for easy access to vital information

- Copy and paste, print, and bookmark content

Did you know that Packt offers eBook versions of every book published, with PDF and ePub files available? You can upgrade to the eBook version at www.packt.com and as a print book customer, you are entitled to a discount on the eBook copy. Get in touch with us at customercare@packtpub.com for more details.

At www.packt.com, you can also read a collection of free technical articles, sign up for a range of free newsletters, and receive exclusive discounts and offers on Packt books and eBooks.

About the author

Herman Fung is an internationally experienced IT manager with hands-on knowledge across the software development life cycle and service management framework. He began his career as a tester and developer with several top-tier IT consultancies, as well as, market leading companies in industry and in government. Since his transition from software developer to manager, he has led global teams and managed notable projects in a variety of sectors, including the first implementation of an open source human resources system with the Ministry of Health in Malawi.

About the reviewer

Tarry Singh is CEO, founder, and AI researcher of AI start-up deepkapha.ai. deepkapha.ai focuses on the following three pillars: AI solutions, AI research, and AI philanthropy.

Tarry has 20 years of experience of working with data and has advised CxOs of global organizations to set up data-driven organizations from scratch. He speaks regularly at global AI leadership summits worldwide and conducts workshops on a regular basis with his **Technical Architects (TAs)** who are currently PhDs in various disciplines such as **Natural Language Processing (NLP)**, computer vision, and robotics.

He also participates in co-supervising deep learning PhD projects related to the previously mentioned areas with the world's leading universities in Germany, US, and China. Tarry is Adj. professor/guest lecturer at University of Texas at Dallas, University of Chicago, Copenhagen University, Charité Berlin, and University of Catalunya at Barcelona. Tarry is a seasoned entrepreneur and is currently also a co-founder of another AI start-up focusing on enterprise data management in the new "dataset economy".

Table of Contents

Preface

This book is a career guide and toolkit for software developers who are considering starting, or have already started, the journey to become a manager. It's a learning experience and journey of discovery on the first read, and a useful handbook containing key information and practical knowledge that you can always refer to throughout your career.

Who this book is for

This book is aimed at software developers and techies who aspire to professionally grow into a more senior position within their organization. It's also for Development Managers, Product Managers, Team Leaders, and Scrum Masters who are settling into their new role.

What this book covers

Chapter 1, *Why Do You Want to Become a Manager?*, asks you a simple yet fundamental question. In answering it, we'll come to understand your "why?" and discuss the pros and cons of embarking on this journey. We'll also address the "imposter syndrome" and, if you're an "accidental manager", discuss how to turn this to your advantage.

Chapter 2, *What Are the Key Skills I Need?*, teaches you the six key skills that I believe all successful software managers need. This includes an introduction to key software and project methodologies, as well as how to land the job of a manager.

Chapter 3, *What is My Job Now?*, is all about getting started as a manager. We'll discuss what to expect in management meetings and how to approach your first day and your first week.

Chapter 4, *A Week in the Life of a Manager*, talks about using a blended approach as the most effective way to learn and build up your manager's toolkit. We'll also talk more about methodologies and introduce the *ITIL Framework*. We start to get really practical and set out a weekly template for how to run a project team, as well as introducing scrum as an effective software development process.

Chapter 5, *Managing Your Team*, is all about managing and dealing with people. We'll discuss the key themes and practical actions of managing your team, lay out some tips for managing your boss, and also introduce ways to manage your peers and customers effectively.

Chapter 6, *Asking the Right Questions to Your Users*, sets the scene for the critical project phase of information gathering. We'll discuss how to define five types of users and the best questions to ask each of them. We'll also use the *five Whys* to get to the root of problems and requirements.

Chapter 7, *Meetings*, is all about the various meetings you will be having as a manager, whether it's an intimate and internal off-duty chat, or a more formal and customer-facing sales meeting and requirements workshop. We'll also discuss how to wow your potential customers with a product demo.

Chapter 8, *Design Techniques*, sets out the various techniques a manager needs to guide their project team to define and design good solutions. We'll also get ultra-practical with tips on how to become a "whiteboard rockstar!"

Chapter 9, *Validating the Solution*, teaches you the different ways to validate your solution. We'll introduce the concept of design thinking and show you how to write a business case and get it signed off.

Chapter 10, *Agile, Waterfall, and Everything in Between*, recaps all of the methodologies we've discussed so far, and introduces the stage-gate process. We'll also set out some proven practical ways to deal with the **Project Management Office** (**PMO**) and how to engage your stakeholders effectively by keeping thing simple and easy to understand.

Chapter 11, *Always Be Shipping*, is about how to launch the product you've built. We'll talk about the importance of the **user acceptance testing** (**UAT**) review and how to sell effectively.

Chapter 12, *The Training Day*, teaches practical ways of approaching the training day and how to handle support requests. We'll also discuss how to approach the problem of a lack of interest in your product from multiple angles.

Chapter 13, *Organizational Management in the 21st Century*, takes you through the important reasons why "the manager who has all the answers" is a myth. The chapter will also introduce five key concepts of self-management, and challenge you to think differently about your own style of management and leadership.

Chapter 14, *Developing Yourself as a Leader*, focuses on the different ways you can improve your emotional intelligence in order to become a better leader. We'll talk about how to establish presence and use nudges to change your team's behaviors. We'll offer some exercises for you to practice and learn more about yourself in the process.

Chapter 15, *Your Next Steps*, addresses the popular query of whether you can still be creative and continue to write code. We'll reference a real-life example to bring this transitional journey to life and prove that it's very achievable. The chapter also contains a comprehensive summary of the entire book.

Get in touch

I'm truly honored and humbled by your interest in this book and I hope that it helps you on your journey toward becoming the successful software manager that you aspire to be. As my valued reader, your honest views matter to me, so I'd be very grateful for your feedback.

General feedback: If you have questions about any aspect of this book, mention the book title in the subject of your message and email us at customercare@packtpub.com.

Errata: Although we have taken every care to ensure the accuracy of our content, mistakes do happen. If you have found a mistake in this book, we would be grateful if you would report this to us. Please visit http://www.packt.com/submit-errata, selecting your book, clicking on the Errata Submission Form link, and entering the details.

Piracy: If you come across any illegal copies of our works in any form on the Internet, we would be grateful if you would provide us with the location address or website name. Please contact us at copyright@packt.com with a link to the material.

If you are interested in becoming an author: If there is a topic that you have expertise in and you are interested in either writing or contributing to a book, please visit http://authors.packtpub.com.

Reviews

Please leave a review. Once you have read and used this book, why not leave a review on the site that you purchased it from? Potential readers can then see and use your unbiased opinion to make purchase decisions, we at Packt can understand what you think about our products, and our authors can see your feedback on their book. Thank you!

For more information about Packt, please visit packt.com.

1

Why Do You Want to Become a Manager?

You're a confident and brilliant developer / coder / programmer / engineer / techie. So, why do you want to become a manager?

If you are on your way to becoming a manager, or you're thinking of starting your journey to become a manager, then this book will give you all the insights, tools, and techniques that you will need for your journey.

This book is your ultimate guide to the journey of becoming a manager and a leader of a technical team. I share my own unique experiences so that you can learn from my own journey. You can take my successes and make them your own, and you can hear learn how to avoid the mistakes I made along the way.

Developers have a wide range of skills, and usually this includes a great capacity for logic. I'll show you how to utilize this key strength, and together we'll plan the *Developer-to-Manager* journey as logically and methodologically as possible.

We're going to launch our journey in this first chapter, by exploring together the fundamental and positive reasons that are driving you forward to become a manager. By taking a balanced view of the pros and cons of becoming a manager, as well as the outcomes and impacts, we'll be able to pinpoint exactly where you are, and how you got here so far, in terms of your career. This will give you a clear sense of what your current course and trajectory are, as well as your natural tendencies, your likes, and dislikes. These are the most important factors for you to think about.

Over the course of this journey, we'll also define what your end destination will be, based on key ideas about what a "manager" really is. By analyzing the more human side of being a manager together and exploring key questions – such as whether being a manager means that you need to be *responsible* for a team of real people – we will also demystify some of the common preconceptions you may have about becoming a manager.

So, let's get started! We asked the question, why you want to become a manager? And what if you're part of the "Accidental Manager" phenomenon where you didn't get to choose? How could you use this to your advantage? We'll be answering these questions by the end of this chapter.

Start with "why?"

You're a confident and brilliant developer / coder / programmer / techie. So, why do you want to become a manager?

Like everything in life – from both a professional and personal perspective – the real reasons behind your motivations, and the ultimate decision you make to really change and move forward, is fundamental to succeeding. As TED speaker and author, Simon Sinek, puts it best:

You must start with "Why?"

Finding your own "why" can be a wondrous journey, but that journey is not a defined process. Unlike software development, this journey is different for everyone. My own journey took five years, three jobs, and four managers. And my journey is still continually evolving even to this day. Every day, I'm still learning to balance a hands-on techie approach, and a hands-off manager approach – and the various combinations in between. In fact, the one thing that I've learned is that different requirements and situations require a different mix.

So, you must be honest with yourself. Do you want a bigger salary? Higher prestige? More learning and development? Or simply the challenge of trying something new? Are you even a little bored with being *just* a developer? Your *why* sits in the middle of your *Golden Circle*, as set out by Simon Sinek.

The *Golden Circle* model can be seen in *Figure 1.1*. It sets out the layers and relationships between your innermost values and your outermost physical behaviors, and it's like an onion. Knowing *why* you are doing something is the most powerful driving force behind any movement:

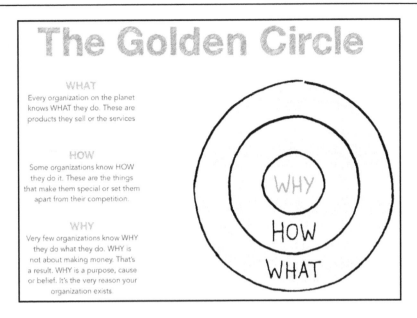

Figure 1.1: A rendition of the *Golden Circle*, as set out by Simon Sinek

Now, feeling bored or unchallenged, and yearning for a new test, would be more of an inner driver, while having more money, a grander title, or greater power would be more of an outer driver. It's vital here to understand what the cause is, and what the effect is, because there's nothing wrong with wanting the results of your labor but you need to be looking in the right places for the rewards you want.

If your singular aim is to earn more money, then there are alternative methods for achieving this – you could work in sales, because, simplistically speaking, more sales will lead to more money.

If you genuinely want to be a great manager, then your journey from *Developer-to-Manager* needs to be a sustainable and meaningful endeavor – because you will need to really know what is your *why*. If you don't, then you you'll run the risk of failing, regressing, and being typecast as a techie who can't do anything else. In short, you must know your inner cause!

The pros and cons of becoming a manager

It's always important to consider as many factors as possible when deciding to undertake this journey. So, let's take a balanced view and explore both the pros and cons of becoming a manager.

The road ahead to becoming a manager is quite complex. The journey requires navigation, planning, and a mindful acceptance that you might make a wrong turn here and there before you reach the finish line. Without this planning, you're likely to get very frustrated and give up at the first hurdle. For some people, that's enough to decide that they don't want to take the journey.

You should certainly consider whether becoming a manager advances your career, your happiness, or perhaps a mixture of both. Likewise, whether your journey will be slow or fast, because balancing your professional and personal ambitions can be difficult to achieve along the road ahead. At times, you will need to concentrate on one of your ambitions and sacrifice or postpone your other ambitions.

This might already be true in your life now as a developer, but by becoming a manager, you risk your work taking over more of your life than you might expect. For example, you might suddenly find yourself bringing home emotional baggage from the office, because being a manager can put you in challenging people situations. While taking these manager type challenges home for some private contemplation may ultimately help you achieve a better outcome, it comes at a price of less personal space and downtime to relax for your own wellbeing. And of course, some situations may also affect you very directly and emotionally.

Another consideration is whether becoming a manager fits your natural talents, and whether you think you'll be any good at being a manager. At the end of the day, we are all different, and our talents are all unique; everyone has their own unique set of strengths and weaknesses, and their own likes and dislikes.

Being a developer is different from being a manager in that your focus will change from writing code yourself to helping others write quality code. As we've already mentioned, people are different – so some of us will naturally be more suited to becoming a manager than others.

It's also quite natural to worry that since you're a good developer you might not be so good at being a manager. Why become a manager and potentially stop doing what you're doing so well? There are so many things that you can learn about software development. But the biggest consideration is most probably, *what if you fail?*

Your attitude and tolerance for risk-taking

Everyone's attitude and tolerance for risk-taking will be different. Some people take a more gung-ho, or "go big or go home!" stance, while others take necessary comfort in making smaller, incremental changes.

It is quite natural to worry that if you don't succeed at becoming an effective and respected manager, then it will be a personal failure, and all the negative things associated with that. You might worry about then being viewed as a techie who just didn't make it as a manager; or having a below-par performance appraisal; perhaps even getting less bonus pay as a result, or a negative mark on your résumé and reputation.

But just imagine that worst-case scenario again, where you don't become a manager, or you fail as a manager. Would it really be considered a setback by others? And, most importantly, by you? There is always a possibility that a future employer will ask you questions such as the following:

- What happened?
- Why did you go back to being a developer?

Sure, it's important to acknowledge this possibility and be prepared to answer such questions directly, even if the answer is that it was not such a positive experience, and you reply with an answer as clear as this: *it just wasn't for me.*

In favor of making the *Developer-to-Manager* journey, there are also numerous things to consider. First and foremost is dealing with the perception of failure. If your attitude to risk-taking is more like the entrepreneurial Silicon Valley style of thinking, then you may acknowledge and accept that failure is part of succeeding. Failing at multiple start-ups is considered a necessary step toward setting up a successful, and hopefully billion-dollar, "unicorn" business.

It's a badge of honor and follows a "you win, or you learn" mindset. When an athlete suffers a severe injury or crushing defeat, they learn from the experience to improve and avoid losing again. This positive mental attitude toward risk-taking is rare and will be recognized by more insightful managers and people in general, which will put you in good stead as a manager or a developer.

Now just for a minute, put yourself in an interviewer's position. One candidate has done the same type of development, at the same level, for their entire career. Meanwhile, another candidate has learned multiple technologies and has also tried becoming a manager. Which candidate would you think has more of a story to tell? Which would you consider to be a more rounded professional? So, whether you absolutely nail becoming a manager first time or not at all, it can still be considered progress.

As former U.S. President, Barack Obama, eloquently puts it:

"Progress is not a straight line."

His takeaway point reinforces the idea that the *Developer-to-Manager* journey is not a predefined process. Imagine the best-case scenario: you've made the successful transition from *Developer-to-Manager*, whenever that may be; and you've obtained the added pay, the job satisfaction, and the recognition you wanted. Now, do a retrospective review and ask yourself: *What was the best part of my journey?*

For me, the best part of my journey was the personal growth I attained by meeting all the new challenges along the way. I was truly stretched beyond what I thought I could achieve. I used to think that I wanted nothing more than to be left alone to write the programs I wanted to write, and to hell with anybody else: my goal was to be the master of my own domain, however large or small it was. However, once I began my journey, I started dealing with people from across a huge spectrum and working on issues not caused or fixed by code. My horizons were broadened as a result, and my confidence to connect with people socially grew exponentially.

Looking back, if I hadn't made the journey, I could easily see myself still doing the same job, albeit as much more of an expert! By understanding these considerations, and knowing the best-and worst-case scenarios, you'll understand all the important steps to discovering your *why*, which is the fundamental reason and driving force behind the *Developer-to-Manager* journey.

Where am I and how did I get here?

Understanding your innermost desires and drivers that lead to you wanting to make this journey is a crucial step. To help discover your inner cause, it's often useful to look back and review your work history.

Let's take a minute to sit back to ask ourselves – and you may even want to write your own personal answers down to these – the following questions:

- How many jobs have I had?
- How often have I changed jobs?
- How many companies have I worked for?
- Have they been in vastly different businesses or sectors?
- Did I instigate these changes, or did they happen to me because someone else made a decision that affected me, such as redundancy?

The answers to these questions are all key indicators. If you have proactively changed jobs frequently, it's a likely sign that you are searching for something more, and is a sign of your curiosity, inquisitive nature, or even that you easily get bored, depending on how positively you choose to look at it! Either way, it's a sign.

If you don't change jobs regularly, or if you've worked in a variety of organizations, then perhaps you love what you're already doing, or simply feel comfortable and safe in your current environment. This is not negative; a safe and secure environment can actually be a wonderful place to start your journey.

Perhaps you've been asked to make the change by someone else. Sometimes, we all need a nudge, a pep talk, or even to be forced into something we didn't think we were capable of or think we would even enjoy. This acts as another possible starting point. The "Accidental Manager," which we'll explore in more detail throughout this book, is often associated with this scenario.

Each starting point has its own merits, advantages, and disadvantages. Whatever you do, don't let your own starting point become a psychological barrier to actually starting. Choose to see it as a springboard, and as a source of infinite possibilities, which it is. It would be extremely boring if everyone's journey started at the same place and followed the exact same path!

It is also important to note that this journey is not a race. Like the projects you've been working on, time is only one part of the *time, cost, and quality* triangle, which is also known as the *Project Triangle* and *Triple Constraint*. I honestly believe that if you focus on quality, your journey will ultimately be more fruitful. After all, this is your career we're talking about, which is not just another project!

Achieving true quality requires commitment in many ways. You will be able to appreciate the quality of your own journey first-hand through your subjective experiences along the journey you're going to take. You'll also see how the reality of your journey compares to your expectations, and you'll experience other people's responses to your journey.

Let's talk about time scale. The *Developer-to-Manager* journey is not a single leap or overnight transformation. It's okay to be spurred on by quick wins and instant gratification. Just understand that they're not the be-all and end-all, since making a change from being a developer to a manager is a journey, and, as with any journey, it's important to have checkpoints and milestones along the way.

All these checkpoints would be useful tools that allow you to gauge your progress, whatever that may mean to you. Overall, you must be willing to be in it for the long haul, because you don't know how long the journey will ultimately be. The adage that *it's about the journey, not the destination,* is absolutely true.

The cost of the journey

The cost of your journey can be considered mainly to be the effort you put in. This is the blood, sweat, and tears you will spill along the way. For instance, even reading this book can be considered part of the cost of your journey! You must decide how much you are willing to spend, or not, or, more sensibly, how much you are willing to invest, in balance with time and quality.

Practically speaking, if you choose to invest in some extra training, which is rarely a bad idea, it may cost you some money. However, one of the more likely reasons why you might be considering becoming a manager is the usually associated higher salary and benefits package. So, in the long term, there shouldn't be much of a direct financial cost.

Whether or not a manager is worth more to a company than a developer is a highly subjective debate and a topic for deeper discussion. By accepting industry norms, it's safe to say that a manager can normally command a higher salary than a developer, whom they may well manage. There are exceptions to this, some of which I have experienced myself, but looking at a respectable independent salary benchmark for the overall picture, then this is a clearly defined position for most companies. If you look at *Glassdoor*, which provides a real-world, data-driven view of the average salaries for various jobs, then you'll see that this is the case.

Are you ready to become a manager?

So, where are you now in relation to the *Developer-to-Manager* journey? If you have been able to answer all the questions at the start of this chapter, then you should have some indicators already in your mind about your answer.

This jumping-off point is crucial to any plan. In Chapter 2, *What Are the Key Skills I Need?*, I will provide you with more answers and also give you clear directions on how to start your journey.

Of course, you may already be more of a manager than you realize! It's quite likely that you already do some of the things that managers do in your current work. This could cover anything from reviewing someone's timesheet, performing a document review, putting together a presentation, or sitting on a committee. This is likely to be informal, and you may not even have noticed or realized that it is managerial work. So, my point is that you may already have started your journey more than you think.

Breaking down your working week

You can analyze how much you might already be a manager, by breaking down your typical week to understand how much of what you do is pure software development versus anything else.

You could try putting anything that is not regarded as pure software development, or personal learning and development, into the "managerial" category. The goal here is to give you a rough idea of how much time you currently spend not doing software development, and how much time you already spend doing management-related tasks.

The answers you get might just surprise you. One tried and tested way to analyze your time is with the Time Log method devised by Peter Drucker in his ground-breaking book, *The Effective Executive.* You can break down your working time into 15-minute units, and you classify them into a particular purpose or category, such as coding and managerial. You may be pleasantly surprised at how much managerial work you already do, and even enjoy!

To make it even more scientific and discerning, you could make a simple side-by-side comparison between the average week of a manager you respect and your own week. Better still, speak with them to understand what their typical week looks and feels like. The idea is to gauge how much overlap there is between you as a developer, and them as a manager.

What jobs are there?

What does the phrase "a manager" really mean anyway? It means different things to different people, and it is often overused for anything that isn't an analyst-level position! So, as common as the term is, it's worthwhile for you to define what the phrase "a manager" really means, especially in the context of software development.

A simple distinction that I have used to illustrate the difference between an analyst and a manager is that while an analyst identifies, collects, and analyzes information, a manager uses this analysis and makes decisions. Or more accurately, a manager is responsible and accountable for the decisions they make.

The structure of software companies is now enormously diverse and varies a lot from one to another, which has an obvious impact on how the manager's role and their responsibilities are defined, which will be unique to each company.

Even within the same company, this is subject to change from time to time, as the company itself changes. Broadly speaking, a manager within software development can be classified into three categories, as we will now discuss.

Team leader / manager

This role is often a lead developer who also doubles up as the team spokesperson and single point of contact. They'll typically be the most senior and knowledgeable member of a small group of developers, who work on the same project, product, and technology.

There is often a direct link between each developer in the team and their code, which means the team manager has a direct responsibility to ensure the product as a whole works. Usually, the team manager is also asked to fulfill the people management duties, such as performance reviews and appraisals, and day-to-day HR responsibilities.

Development / delivery manager

This person could be either a techie or a non-techie. They will have a good understanding of the requirements, design, code, and end product. They will manage running workshops and huddles to facilitate better overall teamwork and delivery. This role may include setting up visual aids, such as team / project charts or boards.

In a matrix management model, where developers and other experts are temporarily asked to work in project teams, the development manager will not be responsible for HR and people management duties.

Project manager

This person is most probably a non-techie, but there are exceptions, and this could be a distinct advantage on certain projects. Most importantly, a project manager will be process-focused and output-driven. They will focus on distributing tasks to individuals. Project managers are not expected to jump in to solve technical problems, but they are responsible for ensuring that the proper resources are available, while managing expectations.

Specifically, project managers take part in the project budget, timeline, and risks. They should also be aware of the political landscape and management agenda within the organization and be able to navigate through them.

The project manager ensures that the project follows the required methodology or process framework mandated by the **Project Management Office** (**PMO**). Project managers will not have people-management responsibilities for project team members.

Being an Agile practitioner

As with all roles in today's world of tech, these categories will vary and overlap. They can even be held by the same person, which is becoming an increasingly common trait. They are also constantly evolving, which exemplifies the need to learn and grow continually, regardless of your role or position.

If you are a true *Agile* practitioner, you may take issue with these three generalized categories, and you'd be right to do so! These three categories are most applicable to an organization that practices the traditional *Waterfall model*. Without diving into the everlasting *Waterfall* versus *Agile* debate, let's just say that these are categories that transcend any methodologies.

Even if they're not referred to by these names, they are the roles that need to be performed, to varying degrees, at various times. For completeness, it is worth noting one role specific to *Agile*, that of the scrum master.

Scrum master

A scrum master is a role often compared – rightly or wrongly – with that of the project manager. The key difference is that their focus is on facilitation and coaching, instead of organizing and control. This difference here is as much about a mindset than it is a strict practice and is often referred to as being attributes of *Servant Leadership*.

I believe a good scrum master will show traits of a good project manager at various times, and vice versa. This is especially true in ensuring that there is clear communication at all times and the team stays focused on delivering together.

Yet, as we look back at all these roles, it's worth remembering that with the advent of new disciplines such as big data, blockchain, artificial intelligence, and machine learning, there are new categories and opportunities to move from a developer role into a management position, for example, as an algorithm manager or data manager.

Does being a manager mean managing people?

Despite what the word itself suggests, being a manager and having to manage people is, in fact, a misnomer. The modern English word is derived from the Latin word *manus*, which means *hand*, as in control, and does not include the meaning of *man*, as in a *person*. The meaning of the word manage in common usage has today evolved to essentially meaning to be responsible for, and in control of, a bunch of *stuff*.

I'll start by saying that managing people is something you should always prepare yourself for, because, regardless of whether direct team management is part of your role, you will always have a part to play in managing stakeholders, who are people. However, it's best not to confuse people management with stakeholder management, which is a topic all on its own and will be covered later in this book.

Back to the original question: does being a manager mean managing people? The answer in fact depends upon your exact job or role. Using the broad categories – Team / Development / Project Manager – that we've previously set out, your involvement and level of people management responsibility will differ at various times. Let's explore this question of people management one step further now by thinking about Maslow's hierarchy.

Maslow's hierarchy of needs

It's vital that you, your team members, as well as other managers, understand and agree on their responsibilities. This means defining what responsibilities people have, and where they begin and end for each person.

This clarity is important because it sets everyone's expectations accordingly. This sounds simple and easy but in reality, it is exceedingly difficult. There are several reasons why it's more difficult than it looks, and not the least of these is because people's needs change all the time!

Specifically, we are talking about higher-level needs, as defined in *Maslow's hierarchy of needs*, of which you can see a representation in *Figure 1.2*. These are essentially emotional needs, which sit above the basic physiological needs such as air, water, food, sleep, and shelter. Our basic physiological needs change all the time, from our choice of food to where we live, so, as you would expect, the higher level needs also change. Moreover, these higher needs are complex and deeply personal:

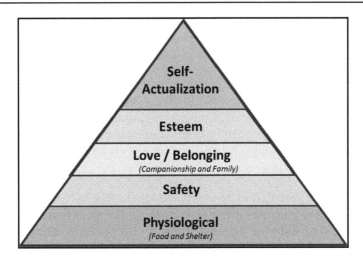

Figure 1.2: Abraham Maslow's hierarchy of needs

An example of applying the concepts from Maslow's hierarchy of needs can be dealing with a friend, because what you do to make them happy is different depending on their physical and mental state.

If they're sad, they may need a shoulder to cry on. If they're happy, they may need someone to share and celebrate with. If they're tired, you might provide them with somewhere to rest. Sometimes, however, what they really need is the opposite of what you might think! Your very tired friend might need some fresh air and exercise to reinvigorate them, rather than you simply providing them with somewhere to rest!

You don't have to be a psychologist

Being a people manager doesn't mean you have to become a professional psychologist or therapist. But like being a good friend, you need to be understanding and adaptable to their needs. It's about understanding their needs as well as your own, and, at times, putting their needs before yours. Knowing the boundaries of both your responsibility as a people manager, and what your team member does and doesn't want to share, is also particularly important. Everyone needs privacy, and everyone's ideas and limits of privacy are different.

I have discussed some very deep and personal thoughts and issues with individual team members, which include positive and negative feelings, ranging from delight and love, to hate and grief.

However, it's important to note that some team members prefer only to discuss work and keep most things private, and in general, there's no right or wrong, or even a magic formula for this. It's about what feels appropriate for you and them.

One aspect that is often forgotten about is the possible gap or overlap between people managers. In an era where we are all constantly busy and time-poor, there is a real risk of having only superficial, ticking-the-box, transactional dialogue. Far worse, a one-to-one meeting turning into a monologue with only the manager talking! Moreover, since people management is all about understanding and giving your team member what they really need, this can be counterproductive.

This is especially true in a matrix management structure, where a person can have multiple managers. If the managers involved are not clear on what aspect they are responsible for, or neglect that responsibility, then the person ultimately may not be managed appropriately. Conversely, as the old saying goes, "Too many cooks spoil the broth." If a person is ill and cannot come into work, having multiple managers call to ask, *How are you?* or *What's wrong?* will most likely be counterproductive.

The art and science of people management is a remarkably interesting and broad topic, and while there is no magic formula or one-size-fits-all approach, there is an entire range of research and tools. Like a good developer, a good manager will also have a suitable toolkit, which we will discuss in more detail throughout this book.

The "Accidental Manager"

The "Accidental Manager" is perhaps ubiquitous now more than ever, but the concept has been around for a long time. The *Peter Principle*, by Laurence J. Peter, introduced the concept that people successful in their role are promoted until they reach a level where they are no longer competent, and that was published back in 1969!

This idea was further popularized by the *Dilbert* cartoons, in which the *Dilbert Principle* mocks the notion that the least competent people are given more managerial responsibilities and power, which is often misused. Quite simply, the "Accidental Manager" can be characterized by a person who reluctantly, unknowingly, unintentionally, or inadvertently becomes a manager.

Perhaps the people management responsibility has defaulted to the "Accidental Manager" because the incumbent manager is too busy, or perhaps the organization has created the new position and has mandated that a person from the existing hierarchy and team takes on the post.

It is of course possible that the manager position has been removed altogether to reduce headcount, but all their responsibilities still need to be picked up by someone, or perhaps the organization has struggled to recruit for this position from the labor market, and "you're it" until they find someone better! There are many circumstances where an accidental manager is created.

In the organization's defense, from their perspective, succession and continuity are rarely easy. Taken to the extreme, the alternative would be to promote someone who is clearly struggling in their current role. Out of the two choices, it's logical to opt for the seemingly more reasonable option. So, if you are an accidental manager, take it as a compliment and confidence booster. It's in your organization's interest to set you up to succeed, and there are people who believe you are capable of becoming a manager.

Rewarding underperformance, as opposed to achievement, could be seen as a blow to the morale of others and a cultural disaster affecting the organization's core people values. It would be a realization of the *Dilbert Principle*! Ask yourself the following questions:

- You're a brilliant developer. Can you manage the team as well?
- You're a brilliant developer. Can you manage some projects, too?

So, what does all this mean to you, and how can you understand it and use it to your advantage? For argument's sake, let's say you are a brilliant developer, probably the best among your peers as recognized by the organization. In that case, there's a chance you could become an accidental manager if the circumstances arise, and perhaps you already are. Being an accidental manager can be interpreted as a purely negative thing, a lesser version of what you may think of as being a "real manager," but let's be clear - it is not!

Circumstances create the accidental manager, but they don't define the person in this position. The key to making this accidental journey a success is to embrace it and get the required training and support – as little or as much as you need, when you need it.

The Johari Window

Recognizing that you may not know what you need is an important first step. It is also an ongoing management skill to learn as you develop, which we will discuss later in the book. So, part of the support structure you will need around you is someone who will constructively point out your blind spots.

Everybody has blind spots, so spot them early instead of ignoring them. In fact, the Johari Window, which you can see in *Figure 1.3,* allows you to think about your own strengths and weaknesses, your blind spots, and ways or people that can help detect them:

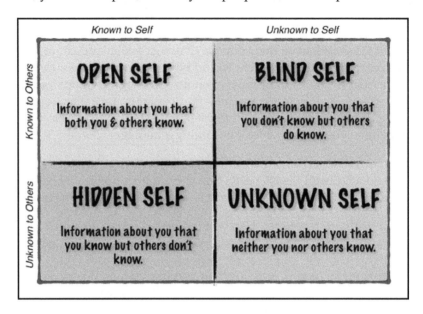

Figure 1.3: Johari Window
Source: https://www.successfulculture.com/build-more-self-awareness-stronger-culture-using-johari-window/

Hacking the impostor syndrome

One key thing for all managers to avoid, but especially for accidental managers, is what technologist and writer Peter Gillard-Moss calls *imposter syndrome*. This is when an often newly promoted manager feels compelled to show that they know everything, even when they don't.

When imposter syndrome sets in for a manager, an array of negative behaviors and impacts can result, including becoming ever more insecure about your position of responsibility and alienating your own team because you're killing their motivation to collaborate and be creative. Not to mention that the manager is stressing themselves out by trying to stay on this treadmill, which only goes faster and faster, even if they're still going at the same speed. The most common way to be a victim of imposter syndrome is to believe that your superior technical ability and/or experience entitles you to be a manager and to lead.

A simple hack to avoid imposter syndrome is to recognize and admit that there will always be things you don't know and aren't even aware that you don't know! This is what makes the journey interesting, and you should never be in denial that there is still so much to learn, no matter how much you think you already know.

The Rumsfeld Matrix

On the other hand, it is important to keep this in balance with what you do know. One of the key tools to achieve this is the Known/Unknown matrix, or *the Rumsfeld Matrix*, which was made famous by Donald Rumsfeld, the former U.S. Secretary of Defense. This chart can be a valuable tool to track your progress and ongoing development as a manager.

The first version you produce will give you an idea of where you need to focus your efforts on learning initially, and, as you repeat the exercise regularly, you can use it to assess your proportion of knowns and unknowns.

As you become more experienced and confident as a manager, you will trend toward more knowns versus unknowns. The idea is not to eliminate all unknowns, but to simply understand what they might be, while affirming and reaffirming the things you are knowledgeable and confident on. Here is an image of the Rumsfeld Matrix:

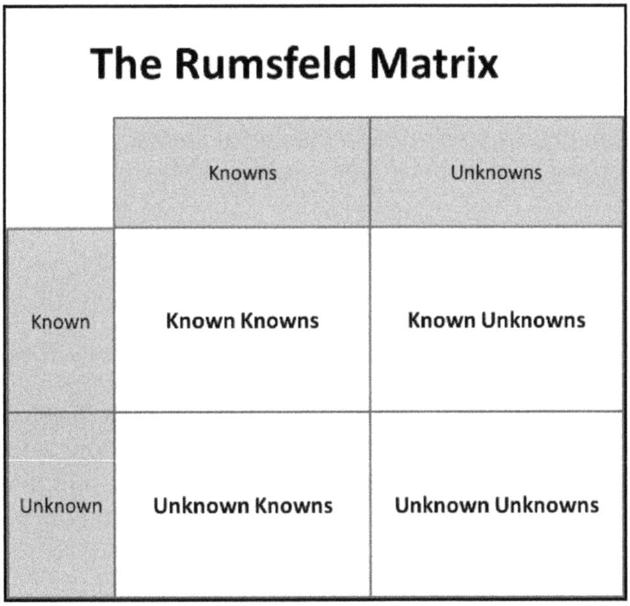

The Rumsfeld Matrix		
	Knowns	Unknowns
Known	**Known Knowns**	**Known Unknowns**
Unknown	**Unknown Knowns**	**Unknown Unknowns**

Figure 1.4: The Rumsfeld Matrix

As an accidental manager, you may not have had the time or opportunity to prepare for the new responsibilities to shape the role before being "it." You can, and should, use this to your advantage. As a newly bestowed accidental manager, you need to maximize the opportunity to ask open and unassuming questions. Tell people that while you don't know something, you want to learn, using open questions like these:

- Where can I get more information on this?
- What are the pros and cons of this process?
- Can you help us to improve this?

Ultimately, as you learn more, your proportion of unknowns will decrease, while the proportion of knowns will increase. As a result, you'll progress along the learning curve, which is no different from learning a new technology as a developer.

When you start, you are likely to have more unknowns than knowns, and you'll be asking more questions than answers. But don't – and never let yourself – be put off! You are still adding value by asking these questions, both to yourself and to the team and organization.

In fact, asking the right questions is often cited as the most important and powerful skill in senior management. This is often referred to as part of corporate governance. Think about the latest corporate scandals and crises in large-scale organizations, which are often traced back to a lack of adequate corporate governance. Those at the very top can fail to recognize the impending cliff edge that the organization is headed toward until it's too late.

To be reasonable, a manager is not expected to know absolutely everything that is happening at any one time. This reinforces the need to ask judicious questions at the right moment, and, in return, getting truthful and insightful answers back. Especially as an accidental manager, one of the key behaviors you should learn and demonstrate early on is the canny shrewdness to ask challenging questions. This has the power to make people respect you, even if your domain knowledge level is low.

Summary

Transitioning, growing, progressing, or simply changing from a developer to a manager is a wonderfully rewarding journey that is unique to everyone. I hope you now have a better idea of your personal response to the original fundamental question that we asked in the introduction.

Just for a minute, think back to the opening of this chapter. It was a thought-provoking statement that said that *you're a confident and brilliant developer / coder / programmer / techie. So, why do you want to become a manager?*

Just as in software development, there is not necessarily a right or wrong way to answer this question. If you are still struggling to answer this, that's perfectly okay. There are a lot more ideas and considerations to think about, which we will cover throughout the upcoming chapters.

It's important to note that it is completely normal to have reservations and even doubts anywhere along the journey to becoming a manager. Having doubts at the start is not only normal, but also potentially advantageous because it's always good to fail fast, learn, and improve. It's the Holy Grail of a more efficient feedback loop, just like in software development.

If you do have a definitive answer to this question and are eager to start your journey, then that's great too. Once you know what *your way* is, that being whatever is at the center of your motivations, everything can be rooted in these foundations. Whether it's more money, power, responsibility, kudos, or something entirely different, it must be clear and convincing enough to keep you motivated for the long haul. *The Golden Circle* by Simon Sinek is a simple model that can help you to frame your thoughts and guide yourself toward your *why*.

Overlaying your risk-versus-reward considerations on top of your *why* will give you a solid base to decide whether, and how, you should set off on your transitional journey to becoming a manager. Most importantly, this will help you understand the impact of your decision. Be prepared to answer the critical question: "What if you fail constructively?" Remember that progress is not a straight line, and you should always be willing to accept that there are risks that go with the rewards.

In planning your journey, knowing where you currently are is a vital step, just like a navigator getting their position and bearings. By doing a focused retrospective review on your career so far, you will learn more about yourself – specifically, your preference and tolerance to less technical, more managerial tasks. By doing a little analysis of your work time, you can gain real insight into whether you are already doing, and enjoying, lots of the managerial tasks.

The legendary management guru Peter Drucker's Time Log method is the perfect tool to quantify and discern your current mix of developer and management work. You will also debunk the notion that becoming a manager is a gargantuan leap, and you can confidently reassure yourself that you already have some experience and achievements to be proud of.

After clarifying what being a "Modern Manager" really means, and the broad categories applicable in software development (Team / Development / Project / Agile manager), the overarching and often key consideration for developers is whether it means they will be managing people and writing less code.

While this is a big and nuanced topic, you can rest assured that it isn't as daunting, or indeed as difficult, as you might think. However, it will require you to be open-minded and receptive to learning new skills along the way, with a focus on fewer technical skills and fewer binary concepts. Consider, as an example, the art of negotiation and stakeholder management.

If the type of manager you wish to become does include the privilege of managing people, then there are extra considerations for you to ponder, because people management is certainly not a trivial responsibility that can be taken lightly.

As a people manager, you have a professional and moral responsibility to lead, protect, nurture, serve, and constructively challenge your team members. This is one of the key areas you will need to have support and mentorship in. So, when you are building your overall support network, finding some extra resources to help you with people management is highly recommended.

To help you tackle each challenge, a comprehensive toolkit for a new developer-cum-manager will be provided and built on across the coming chapters. This is one of the main aims of the book and will include exploring the various elements of managing people in a team. While there's no magic one-size-fits-all formula, there are proven approaches and techniques that can be applied to help you become the best manager you can be.

In today's fast-moving work environment, a common way for a developer to become a manager is often "by accident." The emergence of the "Accidental Manager" is not a new phenomenon. While it is the butt of most Dilbert cartoon jokes, the circumstances in which an accidental manager is created do not define the manager themselves. It can actually create genuine opportunities to ask quality questions from a fresh perspective and add value on a different level.

Look out for imposter syndrome and refrain from succumbing to your insecurities. By using classic and powerful tools such as the Johari Window and the Rumsfeld Matrix, you can become comfortable in knowing your own strengths and weaknesses, your blind spots, and ways that people can help to detect them. Above all, if you do find yourself becoming an accidental manager, take it as a compliment that the company needs you now more than ever, and use it to your advantage!

In the next chapter, *What Are the Key Skills I Need?*, we'll look at the key skills you need to undertake your journey from developer to manager.

2
What Are the Key Skills I Need?

So, you are clear on your *why* – the fundamental reason you want to change your career – and you're now determined to become a manager. You may know exactly which type of manager you want to be, or equally, you may not. But don't worry! There's still time to develop that idea.

Before you can fully prepare yourself mentally, the next set of questions will rush into your head: *What skills will I need*, quickly followed by, *Do I have them?*

Just as in software development, there are no definitively right or wrong answers to these questions. It will be a process to figure out your own answers, and, as soon as you do, the situation will evolve. It's a never-ending cycle of discovery and re-discovery, which is very much a good thing. But to help you to make a start, here is my list of the top six key skills that I believe are most important for a manager:

1. Flexibility and adaptability
2. Communication, communication, communication
3. Team leadership
4. Stakeholder management
5. Negotiation
6. Using a chosen methodology

These six key skills will see you through nearly all the situations you're going to meet. They are also particularly useful for your *Developer-to-Manager* transition, and they've all been learned first-hand through my own experiences. I'm going to share them with you now in this chapter.

Skill 1 – Flexibility and adaptability

Let's start with flexibility and adaptability. There is an important difference between being flexible and being adaptable. To be a successful manager, I believe you need to have the ability to be both, as they go hand-in-hand, and you will need a combination of both in order to make a meaningful and positive impact on your team, project, or both.

Every developer will already think that they're **flexible**, on some level. This line of thinking grows from their own experiences where they have:

- Delivered something a little bit faster when requested to do so by the Project Manager
- Successfully bent logic to allow more permutations
- Made a calculation in a completely different way after a code review
- Allowed for a different exception handling method, even though it may not be used immediately

These are all things an experienced developer will have done throughout their career – some more willingly and happily than others!

Most developers will also think that they're already **adaptable**, on some level. I worked with a consultant developer once who was constantly asked by the team manager to be responsible for unit testing, and only unit testing. This consultant developer didn't actually do any design or coding at all for the entire project! Kudos to him, not once did he complain about it, even though he was clearly frustrated. He had become the "unit test guy," whose task on this particular occasion was important to the overall project, but to him, personally, was very monotonous.

The key distinction between being flexible and adaptable is that being flexible is a reactive and responsive skill, while being adaptable is proactive, affirmative, and actionable. Both are important, and they work well together.

It's also important to note that being flexible and adaptable are not the same as being versatile. To be versatile is to be like a utility player who can perform in different positions on the pitch. That is a quality and skill in itself, but it's not as relevant in our context.

If an urgent new requirement and change request comes in, then flexibility is about having the capacity within your project's contingency or your team's capacity to accept and accommodate this new requirement, without negatively impacting the project. On a personal level, you're also being flexible if, for example, you're booked for a meeting at 9 a.m., but it's rescheduled at the last minute to a less convenient time for you, and you still attend.

If you must deliver a critical change request without delaying the go-live date, and your project contingency has already been exhausted, what do you do? Well, if you're being adaptable in that situation, then you take corrective action and reallocate your resources and even deprioritize other requirements. You take proactive measures to meet the situation.

When I volunteered for an international development charity called **Voluntary Service Overseas** (**VSO**), the top quality they looked for in candidates during the assessment process was flexibility. The selected volunteers may be sent to a variety of developing countries, which may not be known at the selection stage. They may be working with any type of partner organization, ranging from a remote farming village community to the Ministry of Health, which was the case for me. In this case, you could be working in an isolated and difficult-to-reach place, or even dense urban cities. The challenges are varied and unpredictable. Hence, flexibility is vital in the anticipation that expectations will need to be constantly adjusted and even reset.

The extension to flexibility is adaptability. For example, your local community may not speak English, or whatever your native language is, but communicating with them is vital to both your day-to-day living, such as buying food, as well as the success of your project. So, you have to adapt by learning their language and customs, and even resorting to signing gestures if required! You take action to find a way.

A simple but effective technique for a manager to liven up an otherwise dull and laborious meeting is by introducing the positive element of surprise. This could be a simple interactive quiz with prizes to encourage attendees to participate and share their creative ideas – the crazier, the better!

When you are the manager, you absolutely need both flexibility and adaptability. You need the flexibility to understand each situation and constantly draw on your empathy to appreciate things from the other stakeholder's perspective. And you need the adaptability to act in the required role and make the necessary intervention, which may not be your usual role or choice. Moreover, when you are flexible and adaptable, your team will follow and amplify the impact of this key skill.

Skill 2 – Communication, communication, communication

Communication skills are so important that it's worth repeating! I've repeated it three times because there are three logical parts to communication. Of course, you already communicated plenty when you were a developer.

You wrote emails, spoke on conference calls, and maybe even created reports and presentations and gave pitches.

Your communications have a different mission when you are a manager though. Your communications become less about explaining the logic or business knowledge and more about influencing and conveying visions, ideas, and concepts.

It's important to acknowledge the difference between a factual conversation and an opinion-based conversation that might be based on little or no information. For example, a project management meeting about the allocation of key resources is likely to be highly factual; in contrast, a debate about which candidate to hire may be all about opinion.

As a manager, things are less black and white, and are more various shades of gray. Communication is best explained by grouping it into three different parts:

1. Inbound communication
2. Internal (within team) communication
3. Outbound communication

These focus on the overall communication of the team, which the manager is accountable for. But they also reflect the individual skills the manager should exhibit.

The **SIPOC** model is a popular method of basic process analysis. It starts with a **Supplier**, who provides **Input**, which is then **Processed** to produce **Output**, which is consumed by a **Customer**:

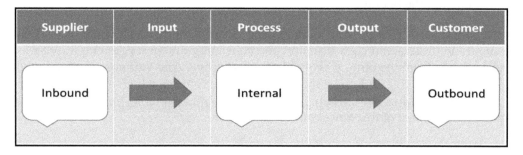

Figure 2.1: The three parts of effective team-based communication can be illustrated by using the popular SIPOC model of analysis

Using the SIPOC model, let's now break down the three key parts of communication: inbound, internal, and outbound.

Inbound communication

Inbound communication is the best place to start because it is often the trigger for internal discussions. The manager's function with inbound communication is not to become the team's only conduit to the outside world, as this would create a single point of failure. It would also create a *Dilbert*-worthy caricature of a micro-manager! However, there is a significant role for the manager to play as a facilitator, interpreter, and, sometimes, moderator.

There are of course very legitimate reasons for some communications to go centrally through the manager of a team or project. For example, work requests can be triaged and shared with the team in a controlled way. This avoids duplication and confusion, which could ensue if the same work request is asked of multiple team members directly without everyone's knowledge.

One of the key inbound communication roles a manager performs is to facilitate the communication process so that the appropriate messages get to the team as quickly as possible. On the other hand, the manager also filters the less-appropriate distractions and not-quite-ready requests, so that the team can focus on what they are currently doing, on the important tasks that are urgent, and, overall, allow them to stay on task.

To be an effective facilitator for inbound communications, the manager must be able to actively listen. The goal here is to spot and, if necessary, debunk any misleading preconceptions. This is a difficult skill to master because even closely aligned colleagues can have very different assumptions about similar things. In an ever-busier work environment, more and more assumptions are made every day due to the pressure on teams to deliver quickly.

I have been on a conference call with international colleagues for 30 minutes before one colleague said they were confused. It turned out that they thought the "DR" meeting was about disaster recovery, as opposed to a dress rehearsal for a go-live date. In this particular global organization, both meanings are used interchangeably depending on context and geography. On this occasion, since the agenda was coordination for code deployment, there was an assumption that this context was understood by a global team who don't work together often. However, it wasn't!

A crucial part of being a manager is being able to discern fact versus opinion and truth versus fiction. This is different from the technical troubleshooting skills you have as a developer, where the answer lies in the code or a bug report, which are both fact-based artifacts.

When you are able to distinguish what and why certain things are being said, your responsibility and challenge are then to understand where the assumptions come from, so you can challenge them constructively if you feel that's appropriate. You can then also re-interpret the message if you need to and convey the right message to the right team members.

As a development team manager, I have encountered situations where a group of project managers all assume that they can secure the same developer to their project at the same time. As difficult as it was, this assumption needed to be challenged in order to avoid mass confusion. Following this, a constructive discussion can determine which projects have highest priority, while also feeding into the developer's view on what is possible.

Internal communication

Once you have facilitated the inbound communication to your team, internal communication is all about opening up enough channels between your development or project team members. This is where it gets really interesting, and where a great manager can add a tremendous amount of value.

Conceptually, imagine a mesh network where all of the nodes are connected to each other directly or indirectly, as opposed to a neat and tidy star shape with the manager sitting in the middle. A manager who is great at communicating will always ensure that every team member can communicate with other team members openly, freely, and quickly, with or without the manager involved.

Depending on the size and complexity of your team, there are various considerations that the manager needs to think about, including geography, language, culture, and personalities. The manager's key role is in enabling meaningful dialog by identifying and removing any barriers that may hinder that process.

For example, it could be as simple as fixing someone's Skype so they can instant message others or establishing a daily huddle for everyone to share what they are working on and what they might need help with. It could even be by enabling them to lighten the mood by giving the team permission to joke around a little in order to break the ice.

This may be a cliché, but it really is good to talk! Even if the amount of talking is taken to the extreme, given a choice between a team who talks too much and a team who talks too little, I would choose the former, every time. In my experience, a lot of talking is a healthy sign and easier to manage than if you were facing the opposite and having to constantly encourage any conversation at all, which could be a danger sign that your team doesn't have a lot in common.

The key to managing the amount of talk or communications within your team to an appropriate level is first of all to be flexible, and then second to know and trust your team to self-regulate that right level. Counter-intuitively, it's actually not your unilateral decision on how much or little the team chooses to talk. However, you do have a say and an oversight for their overall effectiveness.

So, if the team as a whole is ineffective, you can and should provide this as feedback in order to help them to adjust accordingly. By being flexible, it means there is no pre-set level or method of internal communication that is always deemed optimum. Different situations will require different behaviors.

In an "all hands-on deck" situation, you would want an elevated amount of communication and volume, which reflects the urgency and importance. However, a period of less chatter and an overall quieter environment will be more appropriate if there is a critical task that requires individual concentration from separate team members, such as hardcore solo coding to meet a tight deadline.

A nuance to this, which also supports the *more talk is better idea*, is the relationship building effect of more open communication. Something that you may think is uninteresting, insignificant, or inconsequential could be very relevant to another team member. So, while this is not a license to spam other team members, sharing a seemingly minute detail can spark an idea and build rapport. There is a reason why astronauts write everything down in a log, which is then read by other astronauts. When it comes to internal communications, over-communicating is better than under-communicating.

Outbound communication

Getting the outbound communication right is vital for your team's brand and reputation, which contributes to building trust and influence with other teams and stakeholders, as well as your team's own confidence.

After a healthy and constructive internal discussion on an important matter, the outbound message that is then communicated externally should ideally be consistent and coherent. If there is no consensus or agreement internally, then that itself should be communicated, but in an articulate and concise way.

The manager does not always need to be a spokesperson for the team, which would create another single point of failure. Instead, outbound communication can be delivered in a number of ways, and by different team members, which can actually strengthen the message being delivered.

Different people will have different approaches to presenting the same message. Furthermore, the variety itself and simple novelty in having a different person speak up is a powerful tool. A good manager can recognize this phenomenon and the opportunity to use it to empower and develop the team.

Having said that, on some delicate matters, the manager may be the only appropriate person to communicate externally. This can have a big impact on stakeholder management, which we'll come to shortly.

On an individual level, confidence is the key component in delivering an assured and convincing message. The most widely accepted science behind personal communication is the *7-38-55% Rule,* by Dr. Albert Mehrabian. While his research and findings are specific to communications of feelings and attitudes, the simplified formula is still useful because a lot of communication is about feelings and attitudes, like confidence.

When the message is more factual, it's natural that the content or words themselves become more significant, for example, in a release note, bug or performance report, or something more quantitative such as a metrics report. However, how these artifacts are prepared and presented is still important. If a TV newsreader gets their line wrong repeatedly and the line is hesitantly delivered, then you're much less likely to believe the story being reported, even though it may be the truth. Confidence breeds confidence.

If your outbound message to a project steering group is that the project has been delayed, you need to be sure of the reasons and be able to confidently express them and defend them if necessary. Your spoken words, how you say those words, and your facial expression or body language, all affect the audience's confidence level and response, in a ratio of 7-38-55%, respectively.

In the simple pie chart in *Figure 2.2*, you can see that the spoken words element is insignificant in comparison with voice, tone, and body language:

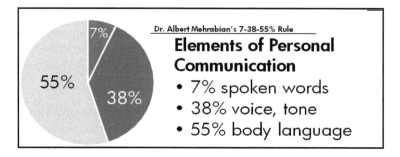

Figure 2.2: The 7-38-55% rule illustrates that how you say something is more important than what you say
Source: http://www.rightattitudes.com/2008/10/04/7-38-55-rule-personal-communication/

Therefore, it is useful to remember that *how* you say something can be more influential than *what* you say. The delivery should always support the content. This makes the recipient's experience more authentic and their impression of the messenger more genuine.

Skill 3 – Team leadership

This skill is particularly applicable to team managers, but a large proportion of it is still applicable and useful for development, and especially project managers, who will be responsible for a project team.

As a new developer-cum-manager, this is likely to be the area where you have the least experience. So, it is vital that you acknowledge and analyze this, through the *Johari Window*, and build and use your support structure. Remember the *impostor syndrome* and consciously work to avoid it through open and honest dialogue with people whom you know well, as well as yourself!

Aspects of team leadership

In our *Developer-to-Manager* context, team leadership is the responsibility and stewardship of a group of developers, where you're looking at the following aspects:

- Wellbeing
- Interests
- Motivation
- Learning
- Development
- Ambitions
- Progression
- Performance
- Value
- Contribution to the team and the organization

This is not an exhaustive list, and it sounds like a lot, which it is! There is a focus here on your team as individuals, and this is because your remit is to get all your team writing more and better code to build a better product. You achieve this by treating them as people and leading the team to become a better version of itself over time.

Don't do everything yourself

There are so many aspects to being responsible for a team of people that the first skill to learn as a manager is to accept that you cannot do everything on behalf of the team.

This also connects back to being flexible and adaptable. Giving yourself permission to not do and complete everything. You should let some things be, and you should occasionally even let something fail, because that can be a liberating experience and a catalyst for better performance and effectiveness – for both yourself and the team.

Similar to starting a new job at a new company, as a newly promoted manager, your natural tendency will be to take on everything, including challenges where others have perhaps failed; work long hours; attend more meetings; talk more; act more like a manager; and generally, take on the world!

This is comparable to the adrenaline rush of an athlete. That initial surge is useful to get you starting out of the blocks fast, but not so useful in the long run. It's certainly not sustainable and can actually be counterproductive in situations where you need composure, calmness, coolness, and clarity of thought.

As the leader of a team, your actions and behaviors set the tone, as well as the boundaries of what is acceptable and unacceptable. You are the example of what is positive and benevolent, as well as negative and malevolent. With this in mind, remember when you were still a developer working for a manager. What exemplified a manager's leadership that was useful to you as a member of their team? Were they frantic, obsessive, and compulsive about every single detailed task? Were they sluggish, dawdling, or indecisive? Or perhaps they were somewhere in the middle and variable according to the situation?

In my experience, finding that middle ground is vital, especially at the beginning of your journey, or at the very least, staying away from being at either end for too long. There may be a time when being more obsessive and devoted is required in order to get an important migration absolutely perfect, or a time when dawdling and being more easy-going is required to enable creativity and unconventional ideas to surface. The key is to be conscious of where you are within the spectrum and deliberately behave in the appropriate way to yield the desired outcome.

Clarity of team responsibilities

Since you will be managing a team of developers, and perhaps some business analysts and architects as well if you become a Project Manager, your individual team members' roles will generally be well defined.

In any case, one of the main responsibilities and essential skills of a manager is to ensure that their team knows what is expected of them. So, establishing a crystal-clear clarity of your team's structure and each member's responsibilities is almost always a valuable exercise.

However, from my experience, I find that new managers have a propensity to shy away from doing this. This can be mostly attributed to the impostor syndrome, where the manager feels it's necessary to assume that everyone knows their role already. With the manager assuming that they themselves already know, or that they need to be seen to know, so then it would be a silly and embarrassing question to ask. But that is exactly what they should do!

Having an honest discussion about the identity and purpose of the team and its members can have multiple positive effects. It improves internal communication by opening up the floor, giving everyone a chance to speak up, and establishing a behavioral norm of discussing anything and everything where necessary. Remember that something obvious to one person may not be to another, and your role as a manager is to facilitate the sharing of knowledge among the team. You may well find that at least one member of your team wasn't fully aware of their roles, or others', and was too nervous to ask.

By openly discussing the team's collective and individual responsibilities, you can also identify and unlock ideas for improvement that were previously hidden.

The only scenario in which reclarifying each team member's responsibilities may not be necessary is when the team and overall organization's culture is so mature that an inherent understanding and fungibility exists without question. This is usually only found in a specialized smaller team, and often in a startup environment, which, by its nature, requires its staff to perform many roles. Therefore, defining an exhaustive list of these roles and responsibilities can be a limiting exercise and end up being counterproductive.

The most widely accepted and well-used method of clarifying responsibilities is the *Responsibility Assignment Matrix*, also known as the *RACI model*. RACI stands for **Responsible**, **Accountable**, **Consulted**, and **Informed**.

ID#	Task Name	Project Owner	Business Subject Matter Expert	Business Analyst	Project Manager	Software Engineer
1	Project Planning and Initiation	A	C	C	R	I
2	Discovery/Inception	I	C	R	I	I
3	Business Requirements	I	C	R	I	I
4	Functional Requirements	I	C	R	I	I
5	Requirements Acceptance	I	C	R	I	I
6	Solution Design and Coding	I	I	C	I	R
7	Solution Testing	I	C	C	I	C
8	Solution Delivery	A	I	C	I	C

Figure 2.3: An example of a project responsibility assignment matrix, or RACI model
Source: http://www.ascendforairlines.com/2016-issue-no-2/right-people-right-places-right-results

If you're managing a large project with many cross-functional team members, it is important that everyone is clear about their roles and responsibilities. The preceding table gives you an example of a RACI table in action.

Document your team services

Last, but not least, and especially for technical teams such as developers, fully documenting the team's service offering and operating model is a great tool to promote your team and engage with stakeholders.

One of the first, if not the very first, thing I now do as a manager is to create a team deck. This is a simple presentation that illustrates what the team does and how it works. It's like a sales brochure, which includes the specifications sheet. It's vital that the deck is kept simple and appropriate for the intended audience, having taken into account their maturity and expectations. But it should also embody and represent the team's own view of itself. So, creating the deck must be a collaborative process, involving the entire team. After all, it is their identity as much as it is yours, and the team as a whole must agree and be proud of it. It is the "team deck," not the "manager's deck."

Like it or not, there will be stakeholders and even colleagues within your department who are unaware of what your team does. So, after the team deck has been created, you have to publish and promote it. This is where your selling skills will be tested. Selling, especially selling an idea, is never easy, especially for a techie developer. So, practice, practice, practice, and refine your presentation until you are confident. Remember the *7-38-55% Rule*, and that confidence breeds confidence. Lastly, keep the deck up to date and current by updating it regularly together with the team.

If you are a Project Manager, you can and should document details of your project team, their roles and responsibilities, and ways of working. This could be included in the **Project Initiation Document** (**PID**) or similar early-stage project artifacts, which will lay out the required resources to complete the project. Such a clear and upfront declaration also helps you to secure those highly valuable resources!

This has a similar effect of both establishing the team as a well-functioning unit, and outwardly promoting it as a group to be respected and listened to.

Skill 4 – Stakeholder management

This is a key skill in most, if not all, careers. As developers or managers, we all have stakeholders to be accountable to and to satisfy by fulfilling their requirements and expectations. Specific to managers, but often forgotten, is the fact that their own team is a key stakeholder. This could be their own development team or a matrix project team.

As we have already discussed *Skill 3 – Team leadership*, which covers the main principles of managing your own team as key stakeholders, for the remainder of this chapter, our focus will be on stakeholder management from a project manager's perspective. This angle covers the remaining key aspects of the essence of stakeholder management, which boils down to building and maintaining relationships, and setting and meeting expectations.

The *Association for Project Management (APM)* explains this best in a simple and logical sequence of four steps:

1. Identify stakeholders
2. Assess their interest and influence
3. Develop communication management plans
4. Engage and influence stakeholders

When identifying stakeholders, you can use a similar approach to the RACI model for your team. But the key here is to make sure that you cast the net wide enough to include the stakeholders who will be indirectly impacted by your work, as well as those directly impacted and actually doing the work; for example, the product owner of an integrated system, and the application support team, if they're a separate entity. All of these people are part of your stakeholder ecology.

The following is a great example of stakeholder ecology for a services company that markets toward travelers. The purpose of constructing a diagram such as this is to widen your focus enough to give yourself as much of a 360-degree view as possible, as well as extending each connection to be long enough to understand the chain reaction and downstream effects of your software products:

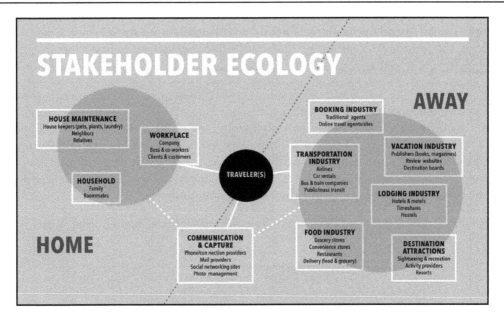

Figure 2.4: An example stakeholder ecology map for a group of travelers
Source: http://sva.isotope221.com/streamline.html

Stakeholder mapping

Once you are confident you have identified all of your stakeholders, the next step is to assess their interest and influence. This is formally known as *stakeholder mapping*, which is a topic of many management studies and papers because it is an important and powerful tool for many professions. It is generally viewed as useful in business and in everyday life improvement advice.

As with most business concepts, it's best illustrated by a classic four-box diagram, with two dimensions across each axis. The most commonly used and best-known dimensions include the following:

- Power
- Influence
- Interest or need
- Support or attitude

My favorite example and application of a four-box stakeholder map is by Vivian Klosterman, the founder of *Continuing Professional Development*, an online academy of professional training and general self-help.

Vivian's model uses influence and interest as its two dimensions. The reason this is my favorite example is because of its simplicity and how easy it is to apply in most contexts, especially in software development. As both developers and managers, we have a good idea of who is interested in our products, and who is influential or instrumental in the products' development and usage. This offers more value by going beyond the general list of the project sponsor, development team, and application user groups, which is still useful for practical purposes, but less insightful in stakeholder analysis.

The following stakeholder map illustrates what each category of stakeholder needs from you:

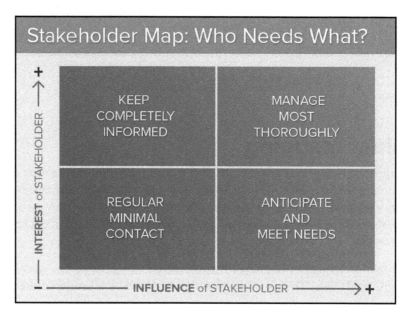

Figure 2.5: A four-box stakeholder map with instructions on how to deal with each stakeholder category
Source: https://www.smartsheet.com/what-stakeholder-analysis-and-mapping-and-how-do-you-do-it-effectively/

Depending on which box your identified stakeholder resides in, you should deploy the appropriate level and type of contact, as well as the suitable amount of thought and attention toward them.

The group to manage most thoroughly is in the top-right corner. For example, if your software product is a consumer app, then this is most likely to include the end user who is the person paying for the app. Therefore, you should pay them the highest level of attention, listen and be responsive to their needs, and keep them completely informed of how you satisfy their requirements.

All of these appropriate considerations and actions go toward building a productive and mutually beneficial working relationship between you and your stakeholders. The key to good relationships is often effective communication. This is the goal of developing communication management plans. It arcs back to the important key skills that we talked about early, of communication, communication, communication, and specifically, the three types – inbound, internal, and outbound.

The layers of a stakeholder relationship

I hope you can now see how stakeholder management skills are built and layered on top of each other, like building blocks. The further you want to build your relationship, the more blocks you will need to advance, and the tighter the blocks need to be. Quite simply, you can't build a relationship with your stakeholder if you're not somehow communicating with them.

Moreover, this communication should be two-way, even if the relationship is between an author and their readers, which may seem like a one-way relationship. There is still dialog and interaction through reviews, comments, and social media, where the author will get feedback and can respond to it.

Remember that stakeholder management is essentially about building and maintaining relationships and setting and meeting expectations. Your communication plan can be as simple or complicated as you wish. The critical success factor is whether or not it ensures that recipients receive and understand the message you are trying to communicate to them. In other words, does your communication plan create relationships and manage expectations?

In a project scenario, the most typical communication methods include the following:

- Regular status update emails or newsletters
- Requirements and design workshops
- Focus groups for feedback
- Steering groups with budget holders
- **Project Management Office** (**PMO**) updates, publications, approvals, and announcements

Within these communications, the basic information of target dates and deadlines, milestones, budgets, commentary on progress, and risks and issues should be included for the appropriate audience. The emphasis is on tailoring your method, as well as content for the target audience, while maintaining a consistent approach and regular cadence, which both help to set expectations. A "weekly project update" should be issued weekly, without fail!

Especially in non-waterfall projects, and for typically more web-based products, I have also seen highly effective examples of more new-age communication methods, including the following:

- Blog posts
- Webcasts
- Show and tells
- Early product demos
- Even hackathons to engage both users and developers

While these may not seem like a logical part of a communication plan, they are all options that you can, and should, think about incorporating. They are not just a novelty, because they can help to make your project stand out, and they really do work.

The goal of your communication plan is to engage and influence stakeholders. This is also the key to setting and meeting your stakeholders' expectations and making sure they know that their expectations have been met!

While your plan, like all plans, will have a start, middle, and end, meaningful engagement and influence are very much a process. You earn your stakeholders' trust and build up your relationship, step by step, little by little. The end goal is to set, and then meet or even exceed, their expectations.

To fulfill their requirements, satisfy their needs, or attain your mutual goals, *APM* lists 10 key principles in stakeholder engagement:

1. Communicate
2. Consult, both early and often
3. Remember, they're only human
4. Plan it
5. Understand that relationships are key
6. Be simple, but not easy
7. Just be part of managing risk

8. Compromise
9. Understand what success is
10. Take responsibility

I've picked out three of these as the quintessential points and central themes to our context of key manager skills in software development, although, they all do play an important part.

As we know, the technology behind our solutions and products are, relatively speaking, simpler than the people involved, which includes ourselves. In other words, it's the people who make developing software complicated. That's not a disparaging comment in any way. It's a pragmatic acknowledgment that stakeholder engagement is absolutely necessary because developing software is a collaborative endeavor.

We have already covered the importance and key requirements for effective communication and how it enables engagement.

The *APM* has a case study on the ground-breaking **National Health Service** (**NHS**) IT program, which was established in 2002. Despite the difficulties and ultimate cancellation of a huge project, there are a number of extremely valuable lessons for all IT projects, especially large-scale programs such as the NHS National Program for IT.

I worked on this program for two years and witnessed some of the very real challenges that the IT and non-IT stakeholders both faced. Most of these were, in fact, different sides of the same trials and tribulations. Some were avoidable, and some were inevitable in such an ambitious program of work to revolutionize the biggest public healthcare system in the world and the world's fifth largest employer. All of these challenges had something to do with engagement and collaboration between people and stakeholders.

Stakeholder management case study – the UK NHS

Stakeholder communication improvements in an IT system delivery project

Abstract

The NHS's *National Program for IT (NPfIT)* was the UK's largest IT project before its cancellation in 2010. Despite the ultimate cancellation of the program, there were many examples of exceptional stakeholder engagement prior to the project's closure.

Background

The *NPfIT* was a **Department of Health** (**DOH**) initiative to centralize electronic patient care records from across the UK to connect 30,000 general practitioners to 300 hospitals, providing secure and audited access to these records by authorized health professionals. As the program progressed from successful procurement through to delivery, a series of technical, political, social, economic, and health issues materialized. The number of stakeholders increased in both size and scope due to these issues and communication and engagement with these parties became an enormous task for the **Connecting for Health** (**CfH**) team.

The issues

To manage this workload, comprehensive stakeholder management tools, processes, and **full-time equivalent** (**FTE**) resources were put in place, but it never was going to be enough. There were too many issues, and the issues were too deep to enable a quick resolution. However, despite the ultimate cancellation of the program, there were some outstanding examples of proactive stakeholder engagement.

The solution

To help resolve some of the diverse range of issues facing the *NPfIT* program, an array of stakeholder techniques got implemented. These included workshops with stakeholder groups regarding the handling of sensitive data, and respected clinical representatives acting as an information conduit between the CfH/DOH/NHS groups involved to ensure clarity and co-operation between all parties. This also extended to within the CfH team regarding the success or failure of the project and the effect it would, therefore, have on the jobs of the employees.

The benefits

This clear, sensible, and pro-active management style is the simplest way to deal with any potential issues. Furthermore, whether in a workshop environment or through a formal review, the *NPfIT* program was constantly seeking opportunities for people to express what their view of success meant. This allowed for a continual assessment of the issues arising within the project and allowed it to effectively address some of the wide range of issues arising from the program.

The learning points

Despite the ultimate closure of the *NPfIT* program, many of the techniques used in stakeholder engagement were hugely successful and transferrable to other projects. However, this study also highlights the possibility that despite best efforts and a well-implemented stakeholder engagement program, the project may still become unviable in light of issues that can arise.

We have also just talked about the fundamental nature of relationships and how they underpin cooperation and collaboration in order to attain common goals and achieve mutual benefits.

Last but not least is compromise. This leads on to the next top manager skill of negotiation, and it arcs back to flexibility and adaptability. Compromise can have a negative meaning in some contexts, but in a real-world project scenario, compromise is simply a necessity. After all, the *Triple Constraint* of time, cost, and quality itself is a trade-off and compromise.

Skill 5 – Negotiation

Negotiations happen every day. People negotiate pretty much anything and everything. It's often quite casual, in a form that we might not even notice, but often it's formal as well, especially in a software project context.

The number, clarity, and feasibility of requirements, bug accuracy, and severity, availability of resources, priority of features, go-live date, release schedule, overall cost, and price, are all usual negotiation points. The agreed figure at the end is rarely, if ever, the original baseline.

For our purposes, and ease of illustration, let's just say there are only two parties involved: a supplier and a customer. As a manager, you will need to understand and appreciate the art of negotiation from both angles.

As the saying goes: *An old poacher makes the best gamekeeper.*

Empathy is a skill often associated with negotiation. Essentially, whether you are the supplier or customer, you can negotiate most effectively if you are aware and understanding of the other party's position, thoughts, and feelings, which ultimately lead to their negotiating actions.

Interestingly, empathy is sandwiched between two topics that we've already discussed: active listening in `Chapter 1`, *Why Do You Want to Become a Manager?*, and rapport as well as influence, which are the focus of this chapter.

In the scenario illustrated in *Figure 2.6* by the **Behavioral Change Stairway Model**, the behavioral change can be interpreted as the other party accepting your negotiation point. This shows how important it is to show empathy toward the other party, even if you are having a hard-nosed and heated negotiation, where each other's motives seem to be polar opposites.

The Behavioral Change Stairway Model was originally developed by the *FBI*'s Crisis Negotiation Unit. Motives and tensions hardly get further apart and stressed than with a hostage situation. See the Behavioral Change Stairway Model in *Figure 2.6*:

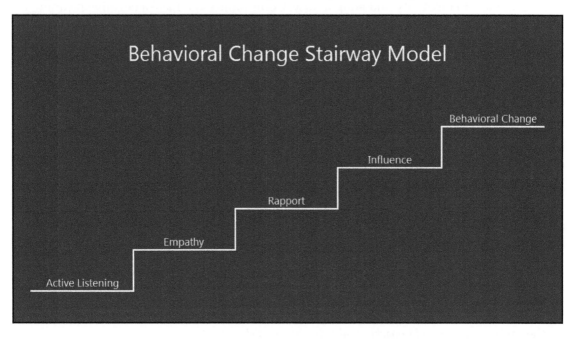

Figure 2.6: The FBI's Behavioral Change Stairway Model, as used in hostage negotiations
Source: https://viaconflict.wordpress.com/2014/10/26/the-behavioral-change-stairway-model/

Building rapport

After you have actively listened and shown empathy toward the other party, you want to build rapport and influence through open communication in order to move up the stairway as quickly as possible.

One of the ways to do this is to open the real negotiation from a sensible and realistic position. Better still, offer the other party something that they find valuable or useful.

> *"Bad negotiators open with unreasonable demands. Good negotiators open with reasonable requests. Great negotiators open by offering something of value."*

> *– Adam Grant*

A classic example of this is when you are discussing the allocation of resources with another Project Manager. If they demand the exclusivity to a key and in-demand developer for a long period without considering your project's needs, it will instantly alienate you. In response, if you offered them a viable alternative solution, such as bringing your need for the same developer forward in time without risking your project. Then that's a great response that will make a mutual compromise more likely, or maybe even a win-win. At the very least it will create a happy-enough outcome for both parties.

From the consumer side, the key concept we will focus on is **BATNA** and **WATNA**, which are acronyms for **Best Alternative to a Negotiated Agreement** and **Worst Alternative to a Negotiated Agreement**.

In layman's terms, BATNA is the point at which you should consider accepting the offer on the table – your best-case scenario. For example, the car dealer has matched the best offer you've seen elsewhere. WATNA is the point at which you should decline and walk away from the deal – your worst-case scenario. In an auction, this is the price at which you would stop bidding.

The terms BATNA and WATNA were coined by Roger Fisher and William Ury in their book called *Getting to Yes: Negotiating Agreement Without Giving In*. BATNA/WATNA often refer to a higher meaning than a simple bottom or top price point. It has built a methodology around the concept, which has a large following in negotiation theory circles.

The deep psychology behind negotiation theory is beyond the scope of this book, but the key point in a software project context is that you should have a set of reasonable BATNAs and WATNAs. The value in learning about BATNA/WATNA, as opposed to the simpler best- and worst-case scenario, is the focus on alternatives.

Focusing on alternatives highlights the need for comparison and perspective, and the bigger picture, based on actual reference points, for example, using the example I mentioned earlier with BATNA, whereby the car dealer matches an offer that was better than theirs. It also emphasizes and encourages looking for different solutions altogether. For example, in the process of finding the best deal for a car, you may see a different model that is actually more suitable.

If both parties take this approach, the likelihood of a more mutually beneficial outcome is much more likely. You may well find that the other project doesn't actually need the in-demand developer for all of that time after all, and there's someone else the developer knows that can do the job!

One piece of advice I would give you is this: always bear in mind your project's triple constraint, which itself is an interconnected trade-off, but don't compromise on your BATNAs and WATNAs when negotiating.

Skill 6 – Using a chosen methodology

Which delivery methodology the project or team uses, if any, is not a manager's unilateral decision. It is the team's collective choice. Therefore, a good manager will not only realize this, but will also be prepared to adapt and embrace it. So, a good understanding of the most common software project methodologies is vital to a flexible manager's toolkit.

An effective Project Manager will facilitate the team's internal discussion to choose their methodology, as well as communicate it externally to inform other stakeholders. In this section, we will introduce the three most common methodologies:

- *Agile*
- *Waterfall*
- *PRINCE2*

There is no de facto best methodology in the real world. These three methodologies aren't even necessarily comparable or like-for-like. But neither are they conflicting or contradictory, either.

Like every person is unique, every project is also unique. So, the key here is to understand the best elements in each methodology, and consciously choose which to adopt and adapt, according to the needs of your project and your team. All three of these methodologies actively encourage its practitioners to adapt it as necessary. It is extremely rare for a popular methodology to be strictly prescriptive, because it will limit its range of applicable situations, and therefore its uptake and following.

While you can, and should, pick the best from any number of these methodologies, it is important that you have an agreed main methodology, even if it's a mix and match of many. This has two main benefits.

Firstly, it encourages all stakeholders to use a standardized vocabulary, especially within the team itself. In the modern work environment, there is a ubiquitous use of acronyms, and there's likely to be people of many backgrounds and geographies involved with the project. The standardized vocabulary levels the playing field and ensures that everyone is talking a common language and, hence, understanding one another more easily, which enables better collaboration.

Secondly, and somewhat of a public relations angle, it helps to communicate confidence and influence on stakeholders, who are very likely to expect the project to use a proven methodology. For this reason, many projects will declare that they are using *Agile*, *Waterfall*, or *PRINCE2*, without really doing so in practice.

For the more discernible stakeholder, if you actually adopt a formal methodology, you are in a better position to give them more meaningful updates and have more effective discussions about progress, as well as challenges, risks, and issues.

Agile

If you haven't read the original *Manifesto for Agile Software Development*, start there. A true *Agile* practitioner will exhibit and demonstrate the four underpinning values:

- Individuals and interactions, over processes and tools
- Working software, over comprehensive documentation
- Customer collaboration, over contract negotiation
- Responding to change, over following a plan

To enact these values, *Agile* has evolved and developed a number of widely accepted, practical methods. To practice, these methods do not necessarily mean you are a true *Agile* practitioner. But a true *Agile* practitioner will certainly understand and is most likely to practice a number of them:

Manifesto for Agile Software Development

We are uncovering better ways of developing
software by doing it and helping others do it.
Through this work we have come to value:

Individuals and interactions over processes and tools
Working software over comprehensive documentation
Customer collaboration over contract negotiation
Responding to change over following a plan

That is, while there is value in the items on
the right, we value the items on the left more.

Figure 2.7: Excerpt from the Manifesto for *Agile* Software Development
Source: http://agilemanifesto.org/

I'll pick out three key concepts and practices in *Agile* that I believe are the most important and practical for our discussion here.

Incremental development, over big-bang releases

This is fundamental to any *Agile* practicing project, because of its suitability for an uncertain future environment, which is a principle assumption for *Agile*. It's logical to work and deliver in smaller chunks when you don't have a definitive target endstate because it's expected to change or it's simply impossible to know.

This is in contrast to large-scale physical infrastructure projects, where almost all details of the end-state are known and agreed before significant work starts. It's not a good idea to start drilling and putting foundations down until you know where, and how high and wide the building needs to be. You can include some scope to compensate for variability by over-specking to some degree. But that will impact your cost and, most likely, time.

So, starting with your **Minimum Viable Product** (**MVP**) or **Minimum Marketable Features** (MMF), and then improving your software through many releases, is preferred over the "perfect first time" mindset.

This is the reason for incremental development's popularity, particularly in web software products. Combined with a flexible technology stack, the time and cost to market and re-market are minimized.

Dynamic daily huddles, over regular static updates

This is one of the most practical methods to build a more effective team, and not just for software projects. It's simple and fun when done constructively. Sharing is the key, coupled with a cadence that encourages incremental progress and improvements from the day before. It arcs back open and honest internal communication within a team.

Every day, at the same time, the team meets for a short period, usually no more than 10 minutes, and preferably face-to-face, but it's still possible over video or audio calls. Each team member takes turns to share what they have completed and what help they need from the team.

An additional custom I recommend is for the huddle to be chaired by someone other than the manager. In a mature team, it doesn't require a chairperson at all. This takes the focus away from what needs to happen on the project, so the huddle isn't just the Project Manager handing out tasks! That is necessary but should be done elsewhere.

User stories, over exhaustive requirements

It's easy to aim to capture all the requirements at the same time but, in an uncertain world, this is not very realistic or practical. So, the purpose of user stories is to extrapolate the same, if not more, information by cutting the requirement elicitation process in a different way.

Create narratives by consulting end users and the product owner. Describe what they need the software to do, and incrementally add more and more detail to the stories until the anticipated scenarios are covered. For non-functional requirements such as supportability and ease of maintenance, the relevant support teams will be the user.

The Waterfall model

The *Waterfall model* is considered the traditional methodology of software development. It is widely attributed to Dr. Winston W. Royce, who published a whitepaper called *Managing the Development of Large Software Systems* in 1970 (`http://www-scf.usc.edu/~csci201/lectures/Lecture11/royce1970.pdf`).

This paper describes Royce's personal views on managing large software systems, but, in fact, does not use the word waterfall to describe the linear process of software development. The seminal point about the paper was the relationship between each stage in the development life cycle. There is a downstream flow, plus an upstream flow, signifying the chance to iterate.

As such, a key difference between *Waterfall* and *Agile* is the focus of *Waterfall* to be iterative between life cycle stages, while *Agile*'s focus is to be incremental in its overall delivery.

An obvious drawback of the *Waterfall model* is the reliance on comprehensive requirements to be known and collected early on in the development life cycle. For projects involving large-scale systems, as declared in the title of Royce's whitepaper, this is still the preferred approach due to its meticulousness. By design, it obliges each stage to be at least confident and complete before progressing to the next, as can be seen *Figure 2.8*:

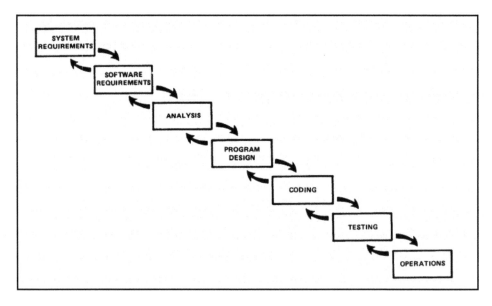

Figure 2.8: The classic *Waterfall model*
Source: http://www-scf.usc.edu/~csci201/lectures/Lecture11/royce1970.pdf

PRINCE2

PRINCE2 is a generic project management method, with a formal set of accompanying certifications. It stands for **PRojects IN Controlled Environments**. Although it was originally developed for IT projects, it's now commonly used in a variety of industries and businesses.

Its basis comprises seven principles, seven themes, and seven processes.

- **Seven principles**: Continued business justification; learn from experience; defined roles and responsibilities; manage by stages; manage by exception; focus on products; and tailor to suit the project environment.
- **Seven themes**: Business case, organization, quality, plans, risk, change, and progress.
- **Seven processes**: Starting up a project, directing a project, initiating a project, controlling a stage, managing product delivery, managing stage boundaries, and closing a project.

For our purposes, we'll concentrate on the key practical and usable elements of *PRINCE2*. The underlying theory and structure are important, but ultimately, it's about the application of the method, which is done via the delivery of artifacts. *PRINCE2* calls these artifacts *Management Products*.

In the early stages of a project, the most important management product is the PID. This is the output of the third process, called *Initiating the Project*. This should include the overall business case, scope, and project team, in addition to setting out the controls to be used during the project.

These controls should include various logs and registers, which are also management products. The issues, risk, quality register, and daily log, as well as other products, are often combined into a RAID log.

RAID stands for **Risks, Actions, Issues**, and **Decisions**, sometimes known as dependencies. This is usually a large spreadsheet with different tabs for each section. Unless there is an extremely good reason not to have one, I would insist that all projects should have a RAID log, and the project team should use and keep it up to date.

The Lessons Log is a management product that's often forgotten about on account of its nature of predominantly helping the next project rather than the current one. However, if it's used correctly through the life cycle, especially for large projects, it can be extremely valuable in the latter stages to help avoid recurring or lingering problems. In a strict *PRINCE2* practicing environment, a Lessons Report must be produced in order to complete the Closing a Project process. This will rely on information from the Lessons Log.

You may have noticed that conceptually and practically, *PRINCE2* seems longer than *Agile* and *Waterfall*. This is because it simply has more entities, products, and processes within its premise of control. This is the reason why only select parts of *PRINCE2* tend to be adopted and practiced. As well as the effort to follow it, there will also be a significant overhead for a PMO to govern it across all projects.

If I'm not ready, then how do I get ready?

So, do you think you have most of these skills already? In the unlikely event that you do have these six top skills already, then that's a great achievement. Do keep in mind that there is always room for improvement, and learning is a lifelong endeavor. So, continue to improve these six skills, in addition to learning new ones as well. If you want to become, and continue to be, a successful and great manager, then this is a necessity, not a luxury.

If you feel you have some way to go, then don't worry; that is completely normal and okay. It's rare for a developer to have mastered these six skills without having real-world experience of being a manager. It is also an unreasonable expectation because even most experienced managers will still have some way to go!

Your task now is to truthfully assess how mature you are at each of the skills and make a plan to increase your knowledge and confidence to practice each skill proficiently.

As with all plans of improvement, you should start with a baseline of where you think you are now. I strongly recommend that you use quantitative measures, as well as qualitative notes. This may seem overly scientific and a complete overkill, but I find that it focuses the mind and helps to carve out time from busy schedules to dedicate to learning and development. Since this practice differs from person to person, you should adopt it in a way that you feel is appropriate to you.

Quantitative measures, or metrics, can be easily compared. Comparing your starting baseline with a later point in time gives you a quantifiable measure of progress. High-performance athletes and their coaches are obsessed with this, and with good reason, because it forms a solid basis for further discussions, such as which areas to focus on.

Qualitative notes are also important. This is your narrative, and where ideas for your actual steps to improvement will come from. This is the insight, reasoning, and background that only you will truly understand and appreciate. So, your own commentary can act like a captain's log, which could be kept private or shared with particular people who can help you to improve.

The easiest and most effective way to record, illustrate, and track your maturity and progress is using a radar chart, also known as a spider chart.

Use a simple five-point scoring system to assess how competent or mature you are in each skill, one being the least mature, and five being the most mature. You can calibrate what this means in real terms by your own standards. The point here is to show gaps and track progress. Clearly, you need to be reasonable and honest about scoring yourself!

This will require a bit of extra effort, but it can be very interesting and even more useful to ask another person to score you as well. Compare their scores with yours and recalibrate accordingly.

Having created a radar chart, make sure you date stamp it. Then, repeat the exercise at a predetermined fixed time interval, which helps to remove the scope for biases. Overlay and compare your charts, and you have your progress!

This is a method you can also employ for your team, and it gives you something more real to consult your mentor on, which is the next step.

Get a mentor

If you don't have a mentor already, I strongly recommend that you think about finding one. A true mentor is tremendously useful in helping you continually learn and develop throughout your career.

Especially as a new manager, a mentor can be an invaluable source of support and guidance. This is the stage where you have more unknowns than knowns. So, it's natural that you have a larger need for extra support, as long as you consciously recognize it.

A mentor is a true coach who holds a necessary mirror up to you, by asking the tough questions. By doing so, they compel you to become much more introspective, and ultimately more insightful about yourself, and the situation or challenges you may be facing.

They can also share their own experiences, lessons, and thoughts, which gives your insight on at least one way of tackling a particular challenge. Note that it may not be the right or only way. How prescriptive they are will depend on your particular relationship with them and your needs to follow their insights. At the beginning of your transition, you are more likely to require more prescriptive guidance and general guidance overall. This will evolve as you become more experienced and confident, and when your challenges change.

In my own experience, mentorship helped me tremendously, especially through the tougher times when I had serious doubts about what I was doing. So, it's something I strongly recommend to all budding managers, as well as developers in general.

You may have heard the saying: *Coaching makes you a better player*. I have found this to be very true. So, as well as finding a mentor for yourself, when you are ready, you should also mentor someone else. Having a mentor and being a mentor is not in any way conflicting or mutually exclusive. You don't need to make an industry out of it. Mentoring can be a 30-minute chat over coffee every so often. The quality is what matters, as opposed to quantity.

Shadowing

Another excellent way to go about acquiring or improving your top skills is to shadow an experienced manager. Consider this like a ride-along. You get the chance to observe and learn from an experienced professional in an environment that you wouldn't normally be in.

It's important that you choose a manager whom you respect and think has the top skills you want to learn, because they will be your role model in many ways. There are good and not-so-good role models, or the outright off-the-wall different type. You should bear this in mind when selecting your manager to shadow and when you're observing them.

Every person is different, and while they may be experienced, it doesn't mean they will execute a skill perfectly all of the time. The most honest and experienced kind of professional will openly and humbly admit that they get a lot of things wrong. The most important thing is that they then learn from them.

Imagine if someone requested to shadow you. Having a fellow professional take notice and wanting to understand a day in the life of you is very much a compliment. It shows reverence and professional regard. So, it's likely to garner positive feelings, especially for your self-esteem and confidence.

Remember this if you are tentative to approach someone whom you might think doesn't have the time or wouldn't be interested. The worst they can say is no. Even then, you will have paid them a sincere compliment, which might lead to another opportunity later down the line.

When you have found someone to shadow, remember to prepare. Make sure you explain your background and motives for doing this. Be as open and flexible as possible. Share your thoughts and expectations, and invite them to share theirs, so you have a mutual understanding. Know where each other's boundaries are, and work around their schedule. If you follow them into meetings with other people, make sure your presence is explained, and observe without disrupting the meeting.

Keep it as formal or informal as you both feel comfortable, but always professional. This is a professional relationship with a defined goal of them sharing and you learning.

How do I get the job?

If you've still not decided which type of manager you want to become, now is the time to make a decision. While it is an important decision, there is always a chance to change even once you are in the role. But ideally, you want to get this decision right the first time, whatever right means for you.

Being a team, development, or project manager will entail similar and transferrable skills, but also a significant amount of role-specific skills, as well as knowledge, which comes with practice and real-world experience.

This section will cover various aspects of job hunting, which may seem general. But we will focus on how to position yourself so that a brilliant developer like you is taken seriously as a managerial candidate.

Internal or external

Is there a manager vacancy at your current organization?

If not, is there a possibility that a new manager position can be created for you?

The answers to these questions indicate whether you need to think about leaving your current organization and finding a new employer, and whether you stay or leave. Each has its own set of advantages and disadvantages, including the opportunity for a fresh start, without baggage, but also, having to learn a lot of new things because every organization does things differently.

If you do decide to leave and go external, you can apply directly to the organizations you desire, or use a variety of recruitment websites and agents, or all of these options.

Remember to use a reliable source of unbiased market information where possible. There's also no substitute to your own personal network, whom you should also reach out to.

When I see an interesting role on a recruitment website, something I find useful is to always cross-check it on another recruitment website. It is often different and there's perhaps more information, which you can piece together to form a clearer overall picture. Job postings are often copied from site to site by time-pressed recruitment agents. There are also many automated platforms that syndicate these postings, with varying degrees of fidelity.

Similarly, if the hiring organization is using multiple recruitment agents, then the agents may have different interpretations of the requirement. So, their job posting will be different, even if it's for the same job and on the same recruitment website.

If there isn't a current manager vacancy, but you decide to stay, there are still things you can do to make the change happen. This is sometimes called "engineering a role." It's essentially influencing the organizational decision makers that there is a need for a new manager position and that you are the perfect candidate for it!

Positioning yourself

Whether you are going for a role that's internal with the same organization, or external with a different organization, you are still subject to an application and interview process.

The good news is that this process itself should not be radically different from the one you succeeded in to become a developer. There are still policies and laws to ensure that it is a fair and non-discriminatory process. However, the focus will be different because the skills and experience required are different. Furthermore, the techniques to test whether you have the required skills will also be different.

The key challenge will be to persuade the hiring manager that you are not just a developer. Remember that you are competing not just against other developers who want to become a manager, but potentially experienced managers as well. So, you need to think about yourself less as a developer, and more as a manager.

Persuading the hiring manager may well be easier if you already work together. So, this is an advantage of staying with the same organization. They will be aware of your reputation and portfolio of work and, more importantly, what you're like as a person and potential manager.

If there is an open manager vacancy within your organization, take the opportunity to find and speak to the hiring manager. Since they are hiring for a role that is a natural progression for you as a developer, the chances are that you already work together, or at least know one another. The hiring manager may even be your mentor! However, I do recommend that you don't artificially reverse engineer this scenario to be the case.

Consider your discussions with them as an informal pre-interview. So, remember to be professional, as well as open and honest about why you want to become a manager.

If there isn't a manager vacancy within your organization and you've decided to stay, this is where you may look to engineer a role. Be aware that there are negative connotations to the phrase *engineering a role*. In some cases, this means artificially manufacturing a bogus situation for your own gains over others'. To do it correctly and ethically, it must be driven by a genuine business need, in which case, you are simply highlighting the fact that there is a gap in the current organizational structure to the organizational decision makers. Therefore, you're making a win-win situation for everyone involved.

Will I like it?

If you have ascertained your why, and you understand the true underlying motives, to make the *Developer-to-Manager* transition, then I can assure you that your journey will be meaningful and rewarding. The journey itself will be challenging and difficult at times, which is to be expected. Whether you will enjoy a professional life as a manager is a great question.

For me, I have no doubt that it has made my career more rewarding and interesting. I had the choice of continuing to test and develop software, which is how I began my career in IT. While I enjoyed writing and breaking code (preferably someone else's), I found myself wanting to learn more and more about the managerial side of the software business: the commercials, the development process, the team, and the people.

In short, I had a natural curiosity toward being a manager in the software business. I found myself with less and less time to write code because I was volunteering for more and more managerial responsibilities, starting with organizing simple team meetings and learning more about tasks and roles connected to, but not actual, software development, such as release and deployment management and configuration management.

As I took on more of these additional responsibilities, I gradually learned more of the skills required to be a manager. My overall knowledge base and confidence also increased, which is both cause and effect. So, ask the *Will I like it?* question differently: *Would you like it if you weren't a manager?*

If your answer is **Yes**, then perhaps you should revisit your *why* to be absolutely sure you have a deep and genuine drive to make the transition. If your answer is **No**, then you should go for it and commit yourself as much as you committed to becoming a brilliant developer.

Life as a team, development, or project manager is genuinely interesting and rewarding in its own right. It's not to be simplistically compared with being a developer or any other position.

There will be days when you hate it, and you wish you weren't a manager, but there will be many days when you absolutely love it and can't imagine doing anything else as rewarding as building a team or delivering a complex project.

The interview and the offer

Perhaps you think you're ready, or perhaps you're not quite, but want to try it anyway.

To best illustrate this part, let's say it's an external position with another organization that you are going for, because that's likely to include all of the aspects of the internal option, with a bit of extra process and rigor.

When you are invited to an interview for a manager vacancy, there are a lot of different ways that the interview can go. But before you get to the interview itself, there are several things you should think about.

First, you should be clear on the type of manager role it is. Increasingly, the manager role is becoming more diverse and hybrid. Such a role usually includes elements of team, development, and project management all mixed in. It's always good to be clear on what this mix is, so that you can assess your own preference and tailor your approach accordingly.

Tailoring your approach, in this respect, means highlighting particular skills and experiences, which are most applicable to the type of role, and what the hiring manager is looking for.

For a team manager, it's likely to have large elements of people management, including a healthy dose of sensibility toward people in general. For a development manager, it could be technical design and hands-on solution delivery. For a project manager, it could be stakeholder management, budgeting, and general organization skills.

Secondly, remember to position and represent yourself as a manager, not a developer. Yes, you are still a developer until you get this job. However, you should fast-forward slightly and think like a manager in answering the questions, especially if they are more hypothetical. If it's more experience-based, such as "Tell me about a time when...", then draw on your learnings from all the managerial responsibilities that you already do, as an accidental manager or when you deliberately volunteered for management tasks, as well as what you learned from shadowing, or your mentoring sessions.

Be super confident in your top six manager skills and remain confident if there are any follow-up or probing questions. This is good practice and an essential demonstration of your behavior as a manager, because a manager is likely to be challenged regularly on various grounds in the real world, sometimes reasonably, and sometimes not. How you react to being challenged is an answer itself, which an insightful interviewer will be looking for.

Think about the value of your *Developer-to-Manager* transition for the organization, rather than yourself. Incorporate the fact that you are a brilliant developer, which helps you to manage a team of developers or a development project.

On the more practical matters, there are typically three main themes in terms of interview content:

- Overview and discussion on your résumé and experience
- Competency-based questions
- Presentation on a pre-determined topic

These are not wildly different from most interviews for any role, perhaps with the exception of the presentation. The topic and guidelines may be given to you in advance of the interview, or you could just be given 10 minutes to prepare as part of the interview itself.

If you are not comfortable with presenting, which is true for a lot of people, then make sure you get help from trusted colleagues and your mentor. Practice the presentation with them and get their honest feedback. Again, think and practice as a manager.

Finally, after you have had a great discussion with the hiring manager, do not be put off if you are offered the job with certain conditions, including an immediate development plan to address your lack of experience as a manager. This is very positive because it indicates they are willing to invest in you as an individual. It will give you the necessary support to learn, which you will inevitably have to do.

Summary

In this chapter, we took a journey through the six key skills that I believe are most important for you to focus on as a manager:

1. Flexibility and adaptability
2. Communication, communication, communication
3. Team leadership
4. Stakeholder management
5. Negotiation
6. Using a chosen methodology

These skills will see you through almost every situation you're ever going to meet. They're also incredibly well adapted for you as a new *Developer-to-Manager*! So, please keep these skills in your mind, and take every opportunity to explore and develop them further – through your own continuous research and the learning you gain every day as a manager.

What Is My Job Now? 3

Whether your new position is external at a new organization, or an internal move; following your successful application and interview, you are likely to have a settling in or transition plan. This plan will be agreed between you and your hiring manager, with the primary purpose of the plan being to set expectations and a reasonable timescale for you to familiarize and truly establish yourself in your new job and environment.

One of the first steps – if not the very first step – will be to clarify what your new managerial role really means. This might sound strange because you've just been through an application and interview process, where you were asked specific questions to ascertain how you would perform as a manager. However, there is another level of detail that needs to be worked out. Unsurprisingly perhaps, in quite a lot of cases, new positions are created and filled without a crystal-clear role profile of task-level responsibilities.

In the real world, especially for managerial positions, organizations often hire on an urgent business need to solve a problem. How to solve that problem has not been fully thought out yet.

As a manager, you have the decision-making scope and responsibility to figure this out. So, one of the key inputs to your plan is what you think you need to do to make this happen. This is true even if your position is a backfill – which could be the urgent business problem itself! The previous person may have moved on, and you were brought in to run an existing team or project. An effective hiring manager will be looking to you to replicate or maintain what is already successful, as well as new ideas to improve and transform the team or project if required.

But if we start with an open mind and a blank canvas, there is clearly a learning and information gathering phase for all new managers to undertake. In our *Developer-to-Manager* context, I would always advise new managers to take the time to understand the wider organization. Even if it's an internal move and you already think you know the organization as a developer, this is still important.

For instance, you will now likely be part of regular management meetings where the management agenda, department performance, people matters, and future project pipeline is discussed. These items are usually not shared with the rest of the organization due to their human and commercial sensitivity.

YOUR MONTHLY MANAGEMENT MEETING AGENDA

Finance

- Review of profit & loss statement for previous month & year to date
- 12-month cash flow - comparison of budget versus actual
- Key Performance Indicators
- Average Daily Production of fee-earners
- Profitability of fee-earners
- Return on investment from marketing activities
- TCO conversion numbers

Marketing

- Overall progress of marketing plan
- Web site review and analytics
- Online Reviews
- Social media connection and engagement
- Word of mouth results
- Testimonials
- Direct marketing review
- Networking review
- B2B - B2C review
- Study Club development

The Patient Experience

- Online booking
- Telephony
- Front Desk
- TCO
  - o Treatment delivered
  - o Up-selling
  - o Pipeline management

Operational

- Clinical issues
- Non-clinical issues
- Governance and Compliance
- Clinical Mentoring

Personnel

- Review of team performance
- Review of individual performance
- Review of bonus system year to date
- Schedule of team meetings
- Training issues
- Personal Progress Interviews

Strategy

- Tactics for growth
- Acquisitions
- Product mix
- Patient demographics
- Delivery models
- Expansion strategy
- Exit strategy
- Personal/professional time management

Figure 3.1: An example of a regular management meeting's agenda and the topics that might be discussed
Source: http://www.coachbarrow.com/blog/monthly-management-meeting-agenda/

In my experience, a management meeting between all manager attendees feels and runs very differently to a functional meeting involving developers and other functional roles. Typically, managers are more expressive and talkative. It is an implicit part of their jobs to participate in, as well as facilitate, discussions. So, that is what they will naturally do. In an all-managers meeting, you are likely to be competing for time to air your views, rather than stimulating the conversation in a battle against awkward silence.

These management meetings are a perfect place to listen and learn about the wider organization from a new perspective. You may be surprised at how freely your fellow managers will share their challenges with you, followed by request for your help to overcome these challenges. This mutual sharing is a positive trait and cultural indicator of the organization. Collective problem-solving is at the heart of good management.

Outside of such meetings, you should also proactively solicit feedback and ideas on an individual basis, to gather information such as:

- What is the organization or department's short-term and long-term vision?
- What are the most critical problems or frequent issues of other managers?
- How can you and your team help them succeed?

Through their collective responses, you can triangulate what and where the business problem you were hired to solve is.

An extra interesting aspect of these questions and their answers will be whether they are consistent between managers. Through this consistency, you can gauge how well the organization's goals have filtered into complimentary or competing individual goals.

In short, the key job change from a developer to a manager is that your primary focus is solving someone else's problem. Therefore, what your job is at any one time is more variable and should be adapted to their needs.

Furthermore, a highly effective manager will be looking to prevent problems from happening in the first place. This will require experience and a savviness to anticipate the likely future needs of the people you work with, and the wider industry.

Figure 3.2: Collective and collaborative problem solving is at the heart of effective management
Source: https://www.cliseetiquette.com/art-business-introduction/

Whether you will still have coding and related developer responsibilities is a topic we'll answer in a later chapter. For now, the focus is on problem solving, which begins with gathering enough information to understand the problem.

Figure 3.3: As a new manager, it is likely to be difficult to code and learn to manage. After all, they are two separate positions and, like all learning curves, learning to manage will take more time and effort, especially at the beginning. So, it's important to be realistic to yourself and others by not trying to juggle too many things at once.
Source: http://community.uservoice.com/blog/scaling-your-product-management-team/

If you are a team manager with people-management responsibilities, then remember to also consult with your team for their input. Their views are vital for you to understand your own team's challenges, as well as creating an open and trusting relationship with your team members by making them feel heard and valued.

These challenges may be similar to those shared by other managers, or they could be different altogether. They could also be different takes of the same problem.

For example, a Project Manager may say to you that their project timeline is slipping. They think it's caused by the development team not understanding the requirements. However, your team's view is that the requirements are unclear and have gaps, and so they need to constantly go back to the business to clarify what they really mean. This elongates the whole development process, which causes the project timeline to slip.

Getting to the bottom of this problem by appreciating and understanding it from more than one perspective is essential to solving it. Finally, while proactively looking to understand the current problems holistically is a great place to start, remember to keep the problems you find in context and balanced with everything else.

It's all too easy to get bogged down and demoralized by the amount and scale of problems. In any organization, there will always be problems. It can seem like a never-ending cycle of problem discovery! But there will also be lots of solutions and more positive wins and outcomes.

Quality dialogue with your team and fellow managers through healthy, sensible, and balanced conversations should also highlight areas that are operating well. This keeps everything in perspective and will give you a better view of what are the real things you need to tend to first, therefore, allowing you to work out: *what is my job now?*

We've talked about what your job is now that you've got it, so let's talk about the seven fundamental roles that you'll encounter, plus what to expect, and what you should do on your first day and your first week.

Figure 3.4: Balancing your workload, as well as tackling problems with adequate solutions, will be a constant challenge
Source: https://www.jashow.org/articles/how-to-live-a-biblically-balanced-life/

The seven fundamental roles of any software project

A software project is a complicated and dynamic process. No matter which methodology you adopt, it's difficult to deliver a software project on time and on budget and to the required quality, not least because seemingly everything changes along the way.

One of the key foundations of any software project is to have all of the necessary stakeholders identified and their roles agreed upon early on. This establishes the purpose and value of each contributor, and when they are required by the project.

Similar to software development methodologies, there are many differing views on this particular topic, partly because software projects are so unique. Each project is so different from another, even if it's being delivered by the same people. No business problem is exactly the same. So, no solution, nor how it's developed and implemented, is ever identical.

However, if you zoom out of individual projects, there are patterns that can be used to generalize some aspects of their commonalities, to some degree, even standardizing their attributes and deliverables. After all, that is one of the key benefits of methodologies.

The classification and definition of the project team members' roles is such a generalization. While it's not a hard and fast set of rules, it establishes a common language, terminology, and understanding, which makes communication and expectation setting easier.

1. Project Manager

If your first step into management is project management, then this is you!

As we discussed in `Chapter 1`, *Why Do You Want to Become a Manager?*, there are broadly three categories of managers in the software development context. Becoming a **Project Manager** (**PM**) is an increasingly popular way for developers, and techies in general, to transition into management. This is because project management is becoming increasingly ubiquitous and intrinsic part of most jobs, in software and IT in general, as well as in other industries.

Although the modern Project Manager is a versatile role, a key distinction is that it has no direct people- or line-management responsibilities. The main role of the Project Manager is to facilitate the process of delivering the project.

To achieve this, the Project Manager has three key responsibilities:

- Planning
- Controlling
- Reporting

Let's have a look at each of those responsibilities.

Planning

Since software projects are complex, planning is essential to ensure there is a reasonable understanding of a project's key aspects and expected challenges ahead of time. This is so that issues can be prevented or solved quickly. It's also important to ascertain whether the project is worth doing at all.

Establishing the **business case** is an essential part of planning. Using simple but effective techniques such as **cost-benefit analysis**, a Project Manager – with input from the project team and stakeholders – can quickly work out whether the project is a worthwhile endeavor for the organization.

Simplistically, if the project is expected to cost £100,000, then it should benefit the organization in excess of £100,000, therefore creating value for the organization.

The quantification of cost is a simpler task, even if it is arduous, depending on the level of detail required, and where most project initially focus. With the best information you have, you estimate what it will take to achieve the project's goal. Like estimating a building project, you guess how much materials and labor you might need, then get quotes for each element and add them together.

However, the quantification of benefits is often more difficult in the real world. This is because there are many forms of benefit, and it's often a potential benefit, which means it may not materialize immediately, or at all. Quite often, a software project is required to mitigate a cost, in which case, this can be used as a good indication of benefit.

For example, if the organization does not upgrade to the latest version of its software, its supplier will charge an additional cost to extend its support. This cost and therefore benefit can be quoted for in advance. But there are also more complex benefits, such as avoiding a potential regulatory fine, or most commonly, investing in a new piece of software in order to expand a business. Business expansion is a complex and risky venture. Having the new piece of software ready is only one part of its chances of succeeding. So, in this wider context, it often comes down to what the Project Sponsor is willing to invest, in relation to the overall business plan of the organization.

If you remember, back in `Chapter 2`, *What Are the Key Skills I Need?*, the business case is a key element within the *PRINCE2* project management methodology. It's normally recorded formally in the management product called the **Project Initiation Document** (**PID**).

With the cost largely considered, a Project Manager will usually then focus on time.

In the cost-benefit analysis, time already has a large part to play. The **End Of Service Life** (**EOSL**) for the existing software has a finite time. The risk of a regulatory fine has a defined point in time when the regulation starts to be enforced.

The overall business plan will have a date when the new business is aiming to launch. So, all of these factors can be used as input to set a deadline for the project's completion.

A Project Manager has to balance this counting back approach, with the practicalities and resource limitations at their disposal.

As the old cliché goes: Everyone knows that it takes one pregnant mother nine months to give birth to a baby. But you can't ask nine mothers to make a baby in one month.

It's the role of the Project Manager to balance this in creating the **project plan**, in essence, deciding and organizing the project's resources in a way that realistically achieves the completion deadline. In other words, this means spreading the work as thinly or heavily as required within the duration of the project, with special considerations for milestones and key events, some of which may be outside of your control, such as external events like public holidays.

The project plan is invariably accompanied by a corresponding **Gantt chart**, which is the most widely accepted way of visualizing a project plan. A good Gantt chart can illustrate the required tasks, who is responsible, the effort required, the timing or scheduling, sequencing, and dependencies all on the same chart!

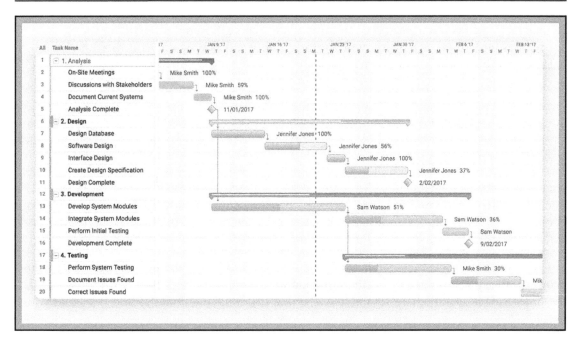

Figure 3.5: A simplified version of the Gantt chart is often a great tool to use for a summary or high-level meeting, like the project steering group, with senior management audience members including the Project Sponsor

Source: http://easybusinessfinance.net/example-of-gantt-chart-for-project-management/gantt-chart-of-project-management/

Controlling

Once a Project Manager has built a plan, as elements inevitably change over the course of the project, they have to control the variables involved in order to stay within the *Triple Constraint* of time, cost, and quality.

In my experience, the focus of control is usually centered around the project's **scope** and **risk** because these two essential elements have the greatest impact on time, cost, and quality, which are the key concerns of all project managers. If the scope increases, the time required will normally increase, and there is a risk of diminished quality.

Scope creep is often cited as the root cause of many project delays and failures. This is when the remit of what the project must deliver changes over the course of the project, often without the necessary adjustments to time, cost, and quality constraints and expectations.

Scope creep itself is often caused by an unrealistic expectation of having all of the knowledge and business requirements upfront. Since this is very difficult to achieve, it's natural that the scope is changed throughout the project life cycle, causing rework at various stages, which requires more effort and time.

The role of a Project Manager is to control this as much as possible. It would be equally unrealistic to expect a Project Manager to prevent any scope creep, as there will be legitimate reasons for scope changes. The key is to keep this to a manageable level, with the agreement of the customer.

It's important to appreciate that the customer is also learning throughout the process. Therefore, it is natural and to be expected that, as the project progresses, requirements evolve due to the clarity of understanding, or a genuine external business change such as pricing updates or even company mergers and acquisitions.

There may also be legitimate technology-led reasons for scope changes. For example, if the project is to replatform an application and soon after starting the project, a new version of the database management system is released that contains functionality and fixes that you would otherwise have to patch manually, then it would be a valid discussion and decision point to increase the scope of the project to include a database upgrade.

When the scope increases, the amount of development and testing work almost always increases as well. In this example, additional regression, performance, and stress testing are likely to be required to make sure the new version of the database is fit for use.

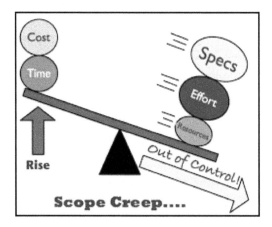

Figure 3.6: Scope creep is the bane of many projects and project managers
Source: https://web.archive.org/web/20171112041209im_/http://www.desaruresorts.com/wp-content/uploads/2017/10/scorecreep.png

Risk is something that requires active management. Being risk-aware at all times is a sign of a good Project Manager, whose role is not to prevent or mitigate all risks, but to meticulously record, track, and ensure they are pursued by the appropriate project team members until their conclusion.

This is most typically done via a detailed **risks, assumptions, issues, and dependencies (RAID)** log. As the name suggests, this is a detailed log of risks, actions, issues, and decisions (sometimes dependencies), which we discussed in `Chapter 2`, *What Are the Key Skills I Need?*. The *RAID log* should be a published document that everyone on the project team contributes to.

Risks should be identified, assessed, and prioritized in a consistently manner as part of its entry into the *RAID log*.

There's a huge variety of risk types and classifications adapted for software projects, but I particularly like the simple yet effective model by technology and project management writer, Balaji Viswanathan, who lists only four types of risks:

1. Scope risk

As the name suggests, this is most associated with a very real risk of scope creep. It also includes a related quality dimension, for example, the number of defects permitted for go-live is very rarely zero. Therefore, this is a calculated risk by the project that the software will operate within a reasonable range of the necessary functionality, accuracy, reliability, and performance.

2. Scheduling risk

This is down to task scheduling and timing. As software projects are complex, with many interdependencies, there is always a risk to cascading impacts and delays. Sometimes unintended or even unknown. For example, testers cannot begin real testing until both the software has been developed and the test environment is ready with suitable test data.

3. Resource risk

This type of risk is most commonly linked to a potential shortage of people with the necessarily knowledge skills, which is a very real possibility in any modern organization with finite resources. An effective Project Manager should be cognizant of this when planning and requesting people's availability. They should also consider other less obvious resources such as a potential lack of servers, storage, test environments, licenses, and so on.

4. Technology risk

The software your project is delivering will most likely sit on top of a technology stack of hardware, operating system, database, server-client, back- and front-end infrastructure. All of these are technology products developed by someone else. The products themselves and their compatibility and integration can present risks to how your software functions and performs. This is also true for cloud platforms because they are inherently complex and have many variations. So, there is always a risk to other layers of the stack, including when any one layer requires a critical update or falls out of service life.

It's the role of a Project Manager to ensure each risk is understood and dealt with appropriately. To do so, they should review the *RAID log* regularly and methodically work through each risk with the rest of the project team to its conclusion.

Good control of the project's risks will result in an appropriate risk option being agreed and an affirmative action being taken. If actively pursued to its conclusion, all risk can be avoided, reduced, shared, or accepted, which means the project does not progress in a haphazard way.

Reporting

Reporting is all about communication, which is a fundamental part of stakeholder engagement and management. This is an essential part of a Project Manager's role throughout the project life cycle.

The goal is to keep everyone involved with the project informed and aware of what is happening. Bear in mind that your project is most likely not the only project they are involved with at any one time. The chances are that you are managing multiple projects at once, too! So, it'd be unreasonable to expect your project team to go out of their way to hunt for the latest information on your project.

Proactively reporting on your project ensures the information they need to know is available for them, when they need it or when the project needs them.

To achieve this, it's the Project Manager's responsibility to establish an engaging and consistent reporting structure.

Reporting methods vary from the mundane tried and tested, to the clever and dynamic.

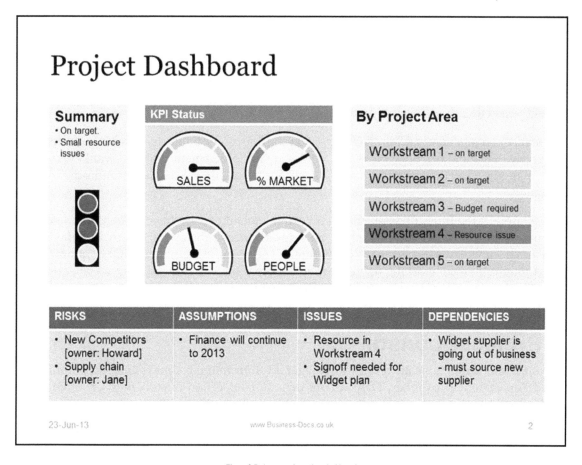

Figure 3.7: An example project dashboard
Source: https://business-docs.co.uk/downloads/powerpoint-project-dashboard-with-status-template/

Most frequently, project status reports follow the same pattern:

- **Cadence**: A report every 1-2 weeks
- **Summary**: Executive and project team level synopsis of the latest updates

- **RAG status**: The useful and often contentious Red/Amber/Green status of the project overall, as well as individual risks and issues
- **Progress against the plan**: Usually a diagrammatic view of the project plan, including the most important information illustrated by the Gantt chart

While it's sensible to be consistent and conform to standards normally set by the **Project Management Office** (**PMO**), I would always advise that a Project Manager thinks seriously about the reaction they are looking to achieve with each update.

The level of engagement and impact that a standard format update achieves is expected to be exactly that standard. So, if there is a significant announcement that you want everyone to sit up and notice, then consider using an extraordinary, or at least, less standard approach.

For example, if the project has reached a milestone, whether it is ahead or behind schedule, the update should reflect the excitement and significance of the event! Again, in today's busy environment, it's important to differentiate your project from any number of others. A little thought to make working on your project more interesting goes a long way to ensure people stay engaged and motivated to do their best work.

2. Project Sponsor

A Project Sponsor is typically a senior manager, both from the business customer and from the IT department or supplier. They are organizational decision-makers who are often short on time and have a wealth of experience, gravitas, and reputation.

If your project follows a formal methodology such as *PRINCE2*, an important distinction of a Project Sponsor is that they should not hold any other role in the project. Specifically, this means that they do not have delivery responsibilities. This is important because it helps to keep them unbiased in their decision-making.

A common symptom of someone actively delivering the project is the *sunk cost fallacy*. Put simply, the individual becomes over-invested into the project because they have worked extremely hard on it. This can cloud their decision-making approach because they are unconsciously looking back at what it's cost them personally.

In contrast, a true Project Sponsor will recognize the cost spent, but more importantly, the future cost and benefit to come, because the overall cost and benefit are what should drive business decisions.

Typically, the Project Manager and the Project Sponsors will meet every 2-4 weeks. These meetings are usually called **steering group** meetings. As a rule of thumb, this period should be every two or more project status updates, the reason being that key business decisions should not be kneejerk reactions, but instead take a longer-term view of events and trends before intervening.

One of the key responsibilities of Project Sponsors, and a likely outcome from a steering group meeting, is the allocation and prioritization of key resources. This could include, the release of funds to continue (or discontinue) a project, or the ringfencing of a key team member's time to work exclusively on one project over others.

Project Sponsors will also have a keen eye on the most significant risks and have input to the project's proposed risk option. In most cases, any significant risks that cannot be mitigated and require accepting will be accepted with the relevant Project Sponsor's approval.

Ultimately, the Project Sponsors will have the responsibility of making or at least supporting the final go/no-go decision for when the project is ready to launch.

3. Business Subject Matter Expert

As the name suggests, the **Business Subject Matter Expert** (BSME) is someone with deep knowledge of the relevant business for which the software is intended to serve.

This person, or group of people, is vital because their early input into the requirements gathering and design process is the starting point for much of the project delivery phase.

Modern business processes are complicated, even those that follow a largely standardized approach, such as, the "Order to Cash" and "Procure to Pay" processes. Assuming that no customization takes place, which would add an extra level of complexity to the requirements, automation of these complex processes requires a great deal of knowledge and insight into how these processes work from end to end. This involves understanding the stories and use cases of all of the users that contribute to the business process.

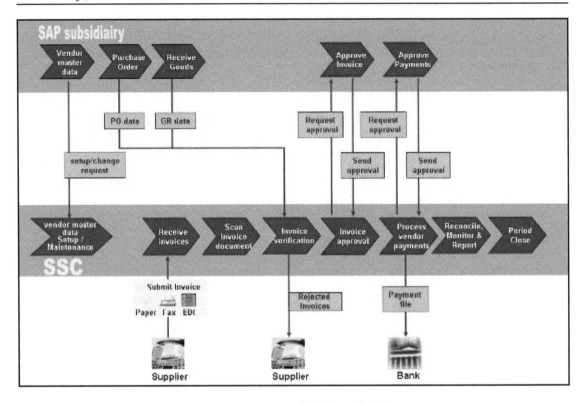

Figure 3.8: An example process diagram of SAP's Procure to Pay (P2P) process
Source: https://wiki.scn.sap.com/wiki/pages/viewpage.action?pageId=14508

If you consider a factory workflow management application, there are likely to be multiple factory operators with unique roles, inputs, and outputs, as well as a monitoring and management information layer to supervise and control overall performance and throughput. Similarly, with consumer-facing software, such as Facebook, there is a complex management and administration layer that only the Facebook engineers see and use to manage their system, including a way to roll out trial features on a user-by-user basis, among over 2 billion users worldwide! Put simply, there are many facets to modern software and its usage.

The Business Subject Matter Expert's role is to represent the business users to the rest of the software project team, taking part in requirements gathering and solution design workshops, as well as end user testing.

4. Business Analyst

The primary role of a **Business Analyst** (**BA**) in a software project is to assist the BSME to understand and document the business requirements in a way that the rest of the project team can use.

In a large organization, a Business Analyst can sit within IT or a business department, depending on how IT is integrated with the rest of the organization. They will be a key contributor in requirements and design workshops, acting as a bridge between non-technical customers and technical designers and developers.

Their first main responsibility is to gather the requirements from the BSME, as well as other sources such as ordinary and power users, IT users, and system administrators. This is formally called **requirement elicitation**, which can be summarized in four steps:

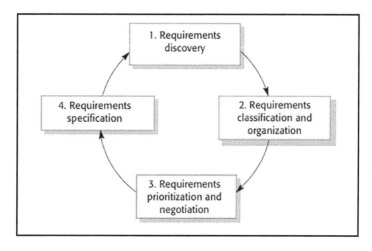

Figure 3.9: The four steps in the requirement elicitation cyclical process
Source: https://medium.com/omarelgabrys-blog/requirements-engineering-elicitation-analysis-part-2-a02db801f135

One of the more advanced techniques used by Business Analysts is **modeling**. This could be process modeling, which simplifies a typical business process in order to make it easier to understand, or data modeling, which rationalizes complex datasets so that it can be represented and illustrated in a summarized format.

There are various structured methods of modeling. Since the purpose of modeling is to represent, illustrate, clarify, and communicate complex concepts, there are standards in place so that the industry as a whole uses a common language.

Unified Modeling Language (**UML**) is the most comprehensive standard for modeling. It's widely used in software, as well as other industries, and has been approved by the **International Organization for Standardization (ISO)**.

On the other hand, **entity-relationship** (**ER**) modeling is most often used to model data. In essence, it is a logical database schema that defines the pieces of data required and how they are connected to each other.

From experience, the humble **flow chart** is most often the go-to format for models. It's versatile, and easy to consume and produce, especially if you're a flexible Project Manager who is filling in as a Business Analyst out of necessity!

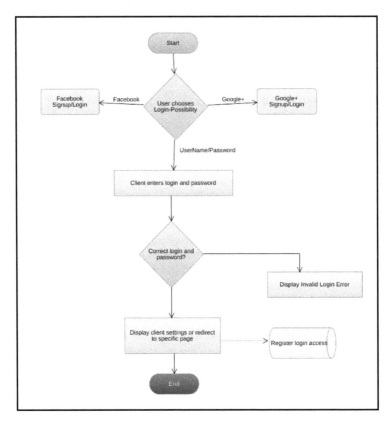

Figure 3.10: Example of a simple flow chart, describing the process of a user logging into Facebook
Source: https://repository.genmymodel.com/alexanderlenz85/Login-Process

As the Project Manager, you should facilitate a discussion between your project team to ensure the choice of modeling language fits the most people. It's a common pitfall that the Business Analyst unilaterally chooses how they model, often because they have a personal preference and expertise. However, it's counterproductive if the rest of the project team does not understand the models produced!

This is why the humble flowchart is often a safe choice, especially in a large-scale software project involving many team members and stakeholders, because it's easily and commonly understood by most people without the need to study modeling. In a positive way, it's the lowest common denominator that connects people and supports their collective understanding.

5. Technical Architect

In a purely software project, the **Technical Architect** (**TA**) can also be thought of as the chief designer or lead developer. The remit of this role is to bridge the gap between the business problem and its technological solution.

It's worth taking a minute to distinguish between an **Enterprise Architect** (**EA**), **Solution Architect** (**SA**), and TA, because these terms are sometimes used interchangeably. However, going by industry best practice, there are important differences in their definition.

EAs focus on a higher, strategic level across the entire organization. Therefore, they concentrate on long-term trends and foundations across all projects and operations; for example, a "cloud-first" strategy, whereby any new solutions being designed should consider cloud hosting as the first option. This supports major commercial activities such as the exit of an on-premise data center-hosting contract.

SAs have a broad range of technical knowledge, including infrastructure, hardware, and software products. They oversee the process of choosing and buying technology solutions. Together with EAs, they create technology roadmaps. For example, when a particular hardware or software product reaches its end of service life, the roadmap plans what the replacement product should be.

Technical Architects have the most focused, in-depth knowledge in a particular technology area because their work is more specialized, for example, Java or integration architecture. In contrast to EAs and SAs, they focus on implementation activities and typically work on a small number of projects at any one time. They work on tailoring the chosen technology products to solve the current business problem. Ensuring that the project designs and implements an application that supports the overall enterprise strategy.

At a project level, the TA is the most relevant and most hands-on in terms of approach. They provide technical leadership for development teams and define best practice standards for them to follow. They also help individual developers to understand and work within the design principles, at times, assisting with technical troubleshooting and problem solving at a code level, if required.

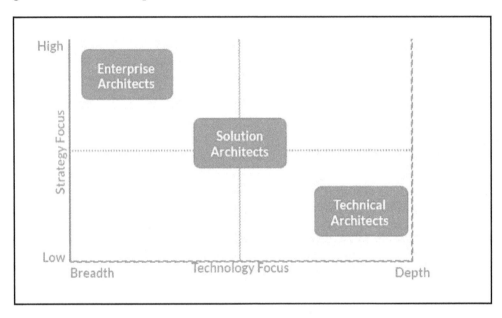

Figure 3.11: A simple chart illustrating the mix of strategy and technology focus by Enterprise Architects, Solution Architects, and Technical Architects
Source: https://blog.leanix.net/en/enterprise-architect-vs-solution-architect-whats-the-difference

The most visible part of a TA's work will normally be done at the application design phase. They collaborate with the Business Analyst and development team to understand the business requirements together and incorporate any technical requirements such as reliability and maintainability, such as **Disaster Recovery** (**DR**), before translating all requirements into a set of actionable technical specifications.

For example, deciding how the data needs to be structured and designing the database accordingly. Or designing the modular structure of the software to ensure it is flexible and performant, such as breaking down the data **Extract, Transform, and Load** (**ETL**) process so that certain extractions, transformations, and loads can share the same modules or use the same code.

An important role of the TA is to ensure any *technical debt* accrued by a project is clearly recorded and explained to the project stakeholders, as well as the SAs and EAs, and that there is a plan to repay that debt. Technical debt, and specifically *code debt*, is essentially a compromise on certain technical aspects of the software product, usually done to save time or cost.

This should not be confused with allowance for more bugs or defects, which is directly related to quality.

An example of code debt would be when there isn't enough time to redevelop and merge two ETL interfaces, which essentially do the same thing but were written at different times, using different adapters. So, a new interface is developed to sit alongside the existing module, which increases overall complexity, maintenance effort, and additional connections.

6. Developer

The humble Developer is central to the software development process, as you well know.

Churning out clever code to meet the requirements and specifications is the bread-and-butter work of the humble Developer. This is what most people think Developers do, day in, day out. While it's not wrong, modern practices have evolved to be much more than that.

Especially in smaller organizations and more specialized software houses, the role of the Developer is increasingly merged with Business Analysts and TAs, adding to the scope and power of the Developer.

Often, the Developer has a larger say in the requirements and design process, which is a welcomed change to the days when "programmers" were asked to hide in the basement for long periods to write programs that are expected to fulfil all of the requirements, seemingly by magic.

Another way the role of the Developer has increased is the amalgamation of the frontend and backend with respect to web development. This is commonly referred to as full stack development.

One of the most common technology stacks for web development is the *LAMP* stack. This stands for Linux, Apache, MySQL, and PHP/Perl/Python. Most recently, the *MEAN* stack (MongoDB, ExpressJS, AngularJS, and NodeJS) has been gaining in popularity. Both stacks are open source and free to use, but you probably knew that already!

If you are a team or delivery manager, it's your responsibility to ensure developers have what they need to deliver. This includes supporting them on technical and social challenges. As with a lot of management responsibilities, they will overlap with those of other management roles, which is why it's important to approach it in a coordinated manner, by speaking to other managers regularly.

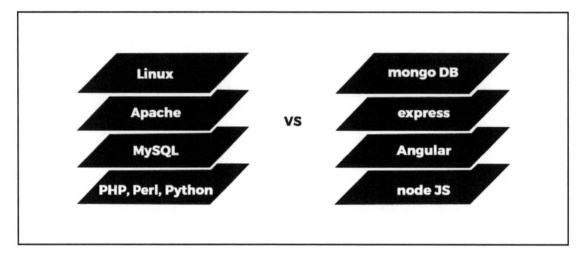

Figure 3.12: LAMP stack versus MEAN stack

7. Testers

Software Testers are primarily responsible for determining the quality of application developed by the project. This involves negative tests, where the purpose of the test is to break the application, as well as positive tests, which proves that it works as intended.

The **V-Model** is most commonly cited by the software testing profession to explain the importance of testing, and the difference between *verification* and *validation*. There are various phases of testing that each relate to a corresponding design phase.

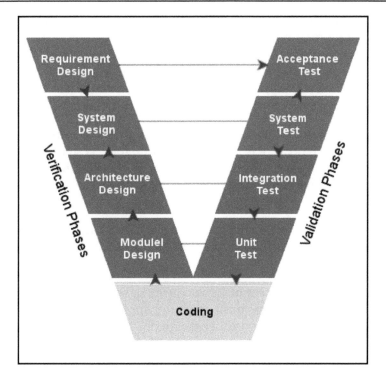

Figure 3.13: The classic V-Model
Source: http://www.professionalqa.com/v-model

The key skill for Testers is in understanding the design of the application from both an end user and technology perspective. Both angles give insight into where there is a high risk of issues within the application.

Software is notoriously impossible to test exhaustively or comprehensively, because there are simply too many permutations and possible scenarios. Certainly, in terms of code coverage, if that's even possible to measure, it is extremely difficult to achieve a high percentage.

Therefore most, if not all, test strategies will use a **risk-based** approach to decide where and how to focus their finite resources to test – positively and negatively. They will also use simple techniques such as *boundary-value analysis* and *equivalence partitioning* to identify values and parameters to test with. This is essentially using variables that are at the cut-off or deciding points, which affect the expected outcome. For example, in tax calculations, you would use income values on either side of a tax bracket boundary.

Another example of a risk-based testing approach is the prioritization of tests which make the biggest technical difference. For example, it'd be rare for a Tester to spend much effort to test that low-level logging is 100% accurate. However, checking that the exception handling functionality displays the correct error code to allow the support team to troubleshoot issues would be a highly valuable test case.

For healthcare applications, functionality that impacts clinical safety, such as patient and medical data, would be highly prioritized because of the potential human and financial cost of any errors.

Increasingly, there is a larger element of security testing, which may include penetration testing and ethical hacking. For some businesses and applications, such as the military and intelligence services, or even mass consumer-facing businesses such as Amazon, it's appropriate to use *Red Team versus Blue Team* simulations of cyber-attacks. This is where an autonomous red team plays the role of an attacker and a separate blue team plays the defense.

As the Project Manager, your role is to ensure that all of the appropriate stakeholders understand and agree with the test strategy, approach, and scope. As with the project scope, there is also a risk of testing scope creep whereby the amount of testing deemed reasonable increases unintentionally. The purpose of the test strategy is to determine this upfront as much as possible, allowing the Project Manager to control the amount of time and resources required for testing, in balance with all other project activities.

Your first day

First impressions matter, because you can only make them once. Starting off on the right foot, and in the right direction, is important to lay the foundations for future success. There are many clichés when it comes to starting something. So, here are some practical things to think about and do on your first day as a manager!

Meet your manager

You've most probably met your new manager because you were interviewed by them. Or, if it's an internal move, you may even have a working relationship with them already.

Your first appointment of the day is most likely to be with your new manager, having been pre-arranged at the end of the recruitment process. The appointment should notify you of where you need to go, when you need to be there, and who you need to ask for at reception.

If any of this has not been pre-arranged, pick up the phone and ask right now!

This part is no different to starting on any other job.

This also applies to dress code. You should know what the organization's standard dress code and culture is ahead of time; specifically, what your fellow managers wear on a day-to-day basis. Typically, customer-facing managers will be required to dress more formally than non-customer facing managers. But practices vary from organization to organization. If in doubt, ask!

Assuming that these basic things have been arranged, you can concentrate on setting your own mind up for success.

Mentally, the most important element is adapting your own sense of role and duty. Remember to acknowledge and conscientiously avoid the impostor syndrome. You haven't radically changed overnight as a person. You still have all of the knowledge, skills, and personality attributes of a brilliant and professional developer. You've been hired or promoted as a result of your good work. So, your new manager believes that you are the most suitable and capable person for the job!

If you're all set to meet your new manager at reception, then that's great!

Speaking from personal experience, there are sometimes mishaps that result in your new manager being absent on your first day.

I once arrived at the new office and asked for my new manager at reception. Unfortunately, no one picked up on their desk phone. It was a rented, shared office facility, so the receptionist didn't know who else to call.

This was before the days of the smartphone and emails on the go. So, I reverted to the paper documentation I had, which included correspondence with someone from HR. The receptionist was able to find the number for this recruiter, but there was also no answer!

After several attempts and a steadily building queue behind me, someone from my new manager's team picked up the call. Although they did not know the details of my arrival, they were aware that I was due to join the organization, so came to reception to greet me and sign me in.

It turned out that my new manager was ill and couldn't make it to work. Since it was a small team and my manager took care of all managerial tasks such as requesting new starter access, no one else had any idea of what was supposed to happen, including where I was supposed to sit. After a little embarrassed laughter, we found a peer of my manager, then my manager's manager, who was able to formally introduce me to the team and tell me where to sit!

Assuming that this sitcom scenario doesn't happen to you, you will meet your manager as soon as you start. A key difference between starting as a manager versus a developer is that you may be asked for your initial thoughts and plans for the team at a very early stage.

My advice on this is to manage your manager's expectations appropriately. Unless a situation is so obvious that it's unmissable, such as a team member who is behaving in a completely unprofessional manner, it's reasonable to stay reserved and conservatively objective.

You can and should be upfront in telling them your initiative observations. But do so without jumping to conclusions, and certainly refrain from selling your five-year plan on your first day.

The most important goal of your first meeting with your manager is to understand their thoughts, intentions, and plans for you and your team or project. You do so by asking them pertinent questions.

Setting an inquisitive and fearless tone early on helps to establish an open and healthy dialogue between you and your manager, in the most important relationship you have in the organization.

Ask questions such as:

- What is your vision for the team?
- What stage is the project currently at?
- What do the overall status, progress, risks, and issues look like?

- Which areas would you like to focus on first?
- What can I do to get up to speed quickly?
- Is there anything I can help with straight away?
- Who are my key stakeholders?
- What is the organization's standard project methodology?
- Why is this methodology used?

If there is an opportunity to talk about yourself, openly share your own background, strengths, and weaknesses. When sharing your relevant experiences, do so constructively and without prejudging or predetermining how you might deal with a real, current situation in your project or team. Remember that this is still your first day!

Also, remember that this is your very first one-to-one. As with your previous one-to-ones, these are regular meetings to catch up and request and receive support. So, also take the opportunity to discuss how you would like your one-to-ones to proceed, how often to meet, and what to focus on.

Figure 3.14: Avoid the awkward handshake
Source: https://web.archive.org/web/20170621115223/http://kjul1047.com/awkward-handshake/

Induction training

In some cases, your first day may involve attending an organizational induction course, instead of meeting your manager or team. If this happens, then simply remember that you are meeting and going through the same process as other new starters and meeting members of the HR recruitment team.

You may well be working with the people you meet after the induction. So, take the opportunity to identify potential key stakeholders, as well as building your understanding of the organization by learning about the jobs of other new starters.

For example, if you know from your interview that you are going to be working on a project to implement a new accounting system, then seeking out and building a relationship with a new starter from the accounting department would be sensible. They may have good information on the current structure and affairs of the department, and so building a relationship with them could be very useful going forward, especially if they also join the project as a business representative.

Meet your team

Whether you are a project, delivery, or team manager, the chances are that you will have a group of people to manage, and be part of a team yourself.

It's important to meet both these groups on your first day, and to do so deliberately rather than by chance. From an employee and career perspective, these are also your key stakeholders and you will be working closely with them throughout your time at the company.

So, proactively go introduce yourself to your peers. Ask your fellow Project Managers what they are working on and what they think of the ways of working. What are the things to look out for?

If you are a Team Manager, make sure you meet each of your development team members individually where possible. Similar to your first meeting with your manager, set an open and inviting tone to establish a good working relationship. Try to understand them as individuals and build rapport with them by active listening and sharing your own background as an experienced developer where appropriate.

As a Team Manager, your team members are your most valuable asset and your biggest responsibility.

The act of taking the time to meet each team member already tells them that you care about them. There's never a bad time to show or remind your team members that you care about them and about the team.

Regardless of style and methods, a caring manager can get the best performance from team members because they can motivate them through more than just reward and punishment, or "carrot and stick". So, show them that you care on your first day, in the same way that your manager has shown you.

The first team meeting

Meeting individual team members is great, but you also need to consider the team as a whole.

Team meetings are your regular one-to-many or many-to-ones, and an opportunity for team members to talk to each other. Take into consideration the size of your team and their locations if they work remotely. This gives you an indication of how practical it is to meet all of them at the same time and how often.

As a new starter and especially from a manager's perspective, it's a chance for you to gauge and assess the team as a collective entity:

- How well does it function or not?
- What are the staff dynamics?
- Who is the most vocal?
- Who is the most thoughtful?
- Who is agreed with and supported the most?
- How does the team react to organizational change?

Your first day is the best day to have your first team meeting. Depending on your organization and team's setup, it's also best to do this in person where possible. Meeting someone for the first time over video-conferencing just doesn't have the same impact. For one, you can't even share a handshake, which is, after all, an ancient custom to build trust by demonstrating to a potential foe that you are not holding a weapon to harm them.

By making an appropriate occasion for the team to meet up, it also sets the tone that you value group communication and collaboration.

In my experience, this is best done as an informal and shorter meeting. There is no agenda other than a gentle introduction and opportunity for everyone to learn a little bit more about you and each other.

I'm not advocating a grand entrance where you make a long speech about you and what you think the team should do immediately. That is most certainly a counterproductive way to achieve the goal of building trust and relationships with all colleagues in general, but more specifically with developers, who are typically creatives at heart, and value respect for their work and opinions. Ironically, I have witnessed this first hand on an applications team!

Your first week

Besides meeting your manager and your team, hosting your first team meeting, and possibly completing your induction training, the rest of your first week as a manager should be spent doing the following three things.

Meet your stakeholders

If you are now a Project Manager, then you may well have a large number of stakeholders, starting with the people who are performing the seven fundamental roles on your software project.

Although your relationship with them will be more transactional in nature, compared to a direct team you manage, when you take the time to formally and purposefully introduce yourself, your working relationship will get off to a better start.

It's not such a nice experience for a project team member to find out they have a new Project Manager through someone else, or at a functional meeting when a stranger presents themselves as the new Project Manager.

A little human touch to introduce yourself before jumping straight into task allocation and delivery goes a long way to earn some professional and mutual respect for each other's time and work.

Formally introducing yourself to a key stakeholder such as your Project Sponsor is vital to establish your own credibility and reputation, because those are the currencies that you will rely on to request for approvals and additional resources.

If you are located at the same office, I strongly recommend that you try to meet in person. Keep it brief and light. It doesn't have to be in a meeting room, but make sure that it's an appropriate and convenient time for them to pause whatever they're doing.

I was once introduced to a colleague at the entrance turnstiles of a large company office, and it happened to be at a busy lunch time! So, it was a disastrous first introduction, which the colleague who attempted to make the introduction and I still laugh about. Luckily, the person I was trying to meet didn't actually work on my project!

Set your own schedule

Time-poverty is an unfortunate theme of life as a modern manager. The importance of setting your own schedule cannot be underestimated.

So, time management needs to be a focus early on, before your calendar starts to fill up by meeting invites, which is an inevitable occurrence for the majority of managers due to the ever-increasing scope of their work, as well as their overall workload.

There is no magic formula or silver bullet to setting your own schedule and keeping to it effectively. But there are actions and habits that can help you to reserve valuable time to your most important tasks. These are highly subjective, and the following suggestions are based on observations from effective managers and my own experience, in a number of different cultural settings.

If you are a Project Manager, begin by finding out the schedule of the project management office (PMO) or project board meetings. If you are joining an existing project, find out what project meetings there are, how often they take place, and whether they're really suitable for every attendee. If anything looks wrong, then your arrival and fresh perspective is the perfect opportunity to change to a better schedule for everyone involved.

Once you have established these mandatory and necessary recurring meetings, plan how much time you need to prepare for them. Block out this preparation time in your calendar immediately before the meetings themselves, so that it can be dedicated to doing this preparation. If you can do the preparation well ahead of the meeting, then great.

If not, this is the last chance you will have to do it, and you really don't want that time to be taken away by something else.

Figure 3.16: The trick here is not to treat your own schedule as a project plan or Gantt chart. Make sure there is a reasonable gap between tasks, so that they do not butt up immediately next to each other.
Source: https://ourcodeworld.com/articles/read/55/top-5-best-jquery-scheduler-and-events-calendar-for-web-applications

If you are a Team Manager, establish the working patterns of your team and design how it needs to be going forward. For example, are there daily huddles or shift handovers? If so, at what time? Is there a better, more appropriate time instead?

From experience, I've found that publishing your team's regular meetings, such as the daily huddles, on collaboration platforms such as SharePoint is a great way to safeguard that time for your team members. Bear in mind that each of them may well be working on different projects. Publishing your development team's huddles as a significant event cuts across all projects becomes regarded as a standard that's valuable for every project, because that's when important development information is shared between projects among your team.

For regular one-to-ones with your team members, make sure you allow sufficient time for each person. Again, try not to schedule them immediately next to each other because there is always the possibility of overrunning.

Due to the potentially sensitive and private nature of the discussions, you should allow the conversation to continue as much as possible by planning in a contingency.

For team meetings, I find that monthly or four-weekly intervals work best. This allows sufficient time for actions and is a reasonable period for genuine newsworthy events to occur, which can then be shared among the team. Team meetings are overly frequent if the same update is given on the same topic, repeatedly.

Make a plan

As a manager, planning is an essential part of your job. It is a basic expectation of a manager to be organized and prepared for most reasonable situations in the near-term. Moreover, this is the planning for yourself and your team or project.

Considering this is your first week, it's reasonable to have only a high-level plan, rather than a detailed, fully formed strategy to take over the world. The important thing is that you have started the process of planning ahead.

When it comes to planning for your team or project, you should first work out where you are now. For a team and its people development, try a technique such as a simple **SWOT** (**Strengths**, **Weaknesses**, **Opportunities**, and **Threats**) analysis or maturity assessment to determine the starting point for each team member and the team as a whole.

One of the first things I always do when building a team from scratch or joining to manage an existing team is to create a "team deck". This is essentially an introductory guidebook to who your team is, what it does, and how it operates. It's also a mini sales brochure that can be used to promote your team to stakeholders and prospective new customers. Your team deck should contain your team's mission, as well as how it's looking to improve.

Once you have a reasonable idea of where your team or project is currently in terms of maturity or progress, you should map out the immediate next steps required to improve or move forward. This will naturally be a list of actions, such as finding training courses or running another design workshop.

Most importantly, keep your plan simple. Write it in a simple way that is easy for you to update and improve on regularly, as well as easily understood by others. As a general rule of thumb, a good first-week plan should fit on a single A4 page, which you can share with your team, your manager, and your stakeholders. Remember to invite them to feedback and openly accept this as an opportunity to improve it.

The underlying idea is to demonstrate your own progress with settling in and adding more value, in order to gain the confidence of your stakeholders.

Summary

When you change roles from *Developer-to-Manager*, it's vital to proactively listen and learn, in order to gain an understanding of your new position as soon as possible. Management meetings are a great forum for you to gain insight into your new management role. Start building a healthy relationship with your peers and fellow managers. A relationship is about more than just simple transactions. So, try to have meaningful conversations focusing on feedback and ideas where possible and appropriate, over simple exchanges of tasks and information.

Be aware of how openly they're likely to share their challenges with you, then request or perhaps enlist your help. Always remember that collective problem solving is at the heart of good management. So, collaborate where possible, but also remember that you have your own priorities to take care of.

No matter which methodology your project adopts, there are widely accepted approaches and seven typical associated roles in a software project, which the project team should all be aware of. A Project Manager is focused on planning, controlling (specifically of risks), and reporting.

The Project Sponsor is the senior key decision maker, who has a big responsibility in approving and steering the project, but isn't concerned with implementing any day-to-day tasks.

The BSME has a deep domain knowledge of the business area of the project and represents the majority of end users at a project level. The Business Analyst has the responsibility of formally discovering, modeling, and recording the business requirements in a way that is pertinent and useful to the project.

The TA is the technical subject matter expert, who brings a solution-oriented view to the project team and is responsible for the overall technical design of the solution. The humble Developer has the critical responsibility of building the agreed solution design. The Tester is responsible for verifying the design and validating the solution to the required quality standard.

It's important to get off to a great start on your first day. Meet your manager to discuss vision, strategy, and urgent priorities. Be mindful of the impostor syndrome and stay confident in your fantastic and unique qualities. Start the conversation about how you, your experience, and key skills can help the team. Don't forget about your induction training.

Meet your team on the first day, individually and collectively, to build rapport and trust with them – your most valuable asset and responsibility. By having your first team meeting immediately, you send a clear message that you value them. It also sets an open tone for responsive and collaborative team-working going forward.

Within your first week, you should also meet your stakeholders. Setting your own schedule is an important step to getting and staying organized. Make a plan and agree this with your manager, as well as any stakeholders, if required.

Then, you can start thinking about methodically building a productive and creative environment for yourself and your team, in order to foster creativity and enable effective delivery, which we will discuss in the next chapter.

4
A Week in the Life of a Manager

Every professional, throughout their career, will encounter both learning and development needs. These needs are typically fulfilled by a combination of on-the-job learning and formal training. Yet, as you begin, and even while you continue your journey as a manager, you will undoubtedly encounter situations where you will need to learn in order to grow and operate effectively.

It's important for you to think of this need to keep learning in certain situations, not as a weakness, or as a sign that you lack skills, but as a positive thing, because it is simply a fact of modern professional life for everyone.

The technologies that we use in our daily lives today are advancing and evolving faster than they have ever done before. This has a profound effect on the software business itself and everything it touches, including the people, both developers and managers, who use it.

The gaps in your skillset, knowledge, mindset, and ways of thinking and working need to be identified and plugged. Moreover, the self-awareness to understand the need to address these gaps is vital if you are going to be an effective manager.

Whether you have the responsibility and privilege of managing people or not, you will still need to be self-aware enough to identify the areas where you can perform better. This could include areas such as technical knowledge as well as softer skills like communication, stakeholder management, and negotiation.

If you're fortunate enough to have funding for formal training, then the type of training tends to split into two main camps: *technical skills* and *soft skills*. Curiously, there are very few training courses that combine both skill sets. This might be because the idea is simply too ambitious and not marketable in today's time-poor environment and competitive training business.

A simple fact of modern professional life is that most individuals and organizations tend to prefer structured training that's focused on a specific area, which is understandable.

This brings us to the focus of this chapter: an exploration of what a week as a manager can look like. Along the way, you'll see how much learning needs to take place every week for a manager.

During this tour of a manager's typical week, we'll look at the *70/20/10* blended learning model and the **Information Technology Infrastructure Library** (**ITIL**) framework, and we'll explore the development process. Our main focus will be on the Weekly Project Template, where we will walk through what an average Monday to Friday as a manager can look like.

The 70/20/10 blended learning model

Before we look at the average week of a manager, I want to place our focus on some different training models that you can implement during on-the-job learning or within more formal training. Whatever model you choose, you'll need to give yourself and any relevant team members enough time to implement it.

To put this into the wider context of your overall work, the most widely understood and followed approach to training is the 70/20/10 blended learning model. Before we break down what that means, *Catalent* has this great graphic, in *Figure 4.1*, which helps to visualize the model itself:

Figure 4.1: 70% experience, 20% exposure, and 10% education
Source: http://www.catalent.com/index.php/about-us/Catalent-Careers2/Overview/Learning-Development

What are the three arcs of the 70/20/10 learning model here? Well, if you are working on this training model then you think of it like this:

- 70% of learning is **experience**, which takes the form of on-the-job participation and discovery learning.
- 20% is through **exposure**, where you will learn through other people's experience, such as coaching, mentoring, shadowing, and other relational means.
- 10% is through **education**, which is where you attend formal training courses and interactive learning, including computer-based training.

For each type of learning, there are some practical actions that you can take in order to maximize the amount, and the pace, of your learning. It will be useful to now explore each of the three types of learning that feature in this training model.

Experiential learning

Experiential learning is all about *doing*. Management is not a theoretical craft. It may have lots of different theories and frameworks behind the science, but make no mistake about it: management is ultimately all about execution and application in the real world and with real people.

The importance of trying, and possibly failing, and then trying again cannot be underestimated. Most seasoned and self-aware managers will be able to tell you their "war stories," or times where they have crashed and burned, but also examples of victories, large or small. These war stories are invaluable experiences that they have gone through, which have shaped them up to the point you see them at today and will continue to going forward.

To maximize experiential learning, you need to simply maximize your experience by being open to defeat and willing to try, and try again and again, if necessary.

Exposure learning

Exposure learning is all about *asking*. The quickest and most effective way to learn through other people is to simply ask them questions like, "Why are you doing this?" and "How did you do this?"

Do you remember when we talked about *impostor syndrome* in the first chapter of this book? Impostor syndrome is one of the biggest barriers to exposure learning because if you are pretending that you know something already, then other people are unlikely to impart and share their knowledge with you.

However, if you openly say you don't know and ask for help, and you actively choose to listen to their answers, then it's more likely that you will learn from what they have to say. As a new manager, you should especially not be afraid to ask lots of questions. What's important here is to remember to do so respectfully and appropriately.

Educational learning

Educational learning is all about *studying*. Either by design, or by formal structured training. Educational learning involves a trainer, a facilitator, and maybe also a teacher figure.

When you are a student taking this pathway of learning, you will need to study in order to understand the content and concepts being taught to you. In today's modern world, education can take several different forms. Some training courses are highly interactive, while others, such as coding-based training, may be more practically based.

If you're reading this and thinking that educational learning is the easiest when compared to either experiential or exposure, then you may need to reconsider that statement. If your educational training leads to an externally recognized qualification, then it will most likely require you to pass an exam.

The impact of your methodology choice

From my experience, a professional organization that takes people development seriously will typically encourage and fund their employees for five days of formal training per year. This formal training time could take the form of one five-day course, which is taken over a working week; or it could be split into multiple training days, across multiple months, and across multiple different topics.

There should always be a valid business case to justify a reasonable value and return on the investment for the organization. You should be able to demonstrate a genuine need to attend such training and you should be able to describe to your boss how the training will benefit you and others in the organization.

That's because whatever you want to achieve, a training request is usually subject to your line manager's discretion and approval. If you are managing other people, then you will find yourself on both sides of this equation!

Let's take some learning here from my own work experience. During my graduate scheme days, I did rotations within a consultancy company – so I would regularly change roles. I spent roughly six months as a developer, tester, business analyst, and **Project Management Office** (**PMO**) analyst, as well as time working in support and operations.

This was an important stage of my career development because, apart from my university course, this was the first time I had received any formal training as a developer. Even though I was in the graduate scheme, where training is accepted as a big factor, I still had to write a short business case to my line manager to justify learning a programming language!

At the time, this seemed nonsensical to me because I would have genuinely struggled to develop code in a slightly obscure **fourth-generation programming language** (**4GL**) called *COOL:Gen*. And yet, in hindsight, writing that first business case was a valuable lesson.

For obvious reasons, including the prospects of long-term employability, most savvy professionals will prefer formal training, which leads to a professionally and externally recognized qualification. This is something for you to take into consideration as an employee, and as a manager, in a very positive way.

While granting unnecessary training that leads to a qualification will incur a needless cost to your company, there is an additional risk to gauge here which is making other colleagues jealous who may not have had formal training.

I personally don't believe that supporting your team members to gain more qualifications is detrimental to your organization. For me, it's quite the opposite! I always prefer my team members to be well qualified so that the entire team, and therefore the organization, is more skilled and marketable. At the end of the day though, it's a fine balance between finite resources and pertinent needs, which is something you will need to consider as a manager.

Even though it's perhaps a throwaway line, and more of a notion than an actual practice, I particularly admire this mindset and approach from Richard Branson, the founder of the Virgin Group:

> *"Train people well enough so they can leave, treat them well enough so they don't want to."*

> *– Richard Branson*

Agile, PRINCE2, and ITIL

When it comes to both software delivery and application management, there are primarily three formal pieces of training that can lead to an externally recognized qualification.

Here are the three methodologies most commonly involved in this training. They are mostly applied to software development, but they can also be used in other industries:

- *Agile*
- *PRINCE2*
- *ITIL*

Interestingly, the *Waterfall model*, which is a popular methodology in our industry, is not included in this top list. My guess is that this is because the *Waterfall model* is now considered the go-to basic methodology that most traditional organizations will use. In which case, while it may require no introduction, you could equally argue that this makes *Waterfall* the most important methodology.

As we discussed in Chapter 2, *What Are the Key Skills I Need?*, the chosen methodology itself is not the be-all and end-all. What is much more important is your team's collective journey and the process of agreeing on which methodology you choose, followed by how you choose as a team to apply that methodology to your work.

All three of these methodologies are both flexible and adaptable. They are, by design, general enough that they can be applied to different industries and contexts. This high level of generalization, or even vagueness, can sometimes be frustrating when all you want to do is follow a simple step-by-step guide to deliver your software project. You therefore also need to be aware of alternatives to these best practices and recognized methodologies.

I'm not saying these three are the only methodologies you can use. Quite often, internally developed project methodologies can be used – which can have their own merits and value. But do be careful because these DIY methodologies are typically a condensed or even debased variation of one of the three main ones. In situations like that, your methodology really should just be called its proper name.

You'll remember from Chapter 2, *What Are the Key Skills I Need?*, that we discussed the merits and practical applications of *Agile, Waterfall*, and *PRINCE2*. We appreciated the true principles behind the *Agile* Manifesto, and we understood the practical benefits of incremental development over big-bang releases, dynamic daily huddles over regular static updates, and user stories over exhaustive requirements.

We also discussed the key difference between *Waterfall* and *Agile*. If you may recall, the focus of *Waterfall* is to be iterative between life cycle stages, while *Agile*'s focus is to be incremental in its overall delivery. With regards to *PRINCE2*, we dedicated a section to identifying the key principles, processes, and themes of the methodology. You'll remember that we put quite a lot of focus on vital management products such as the project initiation document, RAID log, and lessons log.

What you won't remember, however, is the **Information Technology Infrastructure Library** (**ITIL**) methodology, which introduces us now to a new concept called **IT Service Management** (**ITSM**). In *ITIL*'s own words:

   "ITIL is the most adopted and recognized body of knowledge for ITSM."

– *ITIL Mission statement*

The *ITIL* methodology is a broad concept and it isn't exclusive or specific to software applications. Make no mistake though that *ITIL* is a very important methodology that we need to look at in detail, so I will now break this methodology down into more detail.

The ITIL framework

ITIL is often referred to as a best practice framework within the industry. This means that *ITIL* is based on a set of recommended principles and practices, as opposed to a set of strict rules or even guidelines.

In practical terms, this means that *ITIL* represents a set of common processes and a standardized terminology. In the real world, this will help IT departments and organizations to work better with their non-IT counterparts, or "the business" side.

Under the *ITIL* framework, IT solutions and offerings are defined as "services." In contrast to the software development life cycle, *ITIL* will split the service life cycle into five cyclical stages:

1. Service strategy
2. Service design
3. Service transition
4. Service operations
5. Continual service improvement

We will go into more detail on the *ITIL* framework in `Chapter 9`, *Validating the Solution*, where we will explore the concept of technical debt and the long-term total cost of ownership. Back in this chapter, we will focus on the functions and terminologies that matter in delivering a software project, including the overall "service" that *ITIL* provides to "the business."

The five stages of the ITIL life cycle

The five service life cycle stages are central to defining the overall *ITIL* life cycle. You can see these stages, in their cyclical context, in *Figure 4.2*. Here, you can see the five stages arranged in a logical structure, with interconnected processes and functions in each stage connecting them to each other.

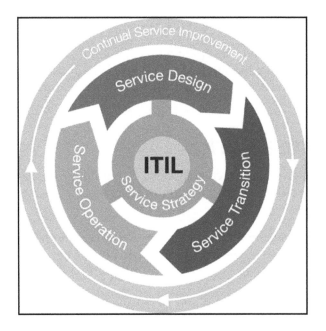

Figure 4.2: The logical structure and flow of the five-stages *ITIL* service life cycle
Source: https://web.fastlaneus.com/blog/cobit-vs.-itil

At the center is **Service Strategy**. This service "ring" is itself then surrounded by a connected circular flow of three elements: **Service Design**, **Service Transition**, and **Service Operations**. Then, enwrapping the entire structure is **Continual Service Improvement**.

This service life cycle concept is most relevant to people like us who are invested in software. We will therefore tend to identify with the **Service Operations** stage. Under this stage, the most relevant function is known as the *Application Management* function.

The **Service Operations** stage is particularly relevant to us in software because the Application Management function is responsible for the following three elements:

- Managing software applications throughout their lifespan, even up to their eventual decommissioning
- Supporting, maintaining, and improving operational software applications
- Helping to design, develop, and deploy software applications

As you can see, the responsibilities of the *Application Management* function are wide-ranging, and go so far as to include elements of design and development work.

ITIL versus DevOps

There is a common interpretation that Service Management, and therefore Application Management, is only responsible for support and/or maintenance work. However, there is an increasingly obvious overlap between these two concepts – which has been made more obvious as DevOps matures as both an operating model and a movement.

DevOps is still a very difficult operating model to implement, especially in large traditional organizations that traditionally prefer a clear split between development and support. But there are a growing number of progressive people and organizations who purposefully amalgamate development and support. This, as you may guess, can sometimes result in a profoundly positive effect or a spectacular failure!

Whether your organization chooses traditional Application Management or DevOps, the value of *ITIL* is in achieving a focus on fulfilling the needs of the business. It achieves this by ensuring that both IT and non-IT people, who you may be managing now, use the same terminology together, so that they can communicate and work better together.

DevOps is a much over-used buzzword. Since the term is still an evolving and maturing practice, it's only natural that there are multiple different interpretations and variations to the phrase.

To explain the more mainstream version of what DevOps is, I want you to take a look at *Figure 4.3*, which is a favorite of mine and which succinctly explains the core activities and responsibilities of DevOps:

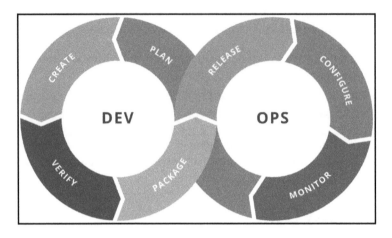

Figure 4.3: The interconnected components of Dev and Ops
Source: https://medium.com/devsondevs/devops-automation-some-tools-weve-come-to-love-8cf7fa6c12da

To finish off our look into *ITIL*, I want to explain to you, in the next section, the three key terms, event management, incident management, and problem management, that you need to know in order to understand this model.

Event, incident, and problem management

When it comes to terminology, there are three key terms-event management, incident management, and problem management-that software teams need to think about.

These three terms, which also come under the **Service Operations** life cycle stage, are referred to officially as processes. As we are only introducing these concepts, we're not going to engage in a deep dive into each of these processes. Instead, we're going to focus on clarifying their definition so that you can use them appropriately as part of the *ITIL* model.

Although these terms are commonly used throughout the industry, they are still often interpreted differently, which somewhat undermines the value of a common language. However, despite this being somewhat of a hindrance, the desired outcome can still be achieved if you're able to invest, even the smallest amount, into trying to understand what the other party really means and having a discussion to clarify your mutual understanding. So, let's break down what we mean by each of these terms.

Event management

An event is defined as a change of state that has at least some form of significance for the management of an IT service. In other words, this could include any occasion that potentially needs requires someone's attention, including when you encounter warnings, exceptions, or acknowledgments.

As an example, the event could be a **System Center Operations Manager** (**SCOM**) alert, a Windows event log entry, a backup completion notification, an exception in an **Enterprise Service Bus** (**ESB**), or an "abend" in a batch management software (such as Control-M). The value of these events is in being able to set alerting thresholds, which can then proactively trigger an intervention before the IT service is disrupted.

Incident management

An **incident** is simply when an IT service is disrupted. This could be an unplanned outage to your application or degradation in its performance or functional quality. When a genuine incident is raised for your application, which will inevitably happen, the goal is to restore normal service as quickly, and in the least disruptive way, as possible. The most basic and common example is a simple restart of the application or its infrastructure.

The difference and segregation between an event and an incident is probably one of the biggest and most common areas of confusion. Clearly, not all events are incidents. However, for convenience, there are a lot of monitoring tools that are set up in a way whereby all significant events will automatically raise an incident. Over time, and because of the way it's set up, people often refer to everything as an incident, even when there has not been any interruption or degradation to the service.

Problem management

A **problem** is a technical statement of an issue that has caused an incident. One problem can cause multiple, reoccurring incidents. A key goal of problem management is to prevent this from happening. When it's not clear what caused an incident, this management process should include a root-cause analysis to identify the underlying cause and prevent any further incidents.

As either a software project or delivery manager, it's important that you understand and use these terms correctly so that you communicate effectively with all the relevant service management teams, as well as your wider stakeholders.

The weekly project template

When it comes to software development and software projects, a lot can happen in a week, which in my view is one of the best things about working with software.

Think about it: between Monday and Friday, you could build an entire system, wipe everything, and rebuild it again in a very short period of time, relative to being in the hardware business. This is especially true if your developers manage to achieve their creative flow state, also known as being "in the zone!"

Of course, gathering the requirements, designing, building, testing, and shipping an entire system week in and week out is not, and should not, be a realistic expectation in most contexts.

You will have stakeholders and users to engage with, and everyone needs time to engage and contribute to the overall goal. With that idea in mind, most organizations and people will think and plan on a week-to-week basis. In most business environments, a week is a natural pattern of planning simply because it fits nicely into people's diaries.

It's also a sensible frequency for most modern professionals from a psychological perspective because, at the end of the week, there's a weekend where you can think about, or more precisely, stop thinking about work. This two-day period (Saturday and Sunday) can act as a natural way to pause to re-evaluate, re-energize, and re-plan your strategy.

Having a weekly routine is a highly productive way to plan and manage your work. This is true for both you as a manager and your team, as it will enable effective team-working, cadence, and regularity, which are all vital for inertia and progress. This is especially true when you need to get through the challenging times where everyone on your team may feel stretched and, as a result, morale is low.

Every project is different, and every team is unique. So, you will always need to tailor your ways of working and managing in accordance to the needs of both your team and the stakeholders. As a starting point, in the next section, I will introduce a simplified weekly template, which has worked well for me across several different environments.

Monday

It's the start of the week. It's time to get organized!

Instead of jumping straight into unread emails, a common exercise is to reflect on the previous week, namely what went well, and equally, what didn't go so well.

While this may seem like a pointless mind game, it's a highly powerful technique that we can use to focus our own mind on learning and improving, based on real experiences that are still fresh in your mind.

There will always be more unread emails to catch up on, which can always be done later in the day and week, but there won't always be that perfect time to reflect on the previous week!

09:00 A.M. to 09:15 A.M. – team huddle

Notice that I've not called this a scrum-something that we will discuss at the end of this chapter-which was a deliberate effort not to label this short meeting as a strictly software development practice. This fact is especially important if your team is multi-disciplined and includes non-developers.

However, both the idea and end goal of the team huddle are very similar to those of a scrum. Ultimately, you want your team to work in a self-organizing manner. If your remit is slightly different, in that your team has chosen to follow the *Waterfall* instead of *Agile* model, then using a simple huddle format to get organized tends to work well. This is especially true for less mature teams.

The rules of a team huddle are simple:

- Everyone speaks and shares for a maximum of 2 minutes per person.
- No interruptions are allowed, and all questions are asked at the very end.
- There's an overall duration of 15 minutes for the entire huddle.

Each team member should provide three pieces of information, all in relation to helping the team to achieve the sprint goal. Teams at *Atlassian*, the global software giant, have dynamic stand-ups and use these three simple questions:

- What did I achieve last Friday?
- What will I achieve/do today?
- What do I need help with?

In the process of establishing this meeting, you will most probably need to, at least at the very start, lead it. Leading it doesn't just involve arranging an appropriate open space or meeting room for the huddle to occur; it can go as far as physically getting everyone to attend and ensuring that everyone follows the rules that we just mentioned.

As the team gets more familiar with this way of working, and they begin to see the positive impact that the huddles are having, then a positive step to take is to try and share the responsibility of leading the meeting with every team member. Remember that the end goal is to build a self-organizing team. So, over time, the team huddle should run effectively without any single point of failure.

10:00 A.M. to 11:00 A.M. – power meeting

The founder of Amazon, Jeff Bezos, is a fan and avid practitioner of making the most important decisions in the morning. The logic behind this is simple. He believes that your energy and ability to think clearly are at their highest in the morning before you naturally get tired in the afternoon as the day draws to an end.

As Bezos puts it:

> *"I like to do my high IQ meetings before lunch, like anything that's going to be really mentally challenging, that's a 10:00 a.m. meeting."*

> *– Jeff Bezos, Founder of Amazon*

By following this logic, this idea of a "power meeting" is even more powerful on a Monday, as it's the start of the week. It's also great because most organizations will have, at any one time, a mixture of ongoing projects and operations.

At this time, both in the day and the week, there should be a natural confluence of these cross-functional teams, including the people who make up those teams. You'll find that it's collectively more productive to have both groups make their key decisions at around the same time so that they are not always waiting on each other.

11:00 A.M. to 12:00 A.M. – backlog/task list review

Whichever methodology your team has chosen, you should have a central product backlog of stories or even a simple task list that isn't just development-focused. This central list should always be readily accessible to and consistently referenced by everyone as the single source of truth.

A quick review of this list will provide you with vital information on what has recently been completed, or is still outstanding, and why that is the case. This information can then be used in planning, while also being shared with stakeholders.

12:00 P.M. onward – stakeholder time

Monday afternoon is a great time to catch up with your key stakeholders. During this time, you should be checking in with them to see whether their priorities and focus have changed. More importantly, you need to use this time to understand their expectations for the project this week and, if required, re-set their expectations realistically too. You can think of this stage almost like a weekly news program.

Getting involved with your key stakeholders is something that will help you and your team to plan. For example, you may find out that there is a major incident with another IT system, or that there's an emergency project required to deal with a regulatory change, which must take priority over all the existing projects.

Alternatively, the idea of stakeholder time could be something quite simple, like your project sponsor expecting to see the product ready to ship by the end of this week!

Tuesday

Build momentum. Get ahead!

09:00 A.M. to 09:15 A.M. – team huddle

If you work in a fast-paced environment, the advantages of a daily team huddle do not need to be explained. However, if your organization and team tend to prefer moving at a slower, gentler pace, then you can adapt your huddles to be a biweekly occurrence.

10:00 A.M. onward – planning time

As a manager, you will have several regular duties and responsibilities to take care of. Aside from attending a myriad of meetings, you also need to plan for your team and your project.

This planning goes beyond simply ensuring a timeline for the project's start and end dates, but also includes planning the financial and resources side, or even producing and updating Gantt and burn charts.

For this stage, where possible, you should get your team involved, not just to supply you with the information that you need, but also to help you to contribute to the decision-making and communication process in sharing the plan.

Burn charts

We haven't talked about burn charts so far, but the idea is simple. You track and plot your current rate of progress in order to work out the trajectory of the project. This allows you to predict whether you're going to finish on time and on budget.

There are two ways to do this, with either a burn-down chart or a burn-up chart. While both methods are important aspects of the *Agile* development cycle and sprint planning, they are also widely used in general project management.

Burn-down charts

A burn-down chart's key strength is its simplicity. It tracks the number of fulfilled story points, use cases, or requirements versus the time or number of sprints spent to achieve it. This chart can also be used to track the financial expenditure of a project.

Starting with your entire budget on day one, you can track how much of it is remaining on a week-by-week basis. Then, by looking at the chart and considering the planned duration of your project, if your budget is decreasing faster than you expected, then you need to investigate why your burn rate is high.

In this case, it may be because a lot of the big expenditures were required in the project start-up stage, for example, initial buy-in costs such as new equipment and licenses, which is in the expected profile. Alternatively, it might perhaps be because of something unexpected, in which case you may need to request an extra budget.

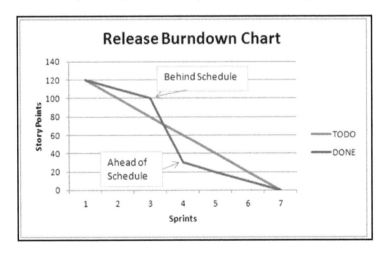

Figure 4.4: An example release burn-down chart
Source: http://www.effectivepmc.com/blog/agile/information-radiators/burn-down-chart

You can see, in the preceding line graph, an example burn-down chart. The graph clearly shows, in a way that is visible to every team member, what is left to be done, what has been finished, and how this is impacting the planned schedule.

Burn-up chart

In comparison, a burn-up chart's key strength is the depth of information that it can present. A burn-up chart effectively illustrates the impact of any scope creep, which is the bane of many software projects.

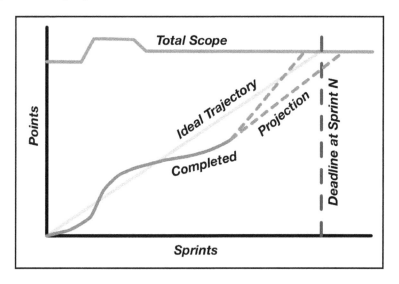

Figure 4.5: A conceptual sprint burn-up chart, showing the ideal and projected trajectory
Source: http://spin.atomicobject.com/2016/03/31/burn-up-charts/

In many ways, beyond just the name, a burn-up chart is similar to a burn-down chart in that it presents the same data, but in an inverted format. The advance is that it shows progress more clearly and logically as it goes up over time.

The main difference is the inclusion of a total scope line, which clearly demarcates where there may be scope creep. This line can also help to explain any significant change seen in the overall progress at that point in time.

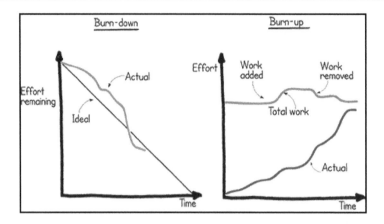

Figure 4.6: A side-by-side comparison of a burn-down and a burn-up chart
Source: http://publications.axelos.com/prince2agile2015/content.aspx?showNav=true&expandNav=true&page=cros_98

Wednesday

Stay focused!

09:00 A.M. to 09:15 A.M. – team huddle

Time for the daily huddle. Keep building and reinforcing good habits!

12:00 P.M. onward – team meeting/backlog review/sprint planning

It's now the middle of the week, and this is the perfect time for everyone to get together to catch up and review progress, but also to start looking ahead to the second half of the week. So, gather your team and create a safe environment where they can share whatever may be on their mind.

There's no magic formula for this team meeting because every meeting will be different depending on your specific requirements. All I can say is that, as a manager, you should lead the way by being both open and transparent and encouraging everyone to do the same.

At these mid-week meetings, you should share the burn charts that you updated on Tuesday, while also sharing your thoughts on the team's progress from your point of view. It is certainly feasible and advisable to mold the meeting to the needs of your team members and to reflect better what's happening on the project, as well as with the wider organization.

This is important because while at first glance some things may seem critical in isolation, as soon as you put that issue into the context of an over-arching shift, such as an acquisition or restructuring plan, then it will begin to put things into perspective.

You should also use this time to openly share any challenges, as well as any achievements. As a manager who is keen to keep the project moving, it can be tempting to put a brave face on tough situations, but this is counterproductive when looking at the longer-term picture.

Accurate forward planning can only be done if everyone has the right information, such as the completeness of the final set user stories to develop. If someone in the team knows that these user stories are the toughest to develop, or if they're actually incomplete, then everyone should know this. If everyone does then know, then collectively, you can plan in extra time for this part of the sprint.

Thursday

Build progress. Maintain energy levels.

09:00 A.M. to 09:15 A.M. – team huddle

It's time for the daily huddle. Build and reinforce good habits!

12:00 P.M. onward – team time

In an ideal world, you should, but more so would, always have time for anyone to approach you and discuss things in detail until everyone is satisfied. This would be especially true for your team members. However, this is unrealistic given the ever-increasing expectations and rapid delivery cycles within most organizations.

So, to reach a compromise with this goal, you should carve out a dedicated and regular time slot where you are free to your team. This is vital in establishing your approachability, which we will discuss more in Chapter 5, *Managing Your Team*.

This is not a Thursday-only event. Any day is a good day for one-to-one meetings with your team members. Thursdays, in my experience, were the best days as they were also when the team was most likely to be feeling fatigued or frustrated at the progress of a project. So, coupling this with a timely one-to-one can be very effective in helping your team to overcome tiredness. It also allows both yourself and your team members to holistically look ahead at their long-term learning and development.

Friday

Finish the week strong!

09:00 A.M. to 09:15 A.M. – team huddle

It's time for the daily huddle. Keep building and reinforcing good habits!

11:00 A.M. to 12:00 P.M. – communication and reporting - project status update

There is certainly an art to providing effective project status updates to the project's stakeholders, which is something that we will discuss more in Chapter 11, *Agile, Waterfall, and Everything in Between*. At this point, it's important to remember to carve out some regular time for this vital activity, communicating and reporting on your project's status.

Whether your project is a business-critical activity or low-priority piece of work for the organization, you should approach it in a consistent and appropriate way. This includes issuing a regular update, which, from my experience, should be done on a weekly basis.

12:00 P.M. to 13:00 P.M. – team washup

In all complex exercises, it's valuable to debrief individually and as a group. The idea of a team washup is to share lessons that have been learned throughout the week. These could be casual observations or an honest disclosure on mistakes made. This washup doesn't have to be a decision-by-decision or play-by-play hyper-analysis of the entire mission.

Everyone in the team, including yourself, can learn a lot by simply taking a little time out from their regular work to both think and talk about what went well this week, but also what could have gone better. In general, this group debriefing exercise is an invaluable opportunity to learn and improve, which software project teams often overlook.

Managing your team with methods and mindsets such as "radical transparency" is something that we'll discuss in `Chapter 5`, *Managing Your Team*. While team washups don't require that level of ultra-transparency and directness, it's your responsibility as the manager and leader of the project team to ensure there is a safe and open environment to discuss mistakes and learning opportunities.

This discussion starts with admitting and candidly sharing any shortcomings you may have felt about your own performance and inviting honest feedback from everyone in the team.

14:00 P.M. onward – try something different

Innovation is not confined to a Friday afternoon, but this time period tends to be the best, or at least the most convenient, point in the week to sit down and try something different.

This activity follows on from the team washup nicely, because you can use the output and feedback from that discussion to think, plan, and go about improving on whatever issues are occurring. This could be trying a new tool, revamping the project team site, revising your own ways of working, or reading and sharing a piece of interesting industry news, or taking some time out for training and learning.

Project management can make it seem like everything important is either a number, measurement, or resource. However, you must remember who the people in your team really are. They're people with moods and feelings and their own identities and stories.

Occasionally, when the project has reached an important milestone, or if it's been a particularly high or low week, don't forget to organize a social occasion to celebrate. Breaking the monotony of rapid and constant delivery cycles is imperative in getting the very best performance from your team of creative developers.

The weekend

Unless you and your team are shipping and deploying your product over the weekend, then these are well-earned rest days! So, switch off and relax, and remember to encourage your team to do the same.

The development process template

As an experienced developer, the development process will already be familiar to you. While there are always new ideas and different ways of doing things, the underlying principles of how software is developed for your customers and end users is almost universal, and this has not changed in decades.

The changing vocabulary used to describe software development practices and its role within the wider industry and even society reflect how the professional is viewed by the public in the mainstream. Whatever the name we are given is, whether it's computer programmers, software engineers, coders, or developers, they all follow the same broad process to create software on time, on cost, and on quality.

The **Software Development Life Cycle** (**SDLC**) is a cornerstone of the IT and tech industry. The SDLC is also what you have probably referred to when you need to explain what you do to a non-IT person. The SDLC is an umbrella term for the logical steps that capture the essence of how you can create software in a purposeful way.

The following chart contains a series of steps or stages, which come together to produce a software product at the end:

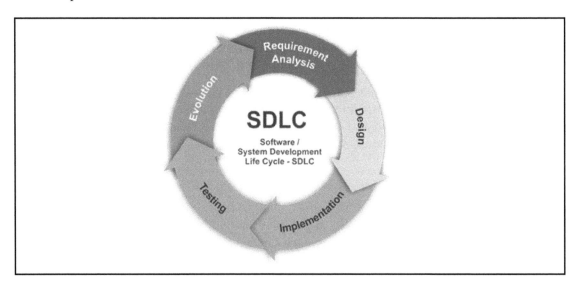

Figure 4.7: A simple, basic SDLC diagram
Source: http://addontraining.com/comparative-analysis-of-different-types-of-models-in-sdlc/

For IT professionals, it is more appropriate to talk on a level beneath the general SDLC, where (as we have seen) there are several practical methodologies, and that's where it gets a lot more interesting, and even controversial, for techies and professionals like us.

Things can become controversial here because seasoned professionals often have an irrational allegiance and bias toward a one methodology or another. This is often based on their war stories of previous projects and experience. However, joking aside, it is important to recognize this bias and loyalty. Especially when you are in the early stages of establishing a new team or facilitating the team's discussion on choosing the methodology for the project. So, it's always worth aligning your understanding with your team's viewpoint before setting up your weekly project template.

A quick visual recap – methodologies

Here is a recap of the two main methodologies, starting with the ubiquitous *Waterfall model*:

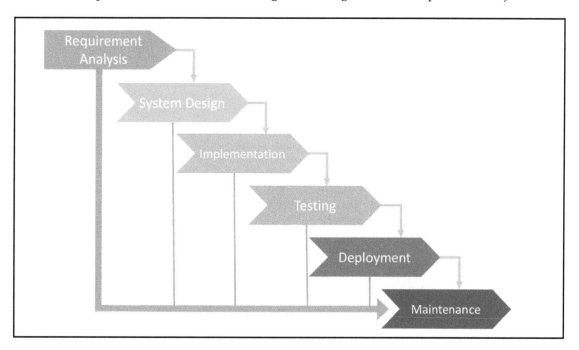

Figure 4.8: Simple traditional *Waterfall model*
Source: http://existek.com/blog/sdlc-models/

Now, here is the increasingly popular *Agile* approach:

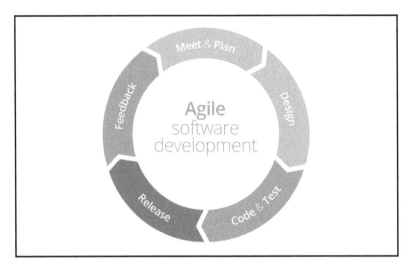

Figure 4.9: Simple *Agile* development cycle
Source: http://bpmmicro.com/bpm-adopts-agile-and-says-goodbye-to-traditional-release-schedule-process/

Where things get even more interesting is with the use of a scrum, which we will now focus on in this final part of this chapter.

Scrum

A scrum is strongly associated but sometimes confused with *Agile*. For me, the best way to explain this is to define Agile as an over-arching mindset and approach to software development. If you look again at the *Agile* Manifesto, it has four values and twelve principles. Meanwhile, a scrum is an actionable series of processes-or a framework-which you can follow in order to develop and deliver software.

If you want a template on how to develop great software, then scrum is what you need! As you may imagine, a successful framework like scrum has been adopted and adapted by countless organizations and industries. As a result, there are now a lot of different and arguably non-essential extensions to its core processes.

For our purposes, we will concentrate on the most common and most valuable processes, which are tried and tested in the software business. In *Figure 4.10* you can see the basics of the scrum process, which have been mapped in a framework form:

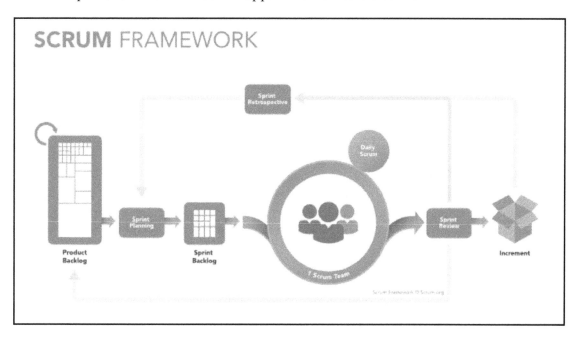

Figure 4.10: A diagrammatic view of the scrum framework, showing the key products such as the product and sprint backlogs, and the flow between each key activity
Source: http://www.scrum.org/resources/what-is-scrum

Before we dive into the four core processes, we need to establish the three essential roles within a scrum project:

- **Product Owner**: This person is responsible for the overall management of the central product backlog. They represent the voice of the customer and communicate this with the Scrum Master and Development Team by acting as the conduit between the project stakeholders including the business and the project team. They also have more traditional project management responsibilities, such as issuing status updates and managing the RAID Log, scope, budget, and schedule.

- **Scrum Master**: This person is the key facilitator for the Development Team. They are responsible for ensuring there is collaboration within the team by running daily scrums and other meetings, protecting, coaching, and training the team to overcome any issues in order to develop software to the agreed scope of backlog items.
- **Development Team**: These are a small group of people who are responsible for building the software that the stakeholders need. Despite the name, this is often a cross-functional team that includes analysts, designers, developers, and testers. The key characteristic of a scrum development team is that they are self-organizing.

Sprint planning

Scrum development cycles are done in sprints. Each sprint, which is a term we have used throughout this chapter, is a time-boxed iteration designed to add value and improve the software product. This is done by fixing bugs and developing additional user stories on the backlog.

At the beginning of each sprint, everyone in the scrum team–the Product Owner, Scrum Master, and Development Team–takes part in a sprint planning meeting. This meeting is crucial to agree and orientate everyone on the goal of the sprint. It's the Product Owner's responsibility to clearly set the sprint goal, for example, to meet the new **General Data Protection Regulation** (**GDPR**) regulations. Once this goal is set, the product backlog is collectively reviewed to identify and prioritize which user stories are required to achieve the sprint goal.

Collaboration is key in this process. The Product Owner must come prepared with a clear picture of the "business" needs. At the same time, the Development Team must have a good understanding of the backlog and be able to provide a technical estimation of the work and effort required to develop each user story.

In the end, with everyone's contribution, the output will be an agreement to deliver a defined scope of stories. To help with this planning process, data should be kept and analyzed from previous sprints. Specifically, this analysis should include the key metric of velocity, which gives the Product Owner an idea of how much work the Development Team should be capable of delivering within a sprint.

What is velocity?

The velocity is the average number of completed user stories in previous sprints. Assuming all previous sprints have the same duration, the velocity would simply be the total number of completed stories divided by the total number of sprints.

Since not all user stories are the same in terms of complexity and the amount of effort required, most scrum teams will use a points system to weight each story appropriately. In which case, the velocity would be the number of story points that the team is theoretically able to deliver over a sprint.

As a general guideline, the duration of a sprint planning meeting in hours should be around twice the duration of the sprint in weeks. To help you to visualize this, I've included a table below, which represents this idea:

Sprint duration (weeks)	Sprint planning meeting duration (hours)
1	2
2	4
3	6
...	...

By using this table, you can ensure that the stories are discussed with an appropriate level of detail.

Daily scrum

We introduced the daily scrum earlier on in this chapter, but as part of the daily scrum and ongoing collaboration, everyone has a joint responsibility to proactively seek help themselves and provide help for other team members.

Each team member must also keep the scrum task board up to date so that the team has the latest accurate information available. The simple fact is that a busy scrum task board, like the one below, is a positive sign of a highly collaborative team!

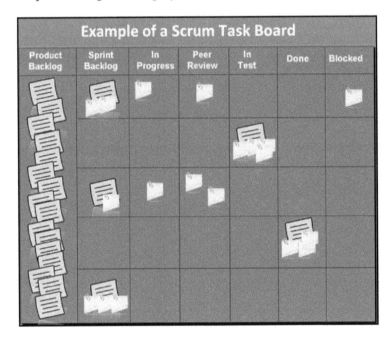

Figure 4.11: An example of a scrum task board, with lots of post-its!
Source: http://www.scrum.org/resources/blog/typical-sprint-play-play

As the sprint progresses, both the scrum task board and product backlog should be continually refined and kept in sync by everyone in a highly collaborative manner. Everyone's input matters and part of the Scrum Master's role is to ensure every team member has a chance to contribute and participate.

Sprint review

Sprint reviews are needed near the end of each sprint. These are informal feedback sessions within the scrum team and an opportunity to ask questions and learn from each other, away from the actual delivery process.

It's also an opportunity to acknowledge and celebrate the achievement of the sprint goal, which is vital after a period of undoubted hard work. Alternatively, if the team did not manage to hit their goal, then the review can be used to collectively work out and understand why it fell short.

To work this out, start with the scrum task board and product backlog. Did the team manage to complete every user story in the scope? If it did, then that's fantastic! If it didn't, then what was outstanding and what happened? In any case, you should thank the team for what they have achieved and celebrate the successes appropriately.

The purpose and value of sprint reviews aren't just to look at the progress and completion status. That's already visible from the task board and backlog. An important aim of sprint reviews is to mark the end of a sprint and to protect the morale of the team.

So, if you are leading the sprint review, make it fun! Keep it light and informal. Tailor the meeting to the needs and preferences of your team. Just as important, instead of setting up potentially awkward questions and answers, try a product demo format, where everyone can contribute spontaneously to ask honest questions and give candid feedback without judgment.

When it is appropriate and safe to do so, the Product Owner may-with the team's permission-invite stakeholders to join in. This opportunity to highlight the improved product and sprint result can dramatically enhance the team's confidence and motivation for the next sprint.

As tempting as it may be, remember to keep sprint reviews separate from sprint retrospectives! Let's explore what a sprint retrospective is now.

Sprint retrospective

As the name suggests, a sprint retrospective is a reflective look back at the team's performance over the sprint. The sprint review has already analyzed and celebrated the work itself within the sprint. The aim of sprint retrospectives is for the team to understand itself better and to improve for the next sprint.

This is a blameless activity that should be facilitated by the Scrum Master. The Product Owner can attend, but this must be agreed upon by the team. For obvious reasons, the Product Owner's presence may be counter-productive, and the personalities of the team and the Product Owner should be taken into consideration before deciding as a group.

The key to a productive retrospective is the interest and depth of conversation. Seemingly trivial points should be explored if the team thinks it's worthwhile because it often leads to greater discovery and more learning. The focus of the conversation should always be the team's process of delivery, captured and framed in these three points:

- What went well over the last sprint?
- What didn't go so well?
- What could we do differently to improve?

As the 12th and final *Agile* principle states:

> *"At regular intervals, the team reflects on how to become more effective, then tunes and adjusts its behavior accordingly."*

This reflective look back is vital for continuous process improvement, the focus of which is the hallmark of any high-performing team.

Summary

In many ways, succeeding as a manager requires similar focus and dedication as you required when you were a developer. Most of all, it is the lifelong-learning mindset and attitude that really stands out and underpins all of the skills you acquire throughout your career and developmental journey. That's why it is so important to invest in yourself, as much as you invest in your team.

Understanding the 70/20/10 blended learning model is certainly a start. This is where 70% of all learning is typically experiential, achieved through doing. The other 20% is exposure, achieved through asking, with the remaining 10% being educational, achieved through studying.

Although your background and most likely focus will be on delivering software projects, you do need to also understand the operations world. Specifically, what the *ITIL* framework for IT Service Management defines as best practices for Application Management.

If you understand the difference between an event, an incident, and a problem in *ITIL* terminology, then this will help you to work better with the operations team whether your organization has a DevOps or "Dev and Ops" structure and culture or not.

Having a regular routine is a powerful force to cultivate and reinforce positive and productive habits. Using a simple weekly template of key activities for yourself and with your team, you can set a good example individually and build a cohesive team that works well as a collective force.

Daily huddles, weekly backlog reviews, planning sessions, team washups, and dedicated stakeholder time are all fundamental tasks you need to think about. These are all practices that have worked well for me and plenty of other professionals. In any case, always remember to be flexible and adapt to your own unique situation and needs.

You can do a lot worse than using a scrum as your development process template. Right now, it is the gold standard. Sprint planning, daily scrum, sprint review, and sprint retrospectives are all common occurrences and the staple of any software team using scrum.

Finally, the one golden rule to remember from this chapter over everything else is this: remember to collaborate with your team and adapt to them continuously!

5
Managing Your Team

As a manager, your team is your biggest asset, but also your biggest responsibility, especially if have line management responsibilities. So, it's right, sensible, and necessary that you prioritize your thoughts and actions to manage the members of your team effectively and get the best performance from them. In this chapter, we will be focusing on the best ways for you to think about and manage your team.

We'll start by talking about how you can build and maintain a healthy team with good communication lines and clear boundaries. I'll then introduce three important lenses through which you should always be looking at your team – culture, tone, and diversity.

But if we take a step back and think beyond your development or project team, there are a lot more people you'll need to influence and proactively manage. You can think of them as your "wider team".

So in this chapter, we'll look at some practical ways for you to manage the following four groups of people effectively:

- Your team
- Your boss
- Your peers
- Your customers

After considering the environment and culture of your team and how to acquire the skills you'll need to manage team, you'll also need to understand how to manage your boss from several different perspectives, including your modes of communication, your mutual expectations of each other, and your shared business vision together.

We'll then move to consider how you can collaborate with your peers and work as a team of managers. Last but not least, we'll walk through how to get to know your customers in order to engage and influence them.

Building and maintaining a team

Building and maintaining a high-performance development team is not an easy task. It takes time, effort, persistence, and a willingness to try, fail, and try again. There are many facets to dealing with people, and there are no definitively right or wrong approaches or answers. Every person is different and unique, every situation requires a fresh new take, and every day is a potential revelation.

Whether you line-manage a project team or a development team, the management principles will always be the same. What will change all the time, though, is how some of the practices within your management role will vary, and how your relationship with the team and other managers will vary.

Roles, responsibilities, and boundaries

It's important to avoid unnecessary overlaps in roles and responsibilities with other managers, because this can confuse those other managers and, most importantly of all, it can confuse the people being managed.

You can avoid this by staying in dialogue with other managers and approaching people management in a coordinated fashion. This, in turn, can be achieved by being upfront and clear about what the boundaries are for you and your team members. Communication and coordination are vital for a trusting and stable working relationship.

Leveraging your experience as an experienced developer is crucial to managing your team effectively once you have transitioned to your new position. You'll remember Maslow's hierarchy of needs, from Chapter 1, *Why Do You Want to Become a Manager?*

Anticipating your team's "higher-level needs" in Maslow's hierarchy is half the battle. Your anticipation relies here on your skill to relate and empathize with your team members on a meaningful level. Moreover, as an ex-developer yourself, you are in a unique position of being able to think and work like a member of your team – but at the same time, you are no longer exactly like them.

Should a manager be at the coalface?

Part of managing a team means that you may be required, from time to time, to fulfill the role of a developer yourself because you really have been there, done that, and got the t-shirt. This is not the case for all managers, of course.

It's unrealistic to expect a Project Manager to be able to fulfill all the roles within their project team. And there are plenty of team managers who cannot perform the role of their team members.

In some ways, managers staying away from the coalface can be healthy. This can encourage more delegation and discourage micro-management on a task-by-task, line-by-line code level, even if that's because the team manager has no understanding of the code. In some cases, a Project Manager may not even understand the technology stack or architecture of the software solution being built.

The exact setup depends on the type of project and composition of the project team and the broader organization. However, I would question the fit of such a non-technical Project Manager, specifically on a software project. I have witnessed the difficulties faced by software projects being managed by generic or infrastructure-focused project managers. While those difficulties themselves are not insurmountable, an effective manager will have to learn and adapt to this situation.

However, if we still accept the premise that software projects are extraordinarily complex, and often convoluted, then clearly, the project is not being set up for the maximum chance of succeeding by appointing a non-technical Project Manager. All other things being equal, it would be irrational to choose a non-software Project Manager over a software Project Manager for a software project!

In short, having first-hand experience of working at the coalface really helps you to become a better manager.

Before we discuss the three most key practical elements of managing your team, there are three general considerations – *culture, setting the tone*, and *diversity* – that you should also be regularly thinking about. Your thoughts about these should feed into your longer-term strategy on how to manage, challenge, develop, and evolve your team.

Team culture and organizational culture

Make sure that you have a good understanding of the culture. This is the culture of your team itself, but also of the broader organization. For example, is it a "*clock in, clock out*" culture, or "*work hard, play hard*," or a "*dog eat dog*" environment where only the strongest survive? Likewise, is there a highly political or highly collaborative ethos, or is there a hybrid mixture of both?

While you should never simply and blindly accept the status quo, you also want to avoid raging against the machine or moving in a different direction or speed to that of your organization, all of which creates friction, tension, and frustration for everyone involved, especially you!

Culture is something that you can influence from within the community that owns it. Yet, in order to do that, you first need to be part of it – to live it and breathe it. So, before shooting from the hip and insisting on ideas without insight or respect for all the history and background that precedes your arrival, show others in your team that you understand the culture. And more importantly, show that you can understand and appreciate them, without any snap judgments or preconceptions.

Team culture – a Malawian example

A great example of working with team culture is from when I worked in the developing country of Malawi, Africa. For context, Malawi has been, and continues to be, one of the poorest and least developed countries in the world. It's consistently ranked in the bottom of the *World Bank*'s **Gross Domestic Product** (**GDP**) per capita rankings. I was there as part of an aid project to implement an open source human resources system for the Ministry of Health. This context was entirely new for me and vastly different then anything I'd experienced before.

Approaching normally quite ordinary, routine topics required the utmost care and respect. For example, when our team was searching for a better data source than the existing *Microsoft Access 2000* database, which was incomplete and extremely out of date because the process for updating it was broken, we identified a more comprehensive and accurate central database of all government staff.

However, this database was maintained by another government department in Malawi. So, in order to even get a copy of this database – and this was not even to integrate or update it in any way – we had to make an ultra-formal request by physically writing – emails were not an official method of communication; think ink stamps and piles of internal memo folders instead – to the Principal Secretary, the highest ranking civil servant at the Ministry of Health.

In turn, this person would physically write to their peer at the other government department requesting permission to gain access to the central staff database! It was only after this permission was granted that we were then allowed to work with the local IT team who managed this database which, coincidentally, was also an Access database, but at least a much more current version.

It was only after several meetings and building a good relationship with this team that we learned how even read-access to this database was extremely sensitive due to the **ghost worker** problem. The ghost worker problem is when the departure or death of a staff member is not disclosed by the relevant, often extremely remote offices. Therefore, that person's salary continues to be paid and collected, possibly by someone else.

So, after knowing about this problem and more general cultural practices, our team of foreign consultants was able to learn and adapt our collective approach to be more sensitive toward local challenges. As the Project Manager, I was able to coach and steer individual team members toward taking a less Western approach where appropriate, which occurred with varying degrees of success.

Where possible, we integrated our local colleagues and stakeholders into the project and development processes as much as possible. We held regular workshops, training, and drop-in sessions to provide the skills and capacity-building specific to our project, as well as general IT support. Extending this example further, there are times and situations where you, the manager, need to set the tone, which, to ultimately do successfully, you need to stand out a little.

Setting the tone

It's important to set the tone for your team. As an example, when my team first arrived at the Ministry of Health offices, it would be an understatement to say that the HR team was not ready for us. Through a breakdown in communication, the HR team was not expecting us that day, or even that week. So, on arriving, we had no office space to work from at all.

We managed to locate our local colleagues and find out where we *could* work from, but it was clear that this was not a suitable space for us. We were looking at a small two-man office that was also storing piles of paperwork, for a new team of six additional people. We were promptly told that it's exceedingly difficult to fix this. It would have to be formally requested to be changed, with new desks and chairs procured through another department. Why? Because that was their process, and their culture was following their process!

Clearly, this was going to be a huge issue for us. So, after careful consideration, I decided to break the rules on this occasion and suggest that we get the new desks and chairs ourselves.

Even though this was early on in the project and partnership with the local HR team, I decided that it was a risk worth taking, partly because it signals to my team, as well as our local colleagues, that we have a "can-do" attitude and are willing to do the hard work ourselves.

So, we rolled up our sleeves, cleared and cleaned out our small room, and found some abandoned furniture in the hallway to create a galley-style office, which accommodated, rather uncomfortably, six new people. To keep our local colleague happy, we kept and cleaned his somewhat oversized desk, in the corner.

We also fixed the only double socket power plug in the whole room. This was done by a Malawian electrician without switching off or isolating the 230 volts mains supply, but that's a separate story all on its own!

The end result was a modest but functioning office space. Despite its modesty, it was a huge improvement on the previous environment:

Figure 5.1: Our remodeled galley style office for up to eight people!
Source: https://hermanfung.wordpress.com/2014/04/28/the-office/

Lastly, let's arc back to how to cultivate and harness your team's creativity. When it comes to encouraging and supporting your team to be creative, setting and managing your team's internal culture plays a large part:

Is your work environment an open culture, where people are confident and free to burst out their wacky ideas? Or is it a "can't do" attitude where there's a problem for every solution?

This is an important question to ask yourself when you consider your team's culture and your part in it.

Diversity

One of the manager's most powerful tools for creativity, originality, and ideation, is valuing diversity over lots of "yes" people. It helps to deter groupthink and confirmation bias by setting up healthy debates and encouraging constructive disagreements within your team. You need diversity in your team in order to work together effectively to solve problems.

Groupthink and confirmation bias are both psychology terms. **Groupthink** is a group of people's irrational decision-making processes and outcomes, caused by an innate desire to agree or conform with each other. **Confirmation bias** is simply a tendency to favor what you already believe to be true, over any alternative reasoning that may say otherwise.

Diversity is often in the news for all the wrong reasons, as it has become a social issue. However, in our context, diversity can come in many positive ways. Specifically, diversity concerns the composition of the team as a group of people, and their respective traits:

- Characters
- Personalities – both introverts and extroverts
- Background, cultures
- Nationalities
- Ethnicity
- Ages
- Genders
- Experience

All these traits play a part in achieving a diverse team. Looking at the following puzzle, you can begin to visualize how all these traits relate to one another, and how no single trait is more important than any other. Equal importance is placed on each trait:

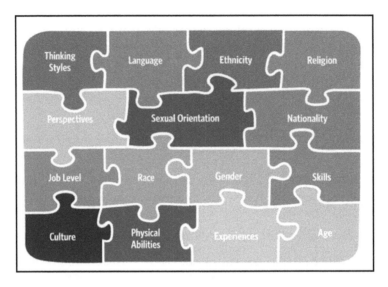

Figure 5.2: A jigsaw diagram showing some common facets of diversity
Source: https://theridgeonline.cc/2018/05/16/05-16-2018-the-gospel-of-inclusion/

Much like having a good trivia team, it's not particularly helpful to have a team full of like-minded experts from the same field, no matter how knowledgeable they are. Each team member should bring something different and complementary to the team's repertoire of knowledge or skill. As the cliché goes: *A good team is much more than the sum of its parts*.

Creating the right mix of these in your team by retaining, hiring, and potentially firing the appropriate candidates should be one of your key considerations for the long-term success of your team. Your team should effectively be the preceding jigsaw, having a broad range of all these traits.

Managing your team

When you have carefully considered how to follow or break a cultural norm and utilize diversity in a positive manner, then there are three practical actions you need to take in order to manage your team effectively:

1. Free up your time.

2. Be approachable.
3. Be transparent, radically.

Let's now go through each of these three practical actions in turn, while bearing in mind the broader considerations.

Managing your team – free up your time

You'll often find that today, most managers individually have a different functional role to the members of their team. This is especially true if you're a Project Manager, for instance. You could also be a team or delivery manager, and yet do no coding at all, which is what your team is mostly doing. So, it's all too easy to spend all your time doing the "manager thing" and forgetting that your team also needs you.

When you spend all your time doing something completely different to your team, it's natural that there is a certain feeling of disconnect. Their understanding of what you do, and vice versa, decreases over time. In turn, this creates a potential misalignment of goals, priorities, and also behaviors. It also sets a negative and inaccurate cultural tone that leading a team doesn't include being part of that team.

To counteract this, it's vital that you take the simple step of freeing up your time. Moreover, it's essential that you do so in a way that's visible to, and noticed by, your team. When you do the exact opposite and begin to run around frantically, reacting to issues haphazardly, it will set a negative example to your team.

We also need to remember that panic spreads like wildfire, especially when the person panicking is also the one in charge. As a manager, it is a fair expectation from your team and your stakeholders that you don't panic under the pressure of a tight deadline or a critical-severity bug. Instead, you should manage your time appropriately and respond to the most urgent and important challenges in a controlled manner.

This is not a book on time management and all of its associated hacks. In my opinion, there are no hacks when it comes to freeing up your time. The insight I've found most useful comes from renowned author and all-around guru, Seth Godin, who advocates a mindset of true focus on what's really important and not confusing activity with productivity.

When you can't help to fix the issue on another project, say that you can't help and stop trying in vain, so that your project doesn't become the one that needs help next! When you can differentiate between activity and productivity, you effectively deprioritize the unnecessary tasks. Therefore, free up time to focus on the necessary tasks such as managing your team.

Managing your team – be approachable

So, you've freed up time for your team. What's next? Being truly *approachable* is more than simply being available. It goes well beyond repeating the rhetoric of having an "open door policy." Although, that is certainly a reasonable place to start.

Being approachable sounds really simple, but it's one of the hardest things to achieve as a manager. Depending on your team's culture, the manager they need could vary from a decision-making authority to a friendly, positive coach. The truth is that you'll need to be a mixture of both at different times, to various team members. Not to mention that there will be times when you are under pressure and need your own space. Hence, becoming truly approachable consistently, and juggling all these different approaches, is no mean feat; in fact, it's quite an elusive moving target!

There is no magic formula on how to become genuinely approachable. Yet there are traits and tools that you should learn to use, which are like building blocks. Firstly, ask yourself: Are you really behaving in a way that is friendly and inviting for your team? Then, answer it not as yourself, but as one of your team. By doing this, you will be testing your empathy skills!

This approach is affected by something as basic as how you greet your team. Do you do so every day without fail, or only when you're not so busy and feel like it? Is it a genuinely warm, "*Good morning? How are you?*" or just something said in passing on your way to another meeting? This is a key difference between being a genuine and affable manager, or not.

One of the best practices I've ever learned from an experienced manager is to check in with my team every morning. It's not necessarily done at the exact same time every day, which makes it overly predictable and robotic. It's done at an appropriate time that has been consciously chosen to avoid interruptions. For some team members, the best time could be when they first arrive in the office. For others, just before the daily huddle may be best. Most importantly, it's done with a genuine purpose to engage with each team member on an individual, human level.

This is not just watercooler talk, either. It's a brief, but sincere, dialogue exchanging information on how you both are feeling, and if there's anything you can help each other with. This simple practice is not another management fad.

After successfully inviting your team to engage with you, you need to ask yourself: *How welcoming are you*? A house with a beautiful frontage is inviting, but it's the actions of the host that determine whether you feel welcome. That is achieved not by simply saying *hello*, but by offering something of value to you.

Typically, this is an open question to your team: *"What do you need to achieve that?"* or *"How can I help to make it happen?"* The next step is to understand: *"Is this actually useful?"*

When your team do ask you for help on a particular task, can you really offer them something useful? This could be an insightful pointer, a piece of information, a contact, a little coaching to approach the problem from another angle, or something requiring a much deeper conversation.

Throughout this process, you need to practice active listening and be prepared to ask for clarification and exploration of any requests, while also not being afraid to challenge your team. As you can see, becoming approachable has suddenly gotten a lot more complicated!

Becoming approachable is not a one-shot trick. Most people are likely to speak openly with you at least once. If you're truly approachable because you've been inviting, welcoming, and useful by being an active listener, then they will come back for more. Like having a loyal base of repeat customers, whether your team keeps re-approaching you or not is a real sign that you are truly approachable.

Managing your team – be radically transparent!

Being transparent sounds pretty straightforward, just like being approachable, right? And yes, to some extent that's true. Simply put, **don't hide anything from your team**! However, as simple as that does sound, it has obvious impracticalities in the real world.

It is reasonable and necessary to set boundaries around what is open for sharing and discussion, and what is not – both on an individual level, including your private life, and on a professional level. The latter could include, for instance, commercially or organizationally sensitive information such as restructures and potential job cuts.

Where these boundaries lie is mainly common sense and not unique to software developers, as long as you are clear on where these boundaries are and demonstrate integrity yourself by not crossing them with your manager and stakeholders. While in conversation with your team, you are also mentally prepared and able to navigate away from these boundaries, and you can achieve a large degree of transparency without compromising privacy, confidentiality, and integrity.

Be conscious and considerate of the cultural norms, such as publishing or opening people's calendars. Instead of being scared of your team asking what you are working on, be encouraged to set up basic collaboration tools that will enable you to share information, instead of locking files on your own computer.

Beyond making things public, make it easy for your team to access information in which they have a stake. When it comes to software development, the source code repository is a classic case of something that should be transparent. Even if that person in your team is working on an early idea or a new feature that isn't ready to be shared, there are clear benefits to at least making their code branch visible to other developers.

Your teammates can only help you if they know a little about the work that you are doing. They may well have had a similar thought, and this piece of work could shape their thinking, or vice versa.

Furthermore, they could volunteer ideas and assistance to this idea, without needing to be asked and persuaded which takes a lot more effort than most people realize! With regard to the code, this transparency is one of the pillars of open source development, which is hugely powerful in harnessing ideas that ultimately result in improvements.

As a general rule, team-tracking tools such as timesheets and reports should be viewable by every member of the team. This is not only transparent, but also equitable and fair. If you get that right, then you can take it to the next level and focus on a more drastic and profound concept, called **radical transparency**.

Ray Dalio – honest improvement

Ray Dalio is the founder of the world's biggest hedge fund, *Bridgewater Associates*, which manages $160 billion. His book, *Principles*, describes his business philosophy of "radical transparency," which he believes is the key to Bridgewater's success.

Before practicing this in the real world, I would emphasize a word of caution. By common standards, this is a set of advanced philosophy and practices. By Ray's own data, it's not suitable for 25-30% of people. We're only going to touch on specific key points here. The concepts presented here are not something that you can implement for you and your team in isolation. The value in discussing this here is in understanding the lessons you can apply from this concept in a more moderate manner within your own team. It should be appropriately tailored for your team and your organization.

The fundamental goal of radical transparency is to create a culture of an "idea meritocracy," where the absolute best ideas always win, regardless of how, where, and who they come from.

Dalio is obsessed with making better decisions, and, in order do that, he believes that anyone in the organization should tell him, the Founder and Chairman, that his performance was poor, or that his idea sucked.

When giving your team feedback, it's often a delicate balance of positive compliments mixed with some developmental points. This is because, while complimenting is easy, giving criticism is hard, even if it's constructive and well intentioned. It's hard for you, the manager, and hard for the team member to receive.

Negative feedback invariably results in an immediate motivational slump, which managers are rarely willing to risk. However, in the long term, this sugar-coated feedback loop does not encourage good ideas or decisions because everyone is too focused on not being wrong.

So, at Bridgewater, in order to be 100% honest and transparent with your colleagues, giving others negative feedback is mandatory! This feedback, and all other meeting notes and minutes, are even made available to everyone in the organization so that everything can be viewed from all angles; a true 360-degree review on everyone! This is coupled with investment in software algorithms that record, analyze, and report on everyone's opinion on each other. This is truly radical, indeed!

So, a gentleman called Jim Haskel, who worked for Dalio, sent Dalio and his other teammates an email, which Dalio then actively and openly shared with the entire company. Dalio did this because he recognized it was important that everyone can and should speak openly, and that Haskel's view was just as important his own, if not more important. Haskel's email gave Dalio a piece of valid criticism to act upon and ultimately do better next time. It was the brutal and honest truth:

> *"Ray - you deserve a "D-" for your performance today in the meeting ... you did not prepare at all because there is no way you could have and been that disorganized. In the future, I/we would ask you to take some time and prepare and maybe even I should come up and start talking to you to get you warmed up or something but we can't let this happen again. If you in any way think my view is wrong, please ask the others or we can talk about it."*

> *– Jim Haskel*

Notice that Haskel himself is being transparent and openly offers to discuss his views with Dalio. The email is direct and evidently between a group of people who have a deep understanding of each other's boundaries and mindset, with a purposeful relationship to help each other improve.

As this quote from Dalio himself illustrates, he is, if nothing else, brutally honest. Considering Bridgewater's success to date, it's safe to say that this honesty and directness has served Dalio and his company well:

> *"Recognize that while most people prefer compliments, accurate criticism is more valuable. You've heard the expression, "no pain, no gain." Psychologists have shown that the most powerful personal transformations come from experiencing pain from mistakes that a person never wants to have again – known as "hitting bottom." So, don't be hesitant to give people those experiences or having them yourself."*

> *– Ray Dalio*

The revelation in this radical transparency is the strong style of the reaction from Dalio, while getting that brutally honest feedback from Haskel. That style is also exhibited in a genuine manner by Bridgewater employees in general. They respond to criticism by saying, *"Thank you!"*

Reacting in this style and with great authenticity opens up the conversation to so many more possibilities. Instead of treating critical comments as negative criticism and naturally jumping to defend your actions, it becomes a constructive discussion on what could have been done better. This becomes a positive for everyone and ultimately benefits the organization as well.

Toyota Production System

What we've just discussed about Ray Dalio reminds me of the proper and original use of the Andon Cord in the world-famous Toyota Production System, which is now ubiquitous in manufacturing.

It's a simple cord that runs along the production line, usually above all the workstations at every stage of the assembly line. An operator pulls the cord when they find a serious quality issue with any aspect of their work. When the cord is pulled, the entire line will stop, and a supervisor will go to the workstation to understand the issue. Profoundly, they begin by saying, *"Thank you for pulling the cord!"*

That one line instantly communicates a true sense of focus on quality and how the supervisor values the operator's actions and views on quality issues. The operators already know that the whole line will stop before deciding to pull the cord. So, there's also an instant bond and understanding built on respect and trust.

The Andon Cord principles have been adopted into software engineering, too. Specifically, within the *Lean* and *Agile* methodologies. They both focus on quality, but also on building an effective method of signaling both issues and feedback, such as test results, to other teams. In software development, teams are often connected in structures much more complicated than assembly lines, such as matrix teams and competence centers in large corporate organizations. The overriding goal and principle are enhancing the ultimate customer or end user experience collaboratively.

Balanced feedback

Do take radical transparency with a hefty dose of reality. Dalio and the Bridgewater group are an exceptional example. They are an extreme outlier in the vast spectrum of companies worldwide. It has taken them decades to develop this profound and intense culture, but their success will also have had many other contributing factors, such as good business fundamentals. So, take elements from it and experiment!

Practically speaking, in the context of the other 99.9% of the world's organizations, the primary use is to get first-hand feedback from your team. After all, they are your eyes and ears. Once you learn to trust them, they are invaluable to you. However, don't forget, that they may also need to be tested and adjusted too.

To moderate this radical approach slightly, I often temper and soften it by asking for "balanced feedback." Basically, something positive, *to build on*, and something negative, *to improve on*, in equal or representative proportion where possible. This makes it easier for your team, who will naturally have serious reservations about telling you that you suck, to open up and give you their true thoughts and feelings. In doing so, you also make them feel heard and valued and establish a healthy culture of constructive dialogue and feedback.

Managing your boss

Managing up, or upward management, is very much necessary. However, it's also a huge black hole for your time and effort. In many ways, this black hole mirrors the relationship and dealings between you and your team. The critical difference is that you're also a manager and have a group of people to take care of, while your team of developers does not. So, there are specific extra considerations and responsibilities you must think about.

As a manager, it would be typical for you to have more diverse responsibilities and less time than your team members. As you go further up the management chain, especially if it's in a large corporate organization, the same can be said for your manager, and their manager, and so on.

There are differences you need to consider that are purely caused by both your own and their organizational position.

However, the way I like to think of this dynamic is that, at the end of the day, you're both human beings. Since the company hired you, it's a reasonable assumption that you are both professional and already have more things in common than in conflict. So, with that in mind, I will highlight three practical actions for you in order to manage your manager effectively. These are about communication styles, expectations, and vision.

Managing your boss – communication

Firstly, understand their communication style. Besides a busy schedule and a lack of free time leading to shorter chats and emails, as a person, a manager will have certain tendencies when it comes to how they like to communicate.

Some managers prefer the details of numbers, facts, and figures, while others like a summary first, hence, the need for a management or executive summary at the top. Some like a summary last, which draws a comprehensive conclusion on all the information included.

Other bosses like visuals, such as graphs and diagrams, while others like wordy narratives. Jeff Bezos, the founder of *Amazon*, is famous for his *No PowerPoint* rule. Instead of glitzy slides, full of bullet points and infographics, he insists on narratively structured memos, which paint a fuller picture with background and context, thereby eliminating, or at least reducing, the risk of misuse or misrepresentation of the underlying data.

> *"No PowerPoints are used inside of Amazon. Somebody for the meeting has prepared a six-page... narratively structured memo. It has real sentences, and topic sentences, and verbs, and nouns – it's not just bullet points."*
>
> *– Jeff Bezos*

To understand your manager's preferred communication style, start by observing how they interact and communicate with their manager, peers, and their team, including you. Bear in mind that they may well tailor this to their intended individual or group, so take a broad sample before drawing your conclusions. Additionally, simply ask your fellow managers and teammates. They may have gone through the same exercise and will generally have more experience of communicating with your manager. This experience, from another viewpoint, is always valuable.

In my experience, there is an obscure but accurate indicator of your manager's natural focus and attention to detail, versus more big-picture tendencies. This is the consistent use of email signatures among the team! I've joined teams where the manager didn't care about this at all. I've also joined a team where the manager asked me to update the signature on my first day. He shared his email signature as a template, and I found that it had a serious typo. The displayed text was correct, but the mailto: hyperlink was for his former company! I quickly learned that his natural preference and communication style was more prone to big picture thoughts and grandiose ideas, over small details and being grammatically correct. So, I always kept my emails to him brief and followed up with a summarized version when discussing verbally, as required.

Of course, you can, and should, proactively talk about the best way for you and your boss to communicate with one another, which actually links this to the next point.

Managing your boss – expectations

Mutually setting and agreeing on expectations is always a good idea, especially at the beginning of an important relationship. Start with the basics, such as reporting and ways of working, or even how they like to be updated.

Some managers prefer a phone call over email, an instant message, or a face-to-face meeting, or any combination of these, whereas other managers prefer to be kept up to date instantly. Some prefer daily or weekly written summaries. However, basic etiquette, such as being on time for meetings and dressing appropriately is generally accepted as the norm!

Getting these basics right will make your life, and that of your managers, much easier, which cannot be undervalued. Good relationships and effective management take effort, but it should never feel like meaningless hard work.

When I was working at a prestigious consulting firm, I once began an assignment at the same time as a group of young graduates. The lead Project Manager arranged an introduction meeting for us on our first day. He methodically explained what the project was trying to achieve, with all the pertinent information about the customer and political background of the relationship, and what was expected of us in making the project a success. When he asked if we had any questions, one of the graduates asked: *What time can we finish on Fridays?*

While I admired this graduate's bravery and clarity, needless to say that this was the wrong type of expectation to be setting on your first day!

A large part of their initial expectations of you should have been covered in the recruiting process and interview where you discussed the role and your suitability directly with your manager. When you start in the role, their expectations of you will normally be encapsulated in your official goals, sometimes known as commitments.

Formal goal setting is the first step toward your performance management, which culminates in your appraisal. This part is the same as when you were a developer. However, you may find that your goals are now more ambiguous, possibly even more vague, and more likely to be broader and change more often.

Even if your goals do not change frequently, it's important to acknowledge that expectations can change all the time, especially the smaller or behavior-related expectations. This could be due to feedback received, or a wider change within the organization, culturally or structurally. For example, if the management agenda changes and your project is now considered as a mission-critical flagship project, then it's rational that your manager may expect you to report and present to a more senior set of stakeholders more regularly.

As you get to know your manager better, explore what they view as good performance. This is the best place to aim for and learn about the visible and tangible indicators of success and a good appraisal. It's often referred to as "*What good looks like.*" Ask probing questions, with a link back to your actual performance. Such questions may include "*In this scenario, how could I have done better?*" This not only gives you an insight into your manager's real expectations, but it also tells them that you are keen to learn and become better.

Managing your boss – vision

Effective managers always have a vision, a vision of what they want their project to achieve, how they see their team working successfully together, or something much bigger, such as transforming the department, or even disrupting an industry. Managing your boss requires you to understand their vision. Of course, this requires them to *have* a clear vision in the first place, and for them to be able to articulate this to you clearly from the outset. However, vision is not always a one-way thing.

You also have a say on this vision, especially as a manager yourself, and through your own vision as a developer. Understanding the manager's vision is often a collaborative process, which requires you and your manager to communicate effectively and have mutual expectations!

If your boss ever consults with you about their vision, then this is an excellent sign that they value your opinion. You should take this opportunity to express your thoughts and input to the process because it also needs to be your vision in order for it to succeed. Your manager is expecting this from you as an engaged member of their team. Removing all functional roles and titles from the equation, you could say that it is the job of *all* employees to support the realization of their manager's vision.

When it comes to vision, the critical point in managing your boss effectively is to do everything possible to stay united and aligned on your collective vision through difficult times. The worst-case scenario is when their vision and your interpretation are not aligned. You could be running off in a complete tangent, or, worse, be working against the vision. For example, if your boss's vision is to transform the department to adopt a true DevOps model, then your role and input as the development team manager must align with that of the support team manager. Both of you must work closely together with each other and your manager to remove any potential politics, to build a workable plan to merge both teams and processes and, most importantly, to help your teams embrace and adopt the shift.

More than anything else, a grown-up conversation with your boss about their vision is likely to be one of the most interesting conversations you will have. The more you understand about the vision, the more you can feed into it, and the more you can help to make it a reality. Furthermore, having this insight also makes you a better manager because you can then spread your boss's message, and, as a result, engage, and motivate your team more. This is also the essence of being a good leader.

Ultimately, managing your boss is about knowing them as a real person and showing them the same empathy, flexibility, and adaptability skills that you show your team. Sometimes, there is simply no substitute for walking in their shoes to really understand why they are the way they are:

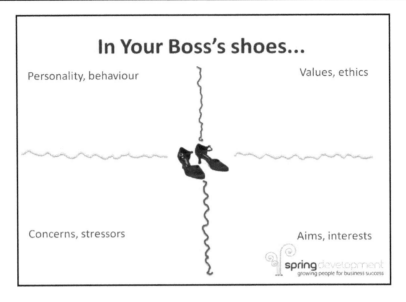

Figure 5.3: In your boss's shoes
Source: http://www.springdevelopment.net/managing-boss/

Being aware of your manager's personality and behavior is a good start, followed by a genuine appreciation and respect for their values and ethics, before recognizing and appreciating their concerns and stressors. Ultimately, you're supporting their aims and interests, which, in turn, will help everyone achieve the collective vision.

Managing your peers

In a lot of ways, being in a *team of managers* is just like being in a team of non-managers. In each case, you still have a role to play and you will need to make a fair contribution to the team. If this team of managers is a high performing team, then it will certainly be more than the sum of its parts.

Team contribution is achieved through **collaboration**, and collaboration is a catch-all term to describe effective interactions that accomplish a shared goal. It's useful to imagine collaboration as a network graph with a bunch of spider webs interconnected among a number of other spider webs.

A team of managers

A team of managers needs to collaborate in the same way as a team of non-managers does. Failing this, the team will risk working in isolation as a loosely connected group of individuals who are not working toward the same goal, which, in turn, creates silos. Furthermore, this cascades down to their teams, which creates even more silos.

One of the first things to observe and consider is how your new team of managers is structured. In the software business, there are two main ways of dividing large teams; the first is according to business areas, and the second is according to roles.

For example, say you work in a company that develops software for financial firms. You're in a team of three dev managers, each with their team of developers, as follows:

- **Team A** may specialize in all retail banking applications.
- **Team B** may deal with all investment banking applications.
- **Team C** may deal with all commercial banking applications.

In this example, collaboration with your fellow managers may focus on the consistency of processes and practices, with performance being measured in a like-for-like manner.

Alternatively, imagine that you work as a Project Manager in a large food manufacturing company. Your team consists of one other Project Manager, a senior business analyst, and a **Project Management Office** (**PMO**) manager. Each has their own team of more junior staff. In this example, collaboration with your fellow managers is more sequential in the delivery process. Their output is your input, and vice versa. Team and individual performance are more complicated to assess because there are many interdependencies involved.

Understanding this structure is crucial because you need to build relationships that are appropriate for the dynamics of collaborating with your fellow managers. Not only do you have to work together with your fellow managers, but your team members will also have to work with your fellow manager's team members. Enabling your team to do this effectively, and ensuring your fellow manager's team does the same, is the shared goal that you should be working toward.

In the following example, you can see a visualization of the network graph that was mentioned earlier. It's a great way to illustrate relationships and interdependencies. The main point here is not the need to produce such a graph for yourself, but to have an idea of your relationships with others:

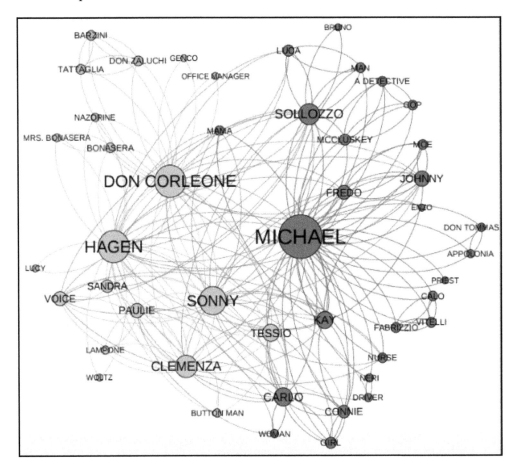

Figure 5.4: A network graph illustrating the links between, and significance of, the main characters of *The Godfather* epic trilogy of films
Source: https://mapr.com/blog/driving-insights-network-graphs/

The key difference with being in a team of managers is the necessary and constant focus on **coordination**. With so many overlapping responsibilities in today's world of business, it's vital for managers to work together in an open and mutually beneficial way. If the managers can't agree and keep each other informed enough to work toward a shared goal, it will be chaos at the analyst level. All of this would result in a disastrous delivery process and end product.

Specifically, if you're a team manager, it's vital to clearly establish boundaries and avoid unnecessary overlaps in terms of people-management responsibilities with other managers so that your team members are not confused as to who is really their line manager.

If you're a Project Manager, it's vital that the roles and responsibilities of your project team members are clearly defined and understood by the other project managers, team managers, and delivery managers. We need to do this so that the other managers can support their teams to fulfill your requirements and support your project appropriately.

If your team's roles and responsibilities are not described effectively, then the delivery process breaks down because the business analyst may think that the developer is responsible for speaking to the users, but the developers believe the business analysts will do that and give them a clear design brief.

In reality, while good coordination is easy to spot, it can be difficult to achieve. It's essentially a well-functioning software development process. Imagine a series of interconnected cogs, all working in synchronization with one another. This idea is the ultimate goal of effective coordination between managers.

Collaboration and coordination

So, how do you achieve effective collaboration and coordination with your peers? The short answer is the same way as you would if you were not a manager. It's about communicating and understanding each other's needs, and then helping each other through a set of agreed actions, and all while still appreciating each other's challenges and limitations, too.

The truth is that most non-managers already do a large amount of coordination. In a complex work environment, it's very much necessary in order to get complicated things, such as developing good software, done! So, bear this in mind and use your team to understand the real interactions between your team and your peers' teams.

Managers tend to be metric-driven. Designing and reporting **key performance indicators** (**KPIs**) and management information is an implicit part of the role of a manager. So, try to understand your peers' KPIs, and truly recognize what they perceive as good performance. This will give you the insight of knowing what's most important for their teams and what they really care about. Moreover, make sure your team also has this information so that they can adapt their work and interactions, too.

At the end of the day, despite the possibly tough management exterior, your peers are also human beings. So, there are practical things you should do to connect with them as normal people, which should, in turn, enables you to manage them more effectively. Get to know them through regular conversations. Be open and share your honest views on the management team's vision and challenges and encourage them to do the same. Build trust through tackling issues together instead of passing the buck.

Lastly, it wouldn't be realistic if we didn't acknowledge the presence of competition and discuss the possible blame between your peers when things don't go quite as planned. Without being cynical, there are positive measures you should proactively take to prevent or avoid getting into the blame game.

In a sticky situation, you should always look to establish the actual data and discern fact from fiction, and truth from rumors. However, especially in the management sphere, this is not always possible. There is a big gray spectrum in most situations, where perception can seem to matter over reality. The best tool to fend off unfair blame and attacks is to establish your credibility nice and early on in your management post.

This benefits you in two ways. It builds respect among your peers, which helps those who respect you to become your allies. With this respect and resultant alliance behind you, it will deter any opportunistic attacks. It's effectively a big sign to would-be blamers that says: *Don't even bother!*

The other tool is the simple humanistic trait of integrity. If you don't throw stones at others, others are less likely to throw stones at you. It doesn't eliminate this possibility altogether, but it certainly helps when you don't start or participate in any negative behavioral cycles at all.

Humility plays a large part, too. When you are humble and don't brag about your successes, especially when others are suffering, this goes a long way to make you a non-target, removing you from the crosshairs of jealous peers. Instead, offer them genuine help.

So, for example, refrain from comparing your good metrics directly with your competitive peer's bad ones. Always use your own team's performance as the reference point for progress and trends where possible.

When you do have to benchmark, be clearly factual, and preempt the likely outcome by sharing this news with your peer first in order to prepare them. Better yet, work together to formulate a remediation plan ready for any hard questions you might get. This is not only moral. It's also highly effective and links back to the need to collaborate and coordinate in order to manage your peers.

Managing your customers

To understand how to manage your customers effectively, first, we need to establish who your customers really are. Software is omnipresent and can be found almost everywhere these days. So, clearly, there are many potential touchpoints between your customers and your products. Hopefully, these are all opportunities for your products to add value to your customers' processes or everyday lives!

One of the simplest and most useful ways to characterize and group your customers is to distinguish between the end users, and the buyers, of your software. Depending on the nature of your product, and whether, for example, your product is for mass consumption by the public, the same person could be both the end user and the buyer. However, in most commercial scenarios, end users and buyers are almost certain to be separate and quite different people.

The most important point of splitting your customers into different groups is to understand better their needs and expectations, which are different. If you understand your users better, then you can serve them better. This is what professional marketers call market segmentation.

The reason I've only used two groups is that this number is sufficient to ascertain the product value matrix for each group. This is the ultimate goal of understanding your users, to know them better and thus to know how to manage them effectively.

Furthermore, I've deliberately avoided confusing matters by including anyone who potentially requests something from you as a customer. That might have been applicable when you were still a developer. For example, in a large organization, if you asked a bunch of developers who they think their customer might be, one of the more popular answers is likely to be their Project Manager. Clearly, that's not so useful now if you are the Project Manager. Thus, the angle I've taken is that your customers are people who are *directly impacted* by your software product.

End users

End users are the people who use your software. Simple! To break this down further, there are three types of end users, these being the following:

- People who voluntarily want to use your software.
- People who don't want to use your product, but who need to in order to do their jobs.
- People who want and need to use your product.

This is important because these groups have subtly different expectations, which can and will affect their scale of satisfaction when they use your product. A person who involuntarily uses your software is unlikely to give it a 10/10 score, even if the real value of your software to them is no less than a person who voluntarily uses it.

The key message here is to calibrate your user satisfaction expectations accordingly. Don't compare your business-critical (but rather boring) accounting application with *Facebook*, for example!

The utility of your product

In contrast to the buyers, the most important thing to end users is **utility**. Marketers call this functional value, meaning the worth of the solution to the user's problem. In other words, by how much does it makes the user's job easier, or their life better?

If your software is functionally valuable, then satisfaction will naturally be higher, and users are likely to use your product increasingly. So, the key to managing end users effectively is to first find out what they need the software to do. To achieve that, you need to involve them early and often throughout the development life cycle. This is vital for your requirement-gathering, and also to truly engage your users even before your product is shipped and live.

Stacy Brown-Philpot, the CEO of *TaskRabbit*, learned a hard lesson when she changed the way the site worked without engaging with its users. To streamline the bidding and accepting process for new tasks, TaskRabbit narrowed all tasks to four categories, which came with a relevant minimum hourly rate. This meant that the "Taskers" wouldn't continually bid to undercut each other's prices, in a race to the bottom to offer the lowest prices in order to win the job.

The importance of making your users feel engaged and consulted is captured nicely by Brown-Philpot:

> *"When people feel ownership, they expect to have input."*

> – *Stacy Brown-Philpot*

This is understandable, since the change significantly affects their day-to-day work and even their livelihood. This underlines how important it is to use the development process to set users' expectations, as well as gather information from them. As a software producer, you very much want your end users to have ownership of your product.

To extend this example further, the problem with TaskRabbit's change wasn't just that the users weren't consulted; it was the fact that they heard about it from the news, instead of directly from TaskRabbit! This lack of meaningful communication undermined the trust and ownership of its user base and caused a user revolt that set the company back significantly.

On a positive note, clearly, this was a necessary long-term change for TaskRabbit. Their intention was absolutely correct. They were focused on the details of their solution, including how truly usable it for to its users in a sustainable manner, over the long term. They also had the strength and courage to stick with the change, even though it was terribly received due to the poor execution.

The user experience

Lastly, unlike the buyers, your users will care deeply about the user experience. This includes the frontend **user interface** (**UI**), as well as general reliability and ease of use. After all, they have to look at it and wait for its screen to load every single day. When your UI doesn't load as they expect or need it to, it's an actual problem that affects them more than anyone else.

When there is a genuine problem, that is where your support service comes in. Surprisingly, this is often forgotten about or left to the last minute! Considering that no software is perfect, setting up a support service is a necessity, not a choice. It's also the last-chance saloon to redeem your frustrated user's trust, engagement, and satisfaction. So, make sure your support is a genuinely useful and customer-friendly service.

All these elements go toward making your end user customers more satisfied. As the TaskRabbit case study shows, the method of engagement can be more important than the engagement itself. In terms of functional features and UI aesthetics, setting a fair expectation and delivering as promised is better than over-promising and under-delivering when it comes to managing your users.

Buyers, budget holders, and decision makers

Buyers are the budget holders and decision makers who give approval and stump up the money for your software. These people are *definitely* one of the most important stakeholders in your software project. They are likely to be part of your software project's steering committee, which holds the power to pause or stop the project altogether, as well as being involved in the decisions on whether to invest more in the project.

In a large company, these are likely to be very senior managers, perhaps including the CIO – especially for large and expensive projects, which can make or break a company's success. In a smaller company, your buyers may also be your users, and there are some software products that almost everyone in an organization will use; for example, email and the much loved and hated Microsoft Office.

The keyword for buyers is **return on investment** (**ROI**). Bear in mind that the buyers are most likely managers themselves, and senior ones at that. Their go-to method is to use metrics and key performance indicators to improve the company's profitability, success, or value in some meaningful way. That is the job of a responsible budget holder.

ROI is a simple calculation of the financial benefit returned by the investment; in other words, the benefit divided by the cost:

$$\text{ROI} = \frac{\text{Return(Benefit)}}{\text{Investment(Cost)}}$$

The way to manage your buyers effectively is to formally communicate with them at consistent intervals, and at key stages and milestones. Note that consistently does not necessarily mean at short intervals, such as every day. This goes back to the principle of setting your stakeholders' expectations. The important element is to have an agreed method and regular schedule for updates.

As a general rule of thumb, weekly communication with your buyers is sufficient and appropriate to both give you and the project the space to progress, and also maximize the use of their time and attention, given that they also have many other responsibilities within their organizations. Depending on the criticality of your software project and the culture of the organization, strike a balance between keeping your buyer up to date with the very latest information versus the mantra of manage by exception, where they are notified less frequently.

In order to maximize the value of your contact with the buyers, make sure you go fully prepared with all the information suitably condensed into a management format, such as RAG status, graphs, and budgets.

Plans and milestones should always be agreed well ahead of time. Always clearly explain the major risks, which should be an integral part of your project deliverables, inside the RAID log. Moreover, request that they agree on the risk response – avoid, control, accept, transfer – and formally record this for future reference.

Overall, treat your buyers with the utmost professionalism and ensure you are formally addressing their focus on the ROI. Gaining their confidence through preparedness and timely communication is vital to ensuring that they become, and stay, your customer.

Summary

As a manager, you now have more people to manage. This is a fact and perhaps a burden, but also an opportunity.

To be a true leader, in the most humanistic sense of the term, managing your team is your most important new responsibility. To do this effectively, you need to understand and appreciate the culture of your team, as well as the wider organization. You need to be able to work with, and within, this environment, but also be equipped and prepared to set the tone, which may mean breaking some rules. Welcoming and valuing diversity will help develop and elevate your team's creativity, productivity, and ability to solve complex problems together.

There are three practical things you can do to manage your team most effectively. Free up your time, exhibiting a true approachability, and using the most appropriate elements of radical transparency to bring your team together as a fully functioning unit of expert developers.

Managing your boss also has three key aspects. Firstly, you should have a good understanding of each other's communication styles. Secondly, you should each have clear expectations regarding one another's performance and ways of working. Thirdly, you should establish a deep, mutual appreciation and agreement in terms of a shared vision.

Since your peers are also now managers, your focus on collaboration must now also adapt. Talk their language, use their experience, and share their challenges. Build a mental image of what your relationships with them look like on a network graph. Recognize that there will be competition and even potential disagreements. Stay humble and refrain from being drawn into rumors. Establish respect and act with integrity. Present and discuss facts where possible, instead of having opinion battles.

Managing your customers first requires an understanding of who your customers really are. End users care most about the utility of your software. Their satisfaction requires a sense of ownership, which means they should have input on the software's requirements and design. They also need a caring and customer-friendly support service to keep them satisfied. In large organizations, buyers are the decision makers. They primarily look at the numbers: benefit value divided by investment cost equals the overall ROI.

6
Asking the Right Questions to Your Users

As little as 20 years ago, the main challenge in gathering information and learning, in general, was the lack of information readily available and easily accessible. The internet and the World Wide Web came along and made it possible to access almost anything a lot more easily for most people.

Furthermore, through always-connected mobile phones and tablets, most people now have the power to do not only basic searching but also contextualized computing, wherever they are. For example, real-time translation from one language to multiple other languages, or how to get to the nearest petrol station. You can even do some of this without being connected to the internet.

I stated that access has become easier for most people, but it's important to recognize that there are still a lot of people in the world who are not always connected to the internet. The United Nations has suggested that only 48% of people in the world have access to the internet. Specifically, the majority of the people struggling are those in developing countries who cannot afford a phone or the often disproportionately expensive network charges.

To highlight this, *Forbes*, with data supplied by *Statista* in 2018, highlights just how expensive the average cost of a broadband plan can be! For example, in some first-world countries the cost is relatively low, with the United Kingdom coming in at $40.62, the United States at $66.17, and Germany charging $33.90, on average. Meanwhile, in developing countries like Burkina Faso (a landlocked country in Africa), the average price is $961.22; in Namibia, it's $440.67; and in Haiti, it is $224.19.

But, in our context, this is not the main challenge that we're facing. In today's working environment and modern information age, there is often too much information.

Information overload

This makes finding the information you need for your software project, which is often something specific, very difficult indeed as you're just looking for a needle in a haystack!

What's more, the advent of fake news is a worrying trend and global issue. Misinformation is unhelpful and potentially dangerous as it helps to perpetuate false notions and skews facts with fiction. As such, it undermines those who are legitimately trying to share genuine information.

When you ask someone on the street for directions, they can cause you a lot of problems by sending you in the completely wrong direction – intentionally or not!

Very few developers would say that investigating a technical issue by examining logs is easy or fun. But, the number of logs you now have to examine is a lot more than a few years ago. Having multiple logs, sometimes for a similar purpose, makes the specific information you're trying to find a lot harder to locate. It can also potentially contradict and complicate matters.

Speaking specifically about the information overload brought on by the volume of information available on the internet, Mitch Kapor, the founder of *Lotus*, the *Electronic Frontier Foundation*, and the *Mozilla Foundation*, ardently puts it like this:

> *"Getting information off the internet is like taking a drink from a fire hydrant."*

With our software development context in mind, this matters a lot because the volume of data that we have to deal with is growing at a rapid rate. *Seagate* and *IDC* published a study titled: **Data Age 2025**, which claims the amount of data created worldwide in 2025 will be ten times the amount produced in 2017. This is true for the subject data our software manages, the metadata around it, as well as technical data such as monitoring information on the entire technology stack. Therefore, there is simply a lot more information that we have to collect, organize, understand, and discern before we can truly understand the requirement we're trying to fulfill or the problem we're trying to solve.

Furthermore, the people we have to deal with are getting increasingly complicated, too. They are better-educated and have much more information at their fingertips than before. This can be viewed as both a cause and an effect of having more data. This can also be viewed as positive or negative, depending on whether it helps solve your problem or deliver your software project.

Remember that your role has now changed from being a developer, who is more responsible for the technical investigation, design, and build of the actual software, to a manager, who is more responsible for facilitating and ensuring this happens smoothly.

As a manager, your most valuable tool to tackle information overload is asking the right questions. This is much harder than it sounds.

When you manage to ask the right questions, to the right group of people, at the right time, you have the best possible chance of obtaining just enough information to do your job!

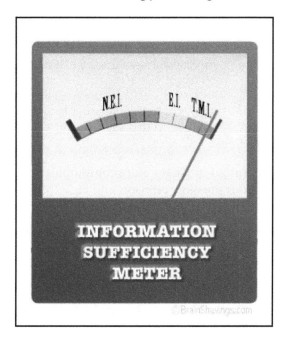

Figure 6.1: A tongue-in-cheek "Information Sufficiency Meter," showing the scale from NEI (not enough information), through EI (enough information), to TMI (too much information)
Source: https://hfboards.mandatory.com/threads/80-flyers-at-islanders-tue-apr-3-2018-7-00-pm-et-msg-2-nbcsp.2471907/page-9

In a traditional software project, information gathering is often associated with a business analyst, who will be responsible for requirement elicitation and analysis, which is a formal step in the *Waterfall model*.

But, asking the right questions is much more than that. It's also a technique to manage other key software development processes, as well as the people involved, including your team and stakeholders. You and those who are working for you can tell a lot about a manager by observing the questions they ask, and how they ask them.

Unfortunately, these days, the busy modern working environment seems to encourage people to only focus on maximizing their output, but being a great manager means maximizing others' output. You can do that by asking the right questions, and also actively listening to their responses.

In an environment where everyone seems to be competing for airtime, you want to avoid ending up in the **too long; didn't read** (**TL; DR**) pile, especially when you are communicating via email. Again, you can achieve this by asking the right questions, succinctly and effectively.

A sign of an unhealthy environment is where the manager is talking a lot more than the developers, users, and other stakeholders. In this case, the manager is not asking their target audience the right questions.

It's not that people aren't interested in what you're communicating; it's just that they're too busy. So, you need to make your message relevant and easy to consume, to avoid disenfranchising people:

Figure 6.2: Picture of a disinterested person bombarded by too much information!
Source: http://brettterpstra.com/2013/12/30/tl-dr-a-jquery-plugin-for-bloggers/

Remember that since everyone has data glut and is time-poor as a result, asking the right questions is necessary to get people's attention in the first place. Only then can you elicit the required information or communicate the required message.

Figure 6.3: Picture of a humorous "time poor" sign: "Please spare some time, I have a young family to see. Thank you!"
Source: https://dingosbreakfast.wordpress.com/tag/time-poor/

The goal of this chapter is to help you ask the right people the right questions, at the right time, so that you can understand the matter at hand and communicate more effectively.

Understanding situational context

Establishing and understanding the context of a question is vital when posing the right questions and communicating in general. There is simply no substitute for recognizing a situation and applying your judgment to it.

This is crucial to knowing what the right questions to ask are, as well as how to ask them, in order to get the desired response. This could be factual information, opinion, or anything in between.

Acquiring this skill takes practice and a large dose of common sense, which is sometimes not that common!

Like an airline pilot speaking on the radio to air traffic control and other support teams, there's a situational context that connects all of it. In this case, the safe passage and management of the flight. The way they communicate, the questions they pose, and the answers they provide to each other are all predicated on this premise and contribute towards the common end goal.

This sets a basic common understanding so that questions and answers are not repeated unnecessarily over the limited radio waves; for instance, every new operator asking the pilot, "Where are you going?" It also sets the boundaries on what is appropriate and expected. As proof that this is an efficient and effective way to communicate and share information, it has been refined over the years into an international standard and protocol.

Like a good detective conducting an interview, their questions are based on an understanding with the interviewee that they are connected to the particular case under investigation. The detective also has to establish a rapport and demonstrate a great amount of tact to encourage the person to open up and talk candidly.

Now, I'm not suggesting that you need to speak like an airline pilot or police detective to ask the right questions; these are just two examples where the communication and questioning techniques are worth highlighting.

If we focus on software projects, the broader context is already set among its stakeholders, with the common goal being the delivery of the software product or solution on time, on budget, and to the required quality. However, within this broad remit, there are many nuances, challenges, and trade-offs to be discussed, clarified, and agreed.

So, asking the right questions is something that's required throughout the project, not just at the requirements gathering stage. For example, simply asking users for feedback during testing is a vital step, which requires a certain approach to get the right type of constructive feedback that you need.

Giving users a blank page to write down all their thoughts might encourage an essay or even no feedback at all, whereas asking users if they "liked" a particular feature is perhaps overly leading and likely to produce a "yes" or "no" response.

As this chapter is about information gathering, the main focus will be on how we extract the right information from the right sources. This is underpinned by truly understanding the situational context of the environment you're in, as well as establishing a working relationship with the people to whom you are asking questions.

Understanding your situational context breaks down into three elements:

- **Appropriate**: Understanding what is appropriate is about knowing what the person asking the question and the person answering the question already know. In other words, what is common knowledge? If something is common knowledge then it would be inappropriate to question them again. Sometimes, double-checking and reconfirming something is legitimate and required. However, this must be done consciously and deliberately.
  In a requirements gathering workshop, it would be appropriate to briefly go over what the overall goal of the project is. This is so that you confirm the context to everyone who may not have worked together before. In a second workshop with the same people, doing this again would be unnecessary and likely to be counter-productive because it would waste everybody's time and alienate them.
- **Pertinent**: Understanding what is pertinent is about knowing what matters to the people involved. A pertinent matter is relevant and applicable to the topic being discussed. For example, when troubleshooting a database performance issue, it's pertinent to check table indexes and resource conflicts, as opposed to talking about the pros and cons of migrating to the public cloud, because it's not helpful to the situation.
  Asking a question about the project budget – however genuine it may be – wouldn't be appropriate or pertinent if users were asked at a requirements workshop, instead of asking project sponsors the question at a steering group meeting.
- **Priority**: Understanding what the highest priority is about and knowing what is both urgent and important. Again, this must be for both the person asking the question as well as the person answering it; only then is it a shared context.
  The *Eisenhower Matrix* is a popular time management tool. Its principles apply here to demarcate between importance and urgency, which then prioritizes what you should do first, last, or possibly not at all.

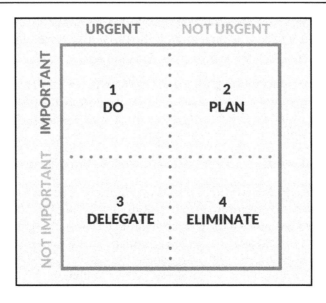

Figure 6.4: The Eisenhower Matrix, with affirmative action suggestions to do, plan, delegate, or eliminate
Source: https://www.developgoodhabits.com/eisenhower-matrix/

Dissecting importance and urgency can also help you understand the priority in which to deal with things, with the important and urgent things at the very top of your list.

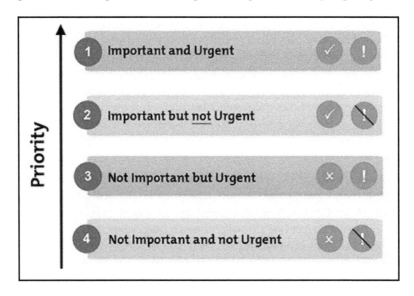

Figure 6.5: A scale of priority, in the context of important and urgent
Source: https://www.mindtools.com/pages/article/newHTE_91.htm

Deciding where to place the vital <**Submit**> button on the final screen of your software is very important from a design perspective. But it's not a priority of discussion at the requirements gathering workshop that takes place very early on in the project life cycle, simply because what the button is submitting hasn't been defined yet.

On the other hand, it's both important and urgent to make sure you have all the right users involved in the requirements gathering stage. This is so that everyone understands the context that requirements gathering is about including the users' views and needs, which makes asking probing questions much more compelling and meaningful.

The five different types of users and what they need

As a general rule of thumb, I find classifying users into five different types one of the most useful elements when looking at requirements and design purposes. If you approach the requirements and design process as a truly collaborative exercise, then you'll understand that it's not just about extracting information from users.

It's important to understand each type of user so that you can tailor your approach, and adapt your questions and your answers, to answer their questions and satisfy their needs.

The key difference between a developer's and a manager's perspective at this stage is the manager's additional responsibility of facilitating the process while also managing everyone's interest, instead of only being concerned with gathering enough information to begin coding. Therefore, managers need to be less transactional and focus more on human elements in order to build relationships that last the entire project lifecycle.

Not only will each one of these five user types have their own needs, but they will also have a unique view on the overall process and other users' needs. Therefore, it's important to appreciate this dynamic and not treat each user type in isolation.

All five types of users will have expectations and a set of "non-negotiables" that they feel the software must do for them:

1. Casual users
2. Business users
3. Power users
4. Management users
5. Non-users

Casual users

These are users for whom your software is not the main application they use in their job or day-to-day life. Although it's not essential to their work, they will use it and have a genuine need for it, albeit somewhat seldom.

A great example of this is a business expenses reimbursement application, which almost everyone in a company will use to claim their travel and accommodation expenses. A casual user is likely to open the application, at most, a couple of times a month, depending on the company's policy and payment cycle.

Likewise, for this user, it's would not be the end of the world if the application is not available to them for a short period of time, but they would be inconvenienced.

As technical writing expert, Mark Baker explains:

> *"Being a casual user is not the same thing as being an infrequent user. Most commuters are frequent drivers, but they have no interest in the art or science of performance motoring. They are casual drivers, even though they spend two hours a day behind the wheel. Many people are casual users of their cell phones, even though they use them daily. Being a casual user is not about how often you use something, but how interested you are in improving and perfecting your knowledge and use of that thing."*
> **Source**: https://everypageispageone.com/2012/05/25/the-difference-between-novices-and-casual-users/

In dealing with these users, you should appreciate that they are not overly engrossed in the software. In other words, they have other things to worry about. In the *Eisenhower Matrix*, it would go in the *not important but urgent* quadrant (box 3: Delegate), because there is a crucial time element to meet the payment cycle deadline.

But, before you discount this type of user, note that they are a potentially great source when it comes to improvement ideas. Therefore, questions that are more useful for casual users are:

- "What would make you use the application more?"
- "How could it help you be more effective?"
- "Why do you think it's good or bad?"

Business users

These are some users who, unlike casual users, use the software as their primary application every workday. In our business expenses app example, the finance team would be considered a business user, because they are responsible for administering and managing the business process behind expenses. In that case, they perform actions that are an additional level beyond the casual user.

Another way to say it is: these people mean business when it comes to your software. They have an incentive to learn how to use the application and become better at using it as it has a direct impact on their productivity and, in some cases, happiness and satisfaction.

For example, this is why some accountants are fiercely loyal to the main software they use and rely on. Some accountancy firms trade on their ability to use particular accounting applications, which are usually **commercial off-the-shelf** (**COTS**) products that are not heavily customized, which makes this even more compelling.

Similarly, healthcare workers, and especially medical doctors, are notably divided when it comes to choosing which software product to use, as well as when deciding on their requirements and which features to include. This was one of the key challenges of the UK's **National Health Service** (**NHS**) National Programme for IT, as mentioned in the case study encountered earlier.

Business users are the largest group of people that your software will need to cater for. Therefore, the bulk of consultation efforts and resulting requirements will be from the perspective of business users.

The most useful types of questions for business users are similar to those for casual users, with one additional thought – it's a reverse take on what would encourage them to use the application more, because you already know that they will be using it:

- "What's the most important feature of the application that you couldn't live without?"

This is a different mindset and prompts business users to review the software they already have in a more realistic light, focusing on the elements that they use. They may find that their initial review needs to be re-tuned, often positively because they now remember why they originally used or bought the software in the first place.

There is a normal human tendency to look for what's wrong or missing. So, an invitation for feedback could turn into a long wish list of new features. By prompting users to think meaningfully about what the application already gives them, it encourages balanced feedback. This is vital to gain a well-rounded view of the entire requirement set. It can also be a good morale boost for your project team, while also making the user constructively re-evaluate the value of what they already have.

If your project is to replace a piece of existing software, then this question also gives you the non-negotiable (must-have) requirements that the new solution must satisfy. The idea of must-have, should-have, could-have, and would-have requirements, has been around for a while and is widely accepted as an effective way of prioritizing requirements. This is set out as the *MoSCoW Method*.

The MoSCoW Method
This is a simple method that can be used to prioritize the requirements of any software project or general product development. It was created by author Dai Clegg in 1994, and since then has been widely adopted throughout multiple industries and practices beyond software development.
MoSCoW is an acronym for:
• **M**ust have
• **o**
• **S**hould have
• **C**ould have
• **o**
• **W**on't have now / **W**ould have in the future

In *Agile* terms, the goal and criteria for the **Minimum Viable Product** (**MVP**) is to satisfy all the must-have requirements, and no more. Remember that the second principle of the *Agile* Manifesto emphasizes how important it is to achieve working software over comprehensive documentation, and that quality is a variable that should be dynamically agreed with stakeholders.

Power users

These are expert users who are more experienced and knowledgeable than a normal business user.

For example, in a team of heavy *Excel* spreadsheet users, power users would be the people who know all the cool keyboard shortcuts and advanced features. Naturally, other users will ask them for help if they get stuck and will look to learn from them if they're inquisitive and engaged.

The type of questions most useful with power users are more in-depth and advanced. They can be designed to be more direct and probing, allowing you to sound out theories and ideas, as well as to gather honest feedback.

Since these users are heavily invested in the software, you can also talk more straightforwardly about the software itself because there is a good shared context about it. This is in contrast to casual users, for whom you need to make the question more relevant to them as individuals, as opposed to the software. Example questions could include:

- "What do you think about this new feature?"
- "Have you seen this done differently elsewhere?"
- "Do you like it? Why?"

It's also important to note that this group of people are powerful change agents because they have knowledge and influence. Therefore, they should be engaged early on in any software project affecting them.

Management users

These are typically managers and approvers within an organization, such as middle and senior managers. Their most typical user story or use case for your software is to review and approve a particular transaction. They may also have more specialized privileges and roles like elevated access to more sensitive information, with the ability to override decisions.

They hold the purse strings and most of the decision-making responsibilities. In that respect, they are likely to be key stakeholders for your project. If the software breaks, it's their business process that will grind to a halt. Likewise, they'll also be the users who will be calling you to escalate an issue when there's a serious problem.

In some cases, management users may think they possess more knowledge than power users, and this may well be true. So, in those scenarios, it's sensible to manage management users in the same way that you would handle a power user. Unlike the other user types, being a management user is not exclusive of other user types. For instance, you could also have management users who are casual users because your application may only be a very small part of their job.

For example, due to the breadth of their responsibilities and delegated authority from senior managers, personal assistants and secretaries could be considered a combination of the casual, business, power, and management user types.

To make questions as useful as possible for management users, they should be tailored according to whether they are also power, business, or casual users. Beyond the questions similar to those for non-management users, the other most useful questions include:

- "Are you happy with the results?"
- "What would you like to see next?"

Non-users

Consideration for non-users may sound strange for a software project, but there is sound logic behind this – especially for consumer-facing applications used by a lot of people, like *Microsoft Office* or *Facebook*.

In a socially connected modern world, not only do opinions matter, but opinions travel fast. Opinions affect reputation; reputation affects trust; trust affects usage.

Any new software is likely to have its non-believers. On an enterprise level, there is an everlasting debate on *Linux* versus *Windows*, or *Apple* versus *Microsoft* versus *Oracle* versus SAP, and so on. In today's world, there's a lot of competition in the software market.

If your project is rolling out a brand-new system, it may well be drawn into at least one of these debates, and so acknowledging that your user pool is already partisan is a good place to start.

Furthermore, tapping into non-users, who are often overlooked, can give your project additional insight and, potentially, a competitive advantage. If your project has a clear remit, such as to acquire new users, then clearly you need to understand this group of people so your software can satisfy their requirements.

If your project does not require winning new users, then non-users can give you a fresh perspective. Either way, it's valuable information. Example useful questions for non-users include:

- "What do you currently use instead?"
- "What would make you start using the app?"

The five whys

Asking "Why?" appropriately is the most powerful discovery and discernment tool in a great manager's toolkit.

This is applicable in not just a project and delivery scenario, but a people management setting as well. Sure, you can do all the investigations and find out the technical answer yourself, if you can do so, but that's not scalable, and it's not an example of leading your team.

Understanding the true reason behind a situation, issue, or decision can be challenging, but also very worthwhile. Besides the obvious reasons behind, and benefits of, simply knowing more, it also builds a deeper relationship and bond with the people you're sharing the experience with.

It's also how children learn a lot about the world in general. A simple "Why?" and "because" conversation between a young child and their parents will satisfy the child's natural curiosity while stimulating their appetite for more knowledge. It's both a cause and effect of wanting to learn more.

Formally, the *Five Whys* is a technique associated with *Six Sigma*, the famous methodology used by many industries to improve their products and processes. A key element of *Six Sigma* is the focus on being data-driven, to understand the cause and effect relationship in any situation. This systematic analysis targets the reduction of defects to achieve the required level of overall quality, cost, and time.

As you might expect, the *Five Whys* is a step in the Analyze phase of a *Six Sigma* project. Specifically, one that uses the **DMADV** method:

- Define
- Measure
- Analyze
- Design
- Verify

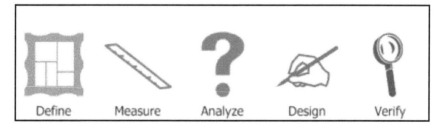

Figure 6.6: Six Sigma - DMADV method
Source: https://en.wikipedia.org/wiki/Six_Sigma#DMADV_or_DFSS

The key aim of the *Five Whys* is to find the root cause of a particular problem or scenario. In the case of business analysis and requirements gathering, it gets right to the bottom of the need the user is trying to tell you about. It filters out and distills the optional wants into real *must-have* needs. Remember the *MoSCoW Method* of prioritizing requirements. As an example, here's a great use case from Business Analysts Toolkit:

User statement: We need a system that will manage and deliver information promptly.
Why? Because information is disorganized, incomplete, or out of date.
Why? Because there are old and varied methods of managing data, that is, no versioning, data, or files are stored on personal drives.
Why? Because rules and guidelines for organizing content are not defined and enforced.
Why? Because there are no intuitive means for enforcing the policy.
Why? Because there's no supporting technology to validate processes for managing content.
Source: http://www.businessanalyststoolkit.com/five-whys-example/

For problems, the output of the *Five Whys* is often captured in a *fishbone diagram*, which also goes by the name of an *Ishikawa Diagram*. This is focused on breaking down and understanding the layers of the cause-and-effect relationships contributing to the problem. In other words, to conduct a **root-cause analysis**.

In essence, a fishbone diagram is a simple way of identifying the likely root cause(s) of an issue; for example, to diagnose the cause of persistent server crashes:

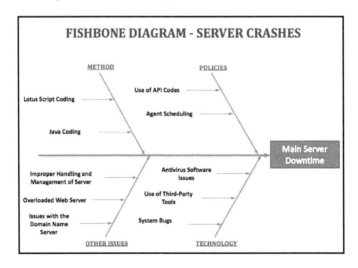

Figure 6.7: An example fishbone or Ishikawa diagram, troubleshooting persistent server crashes
Source: http://www.nagsigs.org/fishbone-diagram-template/

Let's look at an example here – which was provided by *Modern Analyst*:

> **Problem statement**: Employees did not receive their pay stubs on payday.
> **Why?** Because the printing system failed the day before payday.
> **Why?** Because the system could not recover from a hardware fault.
> **Why?** Because the system uses outdated hardware that has no automatic redundant backup.
> **Why?** Because the system hasn't been replaced as it hasn't been identified as a high enough priority to allocate budget to its replacement in the current economic climate.
> **Why?** Because the organization does not have an enterprise planning methodology that weighs the risks of current operational systems failing versus the criticality of those systems and the impact of such a failure.
> So, to tackle the real problem and avoid it happening again, you should focus on implementing a holistic plan for business continuity.
> Interestingly, the analysis of the problem is essentially zooming **in**. But the required intervening or corrective action often comes from zooming **out**.
>
> **Source**: http://www.modernanalyst.com/Community/ModernAnalystBlog/tabid/181/ID/1244/Root-Cause-Analysis-Using-the-Five-Whys.aspx

When troubleshooting an issue that's having an impact on your organization – such as a *live incident* – plainly asking "why" repeatedly can be misinterpreted as an aggressive line of communication of course. To the people being asked "why," it can easily seem like they are being blamed for a mistake, which they don't even know they committed, let alone whether it's a mistake at all.

But used with the right intentions, and used sensitively, the *Five Whys* are not experienced by anyone as an autopsy or a damning investigation. The technique here is simply to uncover data and reasoning, which are often hidden beneath the surface of a situation.

This is why you should also consider the human element. Remember that discovery and learning is much more powerful when it's a shared experience. After all, you are asking another person, colleague, stakeholder, or even customer "Why?" So, to be a great manager, you also need to learn how to ask why, nicely.

Asking why, nicely

I learned an alternative way to ask "Why?" in the strangest place once. I was working away from home, and during that time, I was renting a spare room from a small family. We happened to be all in the kitchen at the same time when the teenage daughter had just baked her first cake.

It was a carrot cake, and she had some carrot-shaped icing to place on the top as décor. She casually placed it on the cake in a neat but fairly indiscriminate fashion. When she finished, her mother asked: "What was the rationale behind placing them like that?" The daughter replied: "There was none. I just did it."

Her mother then went on to explain that placing them strategically would have made it easier to cut the cake later as you wouldn't have to cut through the carrot-shaped icing and there could have been a carrot for each slice.

Figure 6.8: A beautiful carrot cake, with strategically placed carrot-shaped icing
Source: http://www.primrose-bakery.co.uk/shop/carrot-layer-cake

This seemingly innocuous scenario has always stuck with me because the conversation could have gone very differently. Had the mother said, "Why did you do that?" the tone of the conversation would have been changed. The daughter would have instantly felt accused of doing something wrong, and as a result, she would have likely reacted negatively.

By taking a small step back in the question through a different choice of words, the mother pre-emptively disarmed the situation and avoided any possible negativity. As a result, it very much became a positive experience for both of them.

Summary

In today's busy work environment, dealing with information overload is an unfortunate necessity. As you grow and settle into your role as a software manager, this challenge is likely to get worse, before you manage to make it better, or at least more manageable.

The same challenge exists for the people you need to engage with. Your team, your peers, your boss, and most of all, your users and requirement owners.

So, the art of asking the right questions boils down to understanding the situational context. Specifically, knowing what appropriate, pertinent, and high priority is, or is not as the case may be. All the while, balancing a neutral stance by refraining from posing overly leading questions, with sufficient encouragement and guidance for users to coax a more meaningful and specific response, beyond a "yes" or "no."

This requires an empathetic appreciation and understanding of the five types of users and what they need:

- Casual users can be considered a curious group. Although they may not rely on your software in their everyday life, they do use it because they have a genuine need for it. Therefore, they are a good opportunity to engage with users and exploit them further for more insight.
- Business users are the key to knowing why your software is being used (and hopefully loved!) because they rely on it to perform their day-to-day tasks.
- Power users are advanced business users who really know their stuff and are probably quite opinionated about how the software could be improved. So, listen to them carefully and use their insight.
- Management users are typically workflow approvers, budget holders, process owners, and also management information consumers. They are less concerned with the day-to-day stuff, and even the user experience to an extent. They are eager to know that the software is fit for purpose and supports their business process effectively.
- Non-users don't use your software yet! These people represent an opportunity to grow your software's user base and following. If you're not actively acquiring new users, they can still offer you valuable information by giving you a layman's view from the side-lines.

For any of your five user types, use the five whys to investigate, to learn, and understand their needs and requirements effectively. The simple, methodical approach of asking "Why?" in a structured way helps to uncover the real reason for the requirement, request, issue, or assumption. This is necessary to take a holistic view of the situation and conduct root-cause analysis, based on objective information and accurate data.

Last but not least, try rephrasing your "Why?" differently to avoid coming across as being accusatory. Instead, it can be much nicer for someone to be asked: "What was the rationale behind...?" It implies there was a rationale!

7
Meetings

You're going to be attending some new meetings as a developer-manager, and you're also going to be attending some old meetings but in new ways as a manager. In this chapter, we're going to look at the main types of meeting that you're likely to need to attend now as a developer-manager, and how to be successful with those meetings.

We'll start by talking about important "off-duty" meetings, including both one-to-one off-duty chats and the wider-group off-duty chats. These can be very important meetings for your team members, but they can also raise fresh challenges for you as a manager, such as how friendly you can be with your team members while off duty, and how to balance being yourself while holding a certain line as a manager at the same time.

We then move on to "meet and greet" type meetings, where certain protocols and expectations need to be established and upheld. This will lead us through to the often vital "sales meeting," and we'll talk about your role in sales meetings as a manager, and how to prepare, plan, and deliver a successful sales meeting.

While you're probably very familiar with "requirements workshop" meetings, that's probably more as a developer than a manager. So, we'll make take the right amount of time here to help you adjust to now being the manager of the workshop.

And last but definitely not least, in this chapter we'll consider the "product demo" type meeting – the important process of presenting a demonstration of our software to the customer. We'll talk about what to get right and what to not get wrong when it comes to the demo – because we want to impress!

The off-duty chat

Let's start with one of the most subtle and interesting new meetings you're likely to encounter as a manager. Even though you spend most of your workday in the office or "on duty", there are going to be times when you chat informally outside of regular office hours and the office environment.

Whether you count this as "work" is entirely your personal choice and it is different for everyone. What isn't disputed is that your interactions with your team, your manager, your peers, your wider colleagues, and your stakeholders, all matter, whether you're on duty or off duty.

We can usefully split off-duty chats into two categories. The first of these categories is when you're just with your team, while the second is when you're talking to everyone else. The reason for having two categories is that your role is different in each category.

The off-duty chat with your team is important because it's a fresh opportunity to gain experience with your team, and of course to communicate with your team. Given the nature of the off-duty chat, it's quite likely to be with an individual team member, and we will focus on this one-to-one event. However, it can also apply to group events, such as team socials. The setting and dynamics will be different in a one-to-many scenario, which is important to bear in mind. But first, let's set the scene.

The one-to-one off-duty chat

The likely triggers for a one-to-one off-duty chat with a member of your team include particularly challenging or difficult scenarios that they're going through. These can arise from a personal or a professional situation in someone's life, and they can happen to anyone of course. Apparently resilient or very private team members are less likely to reveal much of their issues to others, including you as their manager, in the normal office environment. So, off-duty chats can become very important contact points.

No matter how much you try in your on-duty one-to-ones, most of your team are likely to remain tight-lipped, with their guard up to avoid having to reveal their vulnerabilities. After all, they are still on-duty and will return to work right after your chat, and the location is likely to be in close proximity of the regular office and other colleagues.

Therefore, the off-duty chat is an important – perhaps only – opportunity for you to talk with them openly about their issues and feelings. It's important to note that the off-duty chat is not a substitute for your regular one-to-one. The idea of the off-duty chat is to approach your discussion and relationship with your team member from a different direction in order to achieve a different outcome. It is not an extended opportunity to repeat the same operational stuff repeatedly!

In layman's terms, this can be described as having a "heart-to-heart," of course, where you invite someone to share their feelings and open things up for discussion on sensitive topics, which they may not feel comfortable doing in the regular office.

Naturally, this could include a wide range of topics, from family and personal relationship problems, financial issues, health conditions, motivation, and drive. Topics could even range right through to inhibitions and stress.

Be prepared to talk

It's vital that you are prepared to discuss these topics. Using your listening and empathy skills, you should also be prepared to *just* listen, without judgment, interruption, intervention, or wanting to jump to a resolution. And you should be prepared to share your own issues and feelings.

Although it may not be required or necessarily appropriate every time, having this **open attitude** to sharing is important to establish a certain parity and equity. This helps your team member to open up because it's natural to feel safer when you both lower your guard at the same time. It establishes a primal trust, which is exceedingly difficult to achieve if you yourself remain stiff and closed off, but expect them to be an open book. You may even have to be the first one to lower your guard, in order to persuade them to do the same.

Since off-duty chats are not a substitute for your normal one-to-one meetings, the frequency of off-duty chats is different. In fact, it's vital that you recognize the fact that every person is different and has different needs, not to mention different mindsets, attitudes, and circumstances. Therefore, don't approach all your chats in exactly the same way.

Instead, treat each off-duty chat as a unique opportunity to have a meaningful discussion about something new or a previous topic from a new perspective. As such, it's best to have these chats as and when they are genuinely required, instead of following a set regular pattern. This also helps to keep the entire premise of your off-duty "heart-to-heart" fresh and salubrious.

How to approach your team for an off-duty chat

So, when you see a member of your team struggling and they don't seem like their usual self, and your regular one-to-ones don't have the desired effect, how do you approach them to set up an off-duty chat?

They may well be in a sensitive or even troubled state of mind. So, a formal approach may make them shy away even further. A more practical and subtle way is to arrange a one-to-one at the end of normal working hours, at a location away from the office. Pitch it as a normal meeting over a coffee but do ensure the location itself is appropriate for a private conversation. A quieter café is usually a good choice. **Subtlety** is the key here.

Once you're both settled there, begin your conversation normally but be direct in approaching the difficult topic. Try more sensitive and tactful phrases like: "I've noticed that you've not been yourself recently, and I'm worried about you. Is everything okay?"

Allow them to lead the conversation and listen to intently. Also, **be patient**. If they are not ready to share, then respect their feelings. Offer to be available when they are ready and leave it there without prying further. Difficult conversations often take time to get started, precisely because they are difficult.

To help establish a **safe** environment where they feel comfortable to share their inner thoughts, it's vital to establish **trust** and **confidentiality**. Trust is established through authenticity in your day-to-day behaviors and interactions. When you consistently do what you say and say what you do, people naturally find you more believable and trustworthy. What you discuss should stay confidential between you and them. This is fundamental to both a safe environment to share and discuss difficult topics, as well as your working relationship in the long-term.

While being truthful and respectful of your confidentiality, it is worth knowing your organization's **Human Resources** (**HR**) or people policies, too. There are circumstances where you have a duty to bring in a specialist to help, for example, if there are self-harming or serious wellbeing concerns involved.

The pep talk

Of course, not all off-duty chats are about personal issues. They can also be about achievements, praise, and general positive motivation.

In layman's terms, this is often referred to as "pep talk." The scenario for pep talk can be similar to the "heart-to-heart" in that it's often born from a difficult situation your team member finds themselves in. In contrast with the heart-to-heart, you're likely to be doing most of the talking in a pep talk!

There are many examples of rousing motivational speeches, particularly in sports and in sports-themed movies. Think Sylvester Stallone in *Rocky Balboa* and his one-to-one conversation with his son; Al Pacino's half-time team talk in *Any Given Sunday*, which turns the performance of his American football team around; or even Charlie Chaplin's final speech in *The Great Dictator*, in a political satirical context.

The goal of an off-duty pep talk is to motivate and inspire positive thought and action. This requires a lot of **energy** from you and a willingness to listen from your team member – or members. Otherwise, your best speech, however well you deliver it, will fall on deaf ears and fail to inspire the action you desire. As such, getting the context right is vital.

Assessing the off-duty chat

Assessing whether and how receptive a person is likely to be is a very difficult skill to master. Some people instinctively react and respond quickly to positivity, while others require a sense of shared pain and suffering before coming around to being constructive again. This arcs back to the tendency of most off-duty chats being born out of hardship, rather than victories, as well as the need to truly empathize with your audience.

Throughout the off-duty chat, especially if you are chatting to your team as a whole because your effect is amplified and multiplied, it's important to manage yourself in a thoroughly friendly but professional manner. As you encourage them to lower their mental and emotional guard by being open and vulnerable yourself, it's an easy pitfall to overdo this. It's all too easy to be excessively sociable and overstep the line, which can undermine the manager-team and general colleague relationship, for example, by joining in any negative criticism of your senior management chain.

A pertinent side-note on this matter of criticism or **gripes**. This is one of the most common topics in an off-duty chat. It's a matter you should always be prepared for. There is a timeless scene in Steven Spielberg's *Saving Private Ryan*, where the main protagonists are a squadron of Allied soldiers, and they're complaining to each other about the value of their mission.

Their captain, played by Tom Hanks, calmly explains that while he will quietly listen to their gripes, he never gripes to them or in front of them. Throughout the movie, his character shows qualities of being both part of and the head of his team.

Dialogue from Saving Private Ryan:

Private Reiben: Oh, that's brilliant, bumpkin. Hey, so, Captain, what about you? I mean, you don't gripe at all?

Captain Miller: I don't gripe to *you*, Reiben. I'm a captain. There's a chain of command. Gripes go up, not down. Always up. You gripe to me, I gripe to my superior officer, so on, so on, and so on. I don't gripe to you. I don't gripe in front of you. You should know that as a Ranger.

Private Reiben: I'm sorry, sir, but uh... let's say you weren't a captain, or maybe I was a major. What would you say then?

Captain Miller: Well, in that case... I'd say, "This is an excellent mission, sir, with an extremely valuable objective, sir, worthy of my best efforts, sir. Moreover... I feel heartfelt sorrow for the mother of Private James Ryan and am willing to lay down my life and the lives of my men – especially you, Reiben – to ease her suffering."

Mellish: [chuckles] He's good.

Private Caparzo: I love him.

[they make mocking kissy-faces at each other]

Source: https://www.imdb.com/title/tt0120815/quotes

Although the strict chain of command hierarchy of the military can be viewed of as outdated in today's professional world of much flatter structures, it's a valuable lesson for managers in consciously deciding what to share or not to share, and how to consistently manage themselves in a thoroughly professional manner.

When this is done effectively, it enhances camaraderie rather than diminishes it. One-to-one and team bonding, and an increased sense of togetherness are additional benefits of the off-duty chat.

How friendly should you be?

As a natural pre-cursor or extension to this, the question of exactly "How friendly should I be with my team?" is often asked by new managers. If this is not clear in your mind, the off-duty chat could turn into a complicated situation because the combination of the timing and separation from the normal working environment can introduce additional questions. Is it a purely social occasion? Are you friends first, manager-team second, or vice versa?

There's no doubt that friendships do matter. It captures and shares many of the qualities of a meaningful relationship, which is critical to having open communication and effective collaboration. I have made many life-long friends from work, including members of my teams, as well as my managers. This includes people with whom I have worked extremely well and those I haven't.

On reflection, certainly in my own experience, friendship is not a significant part of professional compatibility. But this is predicated on an ability to segregate the social and professional elements.

In an off-duty chat, it's natural that this line is blurred. After all, you're both off duty. So, strictly speaking, you don't have to be there if you don't want to be!

My rule of thumb and general approach to this conundrum is to keep the social elements light and comfortable for all parties. Don't push their privacy boundary any further than what you're comfortable with. If you feel they're pushing your boundary, be clear that those things are private to you, and bring the conversation back to the topics at hand.

"Work hard, play hard" is a mantra often cited as a badge of honor for an organization's culture. So, the concept of "work" overlapping with "play" is nothing new. However, there should always be a balance between the two. That balance is achieved by an appropriate degree of separation, as much as an overlap.

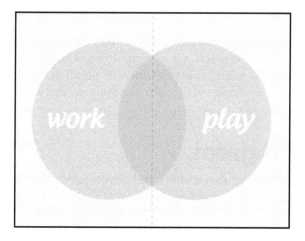

Figure 7.1: A Venn diagram showing the overlap and separation between work and play
Source: http://jewlicious.com/2013/11/where-do-we-go-from-here/work-play-venn-diagram/

Wider-group off-duty chats

The second category of off-duty chats we defined is when you're with everyone other than your team. Many similar rules and approaches that we've talked about so far still apply here, especially the one about not griping about your management chain! Additionally, there are a few extra things to consider and act on.

The office Christmas party is a classic scenario where you often hear horror stories of people letting themselves go a little too much. Whether you're having an off duty chat with one colleague or multiple stakeholders, don't be that person. Remember that the purpose of the off duty chat is to build an extra level of trust and understanding in your relationship with them.

Especially in traditional authority structures, there are certain self-control expectations associated with being a manager. This is in addition to the normal expectations of all employees. Of course, that is not to say you should hide your natural personality and become a completely sanitized robot.

The key is having and demonstrating a maturity that helps you to stay in reasonable control. Should there be a confrontation, you should be in a position to moderate and diffuse the situation. Clearly, that requires a level of self-moderation first so that you're not a participant in the confrontation. Put simply: you need to be able to manage yourself while off duty as if you're on duty.

Furthermore, an off-duty chat with a colleague is an opportunity for you to learn from them and to build your own reputation, which you do by setting a positive example and behaving like a role model. So, take the opportunity to do all of these things, and you will reap the benefits of a better working relationship in your on-duty time, too.

The meet and greet

If you subscribe to the stereotype that techies and developers are an unsociable lot, then this is probably one of the most difficult and arduous things you can think of.

The meet and greet is a customary and necessary step in establishing first contact and introductions to people you've not met before. Like the equally loved and hated "ice-breaker" at the beginning of meetings, it can be a somewhat staged and rehearsed affair. However, it doesn't need to like that. The idea and purpose of a meet and greet are to bring a bunch of people together to develop opportunities for working together, whether you are colleagues or potential customers and suppliers. But if you boil it all down, it's nothing more than a simple get-together of people with a particular shared context.

But what's the goal and role of a manager at a meet and greet? Well, as cheesy as it sounds, it's all about "networking." You may think of networking as an onerous task and a waste of time. But, if you approach it in the right way, I can assure you it can be very productive and fruitful, as well as interesting and fun! The idea is to connect with people whom you wouldn't normally meet, people of different roles, from different sectors, backgrounds, ages, with different views than your own!

I'll stop short of recommending that you meet as many people as possible at a meet and greet because it's also about the quality of your conversations. The key is really about having a meaningful introduction, which leads to more formal and in-depth meetings, not collecting all of the business cards you can.

To help you to imagine making a meet and greet a positive experience, here are some outcomes you can target:

- Acquire a mentor for you or your team members.
- Find a new recruit in your team or company, in particular, if it's a niche skillset you need.
- Find a new strategic partner, perhaps, such as a digital advertising agency to publicize and promote your project or product.
- Develop new business leads. Find new prospective customers.
- Consider it continual professional development to simply learn something new and re-motivate yourself, which we all need to do.

As a general rule when meeting new people, and especially if I'm there with a particular purpose like those above, I always bear in mind a saying by the Greek philosopher, Zeno of Citium:

"We have two ears and one mouth, so we should listen more than we say."

– Zeno of Citium

Without over-emphasizing the need to listen when communicating with people in general, the point here is that an engaging conversation requires a healthy balance of speaking and listening. So, be curious. Share noteworthy news. Ask questions about things they're saying that you find interesting. Tell the other person why that's fascinating to you. Find what's really exciting to both you and them. Strike up a memorable conversation.

What's more, the fact that you could be engaging with someone equally as nervous as you are is itself a good conversation starter! So, the next time you walk into a room full of strangers, remember that they may be feeling the same.

If you're still feeling daunted by the prospect of wandering into a room full of unfamiliar people, try going with someone you know and remember that everyone is there to meet new interesting people, just like you. Just make sure you both meet new people and don't spend all your time just chatting with each other!

The sales meeting

Although a meet and greet is not always sales-oriented, it can be a natural precursor to a sales meeting. This is great because you've just learned how to make the meet and greets into positive and valuable experiences! For the meet and greets that are potential sales opportunities, the next step is the formal sales meeting, which can be daunting even if you're a seasoned sales professional.

As a brilliant developer, you've probably been to a sales meeting before or taken part in the sales process, perhaps accidentally, without you knowing. You could have responded to a simple email from the sales team, who requested some seemingly trivial technical information on a particular product or service. If you can remember such an example, then this will be a great help to understand the end-to-end sales process in more detail. If you can't, that's okay too.

The main point is to understand that selling is a practical exercise. There is no magic theoretical formula because every customer at any one time is different. Therefore, every sale is unique, with different people, dynamics, timings, inputs, information, discussions, negotiations, and actions.

Your role as a manager in a sales meeting

As a manager, your role is also different. Specifically, you are likely to be asked to take a more visible position on the co-opted sales team. Most sales teams are likely to be cross-functional, with commercial and technical people, as well as senior or executive level management, depending on the business importance of the sale.

As such, you will be there more on a leading capacity, as opposed to a supporting one. Remember one of the key differences between a manager and a non-manager is that a manager is responsible for making decisions. In other words, your expected input is more than just facts, figures, and technical analysis. It's also your views, opinions, assessments, judgments, perceptions, and decisions. The latter is much less binary or black and white than the former.

Preparing for a sales meeting

That's not to say all of us who are developer-managers need to become like Zig Ziglar, the renowned *American Salesmaster* – yes, that's a real thing – who revolutionized the sales industry from the 1960s.

> *"Success occurs when opportunity meets preparation."*

> *– Zig Ziglar*

When we think of "salespeople," so many images and caricatures of pushy, passive-aggressive people come into mind. We're not alone in that thought, either. It's very much the popular consensus in wider society thanks to so many infamous and well-publicized Ponzi schemes, pyramid scams, corporate frauds, collapses, and swindles.

Like most things, when sales and the sales meeting is done right, it's a valuable and positive experience for everyone involved. It's also a necessary process. So, suspend your skepticism for now and erase any thoughts of the abhorrent, abusive, and sinister sales coach called Blake, played by Alec Baldwin, in the 1992 movie adaptation of *Glengarry Glen Ross*. At least until we've gone through a more positive example where a sale really is a mutually beneficial transaction where a real business problem is solved by a genuine solution, in exchange for money.

In *Glengarry Glen Ross*, a ruthless Blake lectures the underperforming sales team to:

Always

Be

Closing

Now, if we take Ziglar's quote at face value, then good preparation is a fundamental part of nailing a sales meeting, which is the opportunity. So, it's in everyone's interest that good preparation takes place. In procurement terms, this is called "due diligence," which is mainly financially related, that is, ascertaining whether each party – supplier and customer – is financially viable and legitimate. But preparation is also much simpler and much more than that.

Establishing a human-level connection is a basic communication need. As discussed earlier, this is one of a successful manager's key skill. In this context, being able to connect with your potential customer is obviously vital to establishing a good rapport and relationship, to enable a constructive conversation and to proceed with the sale.

Without over-analyzing the basics, such as speaking the same language as your customer, there are some key things to think about while preparing ahead of and during your sales meeting:

- Research and identify key decision makers.
- Understand the situational context, such as the customer's business environment.
- Pay true attention to the reactions of your customer and adapt accordingly.
- Be time aware.
- Apply the art of pitching.
- Communicate an idea.
- Make a value proposition.

Each of these points should be largely self-explanatory and common sense by now, having come this far in this book and your *Developer-to-Manager* journey. You may have noticed that these points share similarities with some software development processes, such as being time aware, so you don't run out of time with your customer without making your killer points. This has similarities with time-boxing, which helps to focus efforts on delivering the essential must-have requirements by discouraging scope creep and unnecessary tweaking.

The science of the sales process

To understand the sales process more scientifically, we'll borrow a methodology from a non-IT field. Pharmaceuticals is a huge industrial sector that employs and relies heavily on a variety of sales and sales-related strategies and tactics.

One of the most subscribed methodologies in this industry is **Key Account Management** (**KAM**). Before we go too far down the exploration path of KAM, it's worth differentiating between KAM and out-and-out sales only. The *RAIN Group*, an award-winning sales training company, considers sales to be only one part of the overall KAM process. Specifically, it's part of their **Execution** stage.

In short, my non-sales profession interpretation of this is that KAM is essentially a long-term, holistic approach, whereas sales is a shorter term deal-making activity.

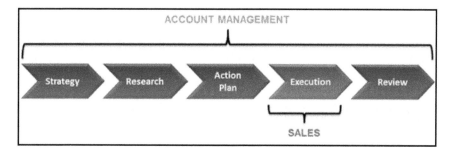

Figure 7.2: The key stages or steps in Key Account Management. Execution is where the key sales activity takes place.
Source: https://www.rainsalestraining.com/blog/what-is-key-account-management

For our purposes, we'll discuss KAM and sales together as a whole, because the humble software sales meeting traverses both, in my humble opinion.

A global pharmaceutical company's more practical take on this process is explained in three circular phases:

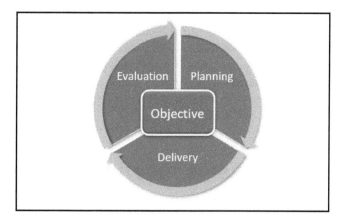

Figure 7.3: The circular process of planning, delivery, and evaluation centered by an Objective

At the center of the circular process is your **objective**. In your sales meeting, this could be to close a million dollar deal to buy your software outright, or it could establish a strategic partnership to supply support and development services for the next five years.

Sales planning

To achieve your sales objective, you first need to complete some detailed planning, starting with your understanding of the customer, your software company, and the wider business environment.

Knowing the answers to these questions will help you and your sales team to frame the conversation with the customer and know what to prepare for the sales meeting itself:

Customer	Your Company	Environment
What's their business? How do they operate? What's their top priority? Why do they need help? Who are the key decision makers?	What's your core business? Which areas are your strengths and weaknesses? What is your current capacity for new work?	What are the current market conditions? Buoyant or quiet? What are your competitors doing? Are there regulatory requirements now or expected in the future, such as GDPR*?

*General Data Protection Regulation (EU) 2016/679, wide-ranging data privacy legislation which came into force on 25th May 2018.

For example, maybe you know that your customer is a fast-growing accountancy firm that has used a particular on-premise hosted, commercial off-the-shelf solution for a long time. You also know that a major version of that solution is coming to its **end of service life** (**EOSL**). And it just happens that your company specializes in the implementation of a **Software-as-a-Service** (**SaaS**) accountancy solution that has the capability to grow into other areas, like corporate audits. And so, you then start to see how they might like a very mutually beneficial partnership, with lots of potential.

How to deliver the sales meeting

Once you've successfully planned for your sales meeting, you need to think about delivery. Delivery is all about engaging with the customer to identify their true needs. This need will be at a high level, because you're not yet at the requirements workshop stage – which will be discussed next.

To get really practical, this is where you have to be precise and comprehensive in your meeting plan about everything from the location, transport, venue, catering, and amenities to your invites and communication throughout.

First impressions matter, and you only make them once! This includes the warm or cold reception your customer receives when they arrive at your office if that's the agreed venue. They may not remember how professional and slick the whole lead-up to the meeting was, but they will definitely remember how unprofessional and chaotic it was if these things were not considered. Even if it's a relaxed meeting, it's best to all arrive at the appropriate location at the same mutually agreed time.

Then, once you and your customer have both arrived at the meeting, it's vital to be professional and confident. You and your team must act together as a sales team, be well-organized and highly competent, to make your customer feel confident that they can rely on your company and trust you as an individual.

Without being overly naïve, clearly, customers who attend sales meeting are not going to be easily wooed and convinced only by a firm handshake. But, every part of this process is required to **engage your customers** and achieve your ultimate objective of closing a sale. After comfortably settling down at your meeting venue, formal introductions always help to establish who's who from all parties. The chances are there will be people who know each other, and those who have never met. So, don't assume everyone knows everyone. Besides, roles and titles might have changed since you last spoke with your liaison.

After introductions, next set and establish the context, the agenda. This is the overarching goal of the meeting, and why you are all there. Your Sales Manager or the Sales Lead on your team might do this if you have one. If it's a smaller, informal sales meeting and you know each of the customers well and vice versa, then you could jump straight into the agenda.

Once you're in the main discussion and talking about what your customer needs, make sure you ask both pre-scripted and ad-lib questions. Asking lots of questions may seem counter-intuitive at a sales meeting. After all, it's a meeting where you are expected to sell yourself, your software products, and services. Contrary to some beliefs, however, positive selling is not about monologues and rants about how great your software is.

Identifying your customer's true needs must be your primary focus. You already know all about your software and what it could do. Understanding your customer's real needs and the business problems they want to be solved most gives you insight into how your software can help them. Furthermore, the process of discussing the business problem itself is a valuable service to you and your customer, because the problems are often complex and difficult to understand, let alone solve. Think of it as free consultancy. That all helps to build rapport with your customer and add value to the meeting itself.

Having actively listened to your customer to explain their business problem, now you can tailor your response to focus on the strengths of your software and company. How you, your company and your software can help them.

You can be precise and specific, down to the very latest function or module, which could be utilized in their business process. This is where you **sell a true solution** to your customer.

Inevitably, there is some degree of a chicken-or-egg dilemma here. Some customers may not know the full extent of their business problem. So, they have approached you to help them to understand it better and to solve it. In this case, you can only act on the information you have, gathered as part of your planning phase, and during the meeting.

The final steps in the delivery phase are to **agree actions**. This is the metaphorical "closing" of the meeting and possibly the sale. Being studious and diligent in recording notes that could be later formalized in a contract is just simple business sense. Mutually agreeing on the next actions is vital to make sure there's a meaningful and well-organized output to the meeting. Remember to share them with the customer afterward!

Evaluate

As you might expect, after an important sales meeting it's important and normal practice to have a debrief, also referred to as a washup. The purpose of the washup is not only to agree and disseminate information internally within your sales team but also as a practical exercise to improve for the next sales meeting. The washup continues the circular process by feeding back into the planning phase, and it's best done soon after the initial meeting, while everyone's memory of the event is still fresh.

The most valuable activity in the evaluation phase is to use all of the information collected from the sale meeting and assess the business opportunity itself. If the sales meeting was a complete success and you managed to close the sale, that's absolutely fantastic. The next steps are to debrief, ratify the contract with legal and finance teams if you have them, and start preparing to ship the product or begin your service.

In the more likely scenario where you've had a positive meeting, and an agreement was reached but only so far in *principle*, then the next steps are to debrief and finalize the requirements, so that another version of the contract can be drafted.

In both scenarios and throughout the sales process, the customer will be evaluating your company, and you should also be evaluating your customer. Like all businesses, including charitable organizations, there are various business risks at any one time. For a software or software services company, there will be a technology focus as you'd expect. For example, if your proposed solution is dependent on another product that has yet to be released, there is a risk that it will impact your delivery timetable unless you can work around it and therefore mitigate the risk.

In regard to the all-important overriding business questions, they are the same:

- **Do the benefits outweigh the cost and risks of doing business with this customer?**
  For example, does the sale price cover the potentially huge fines for non-delivery or operational issues?
- **What is the impact of doing business with this customer, and what is the impact of not doing business with this customer?**
  For example, will this sale exclude you from a potentially larger sale with a competitor? Conversely, will this sale help you to secure a larger sale?
- **How quickly, if it is even possible, can you fulfill the order or contract?**
  For example, do you need to hire a team of people with new skills, and is that realistic in the current job market?

These questions and calculations are all about business value. Bearing in mind your business risks, you need to consider whether this sale is worthwhile and prudent. This may sound a little silly because, clearly, a software company should be selling its software as much as reasonably possible. However, over-promising and under-delivering is not a sensible or sustainable approach. Saying your SaaS accountancy solution is ready for 10,000 new users when it's not is clearly a disaster waiting to happen. Depending on your setup, it may even disrupt your service to existing customers.

Furthermore, scaling up too fast in terms of people can also cause a cultural problem in your organization. Even worse, over-extending your services and going into another business area can jeopardize the stability of the core business, leading to a number of problems such as depleted cashflow. *Zynga*, the mobile games maker behind *Mafia Wars* and other big hits, had to scale back considerably when it became less popular. Granted, these problems are still preferable to a lack of sales.

Looking at this more positively, as a sales team should, after closing a sale, your evaluation should also include assessing where the next sales opportunity with your customer may be. Or, how you can use this as a springboard to lead to more sales with other customers.

Lastly, remember that, throughout the sales process, your customer will also be doing their own evaluation. They may even have a pre-determined checklist to complete during the sales meeting itself. Therefore, bear in mind that your customer is also going through a similar exercise to you, albeit from a different angle. So, remember your empathy skills and put yourself in their position for an alternative view of the situation. Ultimately, it's their decision you're trying to affect in order to close the sale, which is your objective!

The requirements workshop meeting

All software projects have requirements. In fact, modern software projects tend to have a lot of requirements! As an experienced developer, you have probably spent a lot of man-days working with incomplete or ambiguous requirements!

But where do these – clear or otherwise – requirements come from? You'll most probably trace them back to the information and requirement gathering stage of the project, which we started discussing in the previous chapter. The key milestone event in this stage is the requirement workshop.

This is where your experience as a developer is a real benefit. Through your hard graft and many conversations with all five types of users, business analysts, and product owners, you will instinctively know which are the more effective questions to ask that prompt clearer responses. Asking the right questions sounds easy, but in reality, it's extremely difficult, as we've also discussed in the last chapter.

Your role as a manager in the requirements workshop

So, now that you're a manager, what do you need to do in the requirements workshop? For the purposes of this chapter, we'll assume that you are the Project Manager, who will have the most wide-ranging set of responsibilities. So, it's the best starting point to get an understanding, and hopefully insight, into a manager's role at the requirements workshop.

When I reached out to a brilliant developer friend of mine, who has also made the transition into a number of different management roles, to get his take on this, he jokingly said:

> *"Don't forget the biscuits!"*

On deeper reflection, his throw-away comment is actually excellent insight. Because you're here to remember everything and make everything happen. Sure, everyone knows that a software project will have at least one requirements workshop, but how does it even come about? Herein lies one of the key differences between a developer's role and a manager's role. I'm sure you will have attended many requirements workshops as one of a number of attendees. Whereas the manager is the one and only organizer of the event – the one who sends the invites.

The workshop logistics

As the manager, you are the one who sets up the meeting, starting with the logistics of the event, similar to the sales meeting. If you are to successfully facilitate this process, it's vital to make sure the people involved have absolutely everything they need to do their work and be productive. So, don't overlook the details, such as tea and biscuits.

While the requirements gathering process is mainly facts and evidence-based, there is a large part of it that requires creativity and imagination: creativity in producing the right questions and imagination to step into the shoes of another stakeholder or user to give a good, accurate response. This is the type of stuff associated with the cliché; "thinking outside the box."

Also, bear this in mind when you are setting up the event. Make sure the venue is suitable and appropriate to enable creativity to spread and multiply, to maximize creative bursts from your project and requirements team.

Practically speaking, choose a venue that is comfortably large and airy, as well as colorful, instead of drab and dreary. The idea is to inspire and invigorate conversations and to introduce a high level of energy and ordered chaos.

If everyone in your requirements workshop is quiet and reserved, even if the meeting is well organized and runs exactly to schedule, it's a sign that you're missing something. Be very aware that this is likely to cause a set of incomplete requirements, even though everyone will feel that the workshop has gone very well.

Whether your project follows a *Waterfall* or *Agile* methodology, the most widely accepted method of identifying and understanding requirements is *user stories*.

User stories for the requirements workshop

Interestingly, we are talking here about user stories as a method to gather requirements. However, as with a lot of concepts in software development, there are alternative schools of thought, and they often challenge each other, including a distinction between user stories and system requirements.

> *"User stories are often confused with system requirements. A requirement is a formal description of need; a user story is an informal description of a feature."*

> *– Wikipedia, 14 November 2018 revision*

Going by that particular definition, there is a real argument that a system requirement is much more useful and valuable in the design, development, and testing process. So, why use user stories at all? Well, there are several arguments for this.

Firstly, user stories are a great way to engage with your non-technical customer and begin the complex process of software design and development. It is extremely rare for a customer or non-technical user to know exactly what they want or need without a framework and series of prompts and imaginary walkthroughs.

This is especially true when developing a brand-new system. Even if your project is tasked with enhancing or replacing an existing system, this is still very difficult because your users' overall view and imagination are constrained by their own minds after being conditioned in coping with their old system.

Secondly, it's lightweight and fast. Due to its informal nature and use of natural language to capture narratives, it's an easier and much more fun exercise compared to documenting formal system requirements, which is often done in a technical language such as **Unified Modeling Language** (**UML**). This means you can go through the initial requirements process much faster and start designing and developing your MVP. As such, it is a perfect match for a truly *Agile* project.

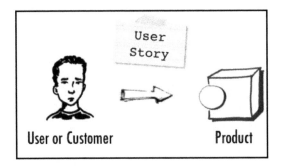

Figure 7.4: A user story is centered around how a user will use the product
Source: https://www.romanpichler.com/blog/10-tips-writing-good-user-stories/

Global software powerhouse, *Atlassian*, is a big proponent of *Agile* and user stories. Their *Agile* coach "no-nonsense guide to *Agile* development," which is available at `https://www.atlassian.com/agile/project-management/user-stories`, says that user stories serve a number of key benefits, including:

- **Stories keep the focus on the user**. A to-do list keeps the team focused on tasks that need to be checked off, but a collection of stories keeps the team focused on solving problems for real users.

- **Stories enable collaboration**. With the end goal defined, the team can work together to decide how best to serve the user and meet that goal.
- **Stories drive creative solutions**. Stories encourage the team to think critically and creatively about how to best solve for an end goal.
- **Stories create momentum**. With each passing story, the development team enjoys a small challenge and a small win, driving momentum.

To present a balanced view on this part of the requirements process, it is important to note that, by design, user stories are not perfect or comprehensive. Therefore, it's equally important to give considerable thought into *non-functional requirements*, especially on business-critical, enterprise-scale systems. After all, end users are important, but it's not just about them.

There are also operations and support teams who have to manage the system to ensure the users have an up and stable system to use in the first place. There are certain standard non-functional requirements, which all business-critical systems will have, such as regular backup and restore and **Disaster Recovery** (**DR**) capabilities, with industry standard measures including **Recovery Point Objective** (**RPO**) and **Recovery Time Objective** (**RTO**).

Personas at the requirements workshop

Simply put a user story is:

"As a <**persona**>, I <want/need to>, so that <purpose>."

Adopting a persona is the first and pivotal part of this formula. This is also where you need your team to be super creative and be able to step out of thinking just in their role but imagine life as another user.

When you're speaking from your own position of knowledge or authority, there is a certain expectation that you have all the answers. So, the creation of personas is the fun part where they can experiment and explore possibilities, without being personally over-invested. Digital product management specialist, Roman Pichler, uses a simple template:

Name and Photo	Bio	Goal

I particularly like the name and photo, because it makes the persona seem much more real. However, there is a danger that too much attention is paid to social and cultural stereotypes. But this is where the strength of your diverse team comes in to counter any overly predictable trains of thought!

The overall result is that you create a more rounded set of personas that is representative, inclusive, and more thorough. This opens up your user stories to many more possible opportunities and relevant scenarios. This is exactly how mass market, consumer-facing software such as *Facebook*, *Twitter*, and all of your popular social media apps are designed. They have to cater to a diverse and endless list of possible unique users.

Workshop epics

Even though user stories are informal and high-level, they can still seem like an endless list of scenarios. This is clearly impossible to capture. Besides the obvious measure of time-boxing the exercise, you can also *frame* your user stories to fit into a larger structure to make better sense, overall. Framing implies an additional connection, over simple similarities. The larger structures, containing connected user stories are called *epics*.

If your project is to develop content for a role-playing video game, then you can easily imagine overall script as an epic, with multiple strands of possible scenes, based on your role and actions, as user stories. Similarly, a series of books and a film saga would be epics, with each individual book and film, each with its own story, as user stories.

Using this approach and definition of epics and user stories, you naturally start from the ground up, using a bottom-up approach. In other words, you make the first *Rocky* film, then *Rocky II*, and so on and so on!

The alternative approach is to think of epics and user stories from a work management perspective. In this case, you would start with the overarching goal of an ambitious epic, then drill down into more manageable pieces of work as your user stories. This would be a top-down approach.

In this scenario, I would suggest that it's more of a *Waterfall* project management methodology, where each user story is no longer about the user but is more of a work package to task out to a particular team or member.

In *Atlassian*'s case, since they produce and provide huge multi-enterprise scale software-as-a-service, there's even a higher level above epics called *initiatives*. The *Atlassian Agile Coach* explains initiatives as a truly colossal piece of work that requires multiple epics.

Example of epics in an initiative:
Let's say your rocket ship company wants to decrease the cost per launch by 5% this year. That's a great fit for an initiative, as no single epic could likely achieve that big a goal. Within that initiative, there would be epics such as, "Decrease launch-phase fuel consumption by 1%," "Increase launches per quarter from 3 to 4," and "Turn all thermostats down from 71 to 69 degrees #Dadmode."

Source: https://www.atlassian.com/agile/project-management/epics-stories-themes

In other words, this is like a program of multiple projects, each of which has multiple work packages:

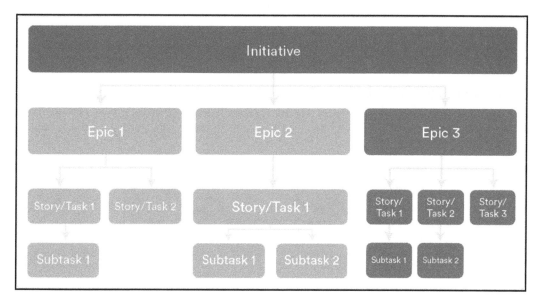

Figure 7.5: A hierarchy of initiative, epics, user stories
Source: https://www.atlassian.com/agile/project-management/user-stories

In both of these approaches, the key to effective user stories is simplicity, which leads to clarity at a user story by user story level. This begins with creating a good set of personas to explore. When your team has creatively invented a set of interesting personas and crafted a set of informative user stories, the next step is to iteratively refine them into being specific enough to start a design or even development immediately.

Prioritization

Humans being humans, we have a tendency to tackle the easiest things first. Sociopsychologists and behavioral economists call this "hyperbolic discounting," where people essentially discount future impact, and so delay taking the more important actions now because they don't benefit the present.

For the good of your company, customer, and project, what everyone needs is a list of requirements that are prioritized by business needs and value, over your team's human biases. I have yet to see a fancy software tool that is better at visualization and encouraging real-time collaboration than a big, plain, perfectly flat wall.

To begin with, write all your personas and user stories on an individual card, and stick them all on to a wall. I really do mean all of them. This is where your large and airy room is useful!

Then, collaboratively with all of your team, move each persona to match the relevant user stories, and together around the wall to frame them into an appropriate epic structure. Make sure that the team as a whole understands each persona, user story, and epic without personal assumptions.

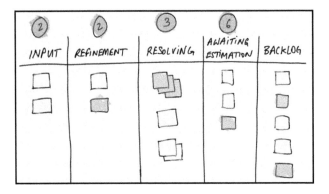

Figure 7.6: A working board of prioritized stories
Source: http://www.anecon.com/blog/user-stories-definition-ready-kanban-board/

Each user story should be the most basic and smallest unit of discussion, work, and requirement. As the team discusses them in a logical, as opposed to arbitrarily sequential order, they will also start to get an idea of how much effort may be required to develop. This will be a very rough estimate because there are still a lot of unknowns at this stage, such as which technologies will be used, and other project constraints such as scheduling. But it's still useful to gauge the necessary inputs into the effort and cost estimation, as well as the technology choice process.

Now, guide your team to identify the user stories that are most realistic within any known constraints of your time, cost, and quality, as well as time-boxed sprints too, if that's what you're using. Then, move them to a separate area of the wall, sorted by true business value and effort required. This will eventually produce a list of user stories that are appropriately prioritized!

Throughout this process, you – the manager – need to coach your team into achieving the goal of producing a reasonable and prioritized backlog, which contains the list of user stories your team has just produced as well as other, non-functional requirements. The backlog will form the basis of your design and development work at the next stage of the software development life cycle.

The product demo meeting

The goal of a product demo is simple: to **wow** your intended audience.

Anything short of this should be considered as being a missed opportunity. In today's world of ubiquitous on-demand videos and webinars, the chance to demonstrate your software product to people you want to impress is rare and must be treasured.

Your audience might be prospective customers, existing key stakeholders or power users, or perhaps a potential investor. By the end of the demo, they should all be compelled to want more, to learn more about the product and also the people who built it; about you, your team, your organization. This is just as important as the product itself because ultimately, it's the people they talk to, deal with, and build a business relationship with. If they are confident in you, then it's natural that they have confidence in your product. Furthermore, it creates the foundations for further products, changes, and general business opportunities.

Of course, not all product demos are sales oriented. However, even in an ongoing business relationship, the principle is largely the same. The aim is not to exhaustively show your audience everything your product does, or even all the changes they've requested in the new release. People's time and attention are too precious for exhaustive lists and aimless waffle. Instead, be specific and targeted in what you're trying to say.

Demos – less is definitely more

There's a natural limit to people's capacity to process new information, like a brand-new software application. Most people who attend product demos expect to see something specific.

Why? Because it is specific use cases that demonstrate real value. So, when it comes to practical experiences like product demos, less is definitely more!

A successful product demo is slick, sharp, and focused, and run by well informed and experienced people who are passionate about the product. The audience is engaged and asks lots of relevant and in-depth questions. They may even interrupt to give instant feedback, whether it's good, bad, or it's plain ugly. They will have a real sense of ownership in the product. Most of all, they will leave the demo interested and feeling positive. Or ideally, even inspired!

On the other hand, an ineffective product demo is dull and meanderingly aimless. However, innovative the product may be, the demo is fishing for reactions and compliments, as opposed being specific and confident in the product's quality, and therefore, its desirability and suitability for its intended customer and user base. The audience will seem distant and generally un-interactive. Naturally, they will leave the demo feeling rather indifferent and ultimately forget about the experience.

To help you run an effective product demo and achieve the goal of wowing your audience, here are some practical steps to make sure they leave satisfied, but also wanting more.

Rehearsing and tailoring the demo

Just like the sales meeting, a good product demo takes good planning. If it's a sales-oriented product demo, then use the same framework as the sales meeting to identify and understand your customer, your own company, and the wider environment.

Start a basic dialogue with your audience in advance of the demo to understand their expectations. If there is a specific area, or process, that they would like information on, then focus on that and tailor your demo according to their needs.

This doesn't mean you have to prepare a completely different demo every time for different customers. "Reinventing the wheel" would be a very time-consuming task. However, having the same demo for every customer would be overly formulaic and presumptuous. Instead, you should strike a workable and sustainable balance between having a completely bespoke demo and a completely scripted, repeated demo.

To achieve this in an effective manner, prepare a main narrative that is suitable, and therefore repeatable, for the majority of your audience. As a rule of thumb, 50% of the demo content should fall into this category.

This means that the **maximum tailoring you have to do is the other 50%**. The tailored portion must be based on the early engagement with your audience and what they've said they're interested in. If you are confident in your understanding of their needs, then you should also anticipate what they might ask next or what they may not have thought about yet.

As the product demo is an important step in the customer engagement process, it's something that you're likely to be doing multiple times. So, it's important to make this valuable opportunity a frictionless and undemanding task as much as possible, for you and your team. The idea is to avoid making everything from scratch every time.

If your demo includes a slideshow presentation, then 50% should be repeatable as is without editing. In general, do minimize your number of slides to an absolute maximum of 5, and concentrate on the demo itself wherever possible.

Lastly, don't forget to practice and rehearse, especially if your demo team consists of many people who may not even normally work together. It's vital to make sure each team member knows their role in the overall context. Conflicting and contradicting information is never good for confidence, so avoid giving such messages at all cost.

A slick product demo with multiple interactions and presenters always require practice. It's naïve to think that it just happens, regardless of how experienced you and your team might be. Your discerning audience can easily tell between a well-rehearsed demo versus an underprepared one. So, make the most of this valuable opportunity by preparing well.

Create a sense of occasion for the demo

Having attended a fair few product demos, the ones I still talk about tend to be those that gave me real sense of occasion. The demo itself may or may not have been inspiring. But overall, it gave me something noteworthy to talk about with my colleagues and friends.

Good preparation is a vital component of this. Whenever the demo is noticeably tailored based on the early discussions with me and my fellow audience, we naturally feel heard and are more likely to engage and stay engaged during the demo as a result.

Furthermore, making the demo a memorable occasion is also about making sure the physical and virtual environment is appropriate. I'm not talking about any red-carpet treatment here. It starts with ensuring that the meeting room or video-conferencing call is ready and open ahead of time. This could be considered basic customer service, but you'd be surprised at how many times the basics are forgotten. As a result, I forgot about the product that was being demoed!

To use the dining out analogy, the demo itself should always feel like the main course of a meal. It's something that you look forward to. It arrives on cue after an appetizing starter and is deeply satisfying, but leaves you wanting more in the form of a dessert!

Set the scene for the demo

When you have your audience settled into the appropriate environment, whether it's physically in person or gathered virtually, always begin by setting the scene. This is just like the starter course. Its purpose is to align and focus your audience to the main point of the demo: to see the product in action.

Simply, always remember to set the scene. Don't be over-presumptuous in thinking that just because your audience is here, they are already interested and engaged in what you're about to show them. Furthermore, it's always worthwhile setting the scene for everyone so that they all start from the same place in terms of understanding and expectations, as much as possible.

Start from the very top. Give a very brief overview of why everyone has gathered here today. Then introduce the basic premise and background of your software product to them, along with any relevant history it has, or that of your team and organization if it's interesting.

As a trick to acknowledge and engage your audience, always thank and reference the pre-engagement questions. Confidently communicate that this session has been tailored to answer these questions, however, many or few these may have been. This small but important detail is the key to creating a sense of significance and occasion for your audience. It captures their attention because they now have something relevant to look forward, not just another set of regurgitated sales patter.

Be specific about a demo

Remember the rule of "less is more." In your demo, be mindful of separating your key message from any noise.

Repetition is not a valid tactic at a product demo. In the limited time you have with this key audience group, you cannot beat them into submission by reiterating the same thing over and over again. If you do find yourself filling for time, simply stop and ask for questions. Instead of repeating the same demo actions, knowingly or otherwise, focus on **two to three specific user stories** to demonstrate in detail.

Ideally, these user stories should be in the areas which your audience has already told you they are interested in. But again, follow the 50% rule of content tailoring and strike a balance with the core stories that are applicable to the majority of your audience and really show the strengths of your product and its unique selling points.

For example, for an **Enterprise Resource Planning** (ERP) product, which manages the day-to-day running of most companies, such as invoices and accounts payable, focus on a key aspect of the order-to-cash business process, such as how easy it is for a budget holder to review and approve a purchase request. Or, how easy it is for a stock controller to run a real-time inventory report. Don't be tempted to go through an entire business process unless that was specifically asked for by your audience or if you anticipate that they would really like to see.

A great example of a specific, engaging, and fun product demo, is *Will It Blend?* This is a viral marketing video series that demonstrates *Blendtec*'s line of premium food processors. It famously blends an *Apple iPhone* and its rival *Samsung Galaxy S*; side by side in a super slow-motion video. And that's it! Weirdly, in an effort to sell you a blender, it doesn't actually try to show you all the features of the blender. But it works!

Also note that the format of the demo is always similar, with a proportion of the content itself actually the same, such as how the "Will it blend? That is the question," introduction at the beginning of every video, and how they ultimately always blend a seemingly unblendable product and show you the result. This follows the maximum 50% tailoring rule and also demonstrates the importance of consistency, which is especially important if you want to build a brand and credibility in the long term.

Pause to engage during the demo

In any presentation, public speaking, or demonstration activity that involves managing a live audience, it's easy to be nervous and hurry through your planned content to the extent where you find yourself needing to pause just to breathe.

Purposefully pausing for breath is a public speaking best practice, and also an effective way to engage your audience. Strategically timed periods of silence allow both you and the audience to gather their thoughts. Especially immediately following an important point, pausing for two to three seconds is vital to let that point sink in. The silence works as an emphasis and tells your audience that this is a key point. If they're taking notes, it gives them time to write and catch up.

When pausing your demo, also proactively ask for questions and feedback. The first invitation to do so may not yield a response, but it sets an open tone for the audience to have interactive conversation with you.

It's a more positive and memorable experience for everyone if the demo is a shared experience, beyond you talking and them listening. At the second or third try, you may well find that your audience does have questions and would like to explore a particular aspect of what you just demonstrated.

Lastly, always **leave lots of time for open questions and free-form discussions**. If you've successfully planned and executed an engaging and inspiring demo, your audience will want to know more, and this is the ideal time for them to learn more. After a satisfying meal, there's always room for dessert!

Summary

In this chapter, we've looked at some of the main types of meeting that you are likely to be attending as a developer-manager, and I've shared with you the important things you need to know to be successful in those meetings.

We started by thinking about those important off-duty meetings that you'll find yourself attending sometimes. The two main categories we talked about where the one-to-one off-duty chats, and the wider-group off-duty chats. These can be very important meetings, especially for your team members if they can't easily share something that's on their mind in normal office hours and environment. These meetings can raise fresh challenges for you as a manager about just how friendly you can be with your team members while off duty, and how to balance being yourself while holding a certain line as a manager at the same time.

We then moved on to the meet and greet type of meeting, where certain protocols and expectations need to be created. This led us naturally on to the even more formal and often very critical sales meeting. We talked about your role in sales meetings as a manager, and how to prepare, plan, and deliver a successful sales meeting.

You're already probably familiar with requirements workshop meetings, but probably as a developer rather than a manager. So, we took the time to help you place yourself in the shoes of the manager of the workshop now, and we looked at all the new things you're responsible for – including the biscuits!

Finally, we considered the product demo meeting – the important process of presenting a demonstration of our software to the customer. We talked about what to get right and what to not get wrong when it comes to the demo, and I offered you my best advice for delivering a successful demo. Your role as a manager will probably make all these meetings feel a little bit different than your previous experiences, so now you know how to think about them as a developer-manager and step forwards!

8
Design Techniques

In the previous chapter, Chapter 7, *Meetings*, we discussed how to practically apply techniques such as personas and user stories in a requirements workshop, which is a key milestone event, of course, during the information and requirements gathering stage.

Once you have gathered your user requirements, it's time to begin defining solutions that you and your team can use to fulfill your project requirements. To help you find those solutions, your development team can use any number of **design techniques**. In this chapter, we will look at the most important design techniques that you're going to use.

These design techniques all have the goal of obtaining user feedback so that you can guide your project toward the needs of your customer:

- Storyboards
- Use cases
- Wireframes
- Mockups
- Prototypes

These design techniques help you move your project forward from the personas, user stories, and requirements that you've already gathered, toward a set of working design definitions. We're going to begin this chapter by considering some of the people and teams you might be working with across an organization during the design phase, and then we'll look into all five design techniques.

Design teams and stakeholders

Within an organization, you and your team won't be working in isolation during these stages – you'll need to work with other various stakeholders, of course. Let's consider some of these now, starting with the architects with whom you may need to work in the organization.

The architects

One of the design roles you're very likely to engage with early on is the architect. As discussed in `Chapter 3`, *What is My Job Now?*, there are three types of architects that you may encounter:

1. An enterprise architect
2. A solution architect
3. A technical architect

Looking from the top of this list downward, you'll see a descending focus in overview and strategy. And looking from the bottom of the list upward, you'll see an ascending focus on technology and delivery.

When you're working with a large organization, you're most likely going to engage with the enterprise architect first. In a smaller organization, one person may well fulfill all three architect roles.

You're going to have the most meaningful and productive engagement with the architect if you arrive ready to present the most pertinent requirements you have gathered from your five types of users, who are as follows:

- Casual users
- Business users
- Power users
- Management users
- Non-users

Your presentation should also include any important decisions that have been made by the project team and stakeholders. This could include the product lifespan, overall budget, and delivery timescales.

The test teams

As well as architects, you will need to engage with the test teams. Again, depending on the size of your organization, you may have to deal with multiple test teams and departments, or you may find there is just one test team.

If you're working in a highly regulated industry, such as aerospace or healthcare, then you will also need to engage with the relevant governance, compliance, and quality teams.

The five design techniques

Even if your organization's **Project Management Office** (**PMO**) and project portfolio planning process are excellent, it's unlikely that all the people and teams in the organization will be aware of your project, let alone understand it.

To help overcome this issue, one of the best ways to initially engage with these people in teams in the organization is to bring them onboard and up to speed with your project. You can do this using the following design techniques: storyboards, use cases, wireframes, mockups, and prototypes.

These design techniques are all perfectly complementary to each other, so you can choose which to use based on both the audience you're engaging with and the outcome you want. So, let's now look at each of them in turn so you can choose the right design technique to suit each of your projects.

Design technique 1 – storyboards

A storyboard is a sequence of pictures that outline a scenario. It's an illustration of a series of events that demonstrates how your software will behave – a visual representation of your software and its process flow, with the appearance of a complete solution.

The pioneering use of storyboards is widely attributed to *Walt Disney Studios*, from as far back as the 1920s. It was used as a cheap and compelling way to previsualize the animated films they were making. The principles and value of this technique have since been adopted by many industries beyond animation and film-making.

In the *Agile* software development process, as the name suggests, storyboarding is synonymous with user stories. It's the technique of choice for documenting and illustrating the assortment of user stories, which are created from the requirements-gathering stage.

The advantages of storyboards

There are many advantages to using storyboards. The biggest advantage in my experience is their sheer **simplicity** and the **clarity** they create. After all, the goal is to capture and then communicate a user story to another group of people. So, the simpler it is, the easier it is for them to understand, and the more effective the storyboard is. In other words, if you can't storyboard it, then it's not clear enough in your own mind to explain to others.

Storyboards create a visceral sense of clarity that can be difficult to achieve with words alone. I would prefer a simple storyboard over a wordy and dry requirements specification any day!

The power of a simple picture cannot be underestimated. Especially in today's world of interactive, responsive, and content-rich **User Interfaces** (**UI**), storyboarding is a highly effective way of describing how a piece of software behaves, looks, and feels.

I should add that there is nothing wrong with a good flowchart or swim lane process diagram – I'm also a big fan of those. However, their application is restricted to formal, and some would say rigid, business processes, which tend to be long and drawn out.

By design, approaches such as flowcharts and swim lane process diagrams will lack the intuitive qualities of a storyboard, and they will often require additional commentary and narration for the audience to truly understand. However, as long as they create clarity for both the project team and their audience, then they serve their purpose well.

As with all communication, you should tailor the content and method of your storyboard according to your audience. Storyboarding is the mainstream tool of choice in most progressive industries. However, there are still plenty of organizations that rely on more traditional techniques such as flowcharts and written documentation, especially those that are highly regulated, as previously mentioned. Legal and audit requirements may restrict them to using a certain method of documentation for contract and regulatory purposes.

Another benefit of storyboards is the real-world context they provide the audience. A good storyboard is a definitive visual aid that brings an imaginary scenario to life. Unlike a flowchart and other diagrams, it's not a notional or conceptual thing that requires explanation. In other words, it's easy to understand and self-explanatory.

As such, storyboards will bridge the gap between concept and reality; the designer's mind and the customer's expectation; the requirement and the design. It provides rich user and usage contexts because it literally draws this out for everyone to see for themselves. By doing this, it also helps to maintain focus on the users as real people, humans in real life, or business situations.

The disadvantages of storyboards

Like all techniques, storyboards aren't perfect either. Critics of storyboards say that it can be a cumbersome process, which adds an overhead to the already significant effort to capture requirements and create designs. To this, I say that I can understand the reason for this. If a storyboard is subject to constant small changes, which can have a ripple effect, it can be a drain on resources.

At the same time, a lot of more traditional developers aren't keen on having to acquire new artistic skills. As with all techniques, storyboards should be used appropriately and as a means to an end.

As you might expect, mobile app development is an area that relies heavily on graphical storyboards to communicate a user's journey, given its emphasis on UX. At the same time, storyboards can also illustrate the look and feel of an app, which is immensely difficult to do with just a written description.

Making storyboards – a growing toolkit

To help you and your team create effective storyboards, there is an ever-growing number of tools out there. The most elaborate ones will offer you integration with wireframing and UI mockup capability, essentially automating some of the processes to make a storyboard into a wireframe or mockup.

The biggest pitfall of relying on these tools is the potential distraction from the human and real-world focus, which is one of the key benefits of storyboarding as a design process. With ever more complicated tools, producing storyboards can become a toolset-centric and technically driven exercise. In other words, you end up producing what the tool is best at producing, or what you are best at producing with a particular tool.

Perhaps this is the reason why a lot of design teams opt to use the ever-present and multi-purpose *Microsoft PowerPoint*. Despite not being renowned for its usability, it is probably one of the most versatile mainstream applications in the world. Interestingly, a lot of storyboarding tools are add-ins for *PowerPoint*. Coincidentally, *PowerPoint* is also many people's preferred tool for wireframes, something we'll get into later.

Remember some of the biggest benefits of storyboarding: simplicity and clarity. So, in the true spirit of simplicity and practicality, we need to go back to basics.

There is nothing wrong with an "old-fashioned" whiteboard as your tool of choice. Effectively using a whiteboard to facilitate collaboration and design is something we'll discuss later in this chapter. It's simple and effective. So, it's a practical skill that all managers should have, and should be using.

Design technique 2 – use cases

Use cases are a systematic way of defining the interactions between actors and the software **system** to achieve a particular goal. It follows a set method of describing how your software will be used.

This concept is best explained with the use diagram of a real-life scenario; in this case, how an ATM machine is used.

Case study – how a bank's ATM is used

There are four common uses and interactions with the bank by a customer to complete the transaction. They are as follows:

- Check balance
- Deposit funds
- Withdraw cash
- Transfer funds

There are also two legitimate uses by a technician, who also interacts with the bank, to achieve their goal of fixing the ATM:

- Maintenance
- Repair

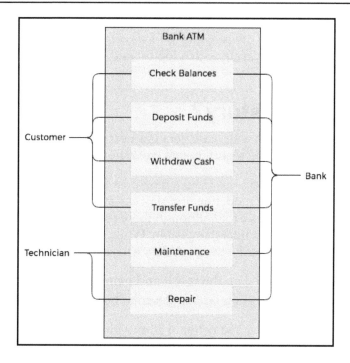

Figure 8.1: How a bank's ATM is used

To make a valid use case, it must have one or more actors, and the relationship between each actor as well as other use cases is also important. Remember that an actor may be another external system, instead of a person, which is especially important when your software is heavily integrated with other software systems.

The human-centric design is important for user experience, but so are the behind-the-scenes system-to-system interactions, which facilitate a myriad of data shares and data flows.

Given their diagrammatic nature, use cases are often used in conjunction with **Unified Modeling Language** (**UML**). However, use cases can also be in a purely written format, as you can see on the following page. As with storyboards, if you work in a highly regulated industry, you may have to follow a strict format and revert only to written words, in order to satisfy the more traditional legal community.

Use cases have an obvious comparison and confluence with storyboards. When both techniques are used well, a storyboard could effectively illustrate each use case.

Depending on the complexity of your software, it could be very strenuous to produce a storyboard for every use case. So, it's sensible to focus on the truly business-critical and most illustrative use cases, showcasing with a logical and beautiful storyboard.

Use case or user story?

So, what's the difference between a use case versus a user story, which we discussed in `Chapter 7`, *Meetings*, as part of the requirements workshop?

The best explanation I've come across is from a blog post by a company called *Visual Paradigm*. It is an award-winning modeling and process-mapping software maker, based in Hong Kong. The company suggests that although there are some similarities between user stories and use cases, they are not interchangeable. While both user stories and use cases identify users, and they both describe the goal, they each serve different purposes:

- User stories are centered on **the result and benefit** of the thing you're describing.
- Use cases can be more granular and describe **how your system will act**.

As user stories are more high level and better at stimulating conversation with your users and development team, it's well suited as a requirement gathering-technique. Because use cases are more formal and structured, they are well suited and detailed as a design technique.

User stories bridge the gap between a real-world business requirement and a technical specification, which a developer can take and code for. This concept is especially important if you have a remote development center, such as an offshore development team, who may not be involved in the requirements-gathering process and have interactions with users directly.

A well-written use case removes ambiguity to provide simplicity and clarity, which is also why it works fantastically together with storyboards. As with all techniques, there are pitfalls and scope for misuse. Renowned software engineer and author, Karl E. Wiegers, lists five self-explanatory and very sensible traps to avoid:

1. Use cases that users don't understand
2. Too many use cases
3. Overly complex use cases
4. Describing specific user interface elements and actions
5. Not using other requirement models

Use cases are a great method to build on your requirements, whether they are in a user story or another format. Storyboards should always be considered in combination with other techniques.

One of the challenges of being a manager is being able to decide which techniques are most appropriate and how to coach your team, as well as your users, to use them effectively.

Design technique 3 – wireframes

A wireframe is simply a diagram of a GUI. It's a visual guide to how a GUI will look, without all of the detail such as images and rendering. Think of it a blueprint to an architect, or as like a wiring schematic to an electrical engineer.

From an end-user perspective, there are very palpable ways of interacting with modern software. This could be through a traditional desktop computer or increasingly, through touchscreen mobile devices. It can even be through virtual and augmented reality, complete with voice commands and haptic feedback.

The commonality between these devices and interactions is that they all have a crucial visual element that is an integral part of the user experience. In other words, very few pieces of software don't have a GUI! So, when you are designing software, the GUI element is something you need to take very seriously. This is where wireframes can help:

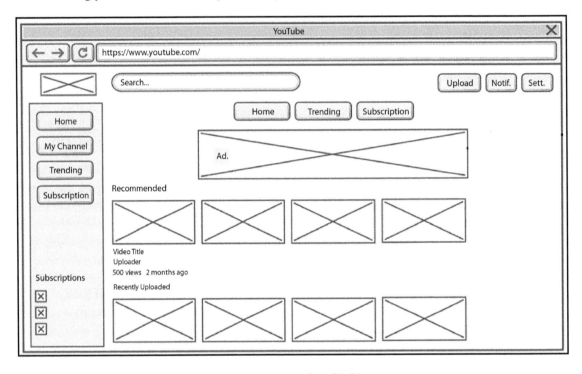

Figure 8.2: An example wireframe of *YouTube*

Wireframes, like the one shown here, are extremely useful as a low-fidelity representation of the GUI you are designing. They create a visual representation of an overall structure, which you can show to other teams and users, with minimal effort. This is the key benefit of wireframes.

If you ever find yourself or your team spending a lot of time drawing and perfecting wireframes, stop! Using wireframes as opposed to just a rough sketch has one major advantage, being that like an architect's blueprint, it follows a consistent set of rules then act as shortcuts to help others to understand what you're designing.

Basically, this is your legend to decipher what each symbol or icon means. This sounds trivial but is actually very important. As you adjust and build on top of your wireframes, there are tools that can automate the process of turning your wireframe into a rendered image or even a mockup, which we will discuss later. The key to using wireframes effectively is to only use it as a guide, an ultra-basic representation of your UI.

While there are many more advanced wireframing tools out there, as bizarre as it may sound, *PowerPoint* is still by far the most popular. For the same reasons as storyboards, the ubiquity and versatility of *PowerPoint* make it an easy and accessible option – as well as a relatively cheap one. *PowerPoint* enables your team to engage with the users more easily because files can be very easily shared and collaborated across. If your team needs more advanced functionality, there are also add-ins available that provide extra templates and icons.

Design technique 4 – mockups

An easy way to explain what a mockup is, in relation to wireframes and prototypes, is to plot these different design techniques on a fidelity-versus-time chart:

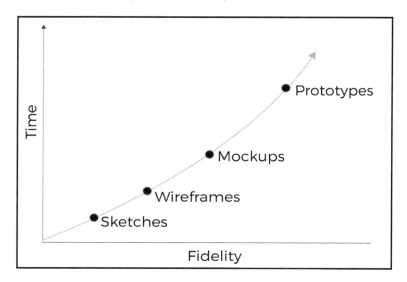

Figure 8.3: A fidelity-versus-time chart, illustrating the difference with sketches, wireframes, mockups, and prototypes

In time and in fidelity, a mockup is another step up from a wireframe, which begins to show how your UI is going to look and feel. A mockup is still a static, non-interactive product at this stage. Its real value is in illustrating to other developers, testers, and users the aesthetics of your software.

Much like storyboards and wireframes, this is all about bringing your intangible software to life, visually, and therefore helping your stakeholders to picture what the finished product will look like and provide feedback to change it, if required, without having to undo any previous work.

The best examples of real and commonly used mockups are for web-based systems or even simple websites. Instead of building an actual working website, you simulate or literally mock up the pages using static objects – images and text. Think drag and drop here, rather than amending the **Cascading Style Sheets** (**CSS**) or the theme within the **content management system** (**CMS**).

Building on the previous wireframe example of an old version of *YouTube*, this is what a mockup might look like:

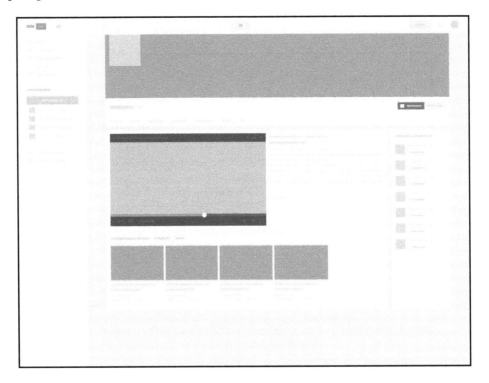

Figure 8.4: A mockup of a more recent version of YouTube

Design technique 5 – prototypes

As you can see in the previous chart, a prototype is the next logical step from a mockup. The key distinction between a prototype and a mockup is that a prototype is interactive. However, it's still not the finished product. It only has very limited functionality, and the interactions are only simulated.

In other words, prototypes don't actually execute the process they are designed for, but they do give the user an instant response, which demonstrates how the real, fully developed system would behave. So, think of a prototype as a mini demo.

Similar to the previous design techniques, the key goal is to obtain user feedback, which helps you to make more informed design decisions and therefore reduce the risk of building something that's not what the customer wanted.

Whereas wireframes and mockups are only for illustrative purposes, prototypes are for demonstrative purposes. In our *YouTube* example, a prototype of the home page will likely provide a number of clickable links and buttons, which can all take the user to other screens, such as the login page. However, there is no actual logging in or account verification process behind the scenes. So, the prototype is rather basic.

This is the point of prototypes, of course, and to bring prototypes back to basics even further, they don't even need to be electronic! This is especially true in mobile app development, where there is a popular practice of handcrafting offline prototypes.

Known as *paper prototyping*, this method is essentially drawing out the UI components by hand, then physically assembling and animating the user journey process. As slow and tedious as this sounds, the results can be very compelling for the user because paper prototypes are tangible and eye-catching. This is especially true if your user is a customer who doesn't want to spend much money at this stage of the project!

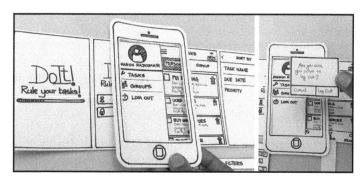

Figure 8.5: An example of a paper prototype
Source: https://sharonmonisharaj.com/power-paper-prototyping

To put prototypes even further into context, we can talk about the ever-popular **proof of concept (POC)** and **pilot**.

As the following chart shows, when a POC is used appropriately, it is a simple isolated exercise that requires minimal time and investment. Meanwhile, a pilot is a larger exercise that requires more time and investment than a prototype, and can serve as an interim stage before the full productionization of your product.

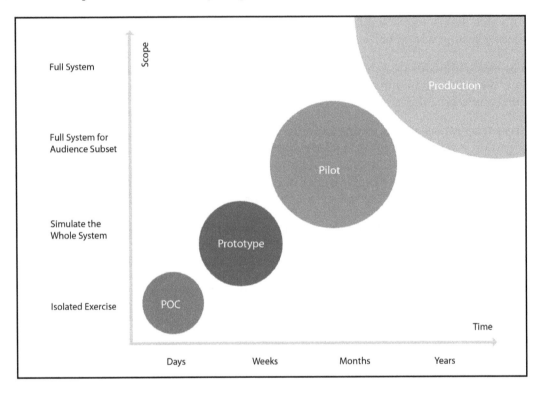

Figure 8.6: A time-versus-scope chart, illustrating the difference between POC, prototype, pilot, and production

How *Facebook* rolls out a new feature or UI is a great example of a controlled pilot. They implement new changes to only a select number of users – with or without their knowledge – before releasing it to all users. This is different from its own development and testing before the pilot, which is done in separate environments.

I've always found it intriguing that another user and I could be sitting right next to each other, but when we both go to *Facebook*, besides the customized content, we could be looking at different UIs.

How to be a "whiteboard rockstar"

Whiteboards are everywhere. Every company has them. You might even have one at home, in the kitchen, or in the office. They're super handy for making quick notes that you can easily rub out and start over.

At the end of the day, using a whiteboard is a pretty simple thing to do, and given your skills and experience as a developer, it's safe to assume that you have some exposure to good (and bad) uses of whiteboards. So, we're not going over-egg it here. However, there are a few useful tips and practical techniques, which you can easily learn to become a "whiteboard rockstar!"

Remember your goal as a manager: to enable your team to do their best work with requirements, analysis, design, development, test, and more.

So, in this context, being a whiteboard rockstar isn't about drawing the prettiest pictures, writing the neatest notes, or grabbing the spotlight because you have everyone's attention. It's about facilitating a group of people and doing the right things to stimulate and encourage the best ideas and discussions with your team, users, and customers.

Let's start with the basics.

Preparation

Not all whiteboards and markers are created equal. Always bring your own markers and eraser or cloth wipe! Besides avoiding the embarrassingly frequent occurrence of dodgy (or even permanent) markers and a dirty whiteboard, this also makes you appear more prepared and professional.

Being professional, rather than constantly blaming the previous users of the board, always helps to inspire more confidence and makes it easier to engage the more skeptical members of your group! In the most extreme case, you can even bring your own whiteboard.

Use block capitals

Writing quickly and clearly in block capitals will take a little practice, but the result is worth it. This is not the time for a fancy calligraphy demonstration. Writing in clear block capitals makes it much easier for everyone to see and read.

Use colors, but write in black

It's really important to use a variety of colors to differentiate and highlight key points, especially if you're drawing a diagram that might need to show different layers or sequences of events.

However, if you're just taking notes or making lists, always write in black unless there is an exceptional reason. Black is the most eye-friendly color for complicated images, which letters are, and most people find other typical marker colors irritating to read. It also reserves the brighter colors for things you want to accentuate.

Use straight lines

This is easier said than done. However, like writing in block capitals, a little practice will go a long way toward achieving a great result. When you write or draw in an aligned fashion, it helps the group to think more clearly and logically. It shows a well-formed concept, as opposed to a chaotic and ill-planned accident.

Furthermore, plan your writing to leave gaps between points or area. Then, use these spaces to encourage discussion and make further anecdotal notes, preferably in a different color.

At the same time, use different letter sizes and larger drawings to illustrate the key points further. Think of the entire whiteboard as a hot spot map for extra impact – be brave and experiment!

Purpose

Once you've got the basics, it's on to the more advanced stuff. Are you actually leading the group and stimulating discussion? Or are you just scribing?

Bear in mind that, in the design stage of a project, there are many decisions to be made. In order to reach those decisions as a team, you need discourse followed by consensus, hopefully. As the manager in charge of the project or team, your input is vital in guiding the group through this turbulent process.

Scribing is an important part of the design process, and a good whiteboard can definitely help with that. However, the real value and opportunity of an effective design discussion are in the debate and sharing of ideas and views, even if they're opposing.

The effective use of a whiteboard is probably one of the simplest and easiest methods of communicating ideas and encouraging debate.

Controlling the room

Running a design meeting or workshop is not easy. First, you need to get the group's full attention and focus. The whiteboard can help with that.

Yes, you can and should consider using it for the agenda and actions. That's what a good, traditional chair and scribe would do. However, there's also a bigger opportunity to really grab everyone's interest and certainly challenge them – maybe even inspire them to do something extraordinary.

I once joined a design workshop where the leader simply put a large question mark on the whiteboard. It happened to be a very nicely drawn question mark, following all of the tips we've just discussed.

As soon as everyone entered the room, the meeting started, and we immediately jumped right into the really important design questions that were outstanding from the previous meeting. These included which technology stack we were going to use and how we were going to coordinate our work with the offshore team.

Handing over control

As counterintuitive as this seems, after you have gained control of the room and the group's focus, you also need to hand over control to someone else. Monopolizing use of the whiteboard for yourself is selfish and self-defeating. There's a real risk that you'll end up with only your thoughts and opinions, which is not the purpose of the meeting.

You can actively encourage collaboration by inviting others to show the group what they're trying to say. Design concepts can be complicated, so drawing it on a whiteboard, even if it's a very rough sketch, is really helpful for the group to understand the idea. A full storyboard may well be too slow to produce in real time, but a simple use case diagram or wireframe can be done relatively easily.

To achieve this active participation from the group, strategically sit down and stand up. In other words, physically relinquish control of the whiteboard by stepping away from it. Offer a marker to the relevant group member and ask them to show the group what they really mean.

You should also refrain from being protective of whatever you have put on the board. Actively ask the group: "Is this what you mean?" and get feedback and suggestions on making the drawing, diagram, or notes better for everyone. Then, empower them to freely mark-up, draw, wipe, and redraw until the group is satisfied with the result.

Visual anchors

Visual anchors are like color to a black and white picture. They add a whole new dimension to your whiteboard artifact and make it a lot more interesting.

Adding symbols to a wordy narration or drawn-out process is a relief for sore eyes and acts as a visual aid, which allows the group, as well as other parties, to interpret the intent and content quickly.

Agile coach and visual trainer, Yuri Malishenko, recommends building up a library of "visual vocabulary:"

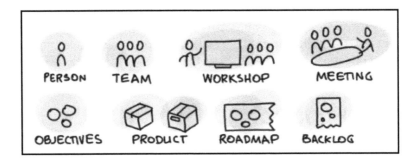

Figure 8.7: Excerpt from Yuri Malishenko's library of "visual vocabulary"
Source: https://medium.com/graphicfacilitation/two-simple-techniques-to-dramatically-improve-your-whiteboard-skills-a391534a8140

Building on the previous example of a business-expenses process map, adding a few visual symbols in appropriately indicative colors makes a big difference to the overall effect of the result. From a somewhat dry and boring series of words, it's transformed into an easily interpreted process flow, on which real analysis and design can be based.

Using visual anchors does require practice and extra effort. However, the ocular improvement is striking, and the ultimate increase in the group's productivity makes it extremely worthwhile. Everything looks more interesting and fun with a doodle or two!

Summary

When it comes to facilitating the design of your software, you're going to be working with various architects and test teams in an organization.

There are five fundamental design techniques you need to have in your manager's toolkit, which will help you communicate with and listen to your users and other design stakeholders. These five techniques are the most commonly used and trusted industry best practices to model and illustrate what your software will look like and what it will feel like to users:

- Storyboards
- Use cases
- Wireframes
- Mockups
- Prototypes

Storyboards are exactly what they sound like, a series of drawings or illustrations with a narrative showing what each step taken by a user and the resulting behavior of your software. They can be as elementary or elaborate as you make them. Their key benefits and advantages are simplicity and clarity.

Use cases are part of a more formal technique that focuses on describing how actors interact with systems in order to achieve a particular goal. They can be captured in a wordy narrative, but more typically, using a basic visual diagram that shows the relationship between actors and systems, supported by some commentary.

Wireframes are low-fidelity illustrations of a **Graphical User Interface** (**GUI**). They are quick and easy to produce and give your audience an estimate of your system's look and feel, instantly!

Mockups are the next step up from wireframes in terms of fidelity and time to produce. They are a more detailed and elaborate representation of your system's GUI.

Prototypes are partially working versions of your software. Building on mockups, at least some of the screens or processes should be functional, which allows your audience to interact with the software and provide more in-depth feedback. Remember that you can also produce handcrafted paper prototypes, which can also be highly effective, especially as an interim step to having the software ready.

Complementary to these five design techniques, it's important to remember the old-fashioned and much-forgotten skill of whiteboarding! In this age of online collaboration, the perception that it's an outdated practice is misguided.

As a low-tech and easily accessible resource, it is the lowest common denominator for almost all organizations and people. It can even cross language barriers and is always relevant as a trusty and productive skill to possess in your manager's toolkit.

It will take practice to be a true "whiteboard rockstar," but there are practical things you can easily do to maximize your effectiveness in facilitating design meetings:

- Prepare well by bringing your own markers and clean the board before starting!
- Use block capitals for visual clarity.
- Use colors freely, but always write words in black.
- Use straight lines, so it's easy for everyone to follow.
- Remember and stick to your true purpose of achieving great design.
- Control the room by grabbing people's attention with bold messages.
- Hand over control to others by inviting them to draw, write, and improve your work.
- Use visual anchors to symbolize more complicated concepts.

By following these eight practices, you can ensure that everyone is engaged and on the same page in terms of understanding. Furthermore, these practices can be used to facilitate a variety of meetings beyond design workshops.

Validating the Solution 9

This chapter is all about how you can progress with your project and your build so that, ultimately, you can start shipping your product. If you've broadly followed the recommended steps so far, you'll have built strong foundations for a great team, a great solution, and a great product.

Your checklist so far...	
Listen and learn; settle into your new role	✓
Build your team	✓
Choose your methodology	✓
Identify your key stakeholders	✓
Gather your requirements	✓
Define your solution	✓

Your work is not done yet of course. Next, you need to validate the solution you've designed. You want to make sure it's refined based on early feedback, and you want to get your stakeholders to sign off that all-important business case so that you have the resources to build it and ship it!

No solution is perfect

Please do remember that no solution is perfect. The notion of a *perfect* solution and a *perfect* product will just hold you back, rather than help you to succeed. So, you need to remove any such ideas from your psyche and just as importantly then communicate this to your team. Don't forget to walk the walk as well in your everyday behavior, in order to set this right tone:

"Progress. Not perfection."

– Robert McCall

This is one of my most favorite quotes because I'm aware of my own tendencies to dwell and procrastinate, over-think, and unnecessarily plan the hell out of something. Back in the real world, though, especially in our time-pressed real world, the most important thing usually is just to start. This is something I wrestle with every day. However, when I remind my team of this, I also remind myself, and vice versa.

This quote, which I first heard in a movie, has always stuck with me. The movie is called *The Equalizer*, and it's particularly poignant because the main character, played by Denzel Washington, is an ex-CIA super-agent who is obsessively dedicated to everything he does, however mundane it is. He always follows a step-by-step approach, which ultimately gives him an exceptionally high standard of results.

To switch to a non-fictional example now, Ben Barry is a famous digital graphic designer and one of the earliest staff members of *Facebook*. He is best known for co-founding the *Facebook* Analog Research Laboratory and developing *Facebook*'s internal culture, voice, and brand. One of his favorites quotes is:

> *"Done is better than perfect."*

> *– Ben Barry*

It's also important to note that focusing on "done" does not mean churning out mediocre work and products. Barry's key point is that you must not become obsessed with perfection and then give up when you can't get everything perfect. Instead, simply focus on finishing the job. You can always come back to improve it later. To press this same message out to a wider audience, rather than just to developers and project managers, there's even a thing called The Done Manifesto.

Technical validation

So, just how do you ensure that your solution is the "right solution?" Well, a good place to start here is by defining and distinguishing the difference between *validation* and *verification*. Barry Boehm, the renowned software engineering academic, explains this in the clearest way:

Validation	Verification
Are we building the right product?	Are we building the product right?

Validating your solution, or more specifically, the design of your solution, is a vital step in any software project. However, this can be a conflicted exercise since it's difficult to impartially assess your own work, both individually and collectively with your team. After all, you've just spent a lot of effort and creative energy on understanding the business problem and designing an innovative solution to this problem. This is exactly the reason why validation should be an objective exercise and ideally based on empirical data, as well as feedback from independent parties.

Unless you are a true one-man-band, you are likely to have a project delivery process to follow within your organization. In this process, which should be owned by the **Project Management Office** (**PMO**), there will most likely be checkpoints or stage gates. From a technical design validation perspective, the most important checkpoints may be called:

- Architecture review forum
- Technical design authority
- Design review board

Depending on the setup of your organization, the focus of these design reviews will be slightly different. For example, if it's a huge corporation with global reach and a suitably large IT department, the chances are that there will be a focus on enterprise architecture. In other words, whether your solution design conforms and supports the wider IT strategy, such as, has "cloud first" hosting been considered?

If so, does the design utilize and leverage Azure or AWS or something else that is already part of the organization's landscape and target state architecture? Does your design use the strategized "N minus one" version of SQL Server or MySQL or Oracle Database, as per the database standards, which makes your solution easier and cheaper to support?

Considering the high number of projects that the organization will have at any one time, these are reasonable questions to ask. As you can imagine, if even a small proportion of these projects do not follow the organizational strategy, the solution landscape can easily become antiquated and a sprawling mess that is very difficult and expensive to manage operationally. Additionally, there may be some specific software products and platforms that are forbidden by enterprise architects, for example, due to security or stability concerns.

To illustrate this further, now is a good moment to consider something that we've not discussed so far and that may not be familiar to many developers. However, now that you're a manager, it's important that you have an awareness and understanding of the role and importance of the *ITIL* Service Management Framework. **ITIL** stands for the **Information Technology Infrastructure Library**.

Under this framework, IT solutions and offerings are defined as "services." In contrast to the software development life cycle, it splits the service life cycle into five cyclical stages:

- Service Strategy
- Service Design
- Service Transition
- Service Operation
- Continual Service Improvement

The following diagram depicts these five stages in their cyclical relationship:

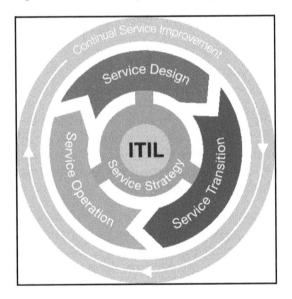

Figure 9.1: The classic *ITIL* V3 life cycle diagram
Source: https://web.fastlaneus.com/blog/cobit-vs.-itil

Without going into too much detail on *ITIL* (we'll go deeper into *ITIL* in a later chapter when the time is right) the key point for us right now is that all solutions or services will have an operational stage on this life cycle.

It is vital that your solution design takes this into consideration. For example, if your solution is designed to run for more than four years, is it built on a *long-term support* version of Java, Linux, or Windows, as opposed to the latest *short-term support* version, which will not have as long of a support period? These things matter.

This arcs back to the accumulation and repayment of technical debt. For various reasons, but usually to shorten the time duration of your project, you may choose to sacrifice some operational benefits, such as enhanced exception handling, to meet a deadline. This decision will have an impact on operational efforts, potentially making it more difficult to support your software. Alternatively, choosing to run on a single server node, without clustering or other high availability measures, maybe a lot easier to develop, test, and implement. However, every time the sysadmins need to patch the server, your users will have to accept the downtime! Similarly, the financial impact must also be thought through. This is especially important now that you're a manager, with more discretion and responsibility in budgeting and financial management.

Financial impact is closely linked with operational impact. For example, patching your non-resilient solution may need to be done outside of office hours, because users need it throughout the day. This may incur an additional higher cost for your organization if they have outsourced support to a third party who charges extra for out of hours work.

Last and not least, the financial impact of your solution should always take into account the **total cost of ownership** (TCO). Within the IT industry, TCO is a concept popularized by the well-known Gartner Group consultancy. Essentially, TCO promotes the analysis of all elements of an IT solution throughout its full long-term life cycle. This includes hardware and software costs; development and delivery costs, as well as operational and support costs; and initial setup and implementation costs, plus eventual exit migration and decommissioning costs. TCO also highlights the need to consider the potential cost of faults and failures.

A project will have a fixed *capital expenditure* budget to deliver and implement the solution. There will also be an even larger, fixed *operational expenditure* budget to support and maintain the solution. Both of these costs must be considered in full, with a sensible balance reached and agreed by key stakeholders. To complicate matters, the *capex* and *opex* budgets are usually owned by separate departments within IT.

Capex is short-hand for capital expenditure, which is essentially the investment budget. Opex is short-hand for operational expenditure, which is the budget for day-to-day costs of running a company.

From a technical and financial perspective, a possible worst-case scenario for an organization is for a flagship project to unnecessarily develop a highly bespoke solution that uses a niche technology that requires a whole new support team to be created and trained, or worse, to be unwillingly locked into a long-term relationship with a single supplier because the solution is proprietary to that supplier. I'd recommend you avoid being that Project Manager who needs to explain this to your enterprise architects and project sponsors!

These are all considerations that your design review and validation forum should question. Your project stakeholders should also be aware of these technical choices and their likely impact. If you are the Project Manager, it will be your job to make sure they understand and accept these impacts.

Business validation

So far, we have talked mainly about validating your solution from a technical perspective. This is very important, not least because this is the bulk of what IT projects do, but also because there is a potential financial impact to consider on the organization over the long-term.

The most critical part of validating a solution is, arguably, from the business perspective. This is because the organization can overcome technical inefficiencies, and even unnecessarily high costs, just as long as it can actually function as a business. The organization must achieve its mission and purpose and create an overall positive business value. This is ultimately the most important and real litmus test, and it boils down to a single question:

Will the solution do what the business needs it to do?

The answer, or answers, to this question are clearly not as simple as the question itself. Similar to the technical validation criteria, the answers to this simple question are multifaceted and not as simple as a "yes" or "no." Getting a business-minded person to validate a largely technical design of a solution is challenging to say the least, even if you've produced a comprehensive set of easy-to-follow, user-centric, and user-friendly storyboards.

Depending on the composition of your project team, you may be lucky enough to have a technically-aware business user or a business-experienced technical expert, or both. Having either of these will be a great help because bridging the gap between the tech and the business is one of the key challenges of any software project.

However, if we take a little step back, business validation should, in fact, be technology agnostic. This is a nice theory, but it does not reflect reality, because business and the technology that supports it are now so intrinsically linked and dependent that it is simply too complicated to unpack and separate their individual inputs.

There's also a large element of "chicken-and-egg" and cause-and-effect. In other words, the software can be made to do what the business needs, but the business may also be led by what the software can do, especially if it's a commercial off-the-shelf enterprise resource planning product such as SAP. Remember the example of software-led accountancy firms who specialize in certain products.

Given all this, the answer to that key question, "Will the solution do what the business needs it to do?" must be broken down into a spectrum of priorities. If we refer back now to the *MoSCoW* method, we will soon ask this instead: "Will the solution design satisfy the must haves, should haves, could haves, and won't haves?" Or put more bluntly, if it's a direct-to-the-consumer software product you're designing, such as the next *Facebook*, or *Amazon*, or *Dollar Shave Club*, then "Will people actually use it and buy from it?"

Michael Dubin, the founder of Dollar Shave Club, remembers his first real customer sale from his website, which was only a **Minimum Viable Product** (**MVP**) and in beta mode at the time. He calls this his first "stranger validation." As an entrepreneur, this gave him a big confidence boost in his overall business, underpinned by his website, which was his only sales channel.

Before launching his MVP website at all, Dollar Shave Club would have gone through something called **Business Process Validation** (**BPV**). Essentially, this is a design walkthrough or even dry run of how the business would work, and specifically, how the website, the sales order, and fulfillment system behind it would work in practice.

This is where your storyboards are vital to give the business users and sponsors a real insight into your solution design, enabling them to imagine what it would be like to have this piece of software working for them in the real world. Better still, you could have a prototype or mock-up of the user interface to provide them with something even more tangible.

Use your whiteboard and storytelling skills to illustrate the design to your stakeholders, what it will do, and how it will do it. Then, use your prototype or UI mock-up to demonstrate how the solution will look and feel. Never underestimate the power of a user's feelings! Remember that confidence is a feeling, and validation requires a level of confidence as much as data and evidence.

Note that BPV is not quite the same as testing of the solution itself. From a software product development perspective, that's regarded as verification. In other words, it's checking that the software functionality matches the design. A great way to think about product or solution validation and verification is that validation is something that happens throughout the development life cycle.

As you can see in *Figure 9.2*, at every stage, you are checking whether you are still building the right product, whereas verification focuses on the design and build. In effect, that's where the real software testing happens:

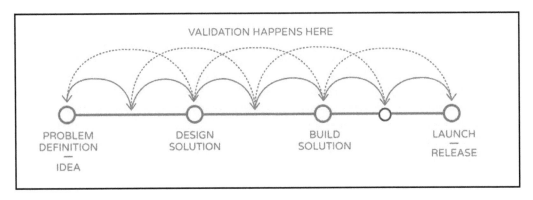

Figure 9.2: A diagram showing where validation happens over the product design process
Source: https://blog.prototypr.io/understanding-verification-and-validation-in-product-design-ef8c993fd496
Credit: Carlos Yllobre

Interestingly, the traditional *V-Model* has a different take on this. It regards verification as the upfront phases, which focus on the design, followed by validation, which focuses on testing:

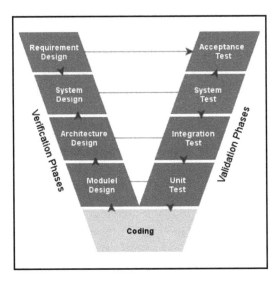

Figure 9.3: A diagram of the classic *V-Model*, which is a favorite of professional testers
Source: http://www.professionalqa.com/v-model

Perhaps this is one of the reasons why the traditional *V-Model*'s popularity has waned. In today's world of "move fast and break things," which was *Facebook*'s early motto, most organizations understandably opt for increased agility over rigidity. That means reducing time-to-market, reducing cost, and reducing risk, which can all count toward competitive advantage.

To be clear, there is no right or wrong way of defining or performing business validation. At the end of the day, it's about designing the most suitable solution and building the product appropriately, all within your project's triple constraint. However you actually choose to do this, you'll most likely find that you need multiple iterations and tweaks to your initial solution along the way.

As discussed during the requirements gathering sections, the business may not know what it needs. Moreover, even when you've created a design based on intently listening to the business to understand its challenges and ideas, they may still not know whether it will do what they need it to do. This is where *design thinking* can help.

Design thinking

When used appropriately, design thinking is a fantastic way to innovate and solve problems that cannot otherwise be solved easily in traditional ways utilizing knowledge alone. Design thinking is certainly not a one-size-fits-all tool, though, and on the downside, it can be conveniently misconstrued as "winging it," in the same way that *Agile* can be falsely used to mask a lack of real requirements and planning.

So, what is design thinking? And how can it help your solution design and validation? Most fundamentally, design thinking is an iterative problem-solving process. Design thinking and real *Agile* are very similar, in that both happen to be a mindset and a set of principles and practices. And put together, they can help you and your team to think and create more productively.

In the software context, design thinking is a focus on being human-centric. Specifically, in the design of user interfaces, it promotes a true user-centered approach, which puts the user first, over the software and its limitations. To achieve this, the *Hasso-Plattner Institute of Design at Stanford University*, also known as *d.school*, sets out a five-phased approach:

- **Empathize** with your users
- **Define** your users' needs, their problem, and your insights
- **Ideate** by challenging assumptions and creating ideas for innovative solutions
- **Prototype** to start creating solutions
- **Test** solutions

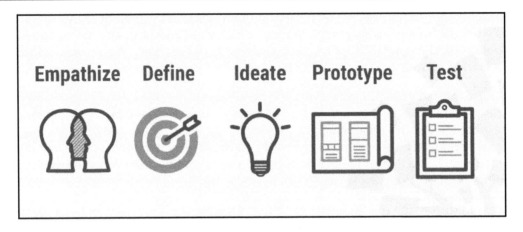

Figure 9.4: The five phases of design thinking set out by *d.school*
Source: https://www.interaction-design.org/literature/article/what-is-design-thinking-and-why-is-it-so-popular
Credit: Rikke Dam and Teo Siang

For me, there's a more profound side to design thinking. A *Waterfall* or even *Agile* project both, to a varying degree, assume that the requirements are clear and understood.

At its core, design thinking is largely a candid admission that both the requirements and the design are nowhere near being clear or understood. As such, the process is geared toward trying to figure out the problem itself and testing it with a possible solution, over and over again, until the solution crosses a quality threshold that finally makes it viable and acceptable.

Clearly, this does not lend itself easily to large-scale IT projects, which involve heavy investment in underlying infrastructure. Architecturally, especially in the lower components of your solution's technology stack, the foundations are much harder and costlier to redo.

On the plus side, there are obvious benefits much higher in the stack at the integration and application layers. That's why the use of more flexible and scalable public cloud infrastructure is increasingly prevalent – especially in the move away from traditional "tin" servers with their own operating systems managed by the customers, to more services-based computing managed by the cloud providers.

In other words, we're moving towards less **Infrastructure-as-a-Service (IaaS)**, and truer **Platform-as-a-Service (PaaS)**. The whole **Anything-as-a-Service (XaaS)** business model is still evolving quickly, which you may argue is iterative like elements of the design thinking process itself. What we witness here is the natural market forces of services adapting to changing user needs.

If your project thinks and works in a truly *Agile* way, then a lot of the design thinking principles should already be incorporated into your methodology, specifically, through shorter sprints and, therefore, shorter lead time from requirement and story to design, build, and ship.

Learning through testing

The unique part of design thinking is learning through testing. Software testing purists may well argue that real testing requires a direct comparison between an expected result and an actual result, which produces a binary outcome of test success or test failure. The purist would say that when we leave scope to learn from testing is not testing, per se.

However valid this argument is, it misses the point of design thinking in that the purpose of the process is to discover, in every iteration, more about the problem and the user. I would say that this is the main goal of "testing," rather than quality checking and scoring the software against its specifications.

Building on this, the five phases set out earlier are in fact are non-linear and non-sequential. At any particular phase, you can feedback or feedforward into another appropriate phase, further emphasizing the discovery and learning theme of the iterative process:

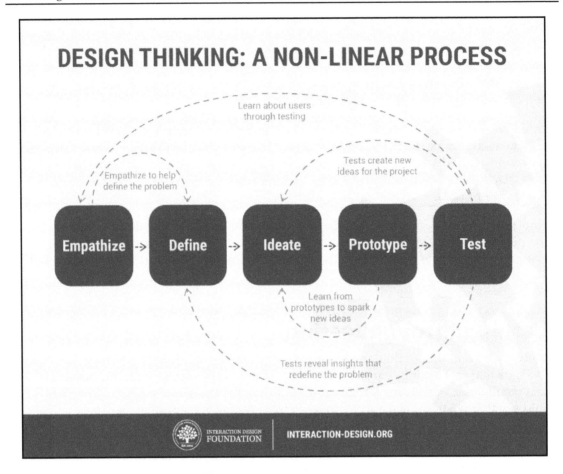

Figure 9.5: The non-linear process of design thinking
Source: https://www.interaction-design.org/literature/article/what-is-design-thinking-and-why-is-it-so-popular
Credit: Rikke Dam and Teo Siang

So, what does all this theory look like in practice? Well, as design thinking encourages and focuses on the creative side of problem-solving, over the traditional engineering approach, it involves a lot of colorful post-it notes and whiteboarding!

To evoke design thinking in the right way, don't think of a software project that might normally take between 3-6 months – instead, imagine participating in a 24-hour hackathon, specifically, the sense of urgency, a readiness to try all possibilities, and a willingness to let go of failures and bad ideas, fast. Moreover, there's a concurrency of multiple parallel workstreams and general chaos, which is ultimately very productive. This will give you an idea of the mindset.

Clearly, for a very complicated project, this frantic pace is not sustainable. However, the idea is still the same. If you can create this type of working environment for your team, one that encourages ideas and acceptance of feedback over a longer term, then that's a great place to start. Process-wise, there are a number of tools and methods that can help you at each stage of the design thinking process. As with the end-product itself, always refine the use of these tools as you progress and iterate.

Empathize

We start design thinking with **empathizing**. You can use a simple empathy map to tease out and categorize a potential user's input and feedback. This is a simple 4-box model of what the user:

- Said
- Did
- Thought
- Felt

This will help your team to establish a common understanding of the user and help them to prioritize the features that matter most to the user, in other words, what they truly need, over what they might want.

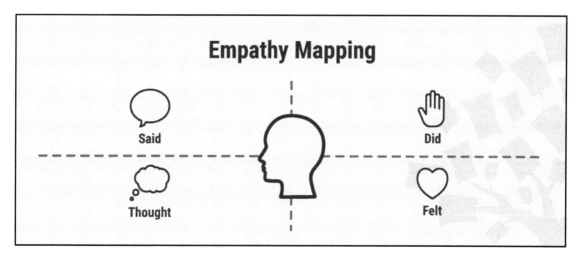

Figure 9.6: The 4-box model of Empathy Mapping
Source: https://www.interaction-design.org/literature/article/empathy-map-why-and-how-to-use-it
Credit: Rikke Dam and Teo Siang

Define

The next step of design thinking is to **define**. To solve any problem, you must first define it and understand it. Even if you accept that it's a moving target, this is an important step in the process. In order to do this, you can use a simple method of problem framing.

The goal of problem framing is for the team to produce and agree on a single problem statement collaboratively. The *Atlassian Team Playbook* has a 30-minute exercise over at www.atlassian.com that breaks down this process:

1. **Set the stage**: Gather and remind the team to define the problem, not the solution.
2. **Draw up a W4 board**: Divide a flipchart into four boxes: Who, What, Why, and Where. Split up groups of four or more into sub-groups.
3. **Talk among yourselves**: Discuss and explore the W4 board. Use post-it notes to record your thoughts on each W.
4. **Come back together**: Consolidate the best post-it notes to a central W4 board. Openly debate which is the best in each W.

Ideate

The next stage of design thinking is **ideation**. Ideation is all about generating fresh ideas and ways of thinking that ultimately lead to a solution to your defined problem. This is much harder than it sounds. In fact, it's probably one of the most challenging activities to facilitate as a manager. It requires a range of people and soft skills, rather than any technical knowledge.

Two of my favorite ideation techniques are well-trodden, much tried, and tested over the years. They're applicable in many contexts, in software, sales, general business, and even at home.

First is good old-fashioned brainstorming. The premise is simple. Follow a few simple rules in order to create as many ideas, as quickly as possible. *IDEO U*, the online school arm of the global design firm *IDEO*, lists seven basic rules to brainstorming sessions:

- Defer judgment
- Encourage wild ideas
- Build on the ideas of others
- Stay focused on the topic

- One conversation at a time
- Be visual
- Go for quantity

My second favorite ideation technique is the worst possible ideas. This is exactly what it sounds like. It's a group of people trying to come up with the worst possible ideas to solve the problem at hand.

In this fun and relaxed exercise, the creativity it generates can spark a great idea! It can also have additional benefits of team building. Any exercise that actively encourages its participants to lose their inhibitions and express themselves freely is good for morale and can help to build trust between teammates, too. It can also be used as an icebreaker exercise.

This has similarities with my favorite time management technique of de-prioritizing, which I find to be more effective than prioritizing. This inverted way of thinking can often yield unexpectedly meaningful results. Thinking of the worst possible ideas can also be easier to execute than the more conventional way.

Prototype

Design thinking is, in many ways, contrary to more traditional engineering methods. Ironically, **prototyping** is something that traditional engineer does all the time! For example, in automotive engineering, there are many early and late concepts and prototypes of new vehicles before car companies even begin preparing to produce the real thing. Or, in construction, the architect often produces physical and virtual scaled-down models of their buildings to bring it to life, something a blueprint simply cannot do nearly as effectively.

In design thinking, prototypes are great for investigation and experimentation. Because it's significantly scaled down, it's an inexpensive way to explore the boundaries and limitations of your design. For example, your UI mock-up would be a prototype, which allows you to demonstrate a super basic product to the customer to get some early feedback. It doesn't have to function and process any data. As a facilitator and narrator, you can fill in the gaps along with the storyline and explain what the software would do when it's been fully developed.

As with all phases of the design thinking process, one of the key goals is to learn from the activity itself and the feedback. This could be internally within the team and externally with users as well as other project teams.

Test

Testing of your design and solution itself can be done in many ways. You can do static walkthroughs of your storyboards. You can plan all your tests in advance and execute them precisely and scientifically when the software is developed.

The trick to effective testing within design thinking is to remember that everything is iterative. So, rather than trying to test for every scenario exhaustively, target your efforts on the essentials and look to move on following the principle of the minimum viable product.

Don't be afraid to go all the way back to empathize and define to reframe the problem. As counter-intuitive as it may sound, this really is progress because you now know more than before, which will ultimately help you to design and develop a better solution. No design or solution is static. So, neither should your thinking and testing be.

Case study – The Finnish UBI

Let's now look at an insightful case study for design thinking. **Universal Basic Income (UBI)** is a socio-economical idea. It proposes that governments provide a guaranteed fixed, regular income to every citizen in order to cover their basic needs, whether they are working or not. The problem it's trying to solve is the widening wealth gap, poverty, and social inequalities.

The UBI design is to simply give people the money to eliminate the most extreme poverty, such as homelessness and hunger. Its intended effects would income a radically simplified and overall reduction in the social welfare system. It would also benefit society because, on average, the population would be more productive, allowing people to study more and take care of themselves better, which also reduces the cost of public healthcare services.

At its core, UBI is an ideological notion that the minimal living standard would be raised, which eradicates the issue of people being trapped in jobs with sub-living standard wages. So, UBI is fairer for all.

Clearly, this is a grand idea. To see any benefits, the proposed solution would have to be implemented for everyone at the same time, through wide-sweeping new laws. This is a monumental task. It's also enormously risky. If it fails, a whole country could potentially descend into chaos. If it works, the social benefits would potentially take years to be realized. This is a truly difficult and tricky problem to solve.

The Finnish Government has chosen to use a design thinking approach to solve this problem. Design thinking is far from the normal approach to making new policies and legislation, which makes this experiment unique and remarkable:

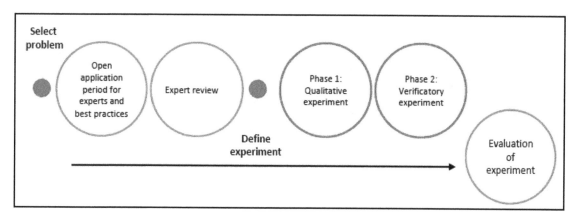

Figure 9.7: A simple diagram illustrating the basics of the design thinking process
Source: https://99percentinvisible.org/episode/the-finnish-experiment/

The Finnish Government has designed and created prototypes of laws to be applied in specific areas only. They will measure the impact of the laws on those specific areas, take feedback, and iterate, before scaling up to a national level implementation. Citizens who are part of the test would receive UBI instead of a combination of other unemployment benefits, which have strict limits on the amount of part-time work they can do. Therefore, they are effectively incentivized not to work.

As part of the validation and evaluation process, the Finnish Government will measure whether recipients of UBI actually change their behavior. Will they feel freer to take on more work and be more productive? Or would they sit back and rely on UBI only?

This feedback is vital to understanding whether UBI has an overall positive or negative effect on the small test population. The Finnish Government is taking an iterative approach to design this law, instead of the traditional mass consultation followed by the one-time rollout approach, which is more like the *Waterfall* or *V-Model* method of software development.

This is a great example of how design thinking can reduce the size and complexity of a problem, and the possible risk of implementing its solution. If something as grand as UBI can adopt design thinking, then design thinking is a process you should consider for your software projects.

Building consensus

Building group consensus is rarely easy. Specifically, when it comes to a software project, there are many stakeholders to engage and gain agreement with. Sometimes, in extreme cases, it may seem like you're herding cats, which is rather futile.

Focusing on the example of getting a design approved, this alone can be a difficult task, just within your own project team. There are always multiple ways of designing a solution. Each with its own unique set of strengths and weaknesses, advantages, and disadvantages. Furthermore, it can be a highly subjective choice, influenced by each team member's past experiences, "war stories," and technology preferences. It's also more of an art form, rather than an exact science.

Nonetheless, building consensus among your team and with your stakeholders is a vital step in progressing your project or your team's mission. Therefore, the ability to lead people to reach consensus is a key skill you need in order to be an effective manager.

What is consensus?

Let's start by defining what consensus really is in our context. One important thing to understand is that the process to build consensus is not the same as a democratic or even meritocracy process. In stalemate situations, people often suggest a vote. However, this naturally produces winners and losers, which you really want to avoid because it harbors disagreement, unless of course, it's a unanimous result.

The idea of unanimity is important because that is the ideal outcome of collective decision making. Short of this ideal outcome, the consensus is when **everyone agrees they can live with and support the final decision**.

True consensus is an alignment of interests, not demands or positions, which are hostile negotiation points. If your group is committed to constructively reaching consensus, it should not be a negotiation process.

Reaching consensus is a seminal point in any creative and problem-solving process, including software design and development. It's the moment when thoughts and ideas turn into action, to start building and shipping.

Building consensus

As a manager, it's essential that you are well-versed in the following basic, practical steps to building consensus with a team or project group:

1. Ensure all relevant stakeholders are included and feel included in the process.
2. Ensure everyone included actively participates and contributes, openly and honestly, to have a stake in the final decision.
3. Ensure there is genuine co-operation to achieving a common goal.
4. Ensure everyone is heard and valued equally.
5. Ensure there is a collective focus on finding a solution that everyone can buy into.
6. Be clear about the proposal and the decision.
7. Invite and allow challenging questions before the decision is made.
8. Ensure everyone understands the consensus and honors the final decision.

If your group is still finding consensus difficult, consider using the following techniques to break down each step of the process further. Also, try to identify any personality clashes and facilitate the conversation to be as objective as possible.

The strengths and weaknesses of each person's idea may largely be obvious to that person and some members of the group. However, it helps all members of the group to understand it better if it's explicitly stated and analyzed by the group collectively. This forms a constructive conversation, which avoids confusion and helps to converge opposing views.

If this is still unsuccessful, you can try a more advanced technique of merging alternatives. This is a simple but structured way of identifying the advantages and disadvantages of the alternatives discussed so far and combining them into another alternative, based on a number of compromises.

If your group still cannot reach a consensus, don't be disheartened. This happens. Having multiple options is a positive thing. Remember this and remind your group that this is also a healthy outcome since you have discovered more possibilities. This is an important step to ensure your group continues to work well together in the future.

A truly collaborative spirit is difficult to achieve overnight but can be destroyed in an instant. Recap the conclusion to everyone in the group and take responsibility for the next step of taking the options to a higher body, such as your project's steering group or board. Be clear with them that a clear consensus could not be reached with the group, but here are the options and their strengths and weaknesses.

Writing the business case and getting sign-off

In Chapter 2, *What Are the Key Skills I Need?*, and Chapter 3, *What is My Job Now?*, we discussed how important it is to build a valid business case to justify and support your project. The business case is an essential element of any successful project, especially those using the *PRINCE2* methodology because it's one of the seven themes. We've also discussed how it comes under the Project Manager's responsibility for planning.

So, how do you actually write a business case? And how do you go about getting sign-off from your key stakeholders? At its core, a business case is nothing more than some logical reasoning to support the investment to initiate and sustain a project. To do that, it must demonstrate a genuine need as well as the viability of succeeding. This boils down to whether it's considered good value for money and a worthwhile risk to take.

Under the *PRINCE2* methodology, there is no pre-set format for a business case. It is, however, listed as a key component of the **Project Initiation Document** (PID). As its name suggests, this document is created at an early stage of a project and required as part of the initiating a project process. In practice, the business case is usually its own separate document, due to its importance.

As a Project Manager, you should be able to create a business case using your organization's template. If there is no template or previous examples to follow, be prepared to incorporate the following elements into a short document between 5-10 pages long. Remember that your intended audience is senior stakeholders. So, tailor your content and writing style to suit their profiles.

I have worked in organizations that focus particularly on numerical facts and figures. So, tables, graphs, and charts were always well received. I have also worked in organizations that prefer more detailed and formal white papers, which paint a more comprehensive picture, complete with academic theories to support financial analysis and key recommendations.

Writing the sections of a business case document

Unless there is an overwhelming reason to do otherwise, always start your business case with an **Executive Summary**. This is a high-level summary of the project, followed by a succinct synopsis of the business case itself. So, in a maximum of 2-3 sentences, outline the project's main goals and key reasons for investment. In other words, explain the problem statement and the recommended solution, followed by the cost and benefit of implementing it.

A good executive summary should be precise and informative. It should take no longer than 30 seconds to read. When writing an executive summary, imagine it to be a written elevator pitch.

Next, include an **Introduction** section to introduce the background and premise of the project formally. Include how and why the project has been commissioned and progressed up to this point. Explain the problem statement in more detail to illustrate the need for this project to proceed.

Then, create an **Analysis** section. This is where all the detailed information should be. However, you should refrain from including all the raw data, which will not be appropriate for your intended audience. Instead, focus on the essential data points and their targeted analysis. For example, establish the total expected cost of the project by listing the big-ticket items such as a large purchase. Also, quantify the expected benefit to the organization on the successful completion of the project. This produces a basic and powerful cost-benefit analysis, which should indicate a positive return on investment for the project.

This should be followed by an **Options** and **Recommendations** section, which explains the possible options available to the organization. Using the output from the building consensus process, make sure you include advantages and disadvantages of each option, as well as the option preferred by your project team, which forms the recommendation. Include information on the expected timescale of each option to clearly show this important constraint, which is often a key deciding factor. For example, what if there is a looming date for a new regulation that fundamentally affects the organization's business?

Next should be a **Key Risks** and **Assumptions** section. Declare what assumptions have been made in creating the business case. Clearly list and assess the key risks to the organization, if the project did or did not proceed.

Together with the previous sections, this should give your reader a balanced view of the cost, benefit, and risk factors for the project.

Similar to the executive summary, unless there is an overwhelming reason to do otherwise, always include a **Conclusion** section to sum up the business case. This is the final chance to emphasize and highlight the most critical points in your business justification for the project.

Remember that the business case is not a business plan. Information such as financial projections and burndown charts are not as appropriate and should be included in the other documents such as the project plan.

Presenting the business case for sign-off

To bring the business case to life and request sign-off, you should present the business case in person at a formal steering committee meeting wherever possible. Furthermore, make the discussion and approval decision of the business case the top agenda item to highlight its importance. After all, if the decision is to stop the project, there wouldn't be much else to discuss besides how to close it down.

The art of presenting the business case is a mysterious one. There is certainly no magic formula. However, preparation is certainly key. As well as rehearsing the presentation itself, you should get impartial feedback on the business case itself. Consider asking a colleague or senior manager who isn't connected to your project to review your business case well in advance of sharing it with your project board.

Use their feedback to adjust the overall message of your business case. Where are the flaws in overall justification? What evidence might be missing? Which information would make the business case clearer? How could the same information be presented differently to make it easier to understand?

As the Project Manager, the confidence you bring to the business case cannot be underestimated. The more confident you are in the contents and its presentation, the more legitimate the whole business case will appear to the audience.

Therefore, as well as producing an accurate and convincing business case itself, passionately presenting it and confidently responding to any questions will make it more compelling. This will have a significant effect on obtaining that all-important business case sign-off and approval for resources to proceed with your project.

Summary

This chapter was all about how to progress your project and your build, so that you can get on with the important business of shipping your product! We looked at how you go about validating the solution you've designed, from both a technical validation and a business validation viewpoint.

Within the context of design thinking, we then looked at how you need to make sure your solution is refined based on early feedback, and how you can learn by testing – right from the ideation and prototyping stages.

Once you have a valid solution, you need consensus with your project stakeholders to implement that solution. It's always useful as a manager to be able to build consensus within your team, of course, but in this chapter, we had our attention very much focused on building a consensus with your project stakeholders. Creating a strong business case document is vital to this process, and so we looked at how to build a business case document, section by section, and how to present your business case for stakeholder sign-off. From there, of course, you will have the resources to build and ship your product!

10
Agile, Waterfall, and Everything in Between

Now that your team has reached a consensus on the design of your product, and your project sponsor has signed off on the business case, you need to start building and shipping!

Across the previous chapters, we've discussed various project methodologies, such as *Agile* and *Waterfall*, and we've established that you and your team can choose, adapt, and apply these methodologies to your projects. We also talked about the skills you need to learn as a manager to work with these methodologies.

Now, fast-forward to this chapter, and you are getting ready to start building your product. Therefore, it's the perfect time to summarize and re-contextualize these methodologies into practical actions that you can take to keep the build focused.

In this chapter, we will be focusing on the following project methodologies:

- *PRINCE2* (PRojects IN Controlled Environments)
- *The Waterfall model*
- *The V-Model*
- *Agile*
- *ITIL* (V3 – IT Service Management Framework)

We'll also visit the **Project Management Office** (**PMO**) and how to assess your local PMO and speak its language. In particular, we'll see how the stage-gate process is so central to working with your PMO and keeping your project moving forward.

To keep the stage-gate process moving forwards for our project, it's vital for you as a manager to report your project updates professionally, cleanly, and in a language that your stakeholders will understand.

We'll therefore discuss some best practices around crafting your project updates and, to round off this chapter, we'll assess how you can challenge the status quo within the organization if something is impeding your project.

Methodologies – A summary and comparison

So, let's begin by reintroducing each methodology and framework along with its key ideas. This following table offers a summary and easy comparison of each methodology and framework we've looked at in this book.

Methodology / Framework	Key Ideas and Practical Actions
PRINCE2 (PRojects IN Controlled Environments)	A popular general project management methodology, centered around: • Seven principles • Seven themes • Seven processes Key management products to produce and use: • PID, including the business case (Project Initiation Document) • RAID log (Risks, Assumptions, Issues, Decisions/Dependencies) • Lessons log
The Waterfall model	Classic and largely linear software development life cycle. The *Waterfall model* is a series of traditional stages organized in an overall downstream flow. It goes from initial requirement gathering through to operations, with an upstream flow between connecting stages, signifying an iterative process between each stage. For example, mini iterations between design and coding, coding and testing. But not between design and testing. Key assumptions and critical success factors are certainty, clarity, and comprehensiveness of requirement at the beginning of the project. Without that, it is extremely difficult for the project to succeed in meeting its objective. *Waterfall* projects are usually much longer in duration and also much riskier than truly *Agile* projects; especially *Agile* projects that look to deliver a minimum viable product first, before additional speedy enhancements.

The V-Model	Variation of the *Waterfall model*. Mainly used by software testers to differentiate verification and validation activities. Verification deals with the checking of the requirements and design against what the customers really need at an overall business requirement, system, architecture, and module level. Validation deals with confirming the developed software actually meets the requirements, design, and specification at a unit, integration, system, and acceptance level.

Agile	The *Agile* Manifesto states four fundamental values (and 12 principles):
	• Individuals and interactions over processes and tools
	• Working software over comprehensive documentation
	• Customer collaboration over contract negotiation
	• Responding to change over following a plan
	Three key practices to adopt and apply:
	• Incremental development over big-bang releases
	• Dynamic daily huddles over regular static updates
	• User stories over exhaustive requirements
	Scrum is the quintessential way of putting the *Agile* mindset into practice. Three essential roles to establish in a scrum team:
	• Product Owner
	• Scrum Master
	• Development Team
	Four core processes to implement on a scrum project, with their key artefacts and activities:
	• Sprint planning
	  ○ Central product backlog
	  ○ Velocity
	• Daily scrum
	  ○ Dynamic huddles
	• Sprint review
	  ○ Demo and feedback
	• Sprint retrospective
	  ○ Continual process improvement

ITIL (V3)
IT Service
Management
Framework
	In contrast with a linear software development life cycle, ITIL is a set of five cyclical, complementary, and comprehensive service life cycle phases, with key functions and processes to note from a software application perspective:
	• Service strategy
	• Service design
	• Service transition
	• Service operation
	   ○ Function:
	      ■ Application management
	   ○ Processes:
	      ■ Event management
	      ■ Incident management
	      ■ Problem management
	• Continual service improvement
	There is an integral focus on the total cost of ownership of services over their entire service life cycle. This includes constant improvements after the service's initial development, as well as its eventual decommissioning and replacement.

Whichever methodology or framework is your personal favorite, always remember that the choice is not solely your decision. As the project or delivery manager, or even a project team member in a non-managerial role, it is your responsibility to facilitate the team's discussion and collective decision to choose and adapt a methodology according to the project and the team's overall needs.

Each software project has complex and unique needs, and because of that, there is no such thing as one-size/model-fits-all. Moreover, it's vital to invest time and effort to reach a team consensus. This avoids any potential resentment in feeling unheard or being overruled. When this process is done effectively, it should also become a fun and productive team building activity.

The language of the PMO

A PMO sounds rather grand, formal, and maybe even a little daunting to deal with. In truth, some PMOs can be quite cumbersome and unwieldy! However, the vast majority of PMOs are a perfectly normal and important function within an organization.

Whichever delivery methodology your team chooses, it's vital to establish good links with your PMO and make sure your methodology and your PMO's ways of working are complementary – or at the very least, compatible.

Most organizations are likely to have a function called a PMO, regardless of whether they're traditional corporates, more modern **small and medium-sized enterprise (SMEs)**, money-making businesses, or not-for-profit charities. But depending on the overall size of the organization, the PMO may not be as large a team of dedicated people as the name might suggest. It's a good idea to find out about the PMO in your organization as soon as you can.

The purpose and value of the PMO

In today's professional world the only way to get anything significant done seems to be through a "project," and so when you visit your PMO you are very likely to find a set of PMO tools and processes, and a group of people who will support, oversee, and govern compliance. In a nutshell, this is what your PMO is responsible for.

The PMO will have a number of ongoing projects to manage at any one time. Therefore, its concern, input, and a lot of its value-add is provided through an overall portfolio view. In other words, no matter how hectic, busy, under-pressure, and messy each project gets, the PMO keeps a balanced view of the world and allocates resources according to the over-arching business priorities of the organization.

For instance, if there is resource contention between multiple projects and the impact on one project is more significant than others, then instead of a knee-jerk reaction to allocate the key resources to that project, the PMO assesses the overall importance and urgency of all projects before helping key stakeholders to make a more strategic decision. To do that, the PMO must also produce meaningful and accurate dashboards, updates, and reports, which we'll talk about later in this chapter.

Another purpose of the PMO is financial control. As the overseer of the overall budget, it is responsible for tracking each project's expenditures and releasing funds appropriately. The PMO really comes into focus near the end of a financial year where it has to review whether or not the overall portfolio is on track to meet its projections or whether it has overspent, and what to do about it!

To achieve this, the PMO must have financial insight and control over all its projects. This is mainly done by releasing capital in a controlled, pre-agreed, well-defined, and timely manner, based on accurate information from each project's budget and burn chart. Otherwise, it's impossible to achieve its objective of overall financial control.

It's important to note that the project portfolio may well include business projects, with and without an IT element, as well as IT-led projects. For example, a project to build a new office and relocate current staff will have an IT workstream, but it's predominantly a business change and facilities project. Though of course, if you work for an IT services company or a software house, then your projects are going to be predominantly IT and software project based.

Learn to speak in the PMO language

If you're a Project Manager, it will be your responsibility to liaise and coordinate with the PMO. You will therefore need to understand and comply with its processes, while also representing your project effectively in order to gain approval to progress and access more funding. To do this, you must be able to understand what the PMO is and learn to speak its language.

Below, you can see the keywords used in the language of the PMO:

Figure 10.1: The language of the PMO illustrated in a word cloud

Besides the usual project terminology like stakeholders, plan, scope, risk, governance, and so on, the best example of some new vocabulary you may need to learn is the fundamental accounting concept of **capital expenditure versus operating expenditure**.

Since financial control is one of the PMO's most important practical activities, it is in your interest to understand these terms and what they ultimately mean for your project and team.

The following table is a side-by-side comparison between capital expenditure and operating expenditure:

Capital Expenditure	Operating Expenditure
Also known as CapEx	Also known as OpEx
Ad hoc investment into the organization	Day-to-day cost of doing business
Recorded as an asset on the balance sheet that depreciates over time	Recorded as a straightforward expense on the balance sheet
Purely project activities such as purchasing new hardware or replacement of a major software system, including non-recurring people costs	Operations activities such as support and maintenance contracts, as well as people and recurring software license costs
Comes out of the project or investment budget	Comes out of the "run" budget

Beyond the financial side of the PMO, there's also a **governance** side. The two are intricately linked because the release of more funding is typically dependent on the passing of predefined "stage-gates." The ability to understand and use the language of the stage-gate process, something we will cover in the next section, is an important part of an effective manager's toolkit.

The stage-gate process

Most PMOs, if not all PMOs, are reliant on a **stage-gate** process (which has also been known as a phase-gate process) to govern their projects. This makes a lot of sense because it's simply too risky to give all the money to a project right at the start of its development.

Instead, it's much more logical and sensible to ration and release funding in tranches, aligned with the project's natural life cycle. This enables the PMO to effectively govern each project, in a controlled and consistent manner, based on its outputs and value delivered to the organization.

There are numerous and various stage-gate processes out there, even within the software project business. A lot of organizations have developed their own models to suit their context and needs, which is perfectly sensible and reasonable.

As we discussed in Chapter 4, *A Week in the Life of a Manager*, these in-house-developed models have often rebranded versions of a wider standard. In which case, they would be better off just calling them by their industry standard name. This would certainly be clearer and easier for everyone to understand and follow, especially new joiners to the organization and newbie project managers!

For software projects, author Robert G. Cooper's logical approach to product development is the best stage-gate standard I have come across. It is also the most commonly used standard in my experience. In his book, *Winning at New Products: Creating Value Through Innovation*, Robert G. Cooper sets out six stages of a project life cycle, with five gates between them:

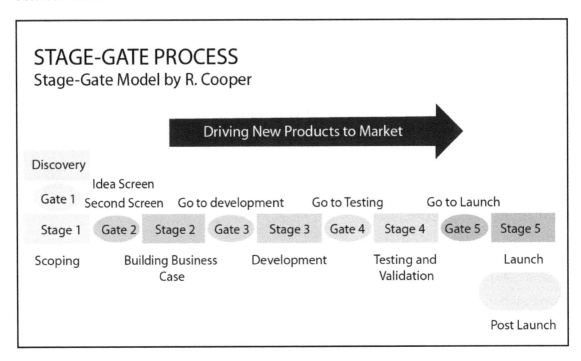

Figure 10.2: A diagrammatic view of Robert G. Cooper's stage-gate process for product development

At the end of each stage (except for the last), there is a stage-gate that requires a pre-agreed combination of the project sponsor, steering group, and PMO to approve before it can proceed to the next stage. So, let's now explore each stage and its purpose and what that means for you and your project.

Stage 0 – Discovery and ideation

In a new product design and innovation context, starting with this discovery and ideation stage makes sense. You start by brainstorming and dreaming up new and novel ideas, especially brand-new ones that your competitors have not yet thought of. It's these brand-new products and innovations that will give your organization a competitive advantage.

However, if you overlay this stage with the *Waterfall model*, it will map to the requirements gathering and analysis stages. These activities are based on real people, real feedback, real data, and real business problems. In today's world of business, projects are only greenlit if they're going to have a positive return on investment and have empirical evidence to prove it.

In other words, the primary purpose of this stage, and the key to passing its stage-gate, is to define the problem statement clearly.

Stage 1 – Scoping

Scoping is all about **finding and defining options**. For example, does the customer need a brand-new bespoke software application or is there a commercial off-the-shelf product out there already that can solve their business problem?

Stage 2 – Building a business case

As part of the PID, the business case is a key management product under *PRINCE2*. This is fundamental to justify the risk and cost of proceeding with your project. As part of the rationale you need to put together, your project must be able to articulate which options it has found and the estimated cost of developing and implementing them.

As such, this stage is actually all about planning and deciding what the project is going to build, how much it's going to cost, and what value it's going to return to the organization.

This also involves potentially conducting a feasibility review, which will assess this business case in relation to other projects. Especially in a large organization, there may be other projects competing to solve the same problem, with them all vying for the same pot of funds in order to proceed to the next stage.

Stage 3 – Development

This is where you get the necessary approval and funding to **start building** your software!

Depending on your project's risk profile and approach, you may choose to only build a prototype or **Minimum Viable Product** (**MVP**). Other projects, especially those strictly following the *Waterfall model*, may require significant development with a lot of sunk costs to reach this stage. In which case, the deliverable may be a more comprehensive product.

For example, a new **Enterprise Service Bus** (**ESB**) platform used to integrate multiple systems will require significant upfront effort and investment to prove its value, as it needs to be connected in order to function, which is often laborious and expensive.

Stage 4 – Testing and validation

After you've built an MVP or even a full system, then you need to **prove that it works and provides the expected value** to the customer, as per the business case.

Typically, this is the longest stage. Therefore, you should use a number of checkpoints and milestones to ensure the build progresses as planned, despite any issues that you may encounter. If your project is using scrum, then each sprint cycle should be considered as a milestone, and you should notify the PMO of the project's progress accordingly.

Stage 5 – Product launch

For software projects specifically, product launch is all about **deploying your tested system**, implementing any process changes through user training, and promoting your product to drive up its usage and adoption.

In most organizations, the outcome of each gate is a basic RAG status of Red/Amber/Green. Some more matured PMOs may have a points-based system, which scores each project across several dimensions, including time, cost, quality, and confidence levels.

In any case, a Project Manager's role is to ensure that all the expected deliverables are produced and ready for presentation. Their role also involves nailing that presentation and getting the approval to proceed.

Death by boring project status update

Let's face it, the world would be a better place if there was even just one less boring project status RAG update!

Joking aside, there is much to be said about projects endlessly issuing rather boring updates. The need for regular project status updates is certainly valid, especially given that your updates can be the trigger for your next project stage-gate.

In today's world of multi-channel rich media, it's no longer necessary or acceptable to send dull, text-filled emails into busy people's already-full inboxes because, the minute it arrives, it's probably out of date – that is, if the recipient even reads it. Just look at this typical, dry, dull, and boring project status update:

> Dear all,
> Project Status: RED
> Summary:
> The project has been delayed by 1 week due to a serious bug found during UAT. A key testing resource is on holiday, and there is no further capacity within the team. Test environment is still unstable and was unavailable for much of this week.
> New issues:
> • BUG1234 raised
> • REQ5678 is incomplete
> Actions:
> • PM to speak to Test Manager about resourcing
> • Deployment of fix for BUG1234 and re-test
> Next milestone:
> • UAT sign-off on December 25th, 2018
> • Stage-gate 4 on January 1st, 2019
> Best regards,
> Your humble project manager

Your project update doesn't have to be like this. In the example above, while all the vital information is there, it's about as uninspiring as you can get. Consequently, people might not even fully read the whole message.

Now, let's try to empathize and imagine ourselves as the recipient. Are you enticed to read more and engage more? The answer is most probably that you are not! Commentary and narrative are always important, but it should never be the audience's initial focal point. Instead, try to use a simple visual aid to attract their attention and make a good first impression. For example, consider a simple doughnut chart:

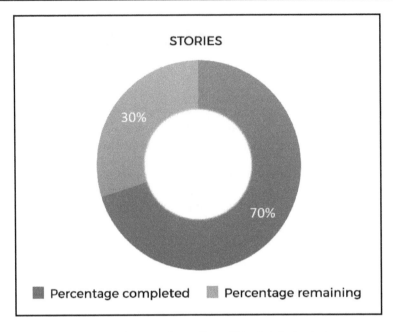

Figure 10.3: Use visualizations where possible, even if it is a simple doughnut chart!

Using the RAG status approach

Depending on your organization's culture, your audience, and PMO methods, you may well choose to use the tried-and-tested RAG status approach. There is absolutely nothing wrong with this. As with all communication, it needs to be adapted to suit its intended audience – the people you are trying to inform or influence.

Given that most of the professional world uses it already, the RAG status is highly likely to be the most appropriate choice for your project too as it's been established across the world. However, always bear in mind that even the basic classifications of red, amber, and green can have many different interpretations.

In our case, it's worth clarifying the definitions of each color with the PMO. This ensures that your project is rated consistently and fairly in relation to all other projects across the portfolio. If you and your team are feeling more adventurous, and with your audience's understanding, a simple alternative or complement to the RAG status is a thumbs or arrows system.

As an example, use the up, down, and horizontal emoji signs to signal positive, negative, or unchanged trends:

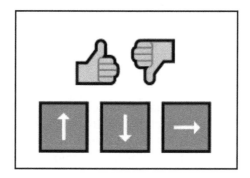

Figure 10.4: If your audience is more accepting of them, try simple alternatives of signaling instead of RAG

This may seem rather strange and trivial, but the idea is not to be different for the sake of it. Instead, try to create a sense of freshness and originality to the well-trodden process to ultimately grab key people's attention in order to differentiate your project among a sea of other projects.

Sending out project updates

When it comes to sending out your project updates, it is the recommended norm to do so on a weekly basis. Every week makes sense because most things, such as sprints, are measured over a week.

Moreover, try to send your updates on any day other than Friday. The reason for this is simple. As the final day of the working week, Friday seems like the most logical day to sum up the week and communicate to stakeholders. The only problem is that every other project is probably doing the same! Therefore, I always recommend issuing weekly updates on a Thursday. Again, this is not to be different for the sake of it, but to genuinely be ahead of the curve in the most positive sense.

If you and your project team are feeling really adventurous, then you can even leverage your project management or collaboration tool to provide dynamic real-time reports and updates. Having true **key performance indicators** (**KPIs**) is nirvana for any Project Manager, PMO, and the overall organization.

This vital information provides insights that will enable better decisions to be made more quickly. This establishes a shorter feedback loop that further enhances the project and the organization's overall ability to make better and better decisions, based on real empirical data. So, it's worth spending time and effort to identify what these may be for your project.

Using a dashboard

When you have real-time data and reports available, you can simply direct your key stakeholders to the dashboard itself, which is usually web-based. Alternatively, you can use the visuals from it and combine it with your more traditional commentary-style status update email, turning something that could be boring into a fun, up-to-date, and informative message.

In choosing which KPIs to include in your project status update, consider the following examples:

- Schedule variance
- Budget variance
- Resource utilization
- Number of open issues
- Number of open risks
- The ratio of bugs per user story
- Customer satisfaction

Here is an example of a comprehensive operations dashboard that includes additional data points, such as **Service Level Agreement (SLA)** compliance:

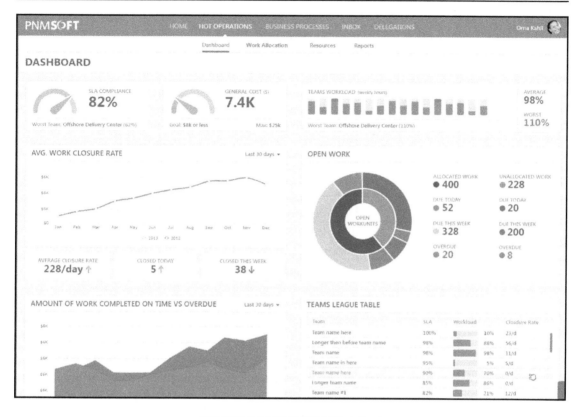

Figure 10.5: A more comprehensive operations dashboard
Source: http://blog.zilicus.com/project-kpis-for-project-manager/

To help you produce more dynamic and inspiring project status updates, you'll find below a list of popular project management tools with real-time reporting capabilities. These can help you engage with your key stakeholders in a more meaningful way.

Project Management Tool	Supplier	Key Features
JIRA	Atlassian	Generally considered the gold standard tool for *Agile* software projects. Great for planning sprints, creating user stories, and tracking bugs. Good built-in reporting and dashboard capabilities.
Office 365, SharePoint, Yammer	Microsoft	All-rounder Office is hard to beat for its sheer breadth and versatility. SharePoint enables collaboration on a basic and advanced level, whichever suits your project and team. Yammer is a novel alternative to mass emails.
Basecamp	Basecamp, LLC	Easy-to-use message boards and task tracking. Good mobile app integration. Built-in project reporting.
Asana	Asana, Inc	Great for organizing tasks between team members. Highly rated mobile app. Ready-to-use project dashboards.
Trello	Atlassian	Simple and visual lists, perfect for tracking tasks. Great for less complex projects and smaller teams. Highly rated mobile app. No advanced reporting functions.
Huddle	Huddle	A general team collaboration platform. Good for projects and operations. Lower complexity alternative to SharePoint. No project reporting capabilities but can be used to present visuals created elsewhere.
monday.com	monday.com Labs	Team working tool with an integrated mobile app. Good for tracking tasks and project milestones. No project reporting function.

These project management tools are popular for both professional organizations and informal groups, such as social clubs. Their versatility is a major selling point because it allows you to plan, monitor, and manage any significant piece of work.

Keeping it simple, stupid

As a manager, one of your key roles within your team and on of your key responsibilities to your stakeholders is to communicate a variety of information on a timely basis. This information could be technical and delivery-focused, such as information about bugs and incidents, or alternatively, it could be more managerial, such as information about risks, budgets, and PMO processes.

To communicate this information effectively, you need to have the ability to "switch domains." What I mean by this is being able to adapt to a different set of phrases and terminology. You need to be able to flip between technical and business; project and operations; software and infrastructure; and *PRINCE2*, *Waterfall*, and *Agile*, back and forth, seamlessly. The ability to explain things in a language your audience can easily understand is a vital skill in an effective manager's toolkit, and like all skills, this requires time and effort to learn.

In earlier chapters, we talked about the importance of active listening, which will help. We also discussed the need for empathy, which most certainly helps too. When you think and act empathically, you naturally recalibrate your style, tone, and language to suit the people you are engaging and communicating with.

The real pillar to all of this is to simply **keep things simple**. When we keep things simple, communicating inherently becomes easier. Paradoxically, making things simple is often neither simple nor easy!

Interpreting between domains

Imagine a good interpreter at the height of their profession. They make translating multiple languages between different contexts seem effortless. This is because they have put in the hard work to acquire the skill of truly understanding what is being communicated. Instead of consciously processing every single word being said, they interpret the content and the context, before relaying the entire message in a listener-friendly and accurate way.

Interpreting between contexts and domains, such as technical and business, is very much the same. You translate a technical person's thoughts and words into a simple layman's terms in order for a non-technical businessperson to easily digest and understand, and vice versa, of course.

Remove the jargon. Remove the complexities. Distill and refine the actual message. Use metaphors and analogies if you need to but put yourself in the non-technical person's shoes and imagine a techie telling you about the nuances of Python. Should you care? The answer is no, but what you do care about is how it affects your product, your project, and your user experience. So, that's where you actually need to focus your efforts and message. If it's still too complicated, then you probably haven't understood the message well enough yourself. So, go back and try to understand it more.

To make things really simple, try going back to your trusty whiteboard. Use diagrams to illustrate concepts, both as an input to learn from someone else and as a way to relay that message to another person.

Making complex things less complex

There are some things that are genuinely complex, such as a software project! So, what can you do about that? Interpreting and re-interpreting something to make it more easily communicated and understood is fine. But there are things that are intrinsically big, complex, and important – things such as your software product, and the process of building it!

This is where your decision-making and influencing skills are needed. As a project, delivery, or team manager, you have the ability and responsibility to make a wide range of decisions and to influence a varied group of people in their decisions.

For example, when your solution architect presents you with a convoluted design that has numerous technical components incorporating the latest cutting-edge technologies, what do you do? Do you accept it and say: That's great! Or do you ask them to explain to you in layman's terms and ask them why it can't be simpler? Of course, there might be very good and valid reasons for this, but how would you know if you didn't ask?

Clarity through simplicity

Looking within your immediate scope of decisions, are you clear on the impact of your decisions? For example, as more and more tasks on your project pile up, it may be tempting to start more workstreams to tackle them, though that's only the case if you have the resources, but there are limits to how many workstreams the project and you can effectively run in parallel, both from a resource and a logical complexity perspective.

There is a definite law of diminishing returns. The more workstreams there are, the more likely they will overlap with, contend with, and confuse each other. In other words, it would be "more haste, less speed!"

If a business user or the product owner gives your team a hugely ambitious and complicated requirement, can it be broken down into smaller stories or dealt with in a simpler way that tackles one business problem at a time?

Constructively challenging key decisions and deliverables to be simple ultimately helps everyone to be clearer on what they need to do and how they can contribute. Confusion triggers more confusion, undermines confidence, and increases the risk of non-delivery of the final product. This is why clarity – through simplicity – is paramount to help to keep your build focused and your project on track!

Past mistakes and changing the status quo

Despite making things as simple as possible, the build process can still be difficult, but there are things you can do to keep the build focused on developing the product your customers truly need. These include learning from past mistakes and changing the status quo.

"Different is not always better, but better is always different."

- Anonymous

Acknowledging that your organization implements projects in a particular way and understanding the reasons why it's historically like this would be a good place to start. As we discussed previously, we are all heavily influenced by our past experiences, and we all have our "war stories" to tell. Consequently, we have our own preferences and biases too.

As the build stage progresses and pressure mounts, we naturally and subconsciously revert more and more into our biased way of thinking and working. When your team is in the midst of an ambitious sprint or busy test cycle, they are not thinking about how to innovate and improve things; they are naturally concentrated on getting the job done.

So, while they're busy doing exactly that, it's your job to think ahead and think differently. Otherwise, things will always be the same, which is another way of saying that it will never improve. Of course, avoiding past mistakes are not confined to the build stage.

There are even formal management products in *PRINCE2* to facilitate this, called the *Lessons Log* and *Lessons Report*. These management products are essentially a detailed record of valuable lessons drawn from other projects in the organization's portfolio.

To learn from the past mistakes of other projects, work with the PMO, and ask:

- What are the lessons learned from other projects and why?
- Does the organization traditionally under-budget its projects and why?
- Where are the most common pain points and why?
- What are the most difficult risks to mitigate within the organization and why?
- Which departments tend to be most risk-averse or difficult to deal with and why?

The what, where, and who gives you the knowledge of past mistakes by other projects, as well as what the status quo looks like. Some of the most frequent and typical excuses used to justify the status quo include statements like: "But we've never done it that way" or "My way has worked fine for me."

The "and why" part of the questions above should give you an understanding of this status quo and insight into how to change it. Challenging and changing the status quo is never easy, but to avoid the mistakes of your predecessors you need to understand why they made those mistakes.

If they are common mistakes made by many projects, then there is most likely an organizational reason as to why this happens. In which case, your role is to highlight this to your team and steer everyone away from these pitfalls while working with the PMO to identify failures and work to address them.

For example, there may be a process flaw where projects are effectively incentivized to under-estimate their resource requirements because they will get the resource anyway without paying for them. This results in the constant over-utilization of key resources and affects the forecasts for additional resources, which are required to back-fill and support other projects.

> *"The definition of insanity is doing the same thing over and over again and expecting a different result."*
>
> *- Albert Einstein (widely attributed)*

When you know what the common mistakes and lessons are, you can effectively avoid making them again!

Summary

Building a good software product is not easy. After you have gathered all your requirements and, as a result, produced a brilliant design, the challenging process of development and coding can start. As the Project or Development Manager in charge, it's not easy to keep the build focused, because there are many common challenges to the software development process, such as scope creep, which we will explore in the next chapter.

The most effective and holistic way to overcome or prevent these hurdles is through the adoption of a proven delivery methodology, which can include:

- *PRINCE2*
- *The Waterfall Model*
- *The V-Model*
- *Agile*
- *ITIL* (V3 - IT Service Management Framework)

Whichever methodology your project team chooses, it is vital that you coordinate your delivery process with the PMO, because the PMO has a responsibility to oversee and govern all projects in a fair and standardized manner.

The PMO's tasks include compiling and maintaining a portfolio view of all projects, as well as financial control of the CapEx budget and releasing funding to projects that satisfactorily pass the relevant stage-gate.

The stage-gate process used by most software projects and software, focused PMOs has six stages in total:

- Stage 0: Discovery and ideation
- Stage 1: Scoping
- Stage 2: Build a business case
- Stage 3: Development
- Stage 4: Testing and validation
- Stage 5: Product launch

To keep your entire project team and stakeholder groups informed, you need to send engaging project status updates regularly.

Please keep in mind that your stakeholders may be from diverse backgrounds. For example, some people will be more technical than others. Therefore, it's essential that you keep things simple to ensure that the right information is received and understood by the key people.

Improving means doing things better, which means doing things differently. Leverage the PMO and use the lessons from past projects to avoid making the same mistakes over and over again!

11
Always Be Shipping

"If you wait until you are ready, it is almost certainly too late."

– Seth Godin

These immortal and provocative words of renowned business guru Seth Godin have been repeated and evangelized by almost anyone who works on products, whether they're software products or otherwise.

A perfect business case, a meticulous project plan, comprehensive requirements, fantastic data models, detailed business process analysis and mapping, amazing user stories, ingenious technical architecture, the latest technological designs, original and inspired code – none of these will matter until, and unless, your software product has shipped!

As Jeff Atwood, the co-founder of *Stack Overflow*, writes on his popular *Coding Horror* blog (`https://blog.codinghorror.com/yes-but-what-have-you-done/`), *Most programmers are introverts*. In other words, stereotypically speaking, programmers can be perpetual procrastinators and perennial tinkerers.

Interestingly, Atwood also references the same "A-B-C. Always Be Closing!" scene from *Glengarry Glen Ross* that we discussed in `Chapter 7`, *Meetings*, in the context of the sales meeting.

Together with Godin's cautionary words, the sense of importance and urgency to ship your software, rather than just sitting on it, is well and truly drilled home. So, remember that in the context of the sales meeting, your goal is to always be closing. In the context of launching your product, your goal is to always be shipping.

The sales meeting	Launching your product
Always be closing	Always be shipping

Confirmation bias considered, I fully agree with Atwood that a lot of developers do tend to have a habit of wanting to perfect their code before releasing it, even if they're only releasing it to other developers. This is despite developers consciously knowing that there is no such thing as perfect software.

My favorite insight from Atwood's blog post – which you can read at `https://blog.codinghorror.com/yes-but-what-have-you-done/` – is on this topic of developers perfecting their code. While I recommend you read the full post, the one area that I would like to draw your attention to is this:

> *It's helpful to discuss features, but sometimes the value of a feature is inversely proportional to how much it has been discussed. Our job as software developers is to deliver features and solve business problems, not to generate never-ending discussion. Ultimately, As Marc Andreessen notes, we will be judged by what we – and our code – have done, not the meta-discussion that went on around it.*
>
> *– Excerpt from Jeff Atwood's blog post on 31st July, 2007*

Developers are ultimately judged by their code, and projects are measured by their delivery. As a manager, both you and your team will be assessed by the product you release. In order to achieve good results, planning, requirements gathering, analysis, and design are all important.

There's really no substitute for just getting on with building the product. Keep the famous Nike marketing slogan in mind:

Nike slogan	Launching your product
Just Do It.	Just code it.

Recognizing a likely tendency within your team, and not just the developers, to dwell, tweak, and tinker is an essential step in your overall contribution to the project's development. As their manager, it is your job to balance this innate need to tinker with the external need to deliver a working product or a solution to the original problem.

To achieve this balance, there are several things that you can proactively do, and they're all associated with the best practices of a software project. When thinking about these tasks, you may not even be aware that they happen to address this particular management challenge.

Creating a delivery-focused team ethos

You need to make sure your team is mission-driven. To achieve this, you must make sure that everybody in the team, including yourself, is 100% clear on the mission from the very start.

Remember the "team deck" concept and the **Project Initiation Document** (PID) that we discussed back in Chapter 2, *What Are the Key Skills I need?*. Your unwavering mission statement and problem statement need to be proudly and prominently.

In the course of achieving your mission, it's also worth remembering that you need to encourage your team to try new and novel things. One of the primary ways that you can establish an area for this is by creating a safe environment that allows them to experiment, but more importantly, facilitate any failures by enabling them to try again. Effectively, you need to harness their creativity to solve complex problems, which you will inevitably encounter over the course of developing, testing, and deploying software.

If the mission is clear, then your team will naturally work toward achieving it. Depending on other factors, this could even happen without you knowing, or perhaps in a way that you might not necessarily agree with. Eventually, this multi-angle approach will yield great results for your team by creating a results-oriented and delivery-focused ethos, rather than an archaic, input-driven one.

Protecting the project from scope creep

We discussed the concept of scope creep previously in Chapter 3, *What is My Job Now?*. Scope creep is the bane of most projects and a significant contributing factor to their failure. Therefore, to enable your team to always be shipping, you must push back on unplanned, disruptive, and unconstructive scope changes, which could haphazardly move the goalposts of your project.

Aside from legitimate and reasonable business reasons, such as having to comply with a regulation change, such as **General Data Protection Regulation** (GDPR), it's never in the organization's best interest to jeopardize a vital project just because someone forgot something that would be nice to be added in. This is true no matter who they are, whether they be the CEO, your project sponsor, or a team member.

Adam Drake (@aadrake on *Twitter*), a data and artificial intelligence expert, has an interesting and insightful take on this challenge, based on real-world factors. He argues that imposing a "feature freeze" to mitigate scope creep will have real political impacts within a project because it will send a negative message to the business, which the project and product are ultimately serving. As such, any feature freeze should be approached with extreme caution:

> *"The feature freeze, in this context, is the equivalent of declaring technological bankruptcy."*

– Adam Drake

While I value and agree with Drake's words of caution, which may seem contrarian, I ultimately believe that there has to be a pragmatic *balance* between the business and the project, and the customer and the problem solver.

If there is no pragmatic balance, then the relationship and ecosystem between supply and demand are fundamentally broken. As such, there must be a little give and take to accommodate the imperfections of all sides. Therefore, it is a practical measure to manage scope creep, which ultimately enables your team to always be shipping.

Maintaining momentum

Delivering anything – and this is especially true in software development – is much easier if you already have momentum that has been built from real progress and the resulting confidence gained through it. This is another reason why iterative methodology, such as the *scrum* methodology, is so effective.

Well-defined – and invariably shorter – development life cycles are naturally suited to respond to rapid business change, which is now the norm.

To maintain this momentum, you need to use the inertia and lessons from cycles and sprints so far to propel the team forward. If the project gets stuck, then draw on previous knowledge, and also prioritize stories and bugs in a way that allows for some progress to be made in parallel to troubleshooting the issues.

In extreme cases, you must be prepared to ship with known bugs – as long as they're reasonably tolerable by the customers and users. If in doubt, you need to get their feedback first.

When times get tough, muck in!

Never be afraid to get your hands dirty! Sometimes, the simple act of rolling your own sleeves up is precisely what your team needs to see in order to get over a particularly tricky challenge. Remember, in this journey, you were once in their shoes, and in many ways, this is going back to your roots!

I'm not talking about trying to solve a technical enigma all by yourself. In itself, that would be a complete fallacy and even potentially detrimental to your team's confidence. The point is that this is simply not the time to remain rooted in your corner office.

Get close to your team. Use the various methods that we have discussed throughout the book, such as one-to-ones, weekly/daily huddles, and enabling team communication. You need to ensure that you take the time and care to understand, from your team's perspective, why progress has been blocked. This is the time to really support them, both as a team and as individuals.

What's troubling them? How can you help? The point is, even if you can't fix the problem for them directly, you're already helping by having these conversations. This is especially true if you use your empathy and active listening skills effectively to discuss and inspire alternative solutions meaningfully.

Continuous delivery

Taking the phrase "always be shipping" in a more literal sense, it naturally means that you are continuously delivering software. Hence, you are practicing the concept of continuous delivery. Before we delve more into this topic, it's worth clarifying the difference between **continuous delivery**, **continuous integration**, and **continuous deployment**, as well as identifying their relationships with each other.

In his *Atlassian* blog post, Sten Pittet, former product manager at *Atlassian* and co-founder of *Tability*, does a fantastic job of explaining these terms in a straightforward way. Of course, there are many interpretations and extensions of these concepts, but Pittet's definitions are certainly my favorite, simply because he clearly explains the essence of each practice at a no-nonsense level, without over-selling or over-complicating.

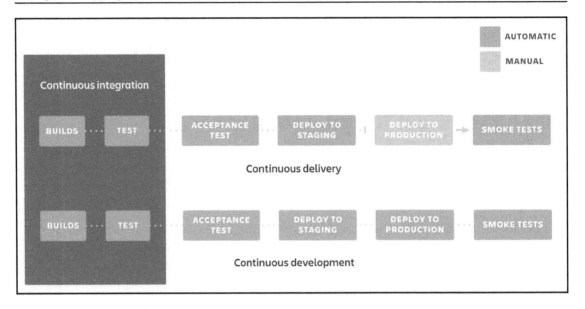

Figure 11.1: A straightforward diagram explaining how continuous integration, continuous delivery, and continuous deployment lead to continuous development
Source: https://www.atlassian.com/continuous-delivery/principles/continuous-integration-vs-delivery-vs-deployment

Working from Pittet's diagram here, we can break these three concepts into the following explanations:

- **Continuous integration** means less code branching and more frequent merging with the main trunk. Overall, your software repository will have fewer orphaned changes that require manual rework, and therefore less maintenance, too.
- **Continuous delivery** means releasing changes to production and therefore delivering value to the customer as quickly as possible. In many ways, this is the antithesis of the *Waterfall model,* where typically, a large number of changes are bundled together in a single release.
- **Continuous deployment** is a way of speeding up the deployment process by automating as many release steps as possible. So, developers can concentrate on pure development, instead of manually testing and deploying changes, too. When this is achieved, you will be practicing actual **continuous development**.

One of the key benefits of continuous delivery is an **accelerated time to market**.

This important idea leads us to the next point: a discussion on what we mean by time to market!

Time to market

To round up and arc back to Godin's quote that was introduced earlier in this chapter, note that his point was originally meant more for a marketing perspective, as opposed to having anything to do with the software development process.

If you wait until your product is fully completed and ready for market, then in all likelihood, somebody else has probably already done it faster and gotten a similar product to market before you. Therefore, you may have just lost your early-mover competitive advantage.

In short, you are no longer the pioneer and market leader for your given product. This point is essential in several ways, whether your product is business-to-business or business-to-consumer.

Dropbox is an excellent example of achieving competitive advantage through an accelerated time to market. It officially launched in 2008, and there is no doubt that it's a great piece of software that addresses a real problem and need. However, arguably, it's not the best or most complete cloud storage and synchronization tool out there.

Microsoft's OneDrive offers almost seamless integration with their *Office* suite of applications. *Google Drive* has cleverly leveraged the popularity of *Gmail* and other *Google Apps*. Meanwhile, *Amazon Cloud Drive* has a compelling commercial advantage because it's bundled with the broader *Amazon Prime* premium service.

By shipping its software faster than its competitors, *Dropbox* has exploited its early-mover advantage well, firmly establishing itself in consumers' minds as well as continuing to innovate and ship improvements.

The User Acceptance Testing (UAT) review

Unless you're working in complete isolation, you will need to test your software products extensively before shipping them. Moreover, there will most likely be multiple phases and types of testing, with most of them being done by someone else other than the developers. These testers may even be independent specialists who could possibly be from a third-party organization.

Based on your experience as a developer, you probably knew all that already, but ask yourself; what's different now that you're a manager?

Well, remember that your role is now to facilitate the development and delivery process of the product, as well as the people behind this, as opposed to doing the development and delivery yourself.

So, your focus as a Project Manager is to facilitate this process and support your entire project team as a whole. Or, if you are a Development Manager, your focus is to support the development team specifically. This is particularly important because a poorly managed test phase of a project – regardless of your choice of methodology – can be a mentally exhausting process for developers, with this pressure coming to a head at the **User Acceptance Testing (UAT)** review stage.

The UAT review itself is an important meeting and project milestone. It may be called different names – such as *Alpha and Beta Testing*, *Business Acceptance Testing*, *Key User Acceptance Testing*, *Operational Acceptance Testing*, and *Black Box Testing* – at various organizations. However, its primary purpose is to confirm and prove that the software that your team has developed is fit for purpose and fit for use.

This is done by demonstrating that an appropriate and pre-agreed level of testing, which would have been agreed upon earlier in the project's life cycle, has been completed successfully, then obtaining the customer's or key user representative's sign-off.

Note that if you're working in a heavily regulated sector, such as aerospace, food, drugs, healthcare, or financial services, there may be legislative regulators involved. This is to ensure that the statutory safeguards and standards are met. These reviews may be done on either a regular basis or via spot audits.

Developer-tester collaboration

If we step back a little, the idea of developer-tester collaboration is an essential theme for you to bear in mind when preparing to ship your product.

This process is essential throughout your project and not just for the UAT review, because while your project takes time to build, it can be destroyed in just seconds. An effective Project Manager ensures that collaboration between developers and testers is established early in the project's life cycle and is harnessed at the critical test phases of the project.

To establish this collaboration, you first have to pick the right people to work together on the team. As the project develops, you need to ensure you continue to pay attention to the composition of both your organization and your project team.

Where possible, you will benefit from choosing people who have a record of working well together, instead just going for the dominant subject-matter experts. As you build your team, pair experienced developers with experienced testers, because overall, there should always be a diverse mix of characters and experience levels.

Secondly, it's vital that you acknowledge that this relationship is going to be strained, especially when there is pressure from senior management to progress. This pressure will inevitably come during a critical test phase, which is likely to be near the end of an already overrunning project!

One of the most practical examples of this in my experience is the simple choice of what to call a "bug." I once worked in an organization where the development team was extremely experienced and influential, while the test team was all either junior and less experienced or external consultants. As a result, the power dynamic between both parties was clearly in the development team's favor, and they were not shy about using it. The result is a historically unchanged process that reflects this imbalance of power, status, and influence.

When do we call it a bug?

The previous example demonstrates the importance of being conscientious in your team's choice of words in raising or responding to questions, test incidents, or "bug" reports. It is normal and expected that testers, developers, and managers would have a different reaction to the word "bug" itself. In that same organization, when a planned and scripted test case failed, the test team was responsible for reporting this to the development team.

In most organizations, this would simply be referred to as a "bug," a "defect," or a "fault." It's any abnormal or unexpected system behavior, or possibly even an error in the test itself, that needs to be investigated. However, in this organization, such reports were referred to as a "test result report," even though that name is both rather long and potentially misleading.

Moreover, this test result report had to come from the Test Manager, as individual test team members were not allowed to contact developers directly. As you can imagine, it was a lot of effort just to protect the ingrained development team from being offended, and therefore defensive about their work and position within the organization.

This is not an example of healthy developer-tester collaboration. As you might expect, the UAT review meetings were a frequent flashpoint for disagreements, as well as political and unproductive arguing, which at that point becomes unhealthy for everyone.

As you read this, either as a project or development manager, there are some practical steps you can take to avoid this and instead establish a more healthy and productive developer-tester relationship:

- **Discourage negative and anti-collaborative behaviors such as boasting**: For example, a tester should not boast that they found a major bug that was a simple "rookie error" by a developer. Conversely, a developer should not boast that a tester messed up a simple test, for example, with bad data. Both of these unkind acts are not solution-focused activities, which we will discuss in more detail later on in this chapter.

- **Create a transparent environment that is conducive for both developers and testers, as well as for those with varying experience levels**: Share development and testing metrics, along with KPIs, with both teams. Encourage both teams to talk with each other about their challenges without unnecessary red tape and hierarchical management interference.

- **Establish an open meritocracy with equitable influence**: Ignore grades, rank, and even reputation. Give everyone a chance to express themselves and base conclusions on evidence and the thoughts of the whole group, rather than just the rank of those expressing them.

- **Get direct buy-in from the business-user community**: In most organizations, the majority of UAT is actually done by a dedicated test team, rather than genuine end users. Getting the actual business user community involved gives both the test and development teams a different perspective, as well as an incentive to work closer together on the entire project.

Learning mindset

Whether you're a developer or tester, a healthy lifelong-learning mindset is always to be encouraged. At the end of the day, the biggest benefactor of this is you! In the context of facilitating and leading a better UAT review, you have the challenge, as a manager, to bring this mindset to both your development and test teams.

It's especially important in this context because of what we touched on earlier. Specifically, the UAT review is often a contentious activity at best, or a downright destructive process at worst. So, bringing all sides together in an open and productive way is vital to ensure your project actually progresses.

This learning mindset involves getting everyone to understand that faults and bugs are an inevitable part of the process of software development. Therefore, by working on this principle, it's never a surprise to anyone, including the customer, when faults and bugs appear. You need to work hard to remove any negative connotations of failure when a bug is found. Instead, you need to focus on it as an opportunity to improve and make the software better.

On a personal level, you need to encourage and facilitate discussions between your developer and testers in an appropriately sized group – small groups for low-impact bugs, and the whole group for potential "showstoppers." You also need to work hard to build enough confidence across the whole project in order to share with, and actively listen to, each other in a genuine manner.

Specifically, for your developers, you should coach them to be more solution-focused, as well as open-minded. Sometimes, the best ideas to improve software can come from the test team, even though, to the developers, the test team may seem like a negative force and distraction, interested only in pointing out the development team's mistakes.

When analyzing bug reports, the default starting position should always be to look for positive truths, even if only a small portion of the report is, in fact, accurate. The development team should start with acknowledging and agreeing on the accurate parts, such as establishing that the right test conditions were set, before disproving and dismissing the testers.

UAT report and exit

If you have managed to implement even some of these mindsets and tasks in a balanced way, then the UAT review preparation and the meeting itself will be a smooth and productive activity for everyone involved.

The preparation should include compiling a report that summarizes all the completed planned tests, as well as the overall success criteria and rate.

As silly and rudimentary as it might sound, remember to always check with the **Project Management Office** (**PMO**), as well as the other project managers, to ensure that you have the correct and latest template. You need to remember that such reports are artifacts whose purpose is to provide confidence to stakeholders.

One of the crucial parts of the report will be the analysis of all the bugs that were found during UAT. As bugs are found, they should be analyzed, classified, categorized, grouped, and then prioritized for investigation and resolving. Achieving this list will drive several decisions, including how and when to design and implement the possible fixes to these confirmed issues.

Predominantly, these decisions are based on business impact and "shipability" (whether the product can be shipped with this bug or not). However, this question is also built on pragmatic matters, such as how many other tests this bug blocks, or how easy it would be to fix it alongside other bugs.

Debugging and refactoring code is a complicated process at the best of times. Coupled with the need to address multiple bugs, which may have the same cause but different effects and impacts, or vice versa, it can be challenging to untangle the cause-and-effect relationship.

However, it shouldn't be avoided, as it's a vital and integral part of the development and testing process. This is also where strong release-management processes can help.

As a result of these factors, the overall triage approach and criteria can often be contentious, causing disagreements not just between the development and test teams, but also with customers, as well as business users.

This is because the key inputs that have a significant bearing on the actions are mostly subjective. It's not always possible to quantify the business impact or accurately assess the effort required to refactor or merge the code change with another fix or release. Therefore, such things are largely a judgment call based on the limited supporting evidence available at the time.

This is the very reason why the source of information and its credibility are essential factors. It's also why it's essential to have established a good level of developer-tester collaboration early in the project, and throughout the project, so that the entire diverse team has a say – as opposed to just one dominant but biased expert.

Another way to address this challenge is to provide as much empirical and objective evidence as possible. Although this will not tackle the nuances of every single situation, it will provide the foundations for a more productive overall debate.

The Test Summary Report

In a best-practice **Test Summary Report**, there are certain types of information that should always be presented. Your stakeholders will most likely be expecting them, and the information should provide a holistic overview of all the test activities that supports a formal decision to accept or reject the software your team has developed.

Here is a typical table of contents for a Test Summary Report:

Test Summary Report

Contents

First of all, I recommend the size and length of the report to be limited to 10 pages or fewer. If the report is any longer than this, it's likely to contain too much information that will take the readers too long to understand and digest.

So, when preparing your report, be sure to distill and refine it until it's sharp and to the point. You can always include any secondary supporting information in an appendix, so nothing is missed.

As with all formal reports, start with an introductory **Purpose** statement. In this case, declare that the aim is to prove that the software is what the customer has requested and obtain the customer's formal sign-off.

The next few sections – the **Application overview**, **Testing scope**, **Metrics**, **Type of testing performed**, and **Test environments and tools** – should provide an overview of the project and software itself.

Remember that your stakeholders at the UAT review may have a non-technical background, and up to this point, may have not been overly invested in the project. These steps are a necessary recap to align everyone's fundamental understanding, which is always a good thing to avoid assumptions and confusion.

Without unnecessarily repeating the Test strategy, which should have been produced and agreed before testing itself, these sections should explain precisely which parts of the software have been tested (in the **Testing scope** section) and how they have been tested (in the **Types of testing** and **Test environments and tools** sections).

The **Metrics** section is key to providing a graphical or numerical representation of critical measurements of the overall test management information. There are three quintessential metrics to include:

1. The number of test cases planned versus executed, as follows:

Test cases planned	Test cases executed	TCs passed	TCs failed
80	75	70	5

2. The number of test cases passed or failed, as follows:

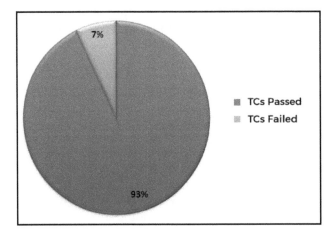

Figure 11.2: Example metric 2 – Number of test cases passed or failed

3. The classification of all bugs according to their severity, as follows:

	Critical	Major	Medium	Cosmetic	Total
Closed	25	15	20	0	60
Open	0	0	0	5	5
					65

Especially if your stakeholders are busy, these are the main metrics they will be looking for. These metrics are easy to understand and give a clear indication of the progress and status of the test activities. They are also essential for your stakeholders to make their decision on whether to sign off the project or not.

The **Test environments and tools** section should also be upfront and clear about the inevitable limitations of the tests executed. For example, maybe integration with specific external third-party systems was simulated by stubbed test environments, or perhaps stress testing was simulated in a test environment with scaled-down infrastructure.

The **Lessons learned, Recommendations**, and **Best practices** sections are more project- and management-focused. These three sections are more quality-related and will provide additional assurance to the stakeholders that testing wasn't just a box-ticking and bean-counting exercise.

The UAT meeting

The UAT review meeting itself should be a walk through of the meticulously prepared and peer-reviewed report, which was shared with the attendees in advance. I strongly recommend that the agenda is kept light and simple. As tempting as it might be, since you will have the stakeholders' attention, refrain from bundling other project-management topics into the same meeting.

During the meeting, you should walk through the report and invite questions along the way to encourage interaction and engagement. Remember to directly, and formally, request the all-important customer sign-off! This is likely to be an official stage gate and even a contractual stipulation. Likewise, after the meeting has taken place, follow up with meeting minutes and written proof of sign-off.

If sign-off has not been obtained, make sure you record the reasons and feedback as to why. Then take actions to address them and respond appropriately. The UAT review meeting is an important project milestone. However, always use it as a positive target, rather than a reverse-engineered date to be hit by compromising quality.

Always be selling – why it's my job, and that's OK

Working in sales and being responsible for selling can be difficult, and it's not for everybody – least of all the introverted developer-now-manager!

However, selling ideas is very much part of a manager's job, whether that's selling ideas about improvement to their team, or selling an idea for a new software product or feature to a potential customer. Besides that, there's always the cliché of "selling yourself," or your team, or the organization you represent.

You have already successfully sold yourself at your interview to secure the manager job, and you may have even made a successful pitch at a sales meeting, as we discussed in `Chapter 7`, *Meetings*.

In short, you've already done a lot of selling, and you're evidently quite good at it. So, there's certainly no need to doubt yourself now. It also does not mean you're anything like the demonic sales coach, Blake, played by Alec Baldwin in *Glengarry Glen Ross*, which we discussed in `Chapter 7`, *Meetings*, with the infamous "A-B-C. Always Be Closing" speech.

On the other hand, whether you like it or not, selling is an increasingly large part of a modern manager's job, whether that's selling ideas, selling value, or actually signing new deals with new and existing customers.

So, you must channel your inner Blake to some extent, to approach the notion of selling with confidence and positivity. It's a delicate balance between having the confidence and courage to share with your audience an idea that is mutually beneficial, without being pushy or arrogant.

The most positive example of this balance is in the product demo, which we discussed in `Chapter 7`, *Meetings*. The best product demos happen when the product really speaks for, and sells itself to, the audience. Your role is to identify the right people who have a need that your product can satisfy, and then engage them.

In other words, it's a **problem-led, rather than solution-led, approach**. It's a needs-based and demand-focused – not supply-focused – mentality. That way, it's not a cold-calling exercise where you are actively and opportunistically trying to push upon a customer a product that may not have any value for the customer.

If you can redefine the idea of selling as this problem-led activity that adds value for everyone involved, then you will find it much easier to accept that selling is now a part of your job – and that that's OK.

Summary

"Always be shipping" is not just another mantra or software management fad. It is an essential software development practice and could even be part of an overall business strategy to establish and exploit an early-mover competitive advantage.

Acknowledge your development team's likely tendency to tweak and tinker, but remind them that the product needs to be launched in order to achieve any value for its users and customers. Then, perform these practical:

1. Create a delivery-focused team ethos.
2. Protect your project from scope creep.
3. Maintain momentum.
4. When times get tough, muck in!

Additionally, encourage your team of to consider and adopt more efficient continuous delivery techniques, including the following:

- Continuous integration
- Continuous delivery
- Continuous deployment

Remind your team the importance of achieving an appropriate time to market. If you hesitate and unnecessarily delay shipping your product, there is always the threat that another organization will launch before you, which will give them a competitive advantage.

The UAT review is a critical milestone in any software project. Your role as a Project or Development Manager is to facilitate a smooth testing process and obtain your key stakeholders' all-important sign-off:

- Foster a developer-tester collaboration.
- Coach developers and testers to adopt a healthy learning mindset.
- Prepare a best-practice UAT or Test Summary Report by illustrating key metrics, including the following:
  - The number of test cases planned versus executed
  - The number of test cases passed or failed
  - The classification of all bugs according to their severity

Although selling may not be your strength, it is an important part of a modern and successful software manager's job. To help you achieve a more positive mindset and a better outcome, adopt a problem-led, rather than solution-led, approach. Listen intently to your users, customers, and sponsors to identify their true needs. Then propose and supply a genuine solution, instead of offering standardized software that doesn't fit their requirements!

12
The Training Day

At this point, you've successfully built, shipped, and sold your software product. However, that's not the end of the journey as there are still things that need to be done to get people to use it, certainly for people to use it correctly - that is, how you intended and designed the product to be used.

Unless you're developing an ultra-simple **business-to-consumer** (**B2C**) app, in all likeliness you and your team will be required to run some form of training to teach your users and customers on how to use it effectively. Even if your product is a self-explanatory B2C app, it's more than likely that you would still have to produce some form of training material, and a self-service-style list of **frequently asked questions** (**FAQs**). So, the topic of training is almost inescapable.

In this chapter, we'll be looking at the training stages in a product life cycle, and we'll see how you - as the manager - play a vital role in the product training day.

Approaching the training day

It's important that you and your team approach the concept of training with positivity and enthusiasm. It's understandable and very much the norm that the people involved with a project hate producing documentation. After all, to the people who have designed, developed, and tested the software, using the software is merely second-nature and requires no rudimentary guidance. It can seem laborious and unnecessary when it comes to creating the documentation and training.

However, as the project or development manager on this piece of software, how you approach and prioritize the essential project task of training sets the tone and sets the example for your team to follow. If you treat this stage as just a tick-in-the-box exercise, the training materials and experience you create for your customer will be sub-standard and practically useless.

On the other hand, if you approach product training and documentation with genuine enthusiasm and excitement, then your team will be more engaged with the work and you'll produce a much better training experience for your users. Genuine enthusiasm and excitement can't be faked. So, you need to be honest and authentic, even if your mind is focused on other important tasks.

To help you achieve this, you must think of training as an opportunity to positively influence your users. The generalized notion of users is that they are a fickle and stubborn lot. This statement is not intended to be controversial in any way, but rather, a cautionary word on how you decide to approach them.

Remember the five types of users, which we discussed in Chapter 6, *Asking the Right Questions to Your Users*. Each of those types of users exhibit an element of potential resistance to change, which has a major impact on how they are going to respond to your product. Since we'll be thinking about these types of user throughout this chapter, let's take a minute to remind ourselves of who they are:

- **Casual users**: These are users for whom your software is not the main application they use in their job or day-to-day life.
- **Business users**: These are users who, unlike casual users, will use your software as their primary application every workday.
- **Power users**: These are expert users who are more experienced and knowledgeable than a normal business user.
- **Management users**: These are typically managers and approvers within an organization, such as middle and senior managers.
- **Non-users**: These are people who are not currently using your software. These people offer you an opportunity for growth if they were to use your software in the future.

User acceptance and adoption can be challenging to obtain from these users, even if it's just for small changes in their business process, like a new validation screen, extra button, or a new click. They can be *particularly* resistant if they feel that your new software has been created without their permission or consultation. Training is therefore a big deal: it's your last opportunity to gain their support.

In this chapter, we will focus on the following topics, which you can combine with the techniques from Chapter 7, *Meetings*, to develop and produce a really effective training session for your product:

- Being realistic about scope and duration
- Concentrating on three key points

- Preparation and setup
- Snappy documentation
- Hands-on demo and practice
- Getting feedback

So, let's look at each of these topics and explore what they mean. Most importantly, we'll talk about how to put them into effective practice.

Be realistic about the scope and length of training

Being realistic in this context really means don't try to cram too much into your training.

Understanding your user is important, but you already know them well because you've designed and developed your software to fulfill their needs and solve their business problems. So, at this point, you should have an idea of what they do and do not care about. You know these people, so don't forget to use this information wisely: plan your training around your users.

Manage the scope of the training thoughtfully as well. If a training session is for a specific user type, then you can and absolutely should focus the entire session on that group alone. Alternatively, if your training session is for all types of users, with no single defined group, then you'll need to identify the most common areas that they all share and allocate the training time accordingly.

One single day is typically the most logical, reasonable, and practical duration for training your users. This recommended duration is primarily due to people's natural tendencies and how busy they are. One key point to remember here is that, unlike a full training course, user training is more specific and targeted.

It can be counter-productive to run user training that lasts for a whole week, but on the other hand, less than one day means that the trainees are splitting their day with their regular workload. This will often mean that you don't have their full and undivided attention. You also need to consider the attention and mental capacity it takes to concentrate and remember everything over long periods of time.

You'll also want to carefully consider whether you want to cover many different topics and the depth at which you go into detail. It's best to keep session topics relatively straightforward. After all, they're only going to use the software, not reverse-engineer it! Getting this depth of knowledge right is a vital part of running a successful training day.

If you provide too little information, then it means that they'll be unsatisfied and leave without the required knowledge or skills; whereas, if you provide too much information, you'll bore them, and they won't remember – nor will they enjoy – your training day! When deciding on where to draw this line for your training session, you'll need to adjust this with the context of your software product and users; but in most cases, a single training day is a reasonable balance for most ordinary circumstances.

Concentrate on three key points

Similar to the product demo that we've discussed throughout this book, limiting the key points in your training day to **three** is vital if you want to make your points stick.

If you try to cover too many different aspects, especially in a scattered or disjointed manner, then your users will not remember what's important and what's not, and most importantly, they won't learn! So, focus on the top three things your users will be most interested in and need most about your product.

This could be three stories or use cases, three business processes, or three different angles on the same business process. Moreover, even within the explanation and walkthrough process, always try to keep to three points. This is an effective way to consistently illustrate a concept and structure it in a way that is easy for those being trained to take in.

To use a non-software example, consider these three Rs: *Reduce, Reuse, Recycle*. It's easy to understand and remember. As an example, for a piece of consumer banking and payments software, your three stories could be:

1. How to create a new payee
2. How to send a payment to that payee
3. How the payee can check the receipt of a payment

Training preparation and setup

Preparation is essential for all important meetings. In the context of a user training day, it's also essential to set up your software and training environment correctly. As simple and rudimentary as this sounds, it's often the one factor that is overlooked! In our case, this setup must include a piece of working software with data that supports the top three things that the training will cover.

For example, one of the best and most logical places to start training around a new product is the new user registration or creation process. But if your training day is geared toward casual or management users, then it might be best to bypass this process and have accounts already created for each user to log into. Why? Because it would be pointless to train casual users on a process that they don't care about. Instead, use the limited time you have to concentrate on a key business process that's important to them. This could be the initial user customization and setup, or management reports and approvals, for example.

To further support your users through the training day, you would also be wise to prepare some documentation for them to reference during and after the training.

Snappy documentation

Snappy documentation isn't a phrase you often hear, nor is it an official term in any methodology or standard. It is, however, the best way to describe some useful documentation that is both insightful and easy to use for the consumer.

The key to producing snappy documentation, which will be used during and after the training day as quick referencing material, is to follow a logical structure that flows consistently. This design requires a well-thought-out arrangement that contains the appropriate level of detail for the given user.

By and large, training content can be quite dry and dull, due to its very nature and purpose. So, instead of trying to fight this, your time would better be spent on focusing on arranging it in an accessible way that makes it useful. As a manager, your goal is not to create a page-turner novel, but to enable users to get the guidance they need with the smallest amount of effort and time required.

Furthermore, your users will benefit more from visual and memory aids than from a wordy description. In other words, an appropriate number of images, diagrams, and screenshots is a lot more effective than wordy narratives describing everything from user actions to the system's behavior itself.

Remember to make sure your screenshots are entirely accurate and aligned with any supporting text. This is an essential part of creating an easy-to-use guide because a typical user is likely to flip, scroll, and skim-read the content to find where they first learned that information during the training day. Therefore, the accuracy of the screenshots in the supporting text is vital to link the training content together. The screenshots act a lot like a memory index.

This stage shouldn't be hard to achieve because if you've designed your software with an optimal **User Experience** (**UX**) in mind, meaning that it's easy to navigate and use, then the documentation for the product will be easy to produce, and even easier to follow.

Remember, the world doesn't need another tedious and dreaded user manual that doesn't compliment the training that the user received, and just ends up getting filed away in a cupboard afterward. What your users need is a lightweight document that they can "snap" to the right page to find the information they want to jog their memory and fix any issue they may have.

Hands-on experience training

If you're going to train your users about how to use your software, then there's no better way than simply letting them get some hands-on time and experience with your product! What's important here is that hands-on sessions should be about your team guiding people through a set of structured steps.

Hands-on demonstrations and practices mean getting hands-on and performing actions instead of just reading about it or passively following someone else's screen. The key here is user interaction, and therefore engagement; this in turn leads to learning and understanding.

Generally speaking, I'm not a fan of the simple "trainer leads, the users repeat" format of training. In these examples, the trainer performs the process on an enormous central screen; then each user tries to repeat the same actions, somewhat by rote. I believe that there should always be a good mix of theory and practice, as well as experimentation, within any form of training.

To achieve this, you first need to establish a solid understanding of some basic user actions so that the users are familiar with the general **User Interface** (**UI**) and workings, such as where the menus are located and what the key functions and buttons do. Then, instead of showing them every step of the process in terms of user actions, set them a task to achieve that uses a combination of the primary user actions they have already learned about.

To make this learning process - which can be challenging - smoother, try pairing up the users in a buddy system. This idea can help ensure that no one is left behind.

Use the lunch break to assess training

To enhance your training day further, there is one additional trick that I want to introduce you to, which is the idea of the lunch break. This one holds a particular place in my heart because I experienced it first-hand as a user and training day attendee, way back in the day when I was making my *Developer-to-Manager* journey.

On that day, the trainer was the Lead Developer from a project that delivered a new payments system - think *PayPal* in its infancy. This Lead Developer was extremely knowledgeable about the software itself and could talk about it for hours on end. However, the training wasn't great, simply because the vital element of appreciation for and empathy with the users they were trying to train was missing.

In short, the trainer was speaking in overly technical terms, in addition to focusing on areas that we, those being trained, didn't need to know that. Metaphorically speaking, they were spending more time explaining how the car worked than how to drive it properly.

What stood out about the training that this Lead Developer gave was their use of the lunch break as an opportunity to get candid feedback on the training event. Instead of using the break as a simple recess to rest and refuel, they actively sought honest reactions and comments on what the users were and were not getting from the training.

Furthermore, instead of sticking to the preplanned script and schedule of the day, they then switched the content focus, as well as the method of the training, based on the feedback they got! That same afternoon of this training day was a lot less theoretical and instead placed focus on the software itself. It was a lot more practical and focused on performing the most common and basic use cases, which is precisely what the users, like myself, said was needed.

This change in focus had a profound effect on the overall effectiveness of the training day and the satisfaction of the users who attended. Not only did we gain a lot more actionable knowledge, which we needed to do our jobs, we also felt valued and heard. So, the simple act of listening and adapting resulted in a shift in this group of users' overall view and sense of ownership of the software that we were there to learn about.

The support request is still training

Once you've shipped your product, managed to convince users to try it, and trained them to use it, you still have an important role to play in your product's success, because all software requires support in one way or another, even after initial training.

Whether your product is a simple website, or a complex enterprise system, users and customers will always require a way to find help because it's inevitable that they will have questions or get stuck in what they're trying to do with your product.

The range of support options varies greatly. On the enterprise end of the spectrum, these are often complicated commercial arrangements, with different **service level agreements** (**SLAs**) that are dependent on the customer's chosen package and contract, often coupled within the license model for the software itself.

The focus of this section is on how you and your team can maximize the opportunity of every support request. Because even if your software is underperforming against the user's expectations, a good support experience can recover some of their lost satisfaction, and in the long term, even make it an overall positive encounter for the user.

In Chapter 4, *A Week in the Life of a Manager*, we discussed the *ITIL* service management framework and the Application Management function in particular. Application Management is considered part of the Service Operations phase of the service life cycle, or put another way, the operational phase of the product life cycle.

Support requests are not exclusive to stable and static versions of the software. You can receive a support request as soon as your product is live and has begun acquiring a user base. Your first support request is always an exciting challenge and a great test of how well your service transition tasks have been completed.

For example, if you have a central IT Service Desk function, was it able to record all the necessary information appropriately and route the request to you effectively?

If you're the Project Manager responsible for delivering a new system, it is part of your remit to ensure that the support model is agreed, understood, and implemented by every team involved with it. In this context, the support model is simply an agreed way of working to respond to requests, as well as events, incidents, and problems, as previously defined.

Typically, this includes a **RACI** table that will broadly illustrate what each team is **Responsible** for, **Accountable** for, **Consulted** about, and **Informed** of. This RACI table will also include some flowcharts to explain how to respond to a support request from a user. *Figure 12.1* is a great example of a support request process diagram involving the User, IT Service Desk, and Application Management (or the relevant apps team):

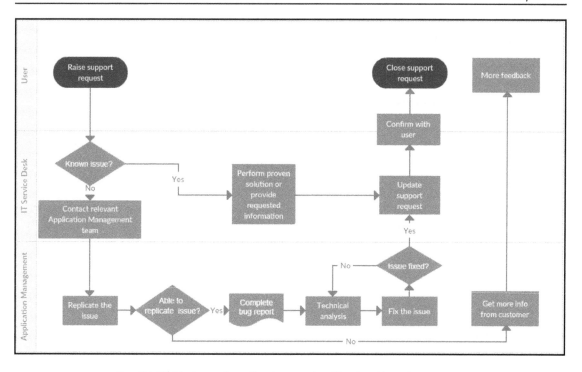

Figure 12.1: A high-level process diagram illustrating an example workflow triggered by a user's support request
Source: http://creately.com/diagram/example/jvp1j0ql1

In this example, you'll notice that most of the actions are performed by the Application Management team. Of course, the diagram could be redrawn with more emphasis and detail on the IT Service Desk. However, even at this high level, it's clear that the Application Management team have the most responsibility for support requests on their application, which makes a lot of sense!

How your Application Management teams respond to each support request determines a large portion of the user's experience and overall satisfaction. The remaining part is played by the IT Service Desk, which acts as a filter and conduit, primarily interacting with the user directly on a more administrative, less technical basis.

To fully make use of support requests as an opportunity to help and satisfy a user, there are three key things to focus on, and in the following sections, we have dedicated a small section to each of them.

Response and resolution time

How long your team takes first to respond to and then resolve each support request and issue plays a huge role in the user's experience and satisfaction. It's also likely to be measured closely as a **key performance indicator** (**KPI**) if you're a corporate service provider.

Instead of just working to avoid breaches of the agreed targets or levels, coach your team to view support request response and resolution as a real opportunity to show kindness and help users who need assistance, especially those who would be completely stuck without it.

Think of it in the same way that we need help from other teams, such as the marketing or finance team. Or put another way, if we see a genuinely needy person on the street, simply offering to help them carry some luggage up a staircase or to cross a busy road is a simple, yet powerful, act of kindness. The response and resolution time targets - where they're reasonable - will naturally be met.

Care and attention

Your team's general attitude toward users and their support requests is very visible. Your users and colleagues don't have to look extremely hard to see whether your team is paying lip service to a user.

Therefore, establishing true customer service orientation within your team is vital to demonstrating a level of care and attention that makes the users feel valued and consequently puts them in a position to enjoy using your software more. You can help your team achieve this by showing empathy yourself and leading by example.

If you get involved in handling support requests yourself, then you can demonstrate this in how you deal with each support request and user. If you are more hands-off, then how you analyze and triage support requests shows your team that you care about the impact of every issue on every user, which will encourage them to care as well.

However, if you're entirely hands-off in the support request process, then how you interact and help colleagues can also demonstrate this value. For example, do you dismiss their issues and concerns without much consideration? Or do you try to ask clarification questions so that you can understand the problem in order to resolve it better?

Quality of communication

When the information provided by the user is insufficient, does your team respond with a "need more info" standard and non-constructive answer, or empathically specify what information they need, and how the user can help get it?

If you don't know the answer to a support request immediately, then say you don't know but be sure to tell your users that you'll look into it and get back to them. Never make a false or unrealistic promise in the hope that the request will magically go away, because it won't, and you've then just squandered an excellent opportunity to win over a user!

The post-mortem

Now, let's say that your product has shipped, and the software is live. However, it's clear that for some reason the project didn't go well, at least in some respects. Perhaps it was over budget, it missed the agreed schedule, or the quality wasn't to the required standard, or any combination of these. Maybe your project did go well from a stakeholder point of view. However, there's always room for improvement. These are all situations where the rather ominous-sounding "post-mortem" is useful.

Before we dive into the post-mortem process, it's worth pointing out that there are two ways of thinking about this topic. A post-mortem could be positive or negative; or constructive or destructive.

If we start with the destructive, or at least non-constructive, way of thinking, then clearly this is a minefield of politics and possible ulterior motives. While this is a fact of modern life, I'm a firm believer that in the long run, the only way to "win" in the blame game is by not playing it at all.

A successful manager should be cognizant of these destructive traps and pitfalls, but never be bounded by or react to them. Stick to the facts, remain positive and confident. Adopt a learning mindset and listen to feedback, even if you don't agree with what is being said.

If you're ever put into a difficult position, focus on maintaining an objective and motive-neutral stance, and think about your team and their work rather than any emotional reaction. It is not worth dwelling on.

Focusing on the constructive side of a post-mortem is where you should always invest the most effort. When it's approached positively and executed productively, this can be a beneficial and valuable exercise for you and your team, as well as the organization in the long-term.

As an experienced developer, you will already be accustomed to sprint retrospectives. In effect, a project post-mortem is a related and comparable activity, only differing in that a post-mortem is related to a specific project instead of a sprint. However, it does have some key differences, which are worth exploring.

To put a formal spin on it, a post-mortem can be considered part of the process that methodically closes down a major project. In the *PRINCE2* methodology, there's even a formal process called *Closing a Project*. This is one of the seven processes, which are accompanied by seven principles and seven themes, that we introduced in `Chapter 2`, *What Are the Key Skills I Need?*

The End Project Report

Within the *Closing a Project* process mentioned in *PRINCE2*, the primary output is the End Project Report. Along with other *PRINCE2* management products, the End Project Report is a relatively well-known and well-used product. This is partly because it's very clear on what it's about, but also simply because of its value, which most mature organizations will recognize.

The ideal End Project Report is a document that can discreetly - by itself - present all of the essential messages and information to a key stakeholder, allowing them to individually consume the information before coming together at a formal meeting. The Project Manager (who could very well be you) is responsible for preparing and producing the End Project Report, with the support of the project team.

The primary purpose of this report is to confirm that the original objectives have been met and review the performance of the project. To achieve this, it should summarize the accomplishments of the original business case as per the **Project Initiation Document (PID)** and provide an objective assessment of the planned versus actual *time*, *cost*, and *quality* metrics.

After all, these three metrics are the things that your customers and senior stakeholders care about. So, you are simply speaking their language and not burdening them with too much information, just the information they need.

The *PRINCE2* wiki - `http://prince2.wiki/PRINCE2` - is a terrific resource for *PRINCE2* followers and practitioners. According to its contributors, and a cited End Project Report template created by a company called *Management Plaza*, there are four essential pieces of information that an End Project Report should include:

- A review of the business case and justification for the project
- Project objectives with their planned and actual measurements

- List of crucial management products (project artifacts) and their statuses
- Lessons learned, including any notable technical debt and recommendations

To conclude a project, it's logical that the original business case is revisited to objectively and holistically assess whether the goals have been accomplished and to see if the target **return on investment** (**ROI**) has been achieved. This is why there should always be a section early on in the report that explains the justification of the project.

This should be followed by a table, like the upcoming one, that displays the metric data measuring each important project objective. *Scope, Time, Cost, Quality, Risks,* and *Benefits* are all vital signs of a project and are something that your stakeholder(s) will be expecting to see.

Risks and benefits are also important, depending on the nature of your project and software itself. For example, is it a flagship project for the organization, which can have a reputational impact? Or is the software delivering a mission-critical system?

Project Objectives

	Target	Tolerance	Actual
Scope			
Time			
Cost			
Quality			
Risks			
Benefits			

Figure 12.2: An example template of the project objective measurement table
Source: https://www.mplaza.pm/templates/prince2/end-project-report/

For the quality objective, which is difficult to quantify and measure at the best of times, this could be a count of the confirmed bugs or defects. If the overall picture is negative - in other words, the numbers don't stack up favorably - then it's necessary to provide commentary around this - and have an explanation ready to discuss in person.

A visual checklist of the key management products is essential information, especially if the organization mandates a particular methodology. More practically, it also signals to the reader of the End Project Report that the project has paid attention to the governance and administrative details, rather than solely working on delivery to the detriment of everything else. In the process of creating and completing this checklist, you will have satisfied the **Project Management Office** (**PMO**) and their processes and criteria!

A summarized view of the Lessons Log, which is another important management product, is an excellent way to round out the report on a constructive note. When producing this summary, include the most noteworthy lessons learned and any outstanding technical debt that is attributed to the project. The idea of doing this would be to provide your stakeholders with an open and honest view of what the project has discovered and learned, not what went wrong and why it went wrong, in the negative sense.

An effective Lessons Log is an accurate and candid record of the significant amount of knowledge gained. It should also be objective wherever possible. For example, if the organization's infrastructure on which the project's software is used is sub-optimal, then the Lessons Log should state the resulting challenges this caused to the project and how the final product overcame them or did not.

In situations where discoveries and challenges were not concluded and resulted in technical debt, for example, then this kind of thing must also be included in the End Project Report. You should also include a list of recommendations that were outside the scope of the project but will benefit other projects and the organization as a whole.

Your role in the End Project Report

So, what exactly is your new role in this kind of documentation? Well, if you are the Project Manager, then you are the person responsible for producing the End Project Report, and you should present that report at the project review or stage-gate meeting. Your job is also to create the document in the first place and collect and collate the required information from the various sources, before then organizing it and presenting it in a way that your key stakeholders can easily consume and understand.

On the other hand, if you are a Development or Delivery Manager, you will have the most information on the technical elements of the project work, such as scope (stories, points), quality (bugs), and also risk (technical challenges) and technical debt (unresolved deferred issues). Therefore, the Project Manager will most likely rely heavily on your input for the content of the report.

However, if you're striving to be a truly effective and successful manager, there's more to the post-mortem than just the report. Besides dealing with any politics, you also need to think of and develop your team in the process. Difficult project closure is one of the best opportunities to learn, from both mistakes made, as well as momentous - but often overlooked - achievements.

You might think that this is putting an overly positive spin on this process. After all, a lot of project closures are difficult because most projects do go over budget and beyond schedule, and miss their quality target. In these common circumstances, it's easy for people to look for fault in others and fall into the blame game in search of excuses to protect their own reputation, ego, and bonus.

This is where there is a real opportunity to do something different and constructive. The most powerful constructive tool you have is to be a positive role model for your team. How you respond to non-constructive criticism sets an example for your team to follow. Your performance when you have to explain the political situation to them matters because it shows that you are transparent, but also that you trust them.

Successfully managing yourself to refrain from the blame game alone can have a profound effect on developing your team as individuals, especially for the more junior members of your team. Coaching them to do the same successfully will reinforce this notion into practice, and through time, it becomes a positive habit.

Whether project closure is politically charged or not, it's still a great learning opportunity, that is, if you adopt an open mindset to actually learn, which is much easier said than done. Similar to a sprint retrospective, a project closure requires a safe environment to be effective. Although you do not have as much control of this activity, you can still influence it by being open and confident yourself, and guiding others to do the same.

For everyone to gain knowledge from setbacks to the project, it requires that the original person responsible has the humility to admit to their mistakes. For example, it's deeply embarrassing for your team member to admit to a simple code change that caused a complete outage. However, admitting it is exactly what they should do. Only then can this be a lesson that results in the appropriate collective action to prevent going forward. For example, implement a double review process for all code changes in critical modules.

This "nobody is perfect" message can be difficult to write in a report and communicate to a customer. As a manager, you first need to guide and support your team to proactively share their own mistakes and shortcomings. Therefore, your team should contribute to the Lessons Log and End Project Report.

From the recipient angle, you also need to find a balance between over-exposing your team to destructive criticism and over-protecting them from genuinely constructive feedback, no matter how difficult that it may be for them to hear. Only then will they benefit from the process.

Supporting your team can be done in many ways. There will be times when you need to defend your team against unfair and unjustified criticism. At the same time, you also need to be conscious of not shielding them too much and trust that they can also stand up for themselves - with facts and evidence, as well as your support.

Nobody cares - what to do about it

Now, let's say that your product has shipped. However, nobody cares, and nobody is buying or using it! For a better illustration and explanation of this, let's use an example of a B2C product.

With any software product, there are different aspects to consider when you design, develop, and eventually launch it. Without over-engineering this, there are three main angles to consider:

- Marketing angle
- Technical angle
- Practical angle

These are not discrete categories, but rather different views of the same object, which can overlap. Each of these angles offers insights into why nobody cares about your product, but can also explain why they love it too!

The first one is the **marketing angle**. To sell a product - in other words, to successfully bring it to market - clearly, marketing is going to be necessary, from understanding the market and identifying your market segment to target, to designing and developing the right product that will serve that market, to finding the best way to reach and tell them about your product. These are all marketing activities.

The **technical angle** should be familiar to you as an experienced developer. This is both an internal view of the software itself (is it a good use of the latest and most appropriate technology?) and an external view of the wider world in which the software needs to operate (is it a good fit with other technology products out there that it needs to integrate with?).

The **practical angle** is something that is often overshadowed by the other two angles, yet it's still a vital part of the overall equation. How adaptable is your product from a customer and user perspective?

In the next few sections we'll now break down each of these angles and explore them in some more detail.

The marketing angle

The science - and art - of marketing is continuously evolving. Even the fundamental concepts in marketing, which you might think of as mainstay pillars, can shift. We've talked a lot about disruption, especially in the software and technology industries, in this book, but marketing is also forever being disrupted because it has a close relationship with technology.

Concepts such as the marketing mix originate from back in the 1940s. The original 4Ps of marketing have since been extended to 7Ps of marketing, and even to the 8Ps of marketing, and different variations of the 4Cs. To represent this, you can see the 7Ps of marketing in *Figure 12.3*, by marketing guru Mark Acutt:

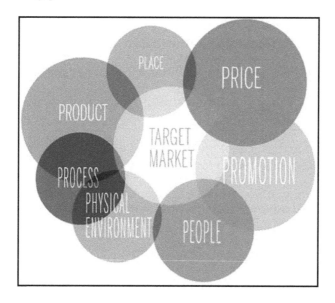

Figure 12.3: A simplified diagram of the 7Ps
Source: https://marketingmix.co.uk/

Here is a more detailed explanation of each version of the marketing mix and a mapping of each element between each version:

4Ps (McCarthy)	7Ps (Booms & Bitner)	8Ps	4Cs (Lauterborn)	4Cs (Shimizu)
Product Price Place Promotion	Product Price Place Promotion People Process Physical evidence	Product Price Place Promotion People Process Physical evidence Performance	Consumer Cost Convenience Communication	Commodity Cost Channel Communication

For our purposes, it's sufficient to stick with the most straightforward and purest form of the marketing mix, the 4Ps. In layman's terms, to successfully bring something to market, you need to answer some fundamental questions, including:

- Is your software **product** what the consumer needs?
- Is your software available at a **price** that consumers are willing to pay?
- Is your software **placed** conveniently enough for consumers to buy it?
- Is your software **promoted** in a way that compels consumers to buy it?

In addition to these, you also need to consider the science of **branding**:

- Is your software product's **brand** strong enough to make it stand out from other software products?

A common comparison in the technology business is often the *Apple* versus *Microsoft* contest. Both brands are strong and always evolving. However, they are quite different.

If you accept the marketing mix as a proven concept, then you must consider the entire mix, rather than just your software product in isolation. Another important concept is the **Unique Selling Point** (USP):

- Does your holistic proposition have a **USP**?

For example, if you offer the same product in the same way as your competitors, but in a brand-new marketplace, then the overall proposition is unique. In the real world, this can be seen for example in *Spotify*'s move into India, which already had other music streaming services, but also had a complex music business structure within a complex legal environment.

There are also potential marketing barriers in the way. Your product could be considered overpriced, simply if there is a comparable product available for less money.

In a more corporate **business-to-business** (**B2B**) context, the marketing mix still applies. However, instead of narrowing in on the sale of your software, the challenge can be about getting people to actually use it. As we've discussed previously, users can be a fickle and potentially resistant lot. So, in response to that, ask yourself: Does your product and overall proposition offer them additional value? In other words:

- Does your software **improve** the user's work, productivity, or happiness?

If you want to successfully launch a software product and sell it to a market, then it is going to be all about how you can make your product stand out against your competition. You need to offer the consumer or user a strong and uniquely compelling reason to buy and invest their time in your software over the option of choosing others.

The technical angle

For a software product, the technical angle is both an internal and external view of the code, the application, and the system itself.

From an internal perspective, the fundamental question you must be able to answer is whether your software product is objectively technically fit and technologically superior to available other software products.

For example:

- Does your software provide the best possible UX through the latest web standards, such as HTML5?
- Does your software performance objectively process the most data compared to competitor software products?

From an external perspective, you need to understand the broader environment in which your software operates. Modern software seldom works in isolation. It's most likely integrated with other software and relies on some infrastructure.

Even if you have built a technically advanced or even superior product, there is always a risk of an external change that might render it useless or lower its value due to an unsupported component in its technology stack. For example, *Windows Phone 8.1*.

Similarly, is your software product compatible with other software products, and even platforms? If not, then this could be a technical limitation that leads to a logical dead end, because it's simply not going to convince people to invest in it and use it when there are other products with much more functionality, possibilities, and longevity. If you can convincingly answer the questions that I've posed to you so far and your software product still struggles, it could even be that your software is ahead of its time.

Back in 2012, I attended a demo for a product called webdoc, which was the most advanced HTML5 website I had visited at the time. webdoc was a rich content editor that enabled its users to create content with a multitude of media - text, sounds, images - then directly post and embed them to other websites.

The problem with webdoc was that most other popular websites were not ready to receive these posts! Therefore, the use of webdoc was limited, and the product was ultimately retired - look at the following screenshot, which is the official website of webdoc. It's now been abandoned!

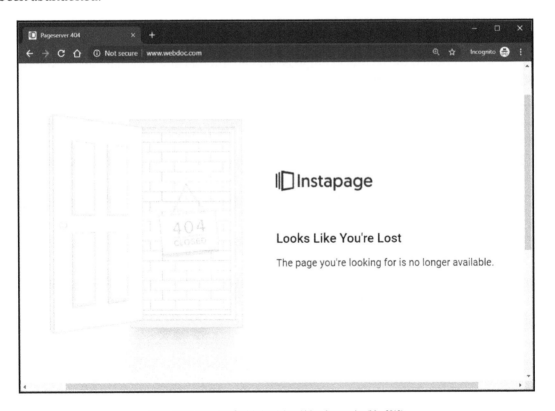

Figure 12.4: A screenshot of webdoc's website, which no longer exists (May 2019)
Source: http://www.webdoc.com/

The last factor to consider is your product's switchability. This has an obvious practical angle, too, which we will discuss in the next section.

In essence, the technical angle is about how easy and realistic it is to change from an existing product to your product. For example, *Gmail* and *Google Calendar* allow you to access and manage emails and calendars from other rival products, such as Microsoft's *Office 365* and *Outlook.com*, and vice versa.

Google also provides extra functionality to transfer essential data such as contacts and photos from a rival cloud storage solution to theirs. Equally, similar functionalities exist for *Apple*'s iOS and *Google*'s Android devices.

In the B2B space, commercial lock-in is common due to contracts that typically run for multiple years. How about technical lock-in? For example:

- How easy and realistic is it to migrate from **SAP** to another **enterprise resource planning** (**ERP**) solution?

This also leads on to the practical angle, which takes a real-world view of these potential barriers and enablers for your software to be adopted.

The practical angle

As discussed in the previous section, clearly there are a lot of possible technical barriers for software products, especially when it comes to the customer switching away from their incumbent solution to adopt yours. In a practical sense, this is a simple exit barrier for the customer to stop using one product and an entry barrier to start using yours, without jeopardizing either their operations or business.

Another entry barrier is that your software product could be too difficult to implement or use. For example, you will have probably worked on many major software upgrades. In general, there are two broad options: an *in-situ upgrade* or a *new install and migration*.

With all other things being equal, such as a stable hosting infrastructure that doesn't need to upgrade, when a reasonable customer is presented with these two options, they are almost always going to choose the in-situ upgrade option. The effort, cost, and risks involved with a new install and migration can be astronomical, especially if it's a business-critical system that's being upgraded.

With today's modern infrastructure in mind, it is commonly assumed that B2C applications are always available. However, (un)availability can be a simple, yet major, barrier to your software product, especially if it's a time-sensitive service that a consumer or user is trying to use.

For example, when Volkswagen launched its ID.3 electric car and began to take pre-orders in May 2019, its website suffered a severe meltdown because it couldn't cope with the volume of traffic. Ultimately, the launch was painted as a success for receiving 10,000 pre-orders, but there is a question mark over whether they could have got more.

The same applies to the adoption of new software. If a new user tries to log in for the very first time, but the software is unavailable, then their experience and overall confidence are severely damaged, and they may not come back.

Summary

Training your users is an important and inescapable task for almost all software projects. Some people argue that it's the most important task of all, because without it even the best software in the world might never get used.

How you and your team approach the training task is vital. It's so important that you inspire and infuse your team with the genuine enthusiasm and excitement that the training task deserves and needs. If you approach training positively, then it can have a major positive impact on your project and team.

Stick to these six practical things to ensure your training day is effective and productive:

- **Be realistic in scope and duration**: It is a training day, after all, so don't try to cram too much in or artificially make it any longer.
- **Concentrate on three key points**: No one remembers the fourth thing you said, so don't say it.
- **Preparation and setup**: Prepare your training materials according to the user type and set up your environments properly, so they work!
- **Snappy documentation**: All training materials, manuals, and guides should be ultra-easy to use so users can snap to the bit they need.
- **Hands-on experience**: There's nothing like a test-drive if you're about to buy a car!
- **Lunch break**: Use it to get near-real-time feedback and adjust your afternoon accordingly.

How your team handles support requests can be a fantastic opportunity to recover user confidence and satisfaction lost through the need for the request to be raised in the first place. It's a real test of how well your processes have been understood and actioned by the entire operations department, especially the IT Service Desk.

Focus on these three key areas to make the support request a positive experience for your team, and most importantly, the user:

- Response and resolution time
- Care and attention
- Quality of communication

The mere prospect of a project post-mortem can be terrifying, especially for a junior manager. Do everything you can to avoid the blame game and embrace it as a learning opportunity. It could even be cathartic!

Set yourself, your team, and your project up for success by compiling a comprehensive and best-practice-packed End Project Report to give your stakeholders confidence that everything has been taken care of. Support your team with an objective, fact-based defense when required.

The success of any product launch and your software's uptake can be meaningfully viewed from three angles:

- **The marketing angle**: Understand your software's marketing mix (7Ps), brand, and USP.
- **The technical angle**: Understand the technical characteristics of your software itself, as well as the integrated technical environment it operates in.
- **The practical angle**: Understand any practical challenges to adopting your software, from the users' perspective.

So, remember to go back to the beginning of this chapter and ensure that your next training day is a success, and that you're thinking about the elements we've discussed from a user perspective.

13
Organizational Management in the 21st Century

Conductal

This is a fascinating topic, and I'm thrilled to introduce to you the brilliant mind of Daniel Ospina, who is the guest contributor to this chapter. Daniel has an insightful and refreshingly different take on what "management" means in today's workplace. Crucially, he uses research and data to back this up! Furthermore, Daniel offers ideas and techniques for you to try that will enable you to maximize your own effectiveness in making sense of what it means to be a manager and a leader.

Daniel's opening story not only resonated with me, but also sets the scene for the challenges faced by a successful modern manager every day. His profound thoughts on how the concept of the manager has evolved – from someone who knows all the answers into a more contemporary, flexible thinker who also nurtures other thinkers – is something that I wholeheartedly endorse. In this chapter, you'll learn about cutting-edge management methods for the 21st century. This will give you a map for understanding what your team needs.

Daniel is an organization designer, a visiting lecturer at the *Saïd Business School* (*Oxford University*), and the founder of *Conductal*. His business facilitates the evolution of teams for a complex and rapidly changing world. After a period managing innovation in one of the world's best restaurants, Daniel worked with *Google*, Boston Consulting Group, New North Zealander Hospital, and the United Nations, as well as numerous **small and medium-sized enterprises** (**SMEs**) and start-ups across Europe and Latin America. His research and insights on the future of work and the leadership frameworks we need to get there have been featured on platforms including TEDx, Tech Open Air, and the Harvard Business Review.

Introduction

I want to begin by telling you a story about me as a rookie manager from my own personal perspective. This sets the scene and brings the themes of this chapter to life.

The first year in the new job was difficult. I had to understand the project, get to know and lead my team, and somehow find time between meetings for my own work. Past developers and architects had left a legacy system, and there were many hard problems to solve. We had to understand the old technology, while also trying to modernize and keep pace with the changing requests being thrown at us.

My team knew I was a first-time manager, but they had heard good things about my coding skills. I wasn't 24 hours into the job before one of them, a young guy named Ed, came to seek my advice. I was determined to be a good leader, and so made some time to work out a solution for what he was asking. I had also been scheduled to attend a meeting of managers and had to rush to prepare some notes. Somehow, I managed to fit it all in.

I was feeling good when I entered the meeting. I was prepared, knew what my team was doing, and had managed to help one of them solve a problem.

During the meeting, we were briefed about some changes and a request for a new feature, and then I was quickly asked how I was doing with my team. I shared what had happened so far, and the other four managers in the meeting seemed to nod. Then, we ran out of time, and I went back to my desk.

Before I was even able to sit down, Jana, another one of my team members, came by. Jana had heard from Ed how I had helped him, and she wanted me to check a piece of work she was about to ship that she had some doubts about. We looked at the code together, and I spotted some unnecessary complexity. There was a whole section that could be refactored, and Jana seemed happy that we were able to find a more elegant solution that later on passed all tests.

By this time, the day was almost finished, and I was yet to type up my notes from the meeting. I ended up having to stay an extra two hours after everyone else had left.

Then, the next morning, another request for help came from yet another of my direct reports, Simon. Some guy had created a custom framework that somehow violated MVC principles, with the business logic written in XML along with the view. It was part of the legacy we were dealing with, and, even more troublingly, it showed that the solution I had given to Ed on the first day was actually not going to work. Sure enough, Ed came by a few minutes later and now it was three of us looking at this thing and trying to find an answer.

One of them suggested calling a colleague, Aseem. Aseem had been transferred to another team, but had been in what was now my team when the previous system was built.

Ed, Simon, Aseem, and I dived into the problem. Aseem was kind enough to get me acquainted with what had been built in detail, and so I was able to work toward a solution. It took me all morning and half of the afternoon, but the problem was solved. I went back to my desk and... suddenly, damn! I had forgotten to share my notes about the briefing of the new feature with my team.

I immediately sent the notes, and then had to rush to another meeting before finishing the day. On the way out, I ran into a colleague who sat next to my other direct reports. He asked me how I was doing, and when I said I was feeling good about my work with the team, he gave me a weird look. It turns out my team had been complaining about me sharing the notes too late, which had led them to waste a whole day of work. My good mood instantly evaporated. Not only had we lost a day of work, but also my team was talking behind my back instead of addressing the issue with me first. I spent most of that night thinking about the issue.

The next morning, I was feeling tired and wasn't particularly happy to discover that Jana and Ed were already waiting to get my opinion on some stuff. Simon also needed to check the requirements of the new feature, and my boss was waiting for a status update. Then, it emerged that my two other reports were unclear about what they were meant to do, and they had accidentally worked on the same thing. This had created some tension, and the mood in the team was quickly deteriorating. Thank God it was Friday!

The next week seemed to be a rerun, but worse. My team needed more support, they had trouble understanding what was being asked of us, and there were more issues with the legacy system, which I was unacquainted with. I was used to being the savvy one, but now, the more I tried to solve problems, the more my team needed help, and the less I felt I knew about the solutions. I didn't have the time to understand all the intricacies and was feeling powerless to answer the requests of my team, coordinate, attend meetings, and deal with them speaking behind my back.

I was being interrupted constantly and couldn't focus on doing my own work. I was annoyed at my team for needing so much help, I was annoyed at myself for the messiness, and everyone was more than annoyed that we were going to have to spend the weekend at work. How could I organize the team to avoid repeating the same thing next week?

I thought that as a manager, I had to know everything. I wish I knew that this is an outdated way of thinking and a complete myth!

An old myth – the manager has all the answers

The manager of our previous story is, unfortunately, prototypical. They are the kind of person that has been promoted thanks to their technical skill. They are used to being hands-on and having all the answers. Because of that, when faced with the complexities and fast pace of modern teamwork, they usually fail.

Part of the problem comes from managers failing to realize that their new job is very different and demands new skills, such as organizing a team to find answers instead of being a know-it-all. As a result, they rely on the behaviors that have brought them success in the past, instead of searching for new mental models.

Unfortunately, most organizations are also stuck in a rather old understanding of management, leading them to divide work in counterproductive ways and be ill-prepared managers. Overwork, stress, disengagement, poor mental health, and mediocre results are the consequence.

In this chapter, we will look at the origins of the type of thinking that leads to these problems, at the way the demands of work have changed in the last few years (faster and more drastically than most organizations realize!), and at the new ideas that have emerged to address the challenges of organizing a team.

By the end of the chapter, you will have learned about several key concepts and discovered some of the most famous methodologies of cutting-edge management in the 21st century. The idea is to give you a map for understanding what your team needs and avoid being sold unrealistic silver bullets.

Management in the Industrial Revolution

Thinkers ≠ Doers

Leadership and management have, until recently, been described as the same thing. For centuries, the only distinction we had was between operations and planning. It came from the Industrial Revolution when assembly lines were invented, and factories blossomed.

The current of thought at the time suggested a division between "doers" (those doing the physical work) and "thinkers" (those who would organize the work). The basic premise was that work could be divided into simple, quick, and repeatable steps, and that even the most basic of workers could be trained to repeat with great efficiency. These were the doers. On the other hand, we had the thinkers. More experienced and educated, they were best suited to divide and plan the work of the doers.

The work itself was rather mechanical, and the pace of life was slower. This was a world where transporting goods from China to America or Africa took months, and even a letter would take several days to arrive. Naturally, innovation was slow. Reliable and predictable output was more valuable than fast adaptation.

And then it all changed

Changing very fast (a reference to The Great Acceleration)

Hyperconnected => complex

After the Second World War, a tipping point was reached, and the pace of change in society exploded. Ever since, advancements in virtually every indicator of human activity have seen exponential growth. This trend, known as the Great Acceleration, continues to intensify today.

The following graph shows how growth across international tourism, telecommunications, transportation, paper production, water use, the number of large dams, fertilizer consumption, primary energy use, urban population, foreign direct investment, real GDP, and the world's population has assumed an L shape.

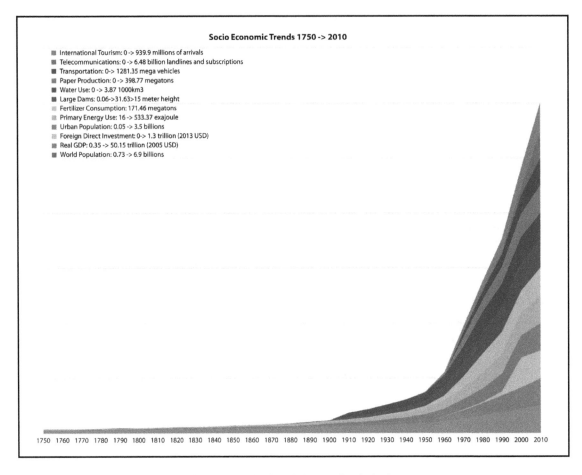

Figure 13.1: A chart showing the Anthropocene Great Acceleration
Source: https://upload.wikimedia.org/wikipedia/commons/6/66/Anthropocene-GreatAccelerationSocioEconomicTrends-1750-2010.png

From an individual perspective, it used to be possible to go to university to study, graduate, and then have a prolific career applying what had been learned. Now, the number of patents filed, and research papers published in virtually every field, has exploded. It is hardly possible to remain an expert in any field without constantly updating your knowledge and re-tooling.

Meanwhile, transportation and communication technologies have connected the world. What happens in Japan or China can affect an organization halfway across the world in a matter of seconds. Constant innovation and change have become a necessity to ensure the survival of an organization.

Simultaneously, the demands of workers have shifted. As society has become wealthier, people are more likely to expect flexible hours, work that feels meaningful to them, career development opportunities, and good coffee, among other trends. This is especially true for developers, and other software engineers, who have seen salaries rise and perks multiply as companies fight one another to attract a scarce pool of talent.

For most organizations, these are seismic changes. The job of thinkers has become increasingly challenging with every passing day. So challenging, in fact, that most managers and executives feel overwhelmed and are constantly playing catch-up, even though they worked many more hours a week than they did a few decades ago.

Separating leadership and management

Society has become more interconnected, leading to greater complexity and faster change. As such, thinkers have been increasingly split into two categories: leaders and managers. This distinction is not about skill or rank; rather, it was suggested that the role of a single thinker now requires two very distinct skill sets.

For academics, the distinction between management and leadership started to take hold around the late '70s, and it has been revisited often with mixed definitions. However, we can generally say that management is about dealing with complexity, while leadership is about dealing with change (reference: *Kotter, J. P. (1990a). What leaders really do. Harvard Business Review, 68, 103-111; Kotter, J. P. (1990b). A force for change: How leadership differs from management. New York, NY: Free Press*). This means that managers focus on planning and budgeting, staffing, controlling against targets, and problem-solving. In summary, managers work to reduce uncertainty and stabilize the organization.

Meanwhile, leaders develop a vision for the future of the organization, align people to that vision through communication, and motivate them through empowerment. Contrary to managers, leaders destabilize the organization, breaking the momentum to foster change (reference: *Vecchio, Robert P. Leadership: Understanding the Dynamics of Power and Influence in Organizations. Notre Dame, Ind: University of Notre Dame Press, 2007. Print*).

The distinction between leadership and management is reflected in the roles of scrum teams. A scrum master facilitates the process because their role is all about organizing. Meanwhile, a product owner will bring in new requests and advocate for the evolving needs of customers and stakeholders; their role is all about fostering change.

Contrary to popular belief, leadership and management are not magical qualities you are either born with or born without. Both leadership and management skills can be learned and developed with practice, just as you can learn to be a product owner or scrum master.

Equally, both polarities – organizing and fostering change – are necessary for a team. A well-led but poorly managed team will be chaotic and fail to deliver on the vision, while a well-managed but poorly led team will become overly bureaucratic and get stuck in the old ways.

Either extreme – too rigid or too chaotic – will frustrate the members of a team, as they will either struggle to adapt and get any work done, or feel trapped in a dull and alienating machine. As a result of either extreme, workers will stop caring for results and disengage, choosing instead to call in sick, cheat on their metrics, keep their best ideas to themselves, or simply do the minimum to get by.

Leadership and management across big and small organizations

Frequently, start-ups are under-managed – there may be few or no processes, and a lot of energy may be spent firefighting and working ad hoc. This often leads start-ups to hire "more senior talent" after they have achieved a product-market fit and can finally raise the necessary funds to build a fully functioning organization and scale.

Meanwhile, big organizations are most frequently over-managed and under-led. They are overly bureaucratic, dismissive of new ideas, and resistant to change. This is understandable when we realize that the modern corporation was born in a time where the world changed less frequently and "leadership," as described above, was less necessary. A second reason is that, as an organization scales, the founders or CEO tend to recruit many manager types, who, in turn, recruit more managers, and leadership gets slowly phased out of the middle and lower ranks.

For big organizations, leadership development has emerged over the last few decades as a way to address the gap in leadership skills. The idea is to teach managers to operate more like leaders.

This is an extraordinarily popular idea, and I am sure you have seen some of the countless programs, courses, and books that promise to teach leadership. However, there are serious problems with it. First, academics argue that exercising both leadership and management is extremely challenging, as one tends toward generating order, while the other tends toward subverting it. The people who are truly capable of both are rare.

Second, both the speed of change and the complexity of markets have continued to increase, creating extra demands for both leadership and management. It is no surprise that a single individual would struggle to do both.

The data about how engaged employees feel in most organizations also leads us to cast doubts on the effectiveness of leadership development programs, as 87% of workers worldwide (reference: *Gallup State of the Workplace Report 2017*) are not engaged with their work. Even more worryingly, there has barely been any improvement in how engaged employees feel over the last couple of decades.

So, if teaching leadership to managers is not enough, what then?

Navigating a new world of work

It doesn't matter how much we teach leadership skills to managers. As the complexity of work continues to increase, and lots of expertise must be routinely pulled together and coordinated to solve problems, having a single thinker (a manager-leader) in a team of doers caps the potential of the team. It is just too much to think about for a single person.

In this day and age, no manager or leader can have all the answers. We need every person in a team to be a thinker. Every team member needs to help with the heavy burden of making sense of the world and figuring out not only how to do the work, but what should be worked on in the first place. Otherwise, we quickly end up like the rookie manager described in the opening story in this chapter, trying to be the hero and running out of hours in the day.

Instead of prescribing exactly how the doers under your command should be organized, it is your role to figure out how to use all your team's capabilities to produce value. This means turning your team members into thinkers too, and leveraging their capabilities for leadership and management to complement your own. You manage and lead as a team.

The importance of motivation

Working with thinkers is very different from working with doers. Thinkers can't be told exactly what needs doing. Instead, they need autonomy to organize their own work and contribute original thoughts. If you try to micromanage thinkers, they will wither and disengage from work.

This makes organizing a team of thinkers very challenging, particularly for software engineers promoted to managers, as they start a career dealing with inert machines. Lines of code don't have a will of their own, and if we simply put the right thing in the right place, everything works.

Humans, on the other hand, are rather unpredictable. We respond to new situations based on patterns that are largely subconscious, learned throughout our lives. We are prone to biases and make systematic errors, such as ignoring evidence that disconfirms our strongly held beliefs or assuming we are in control when we are not (reference: *Nickerson, R. S. (1998). Confirmation Bias: A Ubiquitous Phenomenon in Many Guises. Review of General Psychology, 2(2), 175-220*), and we process information differently in different emotional states (reference: *Loewenstein, George. 2000. Emotions in Economic Theory and Economic Behavior. American Economic Review, 90 (2): 426-432*). At best, human behavior is hard to manage.

When we try to get humans to do something, we discover they have an almost sadistic pleasure in rebelling against what others tell them to do. But, when employees feel engaged with their work, companies are 22% more profitable; sell 20% more; have 21% higher productivity; and experience from 65% to 25% less staff turnover, 37% less absenteeism, and 41% fewer quality defects (reference: `https://www.gallup.com/workplace/236927/employee-engagement-drives-growth.aspx`).

Instead of simply informing a team of thinkers of the "jobs to be done," we need to encourage motivation and provide a structure where teams can take action.

Now, you might have picked up that motivation and structure feel rather connected to leadership and management, which is indeed the case. However, they each come in many flavors. Moreover, as you will soon see, it can become a bit hard to distinguish management from leadership when we go into the context of the new methodologies for teams of thinkers.

So, let's park the distinction between leadership and management as an explanation of how we got to where we are (and why so many people will try to sell you leadership training). Instead, let's look a bit deeper into what motivation and organization really mean in our context. Armed with this knowledge, you will be more able to understand what methodologies are right (or not) for your team and thus avoid being sold any magical silver bullets.

Not all motivation is born equal

Research shows that when a task is simple, meaning it doesn't require imagination or complex problem-solving, we can give monetary incentives to increase performance – that is, to increase the quantity of the output. For example, a worker in an assembly line can be paid by the number of parts they assemble instead of per hour of work. As a result, they will feel motivated to increase the number of parts assembled. This type of motivation is what we call extrinsic – coming from the outside – and is the most widely used type of motivation (for example, in the form of bonuses or disciplinary punishment).

Problematically, when a task is about *quality* instead of only *quantity*, and when it requires imagination or figuring out complex stuff, simple monetary incentives don't work very well. In fact, several controlled experiments have shown that offering too big a reward can even decrease performance! (reference: *Ariely, Gneezy, Loewenstein, Mazar. Large Stakes and Big Mistakes. Review of Economic Studies (2009) 76, 451-469*). A frequent explanation of this is that the possibility of a reward increases the stress related to the task, and the stress impedes our creativity and capacity to learn.

In the case of thinkers, who need to be imaginative and solve complex problems, we are better off encouraging what is called intrinsic motivation. This term refers to the inner drive that someone feels –the passion, curiosity, and sheer pleasure from doing something they enjoy.

Developing software requires solving complex problems and imagining new solutions. It provides countless opportunities to cheat, waste time on distractions, and get away with less-than-stellar work. But if we are intrinsically motivated, we are more likely to dedicate care and attention, look for new ways to solve problems, persevere in the face of difficulties, and generally do a good job. As such, software teams are the perfect candidate for methodologies that focus on fostering intrinsic motivation, instead of ever higher bonuses or other forms of external reward.

Thankfully, intrinsic motivation has been well researched, and if we want to foster it, we have good pointers as to what to look for in a methodology. At a glance, people need to feel they have autonomy (they know the rationale for doing something and have opportunities for choice and input), relatedness (feel warmth and connection from the team), and competence (feel capable of accomplishing the job).

What is structure?

Structure used to refer to hierarchy, or, more precisely, to the rankings in the organizational chart, but, in our day and age, that view is too simplistic and of little use. The reason is that the processes we set to work as a team (for example, a daily stand-up or a retrospective) have more impact on how information flows and the works ultimately happen than where someone sits in the hierarchy. So, at least for this chapter, I'll refer to structure as the sum of the processes the team is using.

Here is where things start to get muddled together. We saw that to get our people to feel intrinsically motivated; they need autonomy, relatedness, and competence. All these three things can be facilitated through processes. For example, when we host a retrospective, we give everyone in our team the possibility for input, or, if we host a regular team bonding exercise (say, some celebratory drinks on Friday), we facilitate the feeling of "being in it together" that is key for relatedness. However, having your team feel autonomy, relatedness, and competence also depends on the hundreds of small interactions that happen outside of the key meetings and in the tone and body language used during meetings.

Think about it this way. For you to like a house, it must have both a nice layout and nice interior design. The processes are the layout, the structure. The daily behaviors are the interior design. They complement one another and also affect one another.

You can set your process "perfectly," but if the daily behaviors don't match, you won't get very far. For example, a bi-weekly meeting for everyone to share their learning or concerns can become counterproductive if people show with gestures that they are not listening or are dismissive of what someone is saying.

That is why we can't just copy a set of processes into our team and expect everything to work out magically. Remember, we are dealing with people, and we humans are very resourceful in finding ways to misinterpret, subvert, or undermine something we dislike. For your team to work well together, it is not enough to create a "perfect" design from the top. Rather, you need to engage, leverage, and develop everyone's talents for management and leadership.

The most challenging aspect is getting everyone on the same page. Some people will find a process too stiff and inhumane, while others will find that it provides the right support for the team. It is hard to strike a balance between trying to please somebody and trying to please everybody. You'll end up pleasing nobody.

To avoid this trap, there is a concept I have found particularly useful when coaching teams: process tolerance.

Process tolerance

Process tolerance refers to the general tendency that someone has to like or dislike clearly stipulated rules for how they should interact.

Process tolerance varies from culture to culture and individual to individual. For example, Swiss and Germans prefer very explicit and structured ways for interacting, while Middle Eastern and Latino cultures find that too much process just gets in the way and hampers the work. Equally, engineer types tend to be more process-oriented than "creative types." But bear in mind that these stereotypes have many exceptions.

More process tolerance is not necessarily better. A team that is too process-oriented can spend so much time designing and redesigning processes that no work ever gets done. Meanwhile, too little process tolerance (that is, process aversion) leads to environments where collective output suffers, and pervasive power dynamics can thrive in the shadows. As in most things, extremes are dangerous.

Process tolerance evolves as people get more familiar with a certain methodology. Just like playing a table game for the first time feels awkward and complicated, we soon learn the rules and start to love the game. Also, the more games we learn to play, the more tolerant we become of the awkward initial phase. The important thing is to address any important differences in your team and choose how many processes (or how complicated a process) to put in place according to your team's process tolerance.

One simple way to check for the process tolerance of the people in your team is to have a one-off discussion about it. Gather your team, explain the concept (or, if you prefer, simply read this section), and let everyone comment on their individual experience and preferences. There is no magic formula for calculating it, but through iteration and being open about it, you will have significantly better chances for finding a structure that works for your team.

Quick recap

Now, we have covered a lot of ground in terms of new concepts and theories, which may seem daunting. It's important to recap before we move on to some of the most influential and practical methodologies out there.

We started with the distinction between doers and thinkers. We looked at how, as the pace of change in the world accelerated and markets became more complex, thinkers got split into leaders and managers. Leaders would foster change, while managers would foster organization. Both traits can be learned, and technically, a single person can do both, but that is very hard. Instead, we saw that we need everyone in our team to be a thinker and contribute some mix of leadership and management to the common pool.

Then, we saw that a team of thinkers works best when motivated intrinsically (by interest, passion, and curiosity) rather than extrinsically (by carrots and sticks). We saw that this is achieved by giving them a sense of autonomy (input and choice), relatedness (connection and warmth), and competence (being capable). And finally, we saw that every person has a different level of process tolerance, and we need to take this into account when implementing processes or rules.

So, now let's take a look at different methodologies and frameworks and see how we can use what you have learned to find what is right for you.

The five key concepts in self-management

Over the last few years, hundreds of frameworks and methodologies have evolved under the loose banner of self-management. Unlike *Agile*, which has a manifesto, self-management is an amorphous cluster. Drawing a difference between *Agile* and self-management would be a challenging exercise and would push us into a theoretical debate of little use.

So, for the time being, let's just say that there is a large group of methodologies that allow those closest to the work to make decisions – they aim to enable everyone to act as a thinker.

First, we will look into the most famous of the self-management methodologies: Sociocracy, Holacracy, and Teal. Then, we will cover Nonviolent Communication – not quite self-management, but a powerful framework to guide the individual transformation necessary for these new ways of working.

Finally, we will look into Dynamic Change – a next-generation framework that, among other things, serves to map the key process of your team, ensure nothing essential is forgotten, and enable a path for purposeful development.

1. Sociocracy

Sociocracy has its origins in social science, with the actual term having been coined as far back as 1851 by a French philosopher named Auguste Comte. He believed that a government led by sociologists would use scientific methods to meet the needs of all the people, not just the ruling class. And to this day, that basic egalitarian idea and faith in the rational discussion are at the core of Sociocracy.

Throughout the 20th century, Sociocracy started to be applied within organizations as a form of management, first by Kees Boeke and his wife, Beatrice Cadbury. Later on, it became formalized in different principles that an organization could adopt by an electrical engineer and former student of Boeke, Gerard Endenburg.

What is Sociocracy?

Sociocracy today has multiple flavors or schools of thought, from the principles Endenburg codified to a collection of patterns recently assembled by **Sociocracy 3.0 (S3)**. With Sociocracy, each organization can apply and experiment with different processes and organically evolve toward a more self-managed form. Nonetheless, a few key principles must be upheld for an organization to be deemed sociocratic:

Organizing in circles

Sociocracy moves from individual roles with authority over a specific area to "circles" composed of the different stakeholders or people involved.

Each circle is semi-autonomous, meaning it has the responsibility to execute, measure, and control its own processes in achieving its goals, but also receives feedback from other circles. When a decision impacts the domain of other circles, it is made in a "higher circle" composed of representatives of each of the affected circles.

Consent over consensus and authoritarianism

All policy decisions, including those that pertain to the allocation of resources and constrain operational decisions (including the election of people to roles), require the consent of all members of a circle.

Day-to-day operational decisions are made by the operations leader within the policies established in circle meetings. This means that, instead of the authoritarianism of traditional management hierarchies, a circle aiming to make a decision on a policy must ensure that all its members find it acceptable.

Importantly, this is different from consensus. According to Reijmer, the co-founder of the Sociocratisch Centrum, "By consensus, I must convince you that I am in the right; by consent, you ask whether you can live with the decision."(*Jack Quarter (2000). Beyond the Bottom Line: Socially Innovative Business Owners. Greenwood Publishing Group. pp. 56-57. ISBN 978-1-56720-414-8*).

Feedback between higher and lower circles (double links)

Each circle will have someone sent by the circle above called an "operational leader" who, in turn, sends a "representative." This double linkage creates a feedback chain and, coupled with the principle of consent over consensus, profoundly alters the power dynamics in an organization.

Why should I care about Sociocracy?

Sociocracy gives everyone ample opportunity to contribute to policy (allocation of resources and directing of operational decisions) as thinkers. As a limitation, however, outside of meetings, regular managers are still in place.

During meetings, Sociocracy leverages the intelligence of the whole team instead of a single leader or manager, which means better decisions and better buy-in from the team. Additionally, through the mechanism of consent, it gives people input (related to the need for autonomy) and, through the circles, encourages relatedness. Autonomy and relatedness, in turn, encourage a lot more intrinsic motivation, which translates to a better mood at work, people staying longer in the team, and higher performance.

In practice, Sociocracy can be tricky to implement as it is a big mindset shift. Sociocracy is based on egalitarianism, while traditional management relies on authoritative power hierarchies. For a successful transformation, some process tolerance, as well as the headspace to study and learn the new system, is necessary.

A transformation into Sociocracy is similar to an *Agile* one, in the sense that both require significant time and attention. Advantageously, Sociocracy, and *Agile* are very compatible and mutually reinforcing, and a team that has taught one will find it easier to learn the other.

Compared to Holacracy, which we will review next, Sociocracy is significantly less cumbersome and can be adopted little by little or experimented with before deciding to take on more elements of it.

How do I use Sociocracy?

The first step would be to familiarize yourself a bit with the principles. There are many resources online you can find through a simple search. I wouldn't recommend trying to adopt it in your first few days as a manager as it is somewhat of an advanced practice. In an ideal world, this would be taught from school, and then the issue of learning new rules wouldn't be such a barrier, but we have to start with what we've got.

Before making any formal changes within your team, I would also suggest discussing the principle of consent over consensus at length. Although it can be summarized in three words, this principle is a radical departure from the way we have been educated and the way most organizations operate. It will require a lot of repetition and several trials and errors before everyone "gets it."

A simple way to dip your toe into the water is to explicitly start using consent as the decision-making mechanism for low-stakes decisions that nonetheless require input from different people. As you get comfortable with the mechanism, you can move to higher stake decisions.

From that point onward, you can begin to implement more formalized practices (Sociocracy 3.0 has a great wiki of practices on their website), although it might be wise to check with your boss and enlist a specialized coach to help you navigate the numerous pitfalls of a large transformation.

2. Holacracy

Holacracy started to take shape between 2001 and 2007 in a small company by the name of Ternary Software. Its founder, Brian Robertson, experimented with ideas from Sociocracy, *Agile*, Lean, and other methods, until he eventually decided to start HolacracyOne together with an entrepreneur by the name of Tom Thomison. Although Ternary Software failed and shut its doors in 2008, HolacracyOne thrived as a vehicle to further mature Holacracy and package it for use by other organizations.

Holacracy surged in popularity in Silicon Valley. Twitter co-founder Evan Williams started his new company, Medium, with it and later introduced it to Tony Hsieh, founder of Zappos. Hsieh loved the idea and Zappos, with 1,500+ employees at the time, became the largest ever company to adopt the system across all its departments. This led to a surge in coverage and attracted even larger clients, including Google, who tested it in one of its teams.

Although Google, Medium, and Zappos have since dropped Holacracy (or their implementation of it), it largely remains the most popular of all self-management systems.

What is Holacracy?

Holacracy is the most extreme of self-management systems. Contrary to Sociocracy's loose set of practices and open intellectual property, the Holacracy brand is well guarded, and they have carefully stipulated all the practices in the form of a constitution.

HolacracyOne claims the constitution should be implemented in full, as only implementing some of the rules will lead to an unsustainable model. They use the analogy of learning to play soccer, where a person starts with a full set of rules. Even if the quality of their playing is poor, with the rules, they can progressively build up the skill to operate within the rule system.

Holacracy borrows heavily from Sociocracy. The idea of circles is taken as is, double links between the circles ("representatives" and "operational leaders") are rebranded "lead links" and "rep links," and consent over consensus is embedded in Holacracy's meeting protocols. Although, that latter point is taken further with something they call **Integrative Decision Making**.

Holacracy places a very strong emphasis on making responsibilities explicit and giving people the freedom to make decisions freely within their area of authority. Its main mechanism to accomplish this goal is breaking traditional job titles into multiple roles, each with clearly articulated tasks and responsibilities. Roles are modified, created, eliminated, or redistributed frequently, but this does not mean a person is necessarily hired or fired. Rather, a change to a role simply signals an addition or subtraction from someone's list of responsibilities.

Holacracy is primarily experienced as a set of recurring meetings. These meetings are heavily structured and fall into two categories, each with a distinct and clearly stipulated format. The first format is monthly governance meetings, where roles are created, modified, and transformed through the processing of tensions that the members of a circle might be feeling. Instead of discussing operations, governance meetings are designed to give the right authority to the right person who will make the decision in their own time.

The second format of meetings is weekly tactical meetings, where regular work is coordinated between roles and work sessions on a particular topic (that are not stipulated in the constitution) can be scheduled. Note that work sessions are discouraged as they can easily allow old power structures and consensus-led decision making to creep back in.

Governance meetings fulfill a similar function to retrospectives in Scrum, while tactical meetings are closely related to *Agile*'s meeting of the same name or weekly stand-ups. The main difference, and it is a crucial one, is that Holacracy gives a very detailed protocol for how to run these meetings. In theory, these detailed protocols safeguard against the pitfalls of power dynamics, office politics, and groupthink.

Holacracy is often perceived as rigid, which, according to Brian Robertson, is a correct criticism. The system tries to "bring polarities together to exploit the benefits and minimize the downsides of each." In this sense, it creates a very rigid process that holds power (instead of the boss being the ultimate source of power), so that everything else can be fluid and change quickly.

Why should I care about Holacracy?

Apart from Holacracy being a word, you will certainly encounter Holacracy if you explore the cutting edge of management, Holacracy is a powerful system. It can foster more autonomy, personal growth, and agility than most management systems or even self-management systems.

It is also useful to know that most people claiming to do Holacracy are not. Rather, they are using a bastardized version or their own construct that is somewhat inspired by the Holacracy Constitution. Most of the criticisms come from half-baked implementations that failed, rather than from a deficiency of the Holacracy Constitution.

How do I use Holacracy?

Because of the large number of complicated rules, Holacracy feels rather awkward to most people and requires an inordinate amount of process tolerance for a team to accept. Even after five days of training (costing more than $3,000), I have seen people criticize the system as being inhumane or trying to repress emotions. In theory, Holacracy's detailed rules create spaces where emotional outbursts are allowed and even encouraged. However, the fact that technical details such as this are frequently overlooked represents Holacracy's biggest challenge. It is too complicated for most teams to afford the dip in productivity that temporarily occurs, as attention is shifted away from work and toward learning the system.

A transformation into Holacracy shouldn't be attempted except by the most committed and process tolerant of teams. Furthermore, it should be attempted only with significant support from an experienced coach and abundant training for as many team members as possible. As a guidepost, training for one individual can take four days and cost between $2,500 and $4,000, not accounting for salary for the week, travel, or accommodation expenses. Consequently, a good practice before such a transformation is ensuring that a large majority of the team is aware of the colossal nature of the challenge and is still willing to attempt it.

3. Teal

Teal usually refers to the work by Frederic Laloux with his book, *Reinventing Organizations*, published in 2014. The use of the word Teal originally comes from integral theory, which inspired Laloux's work.

Integral theory was developed by Ken Wilber, who compared hundreds of models and frameworks of consciousness development to draw commonalities and define a scale of consciousness. Integral theory proposes that consciousness evolves throughout this scale, and, although a single individual will experience back and forth, and generally be inconsistent, we can talk of multiple stages of development within the scale as a useful model.

Laloux used the stages to map types of organizations where, depending on the stage of consciousness, distinct practices and behaviors would emerge. More recently, a community has been formed around a wiki with information on different practices and general knowledge of this approach.

What is Teal?

For his book, Laloux visited multiple organizations that he thought showcased practices that matched a new consciousness paradigm, called Teal. Importantly, none of the organizations used as case studies show all the characteristics of this paradigm. As such, Teal (as self-management) is more of a collection of disjointed practices than a clearly articulated management system.

For a quick overview, the stages are as follows:

- **Red**: Power is exercised constantly by "chiefs" to keep foot soldiers in line. Fear and unpredictability hold the organization together. [...] Wolf packs are a good metaphor for Red organizations.

- **Amber**: Strive for stability and characterized by clear roles and ranks within a hierarchical structure. Leadership is exercised through command, and control and compliance are expected throughout the organization. Stability and order are enforced through rules and processes. Innovation is not encouraged, and competition is viewed with suspicion. The dominant metaphor is that of an army.
- **Orange**: Current management thinking, which is focused on the competition, innovation, and performance [...]. Leadership changes from command-and-control to predict-and-control (management by objectives). The organization as a machine is the dominant metaphor. Most large corporations operate from this paradigm today.
- **Green**: Strive for harmony, tolerance, and equality. While retaining a pyramidal structure, Green organizations focus on empowerment to lift motivation and to create great workplaces. They go beyond the shareholder focus of Orange to embrace all stakeholders. Family is the dominant metaphor.
- **Teal**: Three principles characterize this stage of organization:
    - **Purpose**: The organization is an independent "being" with its own purpose. People's actions are guided not by orders from someone up the chain of command, but by "listening" to this purpose.
    - **Self-Organization**: The hierarchical "predict-and-control" pyramid of Orange is replaced with a decentralized structure consisting of small teams that take responsibility for their own governance and for how they interact with other parts of the organization.
    - **Wholeness**: Assigned positions and job descriptions are replaced with a multiplicity of roles, often self-selected and fluid, and people bring their whole selves to work (emotions, desires, ambitions, and more, not just "the rational mind").

When all three characteristics of Teal (purpose, self-organization, and wholeness) come together, we have an organization that feels and perform, very differently. Instead of a machine dedicated to making money, we have something that feels alive, and is "more than the sum of its parts." This is how we arrive at the type of organization that inspires customers, employees, suppliers, and partners to contribute more and create value together.

Why should I care about Teal?

The link between consciousness stages and organizational practices is useful to strategize around the sort of processes or practices that can be introduced to a team. This link also helps you anticipate the team's reaction to these processes. Teal is a powerful tool to inspire people to explore other forms of organizational management, and its theories can be used to inform personal development. Finally, the online wiki at `http://reinventingorganizationswiki.com` is a good resource to discover practices your team could adopt.

How do I use Teal?

Contrary to Sociocracy or Holacracy, which have clearly defined rules and principles, Teal is more akin to philosophy. In fact, Laloux mentioned Holacracy as an example of practices tending toward Teal.

The ideas that Teal encompasses can be studied, reflected upon, and experimented with. But ultimately, it is more of a lens to understand human behavior (including your own) and inform a path to move things forward.

Because of this somewhat abstract nature, it is easy to start small with Teal and add more practices over time. If you need help along the journey, you can use "Teal coaches," who should be able to support you both on the processes and the consciousness development side. Finally, whether exploring Teal-related practices is right for you and your team depends on your personal development ambitions and capacity to set time and attention aside for it.

4. Nonviolent Communication

The **Nonviolent Communication** (**NVC**) methodology is the brainchild of Marshall Rosenberg, a clinical psychology Ph.D. and peace activist. He developed NVC's basis in the late 1960s while working to reconcile communities after long periods of racial segregation and mediation between rioting students and college administrators.

Marshall started by asking himself why some people find violence so enjoyable that they find it heroic and seek to punish others. He also saw that other people get their joy not in punishing "bad people", but in contributing to others' wellbeing. He noticed that these two groups use very different languages and that these languages are learned culturally.

Marshall explored where the violence-serving language originated. Based on archaeological studies, he found it to be some 8,000 years ago as the concept of "superiority" emerged in society (that is, some people being better than others, for example by divine right). He could also see that nonviolent language, which has always existed and continues to this day in pockets across society, is based on identifying the needs of everyone involved and finding strategies to fulfill them.

Marshall iterated and refined NVC as a methodology to learn and develop nonviolent language in groups, thus transforming the group dynamics from being about competition and oppression to compassion and cooperation. His success led him to become a traveling peacemaker, working in more than 35 countries a year by 2014, and accumulating numerous awards. He passed away in 2015, but the Center for Nonviolent Communication, which he started, continues his mission with a growing global community of trainers and facilitators.

What is NVC?

NVC is primarily a conflict resolution methodology. However, because of its profound impact on those who embrace it, NVC opens an intensive path to personal and group transformation.

NVC supposes that all human behavior originates from attempts to meet universal human needs. Although these needs are not in conflict, the strategies for meeting these needs can clash, or miscommunication can create the impression of a clash.

To resolve the impasse, NVC suggests the following steps in a conversation:

1. **Observe and recap**: Separate the facts from the judgment of the facts.
2. **Describe emotions, not positions**: "This makes me feel X way" as opposed to, "I think that X should be..."
3. **Identify needs**: What is the unfulfilled basic human need that is generating those feelings?
4. **Make a request**: Ask a concrete action that the other person can undertake to help you satisfy your basic human need. Importantly, requests are distinguished from demands in that one is open to hearing a response of "no" (a "no" should lead to further inquiry about the other person's needs).

These steps look deceptively simple. However, adopting a nonviolent form of communication means a dramatic shift in the way we judge other people and their needs. Practicing NVC means practicing empathy and compassion. In Rosenberg's words, "I wouldn't expect someone who's been injured to hear my side until they felt that I had fully understood the depth of their pain."

Why should I care about NVC?

As we have seen, the archetypes of a manager or leader that we learned in old-fashioned hierarchical structures, such as in school or in previous jobs, are rather counterproductive to motivating and working with a team of thinkers. Self-management systems such as Holacracy, Sociocracy, and Teal offer us team processes, but do little to support the mindset and language shift that is necessary, often leading to the benefits never materializing. NVC, while not offering anything in terms of organization design, is a game changer for the individual and interpersonal perspective. As such, it is an ideal complement to any self-management system. I would go as far as to say that either NVC or practice with a very similar outcome is fundamental to work with a team of thinkers.

For reference, Connor, and Wentworth (*Connor, J. M.; Wentworth, R. (2012). Training in Collaborative Communication in an Organizational Context: Assessment of Impact. Psychologists for Social Responsibility 30th Anniversary Conference. Washington DC*) examined the impact of six months of NVC training and coaching on 23 executives in a Fortune 100 corporation. A variety of benefits were reported, including "conversations and meetings were notably more efficient, with issues being resolved in 50-80 percent less time."

How do I use NVC?

An individual or team can benefit from their first contact with NVC through a more extensive program. I have often lead feedback training based on NVC practice with good results in short windows of time (about 2 hours). However, the largest benefits are unlocked with continuous practice over an extended period of time, as NVC is fundamentally about shifting deeply ingrained patterns of thinking and communicating.

The research mentioned previously, where the executives reported massive improvements in their productivity, was based on a program lasting six months and including 10 days of training (a five day kick-off and then one day a month) and weekly peer-to-peer coaching sessions. This represents the most intensive option.

Fortunately, NVC pieces of training are relatively inexpensive. While attending a day of Holacracy training can cost upward of $1,000, attending a two-day NVC foundation training course can be $200 per person (even less for those with financial limitations).

There are also fantastic videos and resources online that you can use and distribute among your team for a free introduction to the topic.

5. Dynamic Change

Dynamic Change was created by me, Daniel Ospina, between 2012 and 2018. Strictly speaking, it is not a self-management system. Instead, Dynamic Change came about after I saw numerous teams fail to scale and transform.

In these teams, managers were often overwhelmed trying to set up a company identity, culture, and vision; update the strategy; coach and support people; and coordinate work. Meanwhile, line workers felt increasingly alienated and confined to accept the problems they could see but have no say on how to solve them.

Many teams were exploring new ways of working to surmount these challenges, but were overwhelmed with the complexity of the topic and the number of buzzwords out there. They lacked a comprehensive approach for how they could evolve. They could either go all the way with Holacracy, and risk discovering that they lacked the process tolerance or headspace to implement it, or go little by little with different processes from, say, Sociocracy 3.0 or Teal, and risk getting lost in details or deviating their attention to something that would have little impact while ignoring a more pressing challenge.

Frustrated with this situation, I searched for a tool that would allow us to map an organization (be it a team or team of teams), identify the key functions, and focus the work where it was most needed to help the team function in the short term and, over time, evolve to thrive in highly complex and rapidly changing environments. I was hoping for something akin to a **Business Model Canvas**, but designed for the internal workings rather than the strategy. Unfortunately, such a tool didn't exist, so I decided to create my own. It turned out to be a titanic task.

In its current incarnation, Dynamic Change is based on development across multiple fields and methodologies, including Lean, *Agile*, design thinking, self-management, cognitive and social psychology, political science, classical management theory, and systems thinking. Dynamic Change has informed our work for organizations such as Google, Boston Consulting Group, the United Nations, and multiple fast-growth start-ups across Europe and Latin America.

What is Dynamic Change?

Dynamic Change proposes that teams need to deliver on six essential disciplines to achieve high performance and evolve with their environment. Each team needs to find out what the best way for them to deliver on each of the disciplines is with their resources at hand and develop their answers as conditions change.

The six disciplines are as follows:

- **Identity**: Define who you are at the core, what motivates you, and what brings you together.
- **Future**: Scan the environment to understand how it is evolving, align around a vision for the future, and enable the emergence of the new.
- **Change**: Create the space to step back and strategize and bridge the gap between the now and the future.
- **Coordination**: Build the tools and processes to coordinate between teams and individuals.
- **Operation**: Identify the areas of everyday work and organize for quality, efficiency, and effectiveness.
- **Support**: Provide the necessary support for your teams and individuals to develop and thrive.

Each of these disciplines can be carried on by an individual, a small group, or even the whole team through a certain process. However, it is important to divide the work according to each individual's talents for the team to thrive now and in the long term.

Importantly, all the disciplines require recurring work, but not of the same nature. For example, identity work (largely related with culture) is relatively slow-paced and requires ample discussion across the team, while operation work is best suited to rapid cycles and the iterations where generally too much discussion can hamper rather than improve outcomes.

Individuals tend to be more skilled and interested in a few of the Dynamic Change disciplines, according to their personality, role models, and experiences. To help people identify and relate with them, thereby facilitating the identification of relevant skills and preferences, Dynamic Change proposes six archetypes that embody the primary type of work of each discipline:

- **Identity**: The Philosopher distills and shapes the worldview of their team or organization (related to purpose, culture, and values).

- **Future**: The Visionary is well connected with the world outside their team or organization, understands what trends are emerging, and how the landscape will change, and can envision an inspiring future for their team or organization.
- **Change**: The Strategist is able to think many steps ahead, preempting moves, and makes change happen.
- **Coordination**: The Coordinator sees all the moving pieces and can coordinate resources and people to succeed despite constantly changing circumstances.
- **Operation**: The Craftsperson is a master of their craft and loves the intricacies and the finer details that make all the difference.
- **Support**: The Carer supports others to give their best, is a confidante and a shoulder to cry on when needed, and ensures that everyone can contribute physically, emotionally, and intellectually to their team's or organization's purpose.

Now, these are not inherent personality traits; they are social roles. We might fulfill one of them in a certain team but act very differently in another, the same way that we behave quite differently with our parents, friends, and colleagues.

Why should I care about Dynamic Change?

We discussed how organizational management has progressed between the basic division between thinkers and doers, with thinkers having been divided into leadership and management. Dynamic Change takes this one step further to suit the complexity and speed of change that teams face today.

By dividing the work of a team down to its six essential disciplines, we can build a map of our team's processes and capabilities, address risks (improving resilience), and spot areas for improvement and innovation (improving performance). We can have all this in the comfort that we haven't forgotten anything essential and are prioritizing for the areas that will have the biggest impact.

Moreover, Dynamic Change allows the liberation of people from ill-fitting roles. For example, a salesperson not particularly talented at closing sales (operation discipline) but with a great mind for strategy (change discipline) will be trapped in a line worker position for years while wasting their other talents. On the other hand, a skilled craftsman, say a graphic designer, is often promoted into a role that takes them away from what they do best and, instead, gives them coordination and support responsibilities that they have not trained for before, might have no talent for, and often don't enjoy.

In traditional management, the skilled craftsman who is promoted to manager is only motivated by a higher salary and an ego boost and thus becomes a mediocre coordinator, supporter, strategist, visionary, and/or philosopher. In Dynamic Change, we are adapting everyone's contribution to their best talents and motivation, thus improving the performance and resilience of our team, and charting a course for its continuous improvement and evolution.

How do I use Dynamic Change?

Dynamic Change serves as an anchor and starting point for many other methodologies, allowing a team to diagnose the root cause of their challenges and figure out where to start creating solutions and new possibilities.

The usual methodology consists of an initial "diagnostic workshop," where the team will assess how much clarity and alignment they have (usually very little), what areas require improvement first, and what strengths and capabilities they can count upon. Based on this diagnosis, the team can pick which methodologies or tools to try out first.

A team can choose to carry this workshop by themselves, and a new book is being developed to facilitate self-help scenarios (`https://www.danielospina.info/book`). However, the support of an expert facilitator is encouraged to smooth the process and ensure it is carried out properly. This is an area that Conductal specializes in.

Management systems – a comparison

It's useful to compare these management systems with each other, now that we've looked at them in turn. Here's a high-level comparison chart:

	Sociocracy	Holacracy	Teal	NVC	Dynamic Change
What is it?	A collection of practices for self-management and a mode of organization based on organizing in circles, decisions by consent, and double linkages between circles.	A fully-fledged system of rules and processes for a self-managed organization.	A stage of consciousness development in an organization based on purpose, wholeness, and self-management and collection of related practices.	A method and philosophy for using compassion and empathy to transform relationships and learn to treat others as thinkers.	A framework to diagnose teams and improve resilience and performance by organizing processes, talent, and attention around the essential disciplines of teamwork.
Why should I care?	An important precursor to many of the other frameworks and a wonderful resource of well-tested practices.	The most famous and perhaps most radical of self-management systems.	An inspirational tool, a fantastic collection of practices, and a way to link personal development with the organization design.	A powerful tool and a necessary complement to enable other self-management frameworks and generally better relationships.	Serves as a map and diagnostic tool to reduce the risks and improve the effectiveness of any self-management transformation.
How do I use it?	Possible to adopt little by little. Multiple resources (training, books, articles, and more) and coaches are available across the world.	Only use if fully committed and use extensive support from specialized coaches.	Possible to adopt little by little. A few resources (workshops, a book, articles, and more) and coaches are available in certain locations.	Affordable and possible to adopt little by little. Multiple resources (training, books, articles, and more) and coaches are available across the world.	As a starting point and guide for team and organization development. Workshops and facilitation available, and a book being written.

Is it safe to try at home?

Many of the concepts we have reviewed might seem blurry at the moment. Organizations are only starting to realize how outdated management practices cap their potential. Our education system is even further behind, so teamwork is rarely taught. Naturally, the number of methodologies out there can feel overwhelming.

There is no reason to feel bad about it, although there is ample reason to take action.

Organizational management is hardly easy to navigate, especially as a newcomer. But burying your head in the sand is hardly an answer. Instead, you can take self-assured steps by focusing on the needs of the people you are trying to serve, whether they are customers, employees, or other stakeholders.

It is too easy to get drawn into the narrative of one of these frameworks and invest all your time and resources in thought experiments with little impact. Instead, start by defining your stakeholders, identifying their needs, and exploring gaps between fulfilling those needs and the current situation. Only then should you start looking for solutions and inspiration across Lean, *Agile*, design thinking, self-management, or whatever else.

When you finally commit to exploring new possibilities, make sure you are bringing your team along for the ride. Spend enough time listening to what they feel and what concerns, hopes, and desires they might have. Good teams can deliver 10x what a bad one can, but going from low performance to 10x is a journey that must be undertaken together.

Evolving your team is a necessity of our times. Focus on your stakeholders and bring your team along for the ride. You won't look back.

Running experiments with your team

Start small and grow your ambitions over time. Unless the situation calls for desperate solutions, a good way to start is brainstorming small experiments to carry out with your team.

Many teams fail because they try too many things and lack continuity. A good practice is to set a small but regular amount of time to implement and evaluate the outcomes of new processes. The name of the game is continuity.

Finally, don't hesitate to ask for help. This is a big and impactful topic, and even seasoned, and talented managers are relatively clueless. Find yourself a mentor, peers you can brainstorm with, and a good sounding board to explore ideas.

Getting expert help

Organizational management is in the middle of a revolution. What was considered good practice for decades is quickly turning outdated, and many new systems rise to fame and are forgotten with equal speed. In this climate, even professionals have to work hard to keep up with new developments. It is only natural that you, with all your other responsibilities, might need some input from a professional from time to time. In a rapidly changing world, collaboration is a necessity.

To make the most of your budget, check for biases, prioritize capacity building, and ensure you have the time to extract value from the engagement:

- **Biases**: Most consultants are not brand agnostic, biasing their recommendations. A design-thinking consultant will try to sell you design thinking, while an *Agile* consultant will tend to preach this methodology as the solution to all the world's problems. A way to face this challenge is to ask them to explain how multiple methodologies compare. If they can't explain the downsides of their chosen one, they are probably religious zealots. Another option is to find brand-agnostic consultants who can give you an overview of multiple options. Unfortunately, we are a rare breed.

- **Capacity building**: Traditional consultancies (for example, McKinsey, BCG, EY, and others) thrive on selling recommendations and working top-down instead of developing the capacity of your team to self-organize. The business of consultancies has historically been that of executing change, rather than of enabling it. The difference is important as teams of thinkers will resent someone telling them what to do, unless they are brought early into the conversation. Whenever possible, choose those who take a facilitation or coaching approach over traditional consultant types. When in doubt, just look for interpersonal clues. Do they listen or ignore what you say to keep on talking? Are they open to new ideas and naturally curious, or do they tend to stick to what they know? Do they care for people or only focus on the numbers on a spreadsheet?

- **Making time**: Finally, a very frequent issue is that no one makes time to work with the consultant. An outsider cannot work with your team unless the team makes themselves available. So, before contracting any intervention, ensure you have at least the same amount of time available as you are hiring them for. This time will be well used to prepare the logistics of any talk or workshop, communicate your needs and get feedback, and generally take as much value from the consultant as possible. Organizational consultants won't free up your time in the short term, but they can speed up and guide your journey to create a thriving team.

Summary

The way most organizations operate is based on thinking that evolved during the Industrial Revolution. This is centered around dividing work between doers and thinkers.

Problematically, the world today is changing a lot faster and is considerably more complex than back then. As a result, many teams fall very short of their potential. This is especially true for software teams, who work within the complex process of software development and need to be continually creative.

In our day and age, a single thinker per team is not enough. That is why thinkers have increasingly been divided between leaders (those who inspire change) and managers (those who systematize and instill order). Both leadership and management are necessary, but a single person trying to do both will struggle as they are two very different activities. It is better to work as a team.

Co-leading and co-managing means everyone thinks instead of just doing what they are told. As a consequence, people need to be intrinsically motivated, meaning that they need to care for the job in itself and not just be doing it for some external reward.

Encouraging people to care intrinsically requires them having autonomy. If they feel something has been forced upon them, they will resist and perhaps even rebel. However, if you give them a real choice and make them feel empowered, then they will take more ownership. There are multiple methodologies that have evolved to make this possible. They are loosely clustered under the banner of self-management.

The five main methodologies of self-management are as follows:

- **Sociocracy**: A flexible approach based on circles of people making decisions together.
- **Holacracy**: A full rule system to be followed to the letter.
- **Teal**: A mindset or state of consciousness and a collection of patterns that match the stages of consciousness.
- **NVC**: A communication-based approach based on understanding our needs and those of others.
- **Dynamic Change**: A framework to embody change and focus on the six essential functions that a team needs to do.

When you start exploring these new ways of working, it's vital that you focus on the needs of the people you are trying to serve in order to avoid getting lost in all the buzzwords. Also, make sure to include your team in the discussion.

Include new practices as experiments, starting with small changes, and becoming bolder as you learn.

Finally, if you get expert help, make sure you check their biases. In other words, don't just buy whatever the expert tries to sell to you, but buy what you need instead! Ensure, the expert will help you build the capacity of your team, instead of creating more dependencies, and dedicate sufficient time to the entire process so that you and your team can genuinely learn and improve.

14
Developing Yourself as a Leader

This chapter has been written by *Matthew Bellringer*, founder of *Meaningbit*.

> *"Watch your thoughts; they become words. Watch your words; they become actions. Watch your actions; they become habits. Watch your habits; they become character. Watch your character; it becomes your destiny."*

> — *Lao Tzu, Chinese Philosopher*

Meaningbit

I'm delighted to introduce *Matthew Bellringer*, the guest author of this chapter, which is all about how to develop your own human potential. Matthew is the founder and director of *Meaningbit LTD*, a British start-up that facilitates organizational growth by unlocking human potential within organizations. Using his experience in IT innovation management, Matthew supports digital transformation projects, productization, and workflow automation.

While Matthew is an academic at heart, he also has a wealth of real-world industry experience. I find his work fascinating, and I know you will too. In particular, the down-to-earth way Matthew explains the differences in psychology between a manager and leader; and how to better manage your own self development.

Matthew is particularly interested in the effect of personal growth on organizational performance, and he has worked alongside personal development professionals to bring about lasting, systemic change for the better.

— *Herman Fung*

You can't separate a leader and their team

Think about the leaders you have enjoyed working for most. What was it about those leaders that made working for them so enjoyable? For most people, it's a leader who is *committed*, *honest*, and *inspirational*.

The hard thing about leading in this way is that it's difficult to fake those skills. You might be able to keep it up for a few days but eventually, you slip. Not only that, but it is really exhausting to maintain the effort. Once people realize that you were not entirely honest with them, it's almost impossible to rebuild the kind of trust needed in a high-performing team.

As a leader, **how you act will have a greater degree of impact on your team than anyone else**. Even if people do not consciously realize what is going on, they will imitate the behaviors, values, and beliefs of the people around them – including you, the manager. Over time, this will have the largest bearing on your team's success and happiness.

Working for a great leader is rewarding because some of their energy – their excitement and passion – gets shared with everybody else. This energy permeates everything the team does and makes work a more rewarding place to be, where challenges are a little less challenging. This is an effective team culture.

Everyone in an organization contributes to the overall culture, with the percentage of that contribution roughly in line with organizational seniority. However, each department has its own subtly different subculture, and within a department, each team then has its own microculture. As the team leader, a significant part of your role is to nurture this microculture. The culture is best if it meets the needs of the organization, of your team members and, most importantly, of yourself.

In an era of *customer first*, and of *servant leadership*, it might seem like an odd thing to concentrate on yourself. You need to concentrate on yourself because your self is the only tool you can use to support your team in delivering value to the customer. So, as the saying goes: spend some of your time sharpening the axe before you begin cutting down the tree.

You must lead yourself before you can lead others. A great saying that supports this was once said by Phil Jackson, one of the most successful professional American basketball players:

> *The strength of the team is each **individual member**. The strength of each member is the* **team***.*

> *– Phil Jackson, former American professional basketball player*

The mindset of a leader – Awareness

To successfully lead your team, you need to have the mindset of a leader. This does not mean that you should seek to dominate or control others, nor does it mean you need to think or behave in a specific way. It means the opposite: that you need to notice what is going on around you and respond appropriately as the situation requires. If you're going to be able to do that *well*, you're going to need to know yourself; and you're going to need to be able to understand yourself.

Noticing what is going on around you is harder than you might think. Your nervous system does a wonderful job of filtering out thousands of irrelevant pieces of data every second. You only become aware of the most important and *salient* information around you.

If I ask you to think of fleas, spiders, or other creepy crawlies, what happens? Do you suddenly feel like there might be something there on your leg, or on your arm, or perhaps in your hair? You can relax – it isn't because there is anything there; you're just experiencing the power of *salience*.

Before I asked you to think about insects, your mind filtered out the small feelings that your clothes create on your skin. After I asked you to think about insects, those small feelings became important, and those feelings were made available to your consciousness – they became salient!

It isn't just the external world that we don't always notice. There's a vast amount of information coming from our internal world – our physical and mental state – that we filter out automatically. This information is vital to building better self-understanding.

Awareness of our filters

Which filter we use at any given time is decided by where we place our attention as managers. Psychologists call this effect *priming*.

If we're hungry, we will be more sensitive to food smells or fast-food adverts. This is one of the reasons that grocery shopping while hungry is a bad idea. Priming happens on an emotional level too. In a good mood, we tend to notice things that are positive. Being in a bad mood makes you see negative things in the environment, and in people.

These automatic filters are vital for our survival. Without them, we'd be overwhelmed by sensory input and thoughts, all colliding at once. Our filters allow us to engage effectively with a complex world. They allow us to concentrate on what really matters. In this sense, they are like scripts, triggered to run at certain times or on certain events.

The problem is that these triggers are automatic, and the scripts run without any checks or error message output. Sometimes, we learned useful automation a while ago, but some aspect of the environment has changed, so it is now suboptimal. The script we are running used to work perfectly, but now it lacks a key component, so its output isn't as good. And sometimes, we mis-learned the automation *entirely*.

Our brains try and solve all problems with the minimum effort necessary, and sometimes over-simplify problems. These kinds of assumptions, over time, can lead to habits that don't serve you as a manager.

Awareness of our automatic habits

We do not think things through from first principles in every situation. We do not build up all our knowledge about the world from scratch every morning. If we did, we'd barely be able to get out of bed. Instead, we operate from mental models that we use to interact with the world. We categorize and then use those categories to inform our behavior. These categories are built over time, from direct experience and from things we've learned. They affect how we respond to the world and how we interact.

The problem is that our mental categories are also built on incomplete information. We haven't experienced every example of a category – there will always be exceptions – and we might have assigned something, or someone, to the wrong category entirely. We're unlikely to know everything about that category of thing in the first place. It's all an approximation created so we can interact.

Our automatic habits, and the thoughts, beliefs, and category judgments by which we model the world, make up a significant part of our subconscious mind. Because these things happen without entering consciousness, they can influence our thoughts, behavior, and responses, without us even knowing they have done so. It is only by becoming aware of the way that you are and the way that you react that you can develop the sensitivity and skills to be an effective leader.

Awareness makes management easier

This approach has a further benefit: by developing knowledge and self-awareness, you don't need to exert as much effort on self-control. Being aligned with the work that you're doing allows you to devote that energy to the work itself. You don't have to spend effort making yourself do the work.

Over time, you can establish a positive feedback loop in which this greater energy can be used to develop knowledge and self-awareness further. As this develops, being the best version of you in the circumstances becomes natural and effortless.

And when things get tough, you will have developed good habits to fall back on. The *Harvard Business Review* found that how a team behaves under pressure (`https://hbr.org/2018/12/when-managers-break-down-under-pressure-so-do-their-te ams`) is what determines the team's view of their boss. Coming over as inauthentic, even if it seems like the right way to behave, can prevent your team from trusting you. By focusing on your own development, you can ensure that your behavior is consistent in all situations, giving your team the foundation that they need to manage issues confidently.

By understanding yourself, you can better understand how you relate to others. This applies when things are going well, and when things are going badly. You can change your approach to meet the needs of the situation you're in. This understanding comes from paying attention to how you feel, how you behave, and how you respond to what is going on around you. That attention is called awareness.

The subconscious mind of a manager

A quick note on our terminology regarding the two words *unconscious* and *subconscious*. You have likely heard that both unconscious and subconscious refer to the parts of our mind where we are not aware. However, there is a crucial difference between these two terms, which I'll explain now.

The *unconscious* refers to parts of the mind that are wholly inaccessible to the conscious self. There is nothing you can do to access your unconscious; it is like trying to lick your elbow. The *subconscious*, on the other hand, refers to those parts of the mind that are filtered out in everyday life, and yet are theoretically accessible to our conscious self.

It can certainly be difficult to bring something that is subconscious right back into our awareness. To bring something back into your awareness you might have to pay attention in a certain way but with practice, it is quite possible for us to access our subconscious.

Throughout this chapter, we are focusing on the subconscious – and how we can be better managers with greater awareness.

Developing awareness as a manager

There is one major problem with developing your own awareness: it doesn't happen automatically. The outside world is distracting – you could spend your entire time occupied with it. You might feel the pressure to be constantly busy, and for sure most people don't have a lot of time built into their day for stopping and taking time to reflect.

The result is that you probably spend most of your time each day on automatic pilot. You are pulled from one thing to the next – emails, a team member in need, a ticket – without ever stopping to breathe. In this situation, there is no chance to develop the kind of awareness that might prevent issues from arising in the first place. You never have the chance to build a better set of tools to deal with them.

There are many approaches to developing awareness, from the ancient to the modern. These range from mindfulness and meditation, to writing a journal, to going for a walk. It is not overly important which approach you choose, or which combination of approaches you choose. What does matter is that you are able to build a strategy for more awareness into your everyday life. This chapter will give you some reflective practices to help you increase your awareness and become a better manager as a result.

The value of reflection for managers

Reflection allows you to explore your subconscious. It allows you to examine how you behave in specific circumstances, and why. Over time, reflection allows you to change your automatic reactions into more helpful ones.

Think of this process as a code review for your internal programming. It allows you to make small, immediate changes and to understand if larger refactoring work would be valuable. In a personal context, such refactoring might mean a holiday, or some work with a coach, or indeed the development of a new reflective practice.

Reflection is incredibly valuable because otherwise our behavior is dominated by the subconscious mind. Without reflection, we will act without conscious awareness for over 90% of the time. So, small tweaks to our subconscious programming can be far more effective than consciously adopting an entirely new approach. By temporarily bringing your subconscious behavior under conscious control – becoming aware of it – you have the chance to modify your habits. You can re-write the underlying code of your mind.

Reflection and awareness

Working with the subconscious mind is useful for another reason, too. The subconscious gets on with most of its work in the background. It is like a service running without any desktop notifications. Unlike a computer, though, resources are not shared between the conscious and subconscious. The subconscious has far more resources to do that work than the conscious mind. If you direct it appropriately and stop to listen to what it is reporting, you can use it to solve hard problems and gain insights.

Have you ever been in the shower, or walking down the street, thinking about nothing much, when the answer to something that has been bugging you for a while just pops into your head? This happens when the subconscious mind has been working away quietly at the problem. When your conscious mind becomes quiet because you're not actively thinking, this solution can float to the surface.

While you cannot guarantee a solution every time, you can increase your chances of gaining this kind of insight. If you give your subconscious mind the tools it needs, it will carry on with a problem for as long as it takes to solve it. You need to prime it by giving it a clear idea of the problem itself.

Once you've done that, do something completely different. If that doesn't work after a few days, have another go at priming the subconscious – focus a little more deeply on the problem, or try and get it out of your head and into a whiteboarding or mind-mapping session.

As you build your ability to reflect, you will find out increasingly more about yourself and your world. However, reflection happens after the event; it relies on memory. In contrast, awareness is the quality of knowing what's going on in the present moment.

What's occurring?

"The past is gone, the future is not yet here, and if we do not go back to ourselves in the present moment, we cannot be in touch with life."

– Thich Nhat Hanh

Awareness is not just about knowing more about yourself. It is about knowing more about what is occurring right now. This awareness is called presence. You can be present in your external and internal world. Presence in the external world gives you information about what is going on around you; while presence in the internal world gives you information about what is going on inside you – how you are thinking and feeling.

Awareness of one of these worlds supports the other. For example, you may be in a meeting and suddenly have a feeling of unease. What does that tell you about what is going on? Conversely, you may be feeling angry right now, and therefore interpreting neutral events as negative. By paying attention to both worlds, you can remain focused on what really matters to you.

This ability to put an experience into context is what allows you to *respond*, rather than *react*. Being able to respond, rather than react, is a key leadership skill. It has the following benefits:

- You can focus on the world as it is.
- You can see opportunities that are not immediately obvious.
- You can behave in a way that is aligned with your intentions.

Your environment presents you with many hundreds of choices at any moment. By cultivating responsiveness, you can be sure you're picking the best ones.

Skillful managers don't react!

Skillful managers respond to situations with the richest information and most meaningful goals in their mind. Skillful managers don't just react. Because when we react, we're just following the learned, unconscious patterns we already have.

When we're focused on only our short-term, immediate problems, our reactions are often self-centered. Our reactions tend to spark conflict and worsen arguments. Some people refer to this as *ego-driven behavior*.

The *ego* is a collection of habits, stories, and behaviors in the mind. The ego fulfills an important role – that of preserving the self. The ego's job is to keep us alive. The problem is that it sometimes does that job at the expense of other, more rewarding choices. It can be hard to fight the ego. If you ignore the ego and do something else, it tells you that you are in danger. If you continue to ignore the ego, then it shouts more loudly and you experience fear.

For example, public speaking is something many people are afraid of. Just the thought of getting up in front of an audience is terrifying to many. If you stop and analyze this, though, it seems odd. There's no physical threat associated with public speaking; after all, the audience is hardly likely to get up and attack you.

Giving a speech is terrifying because of the ego. Your ego is deathly afraid of you making a fool of yourself. There's a good reason for this. In our evolutionary past, and living in a genuinely dangerous world, such a mistake might be fatal. At best, you would reduce your chances of successfully breeding. At worst, you'd be thrown out into the jungle to fend for yourself. So, for many people, public speaking triggers existential dread. However, being so afraid when you're giving a talk, while perfectly natural, doesn't help you today.

Speaking to an audience represents a huge opportunity. It's an opportunity that you'll miss if you're paralyzed by fear. And it isn't the only opportunity that your ego can cause you to miss! If the fear of seeming ignorant holds you back from asking a question, you may miss out on vital knowledge.

All of this is particularly important for you as a manager. You will feel pressure to know all the answers and avoid appearing ignorant. If you give in to that pressure, you'll be acting on low-quality information. That will cause you to make mistakes. Ultimately, if you want to take advantage of everything your environment offers you, you will need to manage your ego effectively.

Be here now

While much of the ego works subconsciously, we're often aware of its warnings and nudges in our behavior. These take the form of your internal dialogue: the voice in your head. Being lost in past regrets or worries about the future are manifestations of the ego. Researchers have found that even positive thoughts about the past and future will make you less happy than spending time paying attention to the present moment.

By paying attention to the detailed, sensory information around you instead of listening to your own thoughts, you can be both happier and more effective. That's not something you can achieve immediately, of course, but with practice, and with reflection, it will make you a better manager and a happier person.

Imagine having a conversation with one member of your team. If you are worried about other things while you're speaking to them, you only have a limited amount of attention to devote to the conversation; you're not giving your team member your full cognitive capacity. If the issue is trivial, this might be okay. However, if the issue is serious, either personally or professionally, then you will miss important details. You will lack the capacity to provide the kind of support that a skilled leader gives.

This capacity to listen and be aware is what distinguishes a *good* leader from a *great* one. In English, the word "presence" has two meanings. Its first meaning is the one we've used thus far – to be aware of the present moment. The second meaning, however, has more to do with charisma. When we say a person has a presence, we mean they command the attention of those around them. These two meanings are far more closely related than most assume. **It is by being aware in the present that you develop the quality of presence**.

By being aware of yourself and the environment, and not your own world of thought, you will be there for other people. While they might not notice it consciously, they will notice that you are more competent, more responsive, and an overall better leader.

You treat others how you treat yourself

Your habits and beliefs dictate how you relate to your colleagues. This happens both consciously and unconsciously. It is impossible to know exactly how this affects other people. You do not know their inner thoughts and feelings. You cannot know if they feel treated fairly or unfairly. You cannot know if they feel treated harshly or kindly. However, there is one person with whom we do have that level of insight: ourselves.

During reflection, we can start to understand how we are treating ourselves. Is our own internal narrative, kind, fair, and generous? Or is it harsh, judgmental, and mean? Almost everyone is tougher on themselves than they are on other people. However, the fundamental habits and beliefs that underly behavior are the same, whether you are thinking about yourself or others.

Consider what happens when you make a mistake. Do you try to make amends, then move on, learning as much as you can? Or do you judge yourself a failure and consider yourself worse for having made a mistake? If you're working at the edge of your capacity and learning as you go, mistakes are inevitable. How you view the making of mistakes has a big impact on how much you can learn. If you judge yourself harshly when you make a mistake, you will likely do so with the rest of your team. By shifting to more growth and a learning-based mindset yourself, you will shift your judgments of others, too.

Admitting mistakes and the limits of knowledge is a key skill in a leader. The ego plays a role in this, too, telling you to appear all-knowledgeable and telling you to have an answer for everything. This is an impossible game to win. After a while, you will find yourself bluffing and making things up. This is an extremely dangerous game to play with your team. If you are caught bluffing, the team's trust in you will rapidly evaporate. No one truly follows a leader they don't trust, except to see what stupid thing they'll do next.

If you don't know something, say that you don't know! This gives others the opportunity to share what they know. It gives you the opportunity to learn and it can create a culture in which not knowing is okay. By fostering that kind of culture, you will both reduce mistakes and increase the chances of exciting discoveries. It is only by changing the way you act yourself that you can give your team the tools it needs to be its best.

Learning from mistakes

Your team members are fallible, as are you. Mistakes will happen from time to time. A small number of mistakes is a sign that you're not pushed to the limits of your skills very often, and hence are not learning as much as you could be. Indeed, learning from mistakes is a key part of *Agile* development methodologies. However, it can be hard to manage the mistakes of others whose work you are responsible for.

The first thing to remember when handling mistakes is that they are not intentional. People are doing the best that they can with the tools they have. When investigating what went wrong, do not assume that the person predicted the outcome, even if it seems obvious in hindsight.

Take a step back and look at the situation that gave rise to the mistake. You can follow this checklist:

- Is your team member or colleague learning a new tool or a new platform?
- Have they had enough training and experience for the level of responsibility they've been given?
- Were knowledge-holders available?
- Did any gateway processes work as they should? Were there too many? Too few?
- Are the deadlines reasonable given the quality of work required?
- Is this work the team member enjoys, or would it be better to offer it to someone else?
- Are they able to devote as much attention as they should to the task?
- Is the physical environment appropriate for the work your team is doing?

You can use this checklist to look at your own mistakes, too. Make a list of your own and add items appropriate to your own workplace.

Sometimes your team will make mistakes that you would not have, and this is the perfect chance for them to learn and grow. A team thrives on the diversity of skills. Knowing what you are good at, and what you are not good at, is vital. You can only discover that knowledge by experimenting and pushing limits, some of which will come with mistakes. It's vital to give your team the space they need to do this for themselves. Otherwise, you will prevent them from developing. By doing this yourself, you set an example they can follow. Own your mistakes to grow yourself and let your team know that this is the best way to go.

Treat mistakes as learning opportunities; embrace them. Explore their causes and what they tell you about the world. The franker and more open you can be about your own mistakes, the more the rest of your team will feel comfortable with them. Your team will take cues from you about how to behave. How you approach your own errors will set the tone for how the whole team approaches theirs.

How to discuss mistakes with your team

Integrate non-judgmental discussions about mistakes into team meetings. Be up-front about your own first. Don't just include technical mistakes, either. As you are developing management skills, you will make many mistakes along the way. Creating a culture of openness will ensure that people do not feel afraid to own up to anything that has gone wrong. A blame culture within the team will only lead to more mistakes down the line and will reduce team engagement, too.

The goal of any discussion about mistakes is understanding. Avoid personal judgment and blame. You should look to understand both the personal and organizational context of errors fully. Think of this process as debugging a system, rather than telling someone they've messed up. You can be confident that anyone who has made a mistake already knows that and feels terrible about it.

The natural response to feeling this way is to get defensive. This defensiveness, however, prevents you uncovering the kind of systematic, underlying causes that are vital for your growth, and vital for your organization. You need to behave in a way that helps your team members overcome their own defensiveness, so they feel comfortable sharing the information you need to move forward. This may not happen immediately and will need a good deal of trust between your team members and you.

When you have investigated a problem and found a systematic cause, you must seek a solution. It's no good going to the effort of finding out what happened and then not doing anything about it. Your team will be watching too; what they see will affect their motivation to raise errors in the future. Even if it is an organizational issue that you cannot fully solve, doing what you can lets your team know that you are supporting them to do the best they can.

That support is more than just practical. Your team members need to feel, as well as understand, that you are looking out for them. To be happy and effective, we need to be comfortable with emotions. That means being able to use the information you hold to make effective decisions and respond well to ambiguous situations. Using emotion effectively – neither ignoring it nor letting it dominate – is a key skill in being a leader.

Rationality and emotion in a manager

You might think that emotions are best kept out of decision-making. You'd be in good company. For hundreds of years, people have emphasized the importance of rational thought. We have systematically misunderstood the role of emotion. Recent research suggests this is a significant mistake.

Imagine you are a chess master. You have played many thousands of games; you can think 15 moves ahead. However, just how are you making your decisions? The chess board has around 10^{120} possible configurations. In order to cope with this complexity, expert players rely on emotion first, and then logic, in order to succeed.

Researchers looked at chess players as they were playing. The researchers observed that chess players use emotion to deal with the huge range of different directions the chess game could proceed in. Emotion is used to filter down to a handful of promising scenarios. Once the emotion has done its job, these scenarios are handed off to rational processing. They enter consciousness, and the player becomes aware of different strategies. Each one is compared; they are checked against the details on the board, and one is selected as the next move.

Such a strategy doesn't just apply to chess players. This is an optimal way for you to think as a manager. You use your **complete** mental capacity by combining emotions and thought. Both emotional thinking and rational thinking are, on their own, flawed. The trick is to choose the right approach for the task at hand.

Rational thinking is logical, procedural, and under conscious control. It is thinking on a small scale and at a very fine resolution. It is excellent at checking details and looking for mistakes. Much of this thinking happens in the neocortex, the most recently evolved part of your brain.

However, rational thinking has some major limitations. Its capacity is limited: on average, we can only hold seven pieces of information in mind at any one time. It takes us a very long time to think in this way. Rational thinking also tends to suffer when we're tired, stressed, or otherwise impaired. With too much information, it gets overloaded and tends to shut down.

Emotional thinking is heuristic, intuitive, and mostly unconscious. It is thinking on a huge scale, but at a far coarser resolution. Emotional thinking is excellent at taking in a wide variety of input and coming to a workable conclusion quickly. It can handle deeply ambiguous, incomplete information.

A lot of this emotional thinking happens in the mid-brain, which evolved much longer ago. This style of thinking has limitations, too. Its use of heuristics means that it jumps to conclusions that may be false. Additionally, it isn't under our direct control, so it can often lead us to thought patterns that our rational brain could tell us are not helpful.

Rational and emotional thinking are complementary. Emotions contain just as much valuable information as rational thought. When you need to make quick judgments, and it doesn't matter a huge amount if you're wrong, you can rely entirely on how you feel. When you need to make detailed, logical judgments and have plenty of time, you can rely entirely on rational thought. However, in everyday life, you must use both in order to be successful.

In technology, we have a lot of practice using the rational mind, and many people rely on rationality exclusively. This is a mistake. If you want to achieve mastery as a leader, you must learn to use emotional thought as well. The key is integrating both rational thought and emotion feelings, so they work effectively together.

How to feel

Feelings and *emotions* are synonyms. That's a big clue about how you can improve your use of emotional thought.

We feel emotions as bodily sensations. Becoming more aware of these sensations can make you more aware of the emotions that you are feeling. By linking these with rational thought, you can use all the processing capacity your brain has available.

It is easy to get stuck entirely in thinking mode: you spend all day in your head, working on complicated problems. This can lead to reduced awareness of your wider context. You fall into the trap of seeing yourself as a brain on a stick or seeing yourself as a complex computer.

This image does not reflect biological reality. You are a whole human being, and your brain is more than just a CPU. Your brain works in a constant feedback loop with the rest of your body. Cognition is embodied. Your rational brain gives explanations of the feelings you experience in your body. Those feelings prime the brain to look for certain details. Your mood dictates the kind of things you notice in the world around you.

If you focus on only half of what you are, you can miss significant information. If you are unaware of how you are feeling, you cannot know why your rational mind has focused on a particular thing. It might be because that thing is the most important work detail that you could possibly attend to next. However, it might also just be because that particular thing was the most relevant to your mood at the time!

This is particularly important when you're making complex judgments, and when not all the facts are known. These are exactly the kind of judgments you will be making as a manager and linking the technical work of your team to the wider organization.

How to manage better using emotions

As a manager you can miss huge opportunities to act skillfully with your team if you only pay attention to the rational, thought-based aspect of your mind. If you work with your emotions, you will not miss any opportunities to influence your pattern of thought in helpful ways. Imagine trying to debug a web app but only having access to the frontend. Without being able to see what's going on server-side, you're left guessing about a lot of what's really happening. Similarly, as a manager you want access to the richest possible information in order to do your job well.

Let's explore this in a scenario where you're the manager. Perhaps you're worried about speaking with a member of your team about a tricky subject. Now, if you can make your body more relaxed, you can make your mind more relaxed. By doing that, you make your team member more relaxed. You are far more likely to have a productive, comfortable conversation this way. Your improved ability to control your level of nervousness then prevents the whole conversation from losing its way.

So, by sending your brain an instruction from your body, you can alter the way interactions unfold with your team. To be able to do this, you need to understand which emotions are associated with which feelings in the body. The body responds in different ways to different things.

Researchers have tracked which areas of the body are more active, depicted by warm colors (lighter shades), and which areas of the body are less active, depicted by cool colors (darker shades), in the following diagram:

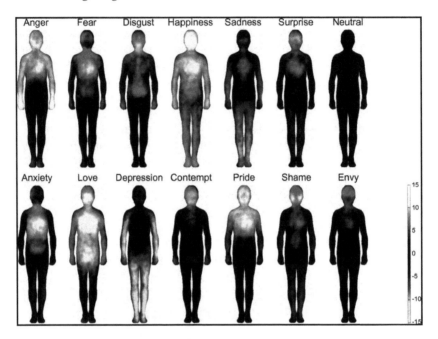

Figure 14.1: Bodily maps of emotions, Nummenmaa et al., 2014
Source: https://www.pnas.org/content/111/2/646

You can use this diagram to examine how different emotions feel in the body. It may be easier to start with more enjoyable emotions, as they are easier to engage with. Over time, though, it's a good idea to aim for an understanding of the whole range of emotions and how they feel in the body. Even the emotions that are unpleasant to experience have an important role for a manager.

All emotions carry important information for us to act on. Anger tells us that someone has crossed a boundary; fear tells us we need to check the environment for threats; and shame tells us we have made a mistake and need to make amends. The sooner you are aware of what you are feeling, the sooner you can respond accordingly.

Think of emotions as a notification message that gets louder and more intrusive over time. It is easy to spot an emotion when it becomes overwhelming and explosive. That is too late. Become aware of your emotions earlier on, because that way, you can respond accordingly. You can act based on the extra information that the emotion gives you, and act more skillfully as a manager.

The information emotions contain is vital for dealing with the kind of complexity you will encounter as a manager. Having a good grasp of your emotional state, and that of others around you is a vital management skill. Like any other skill, emotional awareness can be improved with practice. It may be that you would benefit from developing it further.

Exercise – Assessing your emotional awareness

This exercise is designed to act as a quick test of your emotional awareness. It is not diagnostic, but it should give you an idea of any areas of weakness you may want to work on.

Mark each of the following statements true or false:

1. I can usually maintain a good mood even if something bad happens.
2. Putting my feelings and emotions into words is easy for me.
3. I learn from unpleasant experiences and behave differently the next time.
4. When I don't like something someone has said, I find it easy to tell them.
5. I quickly notice the moods of the people around me.
6. I can tell exactly what emotions close friends are feeling.
7. I can easily talk to someone I am romantically attracted to.
8. I find it easy to buy gifts or plan surprises for those close to me.
9. I can describe my current emotional state – how I feel right now – in detail.
10. I am not afraid of the strength of any of my emotions.
11. I often know when someone is lying to me.
12. Setbacks do not deter me from reaching my goals for long.
13. If someone does something to upset me, I don't brood over what happened.
14. If I feel bad, I usually know why I feel that way.
15. I find it easy to talk to people I have just met.

For each item marked "true," give yourself one point. Add up your scores.

0-5: You have a relatively low level of emotional awareness. You may find yourself frequently overwhelmed by strong and unpleasant feelings. You may also have difficulty interacting with others. You should seek support to develop your emotional awareness further. Doing so will significantly improve your management and leadership.

6-10: You have a moderate level of emotional awareness. You may find your own emotions difficult to handle in more extreme situations. You find some social interactions tricky but can handle others fine. Developing your emotional awareness will increase the number of situations you can handle while staying balanced.

11-15: You have a high level of emotional awareness. You rarely struggle with your own emotions and can respond to them as needed. You are also aware of the emotional state of people around you. You have one of the key skills of leadership and may want to consider how best to put that to use.

Whatever your score, emotional awareness is a vital skill to cultivate. It underpins a wide range of other skills. It will enable you to work confidently across different situations. It will also help you deal with the unexpected. Not only that, but your team will learn from and be supported by your greater emotional ability. They will be able to do their work better as a result.

Leading with intention

The skill of developing our awareness also lets us focus our **intention**. To be able to act with intention, you must have a clear idea of what you are trying to achieve and why you are trying to achieve it. By maintaining awareness of a clear direction for yourself and your team, you know what to do, even in a crisis.

We all know what a day looks like when our intentions go wrong of course. You arrive at work, and as you walk in the door, one of the support team grabs you about a production outage. You scramble to give them a good answer but before you can do that, your manager calls you into a meeting about the problem. You spend the entire day pinballing from one problem to the next, never being able to settle or concentrate on anything. You find yourself saying yes to things you shouldn't and no to things you should. It takes you days to sort out the mess.

Becoming clear on your intentions and remembering to act on them is far from simple. You need to understand what it is that underlies your behavior. Think back to a time when you've worked with an unflappable, steadfast leader. It is their knowledge of the direction of travel and their consistent orientation that inspires confidence in those around them. They can make snap judgments without worrying about consequences, and so respond quickly and effectively.

The catch is that it's too late to come up with that kind of confidence once a crisis has begun. You must be clear of your intentions before it happens – so you can *respond* instead of *reacting*. That way, you will be able to take advantage of any opportunities that arise without getting pushed about by circumstance.

Why are you here?

Do you know exactly why you go to work? What are you managing and why are you managing it? What is it about that work that gives you satisfaction?

Many people assume they just go to work for the paycheck, but research suggests that many people derive much satisfaction from the work that they do. When asked, many people would continue some aspect of their jobs even if they no longer needed money at all.

There are two different kinds of motivation that influence your work: *extrinsic motivation* and *intrinsic motivation*. Extrinsic motivations are those things that come from outside. They might be good or bad. Positive extrinsic motivations include pay, status, and praise from other people. Negative extrinsic motivations are threats or punishments.

Meanwhile, intrinsic motivations are those that come from within our self. Positive intrinsic motivators are things we find inherently enjoyable – things we do for the sake of doing them. Negative intrinsic motivators are things we avoid because we find them fundamentally unpleasant.

The fundamental difference is that to get what you want from an extrinsic motivator, something must happen in the *outside* world: someone must think you have done a good job and they must give you something. To get what you want from an intrinsic motivator, you need to do *work that meets your own standards*; and it needs to be work that you feel good about doing.

In his book *Drive*, the author *Daniel Pink* lists three intrinsic motivations: autonomy, mastery, and meaning. **Autonomy** is the freedom to do as you want, to complete your work in the way that you see fit. **Mastery** is a sense of excellence and skill in what you do. It is the ability to do work, which is of high enough quality to please you. **Meaning** is the ability to do work that connects to the bigger picture. Meaningful work is aligned with your values.

Many people only ever consider extrinsic motivation, and some management theorists considered nothing else for decades. But it's a huge mistake to rely solely on intrinsic motivation because, if you're only motivated by extrinsic things, then you'll need constant external checks and rewards to keep yourself motivated to work. Worse still, you'll get used to those rewards, and you'll need more and better rewards to stay motivated. Over time, you'll become dissatisfied, and the whole thing will feel hollow and repetitive.

To avoid this fate, understand why it is you do the work you do. Get clear on what your extrinsic motivators are. After that, get clear on your intrinsic motivators.

Exercise – Motivator map

Using the following instructions, try creating a motivator map:

1. Take a blank sheet of paper and write down all the things that motivate you to do what you do. Everything that influences you, whether it's something you want to avoid or something you want to get. Don't worry about order, just get everything down.
2. When you have finished, take another blank sheet of paper, and draw lines to divide it into four. This will be your motivator map.
3. Then, label the top-left "Extrinsic negative," the top-right "Extrinsic positive," the bottom-left "Intrinsic negative," and the bottom-right "Intrinsic positive."
4. Write each of the motivators from your first list into the quadrants on the motivator map.
5. When you've written all your motivators on the map, add up how many fall into each category.

You can see an example of a motivator map here:

Extrinsic negative	Extrinsic positive
Avoid getting in trouble with my boss Avoid looking like a fool	Get paid a salary
Intrinsic negative	Intrinsic positive
Avoid being bored	Write beautiful code Solve interesting problems

Ideally, you want more positive motivators than negative, and you want more intrinsic motivators than extrinsic. If that's not the case, try to pick up more work that you find inherently motivating.

Focus your intention as a leader

Examine your intrinsic motivations. How many of them are related to making the world a better place, at least in some small way? These can point you in the direction of what matters most to you. The reason that things matter to you is that they relate directly to your values.

People spend a lot of their time completely unaware of their values. They only notice when something happens, which puts those values under pressure. Once the pressure goes, they forget about them again, and they go back to drifting between different tasks without clear direction.

Instead of letting that happen, take the opportunity to reflect on what matters to you the most. What pleases you when it's present? What angers you when it's absent? These might be things personal to you, such as security or status. They might be things that apply to other people, like fairness or inclusiveness. The important thing is that they matter to you more than anything else.

Aim for a list of three to five things that you really, really care about. If you end up with a longer list, try the values out against each other and see which ones you choose. Read the list back and make sure each of the values resonates strongly for you. You may think that most people share these values, and you're likely right. Where people differ is in the *priority* that they give them. This diversity of values and priorities is important. It's what allows your team members to each focus on their passion without clashing with each other.

By focusing on these core values and priorities, you can get a good idea of exactly what you want to achieve with the work that you're doing. Try and sum up in a single sentence exactly what you're trying to achieve – for yourself, in the work that you do. Make sure that your work covers your core values. You may need to experiment and refine this over time. That's a good thing. Your ambitions grow with you. The key thing is to have a clear idea of why you're doing what you're doing now.

The point of doing this is to become clear about *exactly why* you do what you do. By getting clear on what it is you're doing, you have a fixed point to measure everything else against. This means that, in a crisis, there is no need to work out what matters first, because you already know what your priorities are. All you need to do is select from the available options. You can calmly move toward the best resolution available.

Having a clear idea of your intrinsic motivations – why you are doing what you are doing – is a prerequisite of being an effective leader. Only then can you connect with your team about their intrinsic motivation and work together effectively.

The habits of successful leaders

The challenge most people face once they get clear on their intention is remembering that intention and acting upon it in the short term. It can be easy to forget the big picture when you're in the details. Perhaps you have the intention of setting a good example for your team. You do this is by writing your code according to your organization's style guide. However, you forget and commit poor-quality code to the repository.

To carry through with your intentions, you need to put systems in place to behave as you want. In other words, you must become your own manager. This means working across two separate spaces. The first of these is the outside world. This involves the tools, the systems, and the stuff around you. The second of these is your internal world. To change this, you need to look at building effective habits.

Nudges to victory

The most overlooked influence on behavior is our environment. It's easy to assume that people act as they do because of some innate reason as if it's how they always behave. The thing is, we're all far more influenced by our environment than we are aware. You behave very differently when you're at work than when you're in a bar with friends. You don't have to behave differently consciously. Your past experiences and cues from the environment guide you.

This does not mean you have to be a slave to whatever is going on in the world around you. You can design your environment to help support your plans. You can create a system of "nudges" that give you scaffolding to do the right things. To do this effectively, there are two very human flaws you need to know about.

The first flaw is **forgetfulness**. If you make a plan and then you fail to remind yourself about that plan, you're likely to forget to do it. You might manage a few times, but not enough to make any difference. The way to fix this flaw is to set reminders. These might be scheduled reminders on your phone, or they might be reminders in the physical world that you see from time to time. You might even block out time in your calendar to make space for a task so others cannot crowd it out.

The second flaw is **laziness**. Most people think of laziness as a problem, but it's a natural state of being. It's hard to imagine any animal surviving for long if it spent more effort than needed to get what it wanted. This means that you need to design your environment so that it is easiest to do the right thing. Make it so that the path of least resistance leads you where you want to be – and put barriers in the way of things you want to avoid doing.

A good place to start looking for improvements is the work you do to look after yourself. Remember, your team will follow your behavior, not your words. If you want to build a strong, resilient team, then the first place to focus on is your own wellbeing.

For example, taking regular breaks is one of the most important aspects of working effectively. Set regular environmental cues so that you are reminded to take breaks. Make it easy for yourself to take the right kind of breaks, away from the computer screen, too.

Over time, these little changes add up. Each is a small nudge, but collectively they push toward your objective. You will create an environment for yourself, and for your team, where it is easier to do the right thing. Things will flow, because there's no need to rely on memory or willpower to do what you need to do. Over time, things will become instinctive and automatic. They will become your good habits as a manager.

Habits – Human do-while loops

It's the automatic nature of habits that make them so powerful, and yet such a problem. You can think of habits as cognitive `do-while` loops. They are invoked when a certain condition is met; and then they run and they end when another condition is met. Like all automation, once they are running, they can make life very easy, or wreak havoc, depending on what code they contain.

The first element of a habit is the set of conditions that make it start. Psychologists call this the **behavioral cue**. A cue could be one of a huge range of things, from an external event, such as the time of day, to an internal state, such as feeling tired. The important thing is that when the cue happens, the habit begins automatically, without conscious effort. The cue is the entry point for the loop.

Once the loop has begun, it begins to execute its code. On noticing the cue, you begin your **routine of behavior**. Without consciously being aware of it, you follow the steps that are part of the habit. Once a habit is well-formed, you don't pay much attention to what's going on: you just follow the steps.

Assuming those steps do something useful, you will receive a **reward**. This is the experience that tells you the habit was worthwhile. This is the exit condition for the behavioral loop. Once you've got the reward, you end the habit loop until you next encounter the cue to begin again.

Habits have one important difference from code, however. They self-reinforce. That is, the more a habit is triggered, and the more you get rewarded by doing it, and so the more likely you are to follow it again. You may have already met this concept in modern Artificial Intelligence systems, of course, where neural networks can be taught by reinforcement learning. Unlike a piece of code that is simply being triggered, we are complex beings in a complex environment, and there are many different habits that be triggered every day and every moment by various stimuli. The habits that become ingrained for us are successful habits that have previously gained us rewards. So, we keep doing them of course.

The pros and cons of reinforcement learning

Habits can be a very good thing. You get an awful lot of what you want from the world without thinking about it. Habits guide you where you need to go.

However, this process can go wrong. Sometimes, we follow habits that no longer make sense. This is like trying to run the do-while loop without an important variable being set. In which case, the code runs but the output doesn't really make sense any more. If you have included some error checking – if you are paying attention – then you can spot what's happened and correct it. If not, then the habit continues as before, causing unexpected problems. You waste energy or do something harmful. In short, you then have a **bad habit**.

The other issue with the habit reinforcement mechanism is that some things are just too rewarding. For certain people, at certain times, the reward of a habit is so great that they start to repeat that habit over and over. When that habit starts to push out others, and you no longer meet your basic needs, you're **addicted** to something. The trouble is, every time you perform the behavior, you reinforce that habit again. You can think of addiction as a kind of infinite cognitive loop. All available resources are consumed, feeding something that doesn't help.

To make your life as easy as possible, you want as many good habits and as few bad habits as possible. There are two ways you can achieve this. The first is to use environmental nudges to support your good habits and reduce your bad ones. Refine the conditions in which a loop is invoked. Do things that make it easy to follow good habits, and hard to follow bad ones.

There are some cues that can't be avoided. Maybe you can't avoid that one annoying colleague. The approach then is to change the habitual response into something more helpful. In other words, you still change the code within the loop so that it does something different. To do that requires conscious effort though: you will have to be aware of what's going on and then choose to do something different.

At first, this is hard, but over time, it becomes automatic. It is by repetition that you program your own behavioral loops.

Exercise – Refactoring your habit inventory

The purpose of this exercise is to look at your existing habits and see what room there is for improvement. It is not about doing fewer things that you like! It is about you making it easier to find space in your life for the things that really matter.

Don't be hard on yourself. Remember, many habits were useful once, but no longer serve you. In effect, they have become legacy code. By looking at the habits you have, you're refactoring the unconscious code that you run to become more effective.

1. Find a notebook and keep a record of all the habits you notice for a week. Write them down either as you do them or as soon as you've realized you've done something. Don't worry if you miss a few, or a lot.
2. See if you can break each habit down into its trigger, routine, and reward:
   a. **Trigger** - what is it that starts this habit?
   b. **Routine** - what do I do while I'm doing the habit?
   c. **Reward** - what is it that I get out of doing the habit?
3. Once you've kept the diary for a few days, look at all the habits you've recorded. Try not to judge them as "good" or "bad." Go through them all and decide which ones you'd like to do more, which ones should stay the same, and which ones you'd like to do less.
   a. **Do More**: Look for ways to remind yourself to do this more often and to make it easier to do. Also, look for ways to tweak the habit so that it's more rewarding and makes you enjoy the task more.
   b. **Stay the same**: You don't need to do anything here. Just be aware that things do change, so check back in with these habits from time to time.
   c. **Do Less**: Look for ways to avoid the triggers that start this habit. If those cues really can't be avoided, then look for alternative routines to follow that are rewarding in another way.
4. Repeat this process every few months. Take note of what approaches work best for you and use them to build better habits in future!

Your environment changes you, but you can change your environment. You can also choose to respond differently to that environment. By looking at the way your behavior is automated, or subconscious, you can build more helpful and effective habits. By putting in that effort, you will be able to get a lot more done with a lot less getting in the way.

How leaders use alignment

There are choices waiting for every leader about which directions to take next. This can become something of a problem, because when we're faced with many hard-to-separate options, we tend to pick none of them! Part of your role as a manager is to limit the **choices that your team is exposed to**, so that the problem of decision making doesn't happen to them.

As the manager of yourself, you need to develop a process where your choices are focused. The key to narrowing options down to the point at which you can make a good decision is alignment.

If you are aligned, you know what your strengths and weaknesses are. You know what it is you're trying to do. Then, the people and systems around you will support your intention. Your team then works because everything is lined up and there is little to get in the way. Decisions, and work, and everything else – just flow.

What alignment are you?

One of the first things to consider when you create a character in the RPG *Dungeons & Dragons* is what alignment they are. In *D&D*, alignment has two axes. You can be good, neutral, or evil; and you can be lawful, neutral, or chaotic. What alignment you choose becomes an inherent quality of the character you play, and it dictates how you make a lot of your decisions.

In reality, of course, alignment is more complicated: it is not a fixed trait. In the real world, alignment is the quality that describes how well you fit into what's around you. It's about knowing your internal qualities and creating an environment where these qualities have their greatest effect. It is about working alongside people who share similar sets of values, and who have skills that complement your own. Alignment is about focusing on things that give you the most of what you value. Unlike a game, you do not choose your alignment: instead, you discover it.

The problem is that as you discover your alignment with the world, things change. You grow as a result of your experiences. Your environment changes as a result of your success. You need to adjust how things line up as both you and your situation change. By making this a regular process, you can build a positive feedback loop between your own growth and the situations you find yourself in.

Starting the alignment cycle

If everything will change eventually anyway, where do you start? You start with the one thing you can be sure about: the present moment. Your awareness of what is going on right now – your presence – is the best tool you have. You can, at any moment you wish, stop the automatic flow of events and examine what's going on. This ability to be present in the moment is like having the ability to insert a breakpoint into the code of your reality.

When you first try this, the amount of information can feel overwhelming. There is just too much to focus on, even in a quiet room. But as you practice, you can become aware of more and more. You can become aware of what's going on around you and of your own internal state at the same time. This gives you a place from which you can experiment.

A lean you – Experimenting and iterating

One of the core features of the lean methodology is its focus on testing things. By testing things quickly, you can better understand a complex environment. This avoids costly mistakes. You can approach your own development in the same way. You can experiment and iterate. What patterns of work suit you best? What are your biggest strengths? Who do you work best with?

There isn't one single, ideal solution to be found. However, there are many good ones. The goal is to find one and use that as the basis for finding an even better one. Look at the results of the last thing you did, reflect, and come up with a new hypothesis. Test that and see what happens. Then start the cycle again. The key to doing this effectively is to keep the cycles as short as you possibly can.

Each experiment should give you more valuable information than it costs you in time and effort. That effort might be as small as noticing something that was already happening. It might be altering one small aspect of your behavior to see if that makes any difference. Each experiment should also be low risk, even if it fails. You want to be able to comfortably live with the consequences of any experiment you try.

As you try many small experiments, you'll start to understand how each of the different elements of the world line up and relate to each other. It's not so much about the intrinsic qualities of the nodes that make up the network of you; it's more about how they interact.

Over time, by making many small corrections, you can make the network run more efficiently than you could by trying to implement huge changes up-front. The purpose of these experiments is not just to understand more about the outside world and how it behaves; the purpose is to understand more about yourself and your inner world.

Resistance is information

The biggest clue to what's going on in your inner world is the feeling of resistance. This is the sensation of effort, emotional push-back, or avoidance when you do or think of something. The thing might feel heavy, a huge and high-effort burden. It might rouse strong emotions that create a distraction. Or perhaps you just avoid it altogether, switching to something more comfortable at the first opportunity.

Like other feelings, resistance isn't a bad thing: it's just information. Resistance is a clear message that things are not aligned. Think of resistance as a compiler warning! It's a message to tell you that even if things work, there could be something suboptimal going on. As with other feelings, the key to dealing with resistance is to listen to the message it wants to tell you.

Resistance can be a tricky beast to work with. Sometimes it is a genuine warning, telling you to stay away from something unhelpful. Sometimes, it is your ego trying to protect you from the thing that will allow you to grow the most.

The only way to get good at telling the difference is to practice, but this exercise will give you the tools to start exploring. It is designed to help you approach difficult emotions, so take your time and remember to be kind to yourself. What you find doesn't require any judgment; it makes you neither good nor bad – it's just how things are.

Exercise – Listening to your resistance

This exercise uses a lot of the skills you'll have developed throughout the chapter. It allows you to explore and unlock the stories that don't serve you. It isn't about replacing them with better, more "positive" stories, but about letting go of the judgment that stories bring all together.

That way, you'll spend less time thinking about those stories while events are taking place. That in turn will give you more bandwidth to experience and respond to what is really going on around you.

1. Think back to a time you had to do something you thought was a good idea but felt difficult to do. It might have been asking for a raise, speaking in front of an audience, or raising poor performance with a team member. Try to remember the experience as clearly as you can.
2. How does it feel in your body as you remember what happened? Does anywhere feel tense or uncomfortable? You don't have to understand what these feelings mean; just write them down.

3. When you have explored the feeling, can you link it with emotions? If you find that difficult, use the emotional heatmap from "How to feel." Write down the emotions associated with the event.

4. Sometimes events raise tangled emotions. See if you can approach just one of them, and really feel it. What's the story behind that emotion? What is it trying to tell you? Write down the story that lies underneath the feeling of resistance.

5. Look at the story you have written. How true is it? Is it always definitely 100% true? Can you think of any circumstance, however contrived or unlikely, when it wouldn't be true? Are you making a prediction about how other people or the world will respond?

6. Write down the situation where it wouldn't be true. See if you can produce a story that feels good. Create a scenario that you want to move toward.

7. Try swapping between the two stories, the one that feels bad and the one that feels good. See if you can become comfortable with both of those stories as possible descriptions of the situation.

8. When a similar situation comes up again, try behaving slightly differently. Your reflections will give you clues as to which changes to make. Do you feel differently for having made the changes? Do you want to carry on behaving like that or establish a new habit?

Summary – Work on yourself to lead your team

Management makes new and unexpected demands on you as a person. You can either grow to meet them or shrink away in fear. A big chunk of your success and that of your team depends on how you approach these new demands.

Now you have a range of tools to use that will deepen your self-understanding. Without having yourself as a fixed point of reference, you will not be able to engage with what is going on around you fully. Use your awareness to focus on what matters for you and for your team. Develop the ability to be truly present.

Focus on systematic change, not blame. Use the information that emotions give you to guide this process. Your feelings and your rational mind work best when they complement each other. Be clear about why it is you do what you do, and how that lines up with what other people do. Use the environment to nudge you to where you want to be. Build productive habits to automate your thinking by adjusting triggers, routines, and rewards.

You cannot control external circumstances: organizations and people change. Sometimes, the deserving people suffer, and the undeserving people are rewarded. It isn't that life isn't fair, but fairness doesn't even apply. The one thing you can do in *response* to the unpredictability of working life and a team leader is to work on yourself. That does not mean being selfish. By devoting effort to managing yourself, you can make yourself more effective. The more effective you are, the more you can help other people. And the people who depend on you most at work are your team.

15
Your Next Steps

You have learned *why* you want to change from being a developer to a manager.

You have learned *how* to be a Successful Software Manager.

You have listened to your users and designed a great solution for your customers.

You have even built a great team, who have developed a great software product, and launched it successfully!

So, what's next?

First of all, take stock and be proud of how far you've come. As we discussed at the beginning of this book, the *Developer-to-Manager* journey that you've been on to become a successful software manager is a long and, at times, undefined process.

There is no doubt that you will have been challenged in new ways since your days as "just a developer." Yet, what this means is that you've grown significantly as a professional. The good news is that this is not about to change. To stay successful, you must carry on learning and developing yourself because the entire process truly demands a lifelong learning mindset.

By using the practical suggestions and recommended templates found throughout this book, you will soon be delivering your first (of many) successful software projects. You might have even already done so. If that's the case, then great!

In some cases, despite this confidence–boosting success, I still get approached by a lot of developers and junior managers who are worried about losing their coding skills. The ask me, "Can I still be creative?" Let's get this question answered once and for all, because it's a pivotal factor in maintaining your personal satisfaction and motivation in the long-run.

Can I still be creative?

Yes. Absolutely, yes!

In fact, being creative is an incredibly important skill to have as a manager. With this new position you find yourself in, you need to be flexible and adaptable, and, at times, be able to create something out of nothing, such as having to invent solutions to problems that others may have simply not even seen.

Your role now is to focus on generating ideas to inspire and motivate your team, who may be thinking that they've seen it all. That may not be the definition of being creative that you had in mind, but as a manager, your job is now supporting, empowering, and enabling others to not only write more code but to write better code. It also means that the focus of your creativity needs to shift from purely focusing on writing ingenious code that leverages the latest technologies, to seeing and understanding what the obstacles to achieving this may be for other people, in both the present and the future.

So, your first-hand experience of being a brilliant developer is invaluable. You have seen and painfully experienced all the likely roadblocks to a developer's creativity yourself. Perhaps, through this, you might have a good idea of the more unusual and exceptional challenges that you're going to face. Whatever your situation, this will help you to anticipate any issues that you or your team may face, before allowing you to solve them quickly, or preferably avoid them altogether in the first place.

Having said that, there is always the opportunity for you to still think like a developer and to be in touch with the code. Whether you're a team, project, or delivery manager, you can, and should, still know what is happening on your software project at even the code level, and, more importantly, how the people working on it are. You should never be that far from the code; after all, it is your primary deliverable!

As a manager, you can still be involved in several different hands-on matters, including:

- Code reviews
- Design meetings
- End-user testing feedback

In fact, and especially on a large-scale project, it's likely that you're the person who makes these things happen. So, because of that, you'll have some choice or, at the very least, some input into how hands-on you are with each step.

From a more delivery and team management perspective, looking after your team of developers will involve knowing and understanding what they're doing. There are elements of the software development process that are central to many projects. So, a savvy Project Manager such as yourself will ensure that their project is not lumbered with the responsibility and cost of setting those elements up.

These costs include elements such as a central software repository or a shared test environment. This is the point where your managerial skills, technical creativity, and experience of development all come together.

In a perfect world, a senior developer can and will probably take care of this, which diminishes the role of the manager in at least this scenario, which is not necessarily a bad thing. However, in the real world, developers are often inundated by multiple projects and engrossed by what they're doing individually. The responsibility, and certainly the accountability, of setting up shared resources such as repositories and test environments will default to you, the manager.

Without your oversight across the project landscape and your team's workload, there is a distinct probability that individual developers and projects will work in isolation. This is not ideal as this would directly lead you to be in a situation where you're creating duplicate solutions and disparate ways of working that, in turn, will diverge increasingly over time. These elements will make the overall maintenance and management of all the software increasingly cumbersome and difficult.

The creative work ahead of you

As a manager, your creativity in finding the solution, while supporting everyone else with their issues, is the key to enabling your developers to write both more and better code.

From a pure people-management perspective, your creativity will probably be focused on the softer, human needs of your team. This could be something as simple as trying to persuade a team of entrenched developers to switch tools that will allow you to test your creativity to the limit!

Perhaps you bring in a product evangelist from the new tool's manufacturer to sell the idea, or even an existing customer to give the team a testimonial review. You may even find yourself creating a scenario where the new tool is evidently better placed to serve your team's needs.

In your role as a manager, you might even break down all the pros and cons of the change in a beautifully hand-drawn illustration, one that catches everyone's attention. While this may seem rather weird, I have seen it work in action before!

Motivating a group of hard-working people who are currently feeling bombarded by incomplete requirements and over-ambitious deadlines will need some magical creativity from you. Relieving an overworked developer of their support duties, or even helping them with their errands to give them more time and space to focus on coding is a simple yet effective way of doing this.

As a manager, you need to be creative about being creative. A successful manager is also a creative manager who can generate new ideas, but at the same time encourages their team to do the same. At the end of the day, idea generation is integral to the effective management of your team and the delivery of good software.

Figure 15.1: A successful manager understands that a good idea is bigger and more important than just the person who created it
Source: http://www.jetsetmag.com/exclusive/business/finding-the-magic-in-collective-creativity-what-we-all-can-learn-from-pixar/

The idea of being creative is about more than just yourself. So, it's vital that you use your listening skills to spot and capture a good idea, which can come from anyone and anywhere. A successful manager will always check in on their own ego to enable other people to flourish; this can include embracing their ideas over your own when it's the right thing to do.

Stop coding!

When you first take on the challenge of being a manager, you're likely to become so time-poor that coding will be an extremely low priority item on your to-do list. So, naturally, your coding time is likely to be next to zero, if not completely zero. If you expect and anticipate encountering this wall, then it will help, psychologically, to make your transition from a coder to a manager easier.

Expecting to keep up your coding and be an effective manager, certainly at the beginning, is ambitious at best, or foolish at worst.

One of the very first challenges you will face as a manager is figuring out how to divide your time: identifying which bush fires need to be put out first, and which you can let burn, let alone the fact that you'll need to be able to identify whether they are even genuine fires. In your new role, this translates to how to prioritize – or, most importantly, de-prioritize - your tasks. Remember the Eisenhower Matrix of important versus urgent tasks that we've referred to throughout this book.

Reid Hoffman, the co-founder of *PayPal* and *LinkedIn*, has famously told – you can read its context here: `https://mastersofscale.com/reid-hoffman-make-everyone-a-hero-part-two/` – of an extreme case where thousands of complaint emails and calls were deliberately left unanswered at *PayPal* during its early days. This wasn't because they weren't urgent or important, but because the team had identified even more important fires that needed to be tackled first.

The scale of your time-poorness as a new manager should not be underestimated. Of course, it's not absolutely the case everywhere, and there will be exceptions.

However, in every organization where I've joined as a manager, my first weeks have always been spent listening and learning, which was always done according to other people's timetables. Effectively, you're adapting and working to the organization's schedule, which leaves little time to dedicate for focused, largely solo activities such as coding.

Besides the time factor, whether or not you continue to code should be a conscious decision. As a manager, and with the agreement of your upper management, it's at your discretion how hands-on you need to be to achieve your goal of delivering the required software on time, on budget, and to the agreed quality to the company.

In some cases, it may be appropriate for you to stop coding altogether, for example, on a project that is staffed by a sufficient number of developers. Why? Because it simply wouldn't be an effective use of your time to do what is already being done efficiently by your team. Alternately, on a particularly large project, you may stop coding because there are clearly defined roles and you're only the Project Manager, and not a coder.

The customer's expectation has been clearly set, with you as the single point of contact between them and the company, and the project your working on requires extensive budgetary control and risk management. In this case, the customer may find it confusing if you are also delivering the code yourself, and in all likelihood, it may set up a situation where your role as a manager is questioned. This is especially true when the budget and risk-based issues begin to creep up.

All of this is different to those managers who don't come from a software development background and therefore can't code, even if they wanted to.

Figure 15.2: "Can't code, won't code"
Source: https://hackernoon.com/the-government-cant-code-dd0a7250f46c

When conscientiously deciding to stop coding or not, take the time, effort, priorities, roles, and customer expectations into consideration.

However, there are also other considerations and tools in your manager's toolkit to think about, in this case, the ideas of **delegation** and **accountability**. Both of these are measures that you can and should take to manage the coding process, without getting overly involved yourself. So, let's look at delegation and accountability right now.

Delegation

One of the key skills of an effective manager is delegation. Again, depending on the situation that you face, it may simply be more appropriate and effective for you, and the project as a whole, to delegate all of the coding to other party members.

For example, if the project is sufficiently staffed by several developers. In this case, and in agreement with the development team, you may choose to nominate a Lead Developer. This person can ensure that all the necessary design discussions happen, they are productive, standards are followed, and reviews and quality checks are fully completed. This also has the added benefit of developing the person in the Lead Developer position, as they will be motivated and stretched as a result of having the extra responsibility-you'll remember the discussions that we've had regarding the Accidental Manager.

Think carefully, then, when you are nominating who the Lead Developer will be. Understandably, it is often easier when making the decision to opt for the most experienced/senior developer on the team, especially if they have the organizational title of Lead Developer or Senior Developer, as they'll generally be considered a pair of "safe hands" when dealing with such occasions.

In my experience, this easier option of automatically making the *Senior Developer* the *Lead Developer* is not always the best one to take. By conveniently choosing the nominally most senior developer, you are reinforcing a preconceived notion that this person is always the best choice. This approach can be counterproductive if they are not the best-placed person, which can occur for any number of reasons.

By flipping the structure of "senior equals lead", you also create a different dynamic within the team. From my experience, a lot of senior developers prefer not being in the spotlight and the spokesperson for their team. Instead, they would rather work studiously in the background to support a more vocal member of the team.

Without stereotyping, there should be an honest assessment of the personalities involved before making your decision on who should take up this new role. A vital but often forgotten consideration in choosing the senior developer as your lead is that you are missing the opportunity to develop another team member's skillset and personality.

Developing other team members is a topic that we will discuss later on in this chapter. However, back to your role as a manager; the need to develop others is the duty of a manager who cares about the organization's long-term success.

Delegating in a considerate and controlled way

When you decide to stop coding and begin to delegate the tasks, it's important to action this in a considerate and controlled way within your organization and/or team.

This is something that can be applied to any type of delegation. However, in our case coding is a specialized discipline and a fundamental process that is central to your software deliverability. Therefore, it is especially important to consider some extra factors, tailored toward the developer community that you're trying to delegate to.

Given your own profile of being a new developer-cum-manager, it is quite rational for others, in your team and company, to think that you are still responsible for coding. Therefore, when they receive your request to code, they may be thinking: "Why are you not doing it?"

While this is a somewhat negative view, it has happened to me in the past, soon after changing roles within the same organization. This view has more to do with a lack of clarity in the roles given, and with your reputation as a developer rather than manager, as opposed to an age or seniority reversal, but these can also be a factor in some cases.

To that extent, establishing your role within your project or team is vital. Furthermore, you should only delegate responsibilities, not tasks or accountability. You'll remember the often-referenced RACI model – **Responsibility**, **Accountable**, **Consulted**, and **Informed** – and the difference between responsibility and accountability.

In terms of coding, I have learned through my experience that it's more effective and amenable for the recipient to delegate the responsibility of writing quality code, as opposed to the act of coding a particular set of functions or programs. This may seem like little or no difference at all to you, but to the recipient, it could be interpreted very differently.

Giving someone within your team a form of responsibility implies **trust**, and they have the scope to make decisions. They are empowered to do what they think is best for the project, team, and company. In this approach, coding in the best way they see fit, in accordance with the agreed standards, promotes creativity, rather than stifling it!

Rick Baker, the founder and CEO of *NeuStyle Software & Systems Corporation*, illustrates this effect beautifully in a graphic, which we can see in *Figure 15.3*. It highlights how delegation means releasing control and growing trust. On a very practical level, I also love his "80% Rule," which states:

"If someone else can do the task 80% as well as you can do it, then delegate."

-Rick Baker

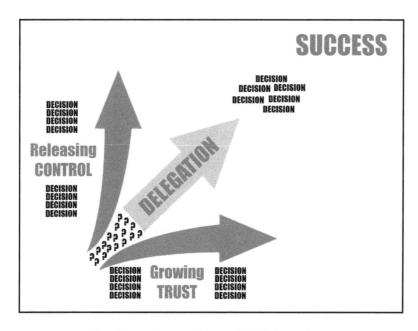

Figure 15.3: Delegation means releasing control, which leads to growing trust
Source: http://www.rickbaker.ca/post/2013/11/13/Delegation-The-Decision-Making-Engine-of-Business-.aspx

Giving someone a task can be demoralizing, especially for a person expecting more responsibility. When this is done badly, it's also a symptom of micromanagement, even if your task-level intervention is intended to support them.

The amount of scope and support you should give needs to be tailored according to the recipient. For example, less scope and more guidance may be appropriate for a less experienced or less confident developer, until they can make those decisions. In short, you are setting them up to succeed, not fail.

Prescriptively telling someone how to code something is a task within itself. This approach assumes that the person doesn't already know how to do it, which is not particularly productive for everyone, even if it is true. It's an instruction, not effective delegation. Your way is not necessarily the only or even the best way. Not to mention that by choosing this pathway, you've just effectively ruled any other way of coding the requirement.

Accountability

Giving someone the accountability of coding is likely to seem like an abdication of your responsibilities that have been given to the poor developers on the receiving end. Given the complexity of the coding phase of any software project, the developers are certainly going to be responsible for the coding but making them accountable for that could be a bridge too far.

I have never been on a successful project in which the leadership openly places the accountability of coding on either a developer or the RACI table. The manager, and if you're reading this, then it will likely be you, should be accountable for this key phase of the project and do everything necessary to support the developers who are responsible.

The *Centre for Management Development at Wichita State University*, USA, explains and illustrates the key difference between **delegation** and **abdication** in terms of the work that is required by the manager:

Figure 15.4: Delegation takes work, versus abdication that doesn't
Source: https://cmd.wichita.edu/hackett-in-management-delegation-vs-dumping/

The best visual metaphor for effective delegation is a relay runner handing over the baton to their teammate. The process is a safe and mutually agreed transaction, with an agreed upon set of boundaries. Although the runners are, strictly speaking, peers of one another, this should be how a manager also approaches this skill. Why? Because hierarchy is not a factor in effective delegation.

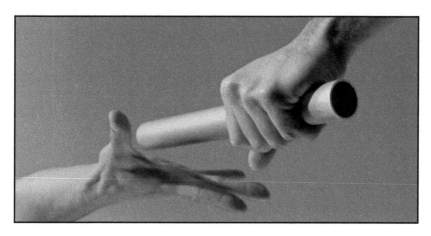

Figure 15.5: A relay runner handing over the baton is a great metaphor for effective delegation
Source: http://www.markgarretthayes.com/5-ways-you-can-delegate-work-more-effectively/

Even after the handover, you are still supporting them. You're also part of the same result and share the same failure or success, so you have a vested interest in making sure this delegation works well.

Actually keep coding!

As we've just read, there is undoubtedly a bunch of reasons to stop coding when you become a manager. However, there is also a bunch of reasons, with some being contrarian and counter to those to stop coding, to keep coding!

Some of these reasons are alternative views altogether. Since neither software development nor management are binary concepts with definitive rights and wrongs, both effective software development and management require the ability to work with ambiguity and, sometimes, conflicting points of views.

It's a balance between science and art, dealing with pure logic and real people. In short, there are no absolutes.

From a personal perspective, one of the main reasons to keep coding is simply to stay relevant. After all, you are still working in the business of software development. Knowing about the latest technologies, techniques, and practices of coding is really a necessity, not a luxury, especially in the field that we're talking about.

Keeping your coding skills up to date is valuable in many ways. For example, it means that you can still code and "do it yourself" if that is ever called for by a project. Although this is something I tend to discourage, there is value in being able to support your team directly by filling in any missing gaps.

Most managers I know cannot do this, simply because they may not come from a developer background or they didn't keep their skills up to date. Therefore, keeping up to date on coding is something that could be considered a special and more unique skill for you, which is a positive differentiator.

Furthermore, with this approach, you can offer more value in the deep, technical, and meaningful conversations with your developers simply because you share a similar reference point – or in this case, a literal language. You can understand them better, and; they can understand you better, and through that, you can support them better.

By having those conversations, you will earn the respect of your technical teams. As you know from being a developer, trying to explain something technical to a non-technical manager can be challenging!

Lastly, it helps you to maintain your reputation as a brilliant developer, or at least as someone who knows what they're talking about but now is a manager, too. Psychologically, this will also help you to avoid impostor syndrome, namely, feeling insecure about your own status.

Even though you're now officially a manager, the person who you are has not changed overnight. Your natural tendencies, curiosities, and preferences are still fundamentally the same as they were before.

You can still think like a developer

It's only natural that you will approach most situations still thinking like a developer. This can be a good thing because it means you have an urge and fondness for creating beautiful code and programs. If you don't satisfy this urge somehow, you are likely to become less happy in your job.

Many of the most brilliant developer-cum-managers I know still have their own geeky projects at home. It could be a *Raspberry Pi* project, or perhaps even teaching their children to code. They keep their inner geek spirit alive, and always have some retention of their roots!

In the unlikely case that you absolutely hated coding and couldn't wait to become a manager, you may want to close down your coding activities in a controlled way to avoid this classic comedic example:

```
8    // Dear programmer:
9    // When I wrote this code, only god and
10   // I knew how it worked.
11   // Now, only god knows it!
12   //
13   // Therefore, if you are trying to optimize
14   // this routine and it fails (most surely),
15   // please increase this counter as a
16   // warning for the next person:
17   //
18   // total_hours_wasted_here = 254
19   //
20
```

Figure 15.6: The immortal comments of a developer who has forgotten how their code works!
Source: https://www.reddit.com/r/ProgrammerHumor/comments/8pdebc/only_god_and_i_knew/

We've talked about the reasons for both continuing and stopping coding once you become a manager. One of the most obvious reasons to stop coding as a manager would simply be because it's no longer your role.

Delegation and being busy

In a world where roles are rather flexible and fluid, this translates to having a lot of other things to do, so you simply don't have time to code as well. Being in this position, which we often refer to as being time-poor, seems almost unavoidable in today's working environment. In fact, a successful TV producer and businessperson, Remy Blumenfeld, put it like this:

"There is no question that the currency of 'busyness' is at an all-time high."

There's a deeper point to Blumenfeld's statement, which is that many people are now commonly mistaking being busy with being successful or important. Often, people are masquerading as busy to confer status. So, if you accept that being time-poor is simply the norm for everyone, it is no longer a reason to stop coding as a result of being busy.

However, the real insight that Blumenfeld offers is the need to challenge this idea of busyness. Specifically, being busy does not necessarily represent any real demand for the busy person's work or even their success. In fact, they might be busy simply because they are inefficient or ineffective.

So, turning busy on its head, the measure of success is to be not busy, which is perhaps overly idealistic in most organizations. Yet, now that you are a manager, prioritizing, and more importantly, de-prioritizing, is vital. If you are efficient and effective, then you will have time to code. If coding that has been done by you is what is required by your project, then that is what you should prioritize and do. The key here is to be situationally aware and adapt accordingly. You should refrain from simplistically citing that you're a busy manager as a reason to stop coding.

One of the biggest reasons for a manager to stop coding is the need and opportunity to delegate to others. Delegation can be done out of necessity to maximize all your resources, which are primarily people, and to take the opportunity to develop others.

In general, delegation is no doubt necessary. One manager, however brilliant, cannot manage and deliver every aspect of a project on their own. That is why there are defined roles, which should be performed by the right number of people, which leads us to the idea that delegation requires effort.

Sometimes, it's more important to get it done, rather than go through with the delegation process. Likewise, some responsibilities are not significant enough to warrant delegating or need to be done urgently, even if they qualify for Baker's 80% rule and should firmly be performed by another person in the team.

For example, I was once involved in a high-severity incident, which was reported near the end of the working day. The support analyst had identified the issue to a particular functionality, which was new. It was clear that the root cause of the problem was a simple typo in one particular line of code.

As the manager of the team responsible for the app, I had the knowledge and access required to make a hotfix. Due to the severity of the impact, and the agreement with all of the incident stakeholders, I made the simple code change, which fixed a problem that would have significantly impacted the business.

Was this the correct procedure? No.

Was this effective in resolving the incident? Yes.

Of course, as part of the cleanup, this knowledge was shared with the team, and all the code was checked and then all the test environments were realigned. This example was far from an ideal situation. However, it illustrates the point that you should not delegate for the sake of delegating.

A real-life delegator – Anthony Casalena

In 2003, Anthony Casalena started the website development and hosting company giant *Squarespace*. For the next four years, Anthony was the only employee, developer, support guy, marketer, and business director. Fast-forward to 2018, and *Squarespace* was valued at 1.7 billion US Dollars, with 800 employees.

Not only did *Squarespace* go through phenomenal growth and development, clearly Casalena, as a person, had to and did. By his own admission, he had made many mistakes and simply didn't know how to manage anyone before because he had never professionally worked for another company.

Through these mistakes, he learned how to manage himself and others better. Now, in 2019, Casalena focuses on creating an organizational environment that is transparent and responsive to feedback. This was all done by Casalena developing into a more effective manager and leader of people by listening to their feedback and ideas, primarily so he could then see the upcoming opportunities and challenges, instead of being hit by them unexpectedly.

It was through gradually delegating his one-man show of responsibilities to others that he managed to find time to stay involved in the technical side, which was where his natural genius lay and was what he personally wanted to do most. After all, the early versions of *Squarespace* were his software and only he – and God only knows how – knew how it worked!

Despite a management power struggle at the top and the company's continued growth, he still managed to stay pivotally involved in the complete redevelopment of the *Squarespace* platform in version 6 – `https://www.squarespace.com/blog/introducing-squarespace-6` – which was the most fundamental and radical rewrite since its creation.

Through these challenges, it's clear that both *Squarespace* and Casalena went through significant growing pains. Yet, as the success of *Squarespace* and Casalena proves, this transitional journey can also be a deeply rewarding one.

Figure 15.7: Anthony Casalena, the founder and CEO of *Squarespace*
Source: https://medium.com/the-lindberg-interviews/interview-with-squarespace-ceo-anthony-casalena-bec11b6eaf4d

To drive this point home even further, Mark Zuckerberg, the CEO and founder of *Facebook Inc.*, is another example of a talented developer and engineer who clearly stays in touch with his techie side and knows how to delegate, too.

Zuckerberg is equally adept at talking about the technical intricacies of a new service, as well as the geopolitics and social issues within civil society, such as fake news, potential political interference, and cyberbullying, all the while heading up one of the biggest companies in the world.

Developing others

Doing something yourself versus coaching someone else to do it is quite different. Just because you can code and develop software, it doesn't mean you can coach and develop others to code.

Developing others involves a lot more than just helping them to code. Since coding is the main body of our work, it's obviously going to be important to help your team to code but remember that your goal as a manager now is to enable developers write more and better software.

As an ex-developer, you have the inside track on life as a developer, from starting out as a junior developer to being more experienced and confident, and maybe now being your company's most senior and go-to guru. This experience is extremely valuable to another developer, especially one who is just starting out.

Whatever your situation, you can simply share your experiences, good and bad. Others can learn from those good lessons. In turn, they can replicate and incorporate them into their own careers. They can also learn from the bad experiences and avoid the same pitfalls, which is often the key focus for most experiential teaching and learning.

However, the most compelling and valuable use of your experience is that you can feel and truly empathize with what your team is going through because you have been through all those trials and tribulations, hard knocks, and successes.

Relating to others

Relating to others is a great precursor to developing others. This is the difference between you simply getting someone past their current roadblock and helping them to overcome the underlying problem that might cause more roadblocks in the future.

For example, when a junior developer asks for your help because they cannot build the interface to meet the look and feel of the design brief, you may want to focus on the technical reasons why they are unable to achieve this. Could it be that they're using the wrong template, or not using the right tool for the job?

Now, a more insightful approach would be to relate to their experience and understand why they hit that roadblock in the first place. You may well have had a similar experience when, as a newbie yourself, you didn't know where to get the necessary resources, such as templates, from.

You may find that they were too afraid to bother busy teammates to ask. Therefore, a better way to help them is to share that you were also once too afraid to ask, but when you did, your teammates were more than happy to help.

Sharing real experiences that resonate is always better than getting information that is requested. That's the true wisdom in developing others. It's like a wise old grandfather teaching his grandson about baseball, something that the grandfather has loved all his life:

Figure 15.8: A grandfather talking to his grandson about baseball, sharing real experiences and wisdom in the process
Source: https://www.southernliving.com/home-garden/grandfather-names#grandfather-names-image

When you are sharing your own experiences, take care to ensure that it's both relevant and current to your situation. A common pitfall of received wisdom is that it's simply outdated. This is especially true when it comes to software development, which is constantly evolving. Just remember, don't teach something that's outdated!

Unfortunately, teaching something that's outdated is a common pitfall, with antiquated development standards blindly being taught and followed. Why? Simply because, "that's the way we've always done it."

One of the most valuable lessons you can give to a junior developer is to have an open and inquisitive mind in order to encourage them to understand and also constructively challenge the standing practices so that they evolve, and everyone benefits, including the overall company. This is a level of critical thinking that is useful in coding and life in general.

This is a great example of how you might go about modernizing a development team's standards and practices. When a new team member joins, it's the perfect opportunity to revisit and update these accepted norms from a fresh new perspective, so that everyone stays current and on the same page.

CLEANING UP THE MESS
: Modernizing Your Dev Team's Outdated Workflow

- Bohyun Kim, Associate Director for Library Applications and Knowledge Systems
- Brad Gerhart, Web Developer
- Zak Burke, Senior Web Developer
University of Maryland, Baltimore - Health Sciences and Human Services Library
ALA Annual Conference, Chicago, IL - June 25, 2017.

SOME COMMON PROBLEMS IN APPLICATION DEVELOPMENT

- What happens when you join a development team that went through many changes in personnel and team workflow over time?
- What will you do if there is no consistent and streamlined workflow for application development and deployment?
- As either a new manager or a member of such a development team, how would you go about modernizing the development process and creating a collaborative and efficient workflow?

OLD PRACTICE aka 'THE MESS'

- No collaborative workflow
- No separate environment for dev / testing / staging / prod
- No version control
- No standardized or automated deployment process

Figure 15.9: An excerpt from a presentation given at the 2017 ALA (American Library Association) Annual Conference, by Bohyun Kim, Brad Gerhart, Zak Burke
Source: https://www.slideshare.net/bohyunkim/cleaning-up-the-mess-modernizing-your-dev-teams-outdated-workflow

When you delegate effectively, you are also giving the recipient a chance to learn and develop. That's why the example of me – as a manager – personally implementing a code fix for a high-severity incident is far from ideal and is actually something I would normally discourage. By doing the code change myself, I effectively denied someone else the opportunity to go through that experience first-hand.

This point is like if you saw a senior doctor doing all the procedures in a teaching hospital, where part of the mission was for students to learn. If you are truly serious about developing others, it is vital to delegate effectively. The manager must trust the recipient to make the necessary decisions without micro-managing their coding. They also need to support their team by sharing insightful experiences over transactional information while still maintaining accountability for the outcome.

Creativity bursts

Okay, so we've established that when you transition to a manager, you can still be creative. Let's move on to look at the other side: what about your team's creativity?

If you have found a balance between personally coding or not coding, knowing when and what to delegate, and created a culture of actively developing others, how can you tell if it has increased your team's effectiveness and creativity?

Software development can be a convoluted process, which makes it not particularly conducive to creativity, which is especially true in the group context. Even in a truly *Agile* environment, it's difficult to create and sustain an innovative mindset and approach. It takes everyone to get it going and to even keep it going, but only one member or moment to stop it.

Anita Wooley, from *Carnegie Mellon University*, USA, studied software teams working in different places around the globe. Ultimately, she found that the most innovative and productive teams were "bursty," which unbelievably is a real psychology term!

When a group of people get really creative, they tend to communicate in bursts. This happens to the extent where they might constantly be interrupting each other. This spontaneous and direct way of communication is a sign that there is a meaningful conversation happening, where the goal is to create, invent, and generate something original. It's like a group scribbling together and drawing on top of each other's doodles without permission.

Figure 15.10: A team doodling in real-time collaboration
Source: http://techzulu.com/software-development-how-to-collaborate-as-a-team/

In a formal design or troubleshooting meeting, you'll typically see a linear format where each attendee is consulted and speaks in turn. Yet in a truly creative environment, you'll see a preference for chaos and randomness over order.

Now, while this is not appropriate for all occasions – I wouldn't advise it as the default meeting format! – it is particularly useful when the goal is to solve a specific problem as a group.

By far, the most common method of generating new ideas is through brainstorming. A Project Manager will typically assemble their team, start with a blank flipchart, formalize and present a problem statement, before then asking their team to brainstorm ideas to solve it.

Participants are encouraged to think out loud, with the emphasis on no critiquing or criticizing. However, this is often a painstaking exercise. While no critiquing is an important rule to ensure people feel safe to share their ideas, it can also mean no interruptions.

As a manager, you can create a better and more productive environment that spawns innovation by encouraging your team to be more "bursty" in everyday interactions. When used in moderation and consistency, it helps to build a cultural atmosphere where more ideas are created, and people are generally more open to trying new and wacky things.

So, the next time you come across a difficult problem, your team's thoughts will be more free-flowing, which leads to ideas, and which leads to a real plan of action, and at no point will you be stuck with a blank flipchart.

Looking towards your future

The mission of this book has been straightforward: looking towards your future as a manager. We started the journey with this simple question:

You're a confident and brilliant developer/coder/programmer/engineer/techie. So, why do you want to become a manager?

Knowing your "why" – your inner cause, reason, and driver – to make this career change into management is a critical and fundamental step to the process. Everyone's "why" is different, and you must figure out yours to satisfy yourself that what you're doing is the right choice for you.

To do this, you need to start by analyzing the risks and rewards. Remember to always keep in mind that "progress is not a straight line" and be prepared for setbacks and challenges you've never faced before.

Getting the manager job

You need to understand what types of manager jobs are out there and suitable for a developer such as yourself. Team Manager, Development Manager, or commonly Project Manager are all roles that you can consider as good starting points because your skills already overlap, with or without you knowing it.

Being an Accidental Manager is not necessarily a bad thing. On the contrary, it simply means you already have experience of doing many of the tasks that your future self will do officially. This may include having the privilege and responsibility of managing people. Yet in today's common matrix organizational structure, there are plenty of manager roles that don't include people management.

Getting started

Once you are sure of your "why", you need to know "how" you become a successful software manager. As you make the first steps in your *Developer-to-Manager* transition, there are six key skills you need to learn.

These six skills support the shift in your focus from writing the brilliant code yourself, to enabling your team to write more code, to write better code, and ultimately to deliver a piece of great software for the customer.

These six skills are:

1. Flexibility and adaptability
2. Communication, communication, communication
3. Team leadership
4. Stakeholder management
5. Negotiation
6. The methodology of choice (by the team)

Understanding the foundations of the most commonly practiced software development, project management, and service management methodologies is also essential. You'll remember that we have constantly referred to these five methods as the most popular and accessible methodologies:

- *Agile*
- *Scrum*
- *Waterfall model*
- *PRINCE2*
- *Information Technology Infrastructure Library (ITIL)*

You must be able to support your team to choose and adopt one or a combination of these methodologies. Furthermore, you need to be able to represent them to your stakeholders.

A manager's toolkit

When you start your new manager role, remember to meet your team – your biggest asset and responsibility – on the first day. Be sure to introduce yourself to your stakeholders within the first week and plan to start owning your own schedule.

If your role is in operations or services, then it's important to be mindful of the ITIL framework and its key terms for software teams: *events*, *incidents*, and *problems*. Remember the wide-ranging roles of the Application Management function, and how that compliments the DevOps mindset and approach.

If your role is in projects or delivery, then prepare a suitably flexible but consistently applied weekly template, which should include daily huddles with your team. Important power meetings should occur at the beginning of the week, preferably in the morning, with a focus on people and delivery in the middle of the week. You should aim to round the week off with meaningful reviews and regular reports, as well as some time to innovate and possibly learn.

Managing your team means being available and present to support them as individuals and as a team. So, you must purposefully free up your time and make yourself approachable by actively seeking and providing what they really need.

To manage your boss effectively, you must understand their preferred communication style, mutually set expectations, and understand the vision for their team of teams.

Understanding who your customers are and what they need is the key to managing them successfully. End users want utility and functional value – something to make their work easier and their lives better, while buyers want financial value and return on investment.

Extracting information – information gathering

People's time-poorness and the abundance of information mean that it's never been more important to know how to ask the right questions. You need to make sure your interaction with your team, boss, stakeholders, customers, and users are appropriate, pertinent, and priority-based.

A productive way of eliciting information from users is to first classify them into five types, then ask each type the questions most relevant to them, including:

- Casual users
- Business users
- Power users
- Management users
- Non-users

You can borrow a simple but effective technique from *Six Sigma* and ask "The Five Whys" to systematically analyze problems right down to their root cause. Remember that you can use a fishbone diagram to do this.

With the shift in focus and responsibilities, a manager's meetings are naturally different from those of a developer. An off-duty chat is an important way to connect with your team informally and manage their motivations and gripes.

Meet and greets can be productive and fun if you approach them with a target outcome in mind and actively listen more than you talk. The sales meeting will also be more effective if you use key account management principles to plan, deliver, and evaluate. Releasing your inner Alec Baldwin to hard sell is completely optional!

The requirements workshop is a key meeting for all software projects. It requires know-how and preparation, and lots of biscuits! Here, you should apply user stories and personas to extract and capture valuable information from multiple perspectives. Then organize the requirements in a prioritized fashion that acknowledges your individual and your team's innate biases, such as hyperbolic discounting.

The product demo is all about wowing your audience. Basic preparation is essential. As is creating a sense of occasion that equates to a good dinner main course that leaves you wanting the dessert. Be specific and keep to three or fewer specific points and stories, because less is more in this context. Most importantly, always allow lots of time for interactive questions!

Defining solutions

Storyboards are a simple and clear way to design software, especially a piece of UX-critical software such as a mobile app. User cases are more formal with actors, relationships, and interactions, while wireframes are great for software with a **Graphical User Interface (GUI)**, which is pretty much used in everything these days!

Mockups require a little more work than wireframes, simply because it include a visual render of how a GUI might look. A prototype is a little bit more advanced, with a limited set of simulated actions available to demonstrate how the full software will behave.

When it comes to designing software and stuff in general, the plain old, but mighty, whiteboard is an often undervalued and overlooked tool. Spend time to practice, experiment, and persevere to become a whiteboard rock star.

All designs and solutions need validation to ensure that they are the right product. Technical and business validation are both important and should be conducted following the organization's standards and processes, as set out by the project management office.

Design thinking and insisting on a full consensus is not always the best way to achieve progress. However, they can be great in the appropriate situation and circumstance. A non-linear process, such as design thinking, is not naturally suited to large-scale projects that tend to follow the *Waterfall model*.

The key is a five-phased approach:

- **Empathize** with your users
- **Define** your users' needs, their problems, and your insights
- **Ideate** by challenging assumptions and innovating new ideas and solutions
- **Prototype** to start creating solutions
- **Test** solutions

The Finnish Universal Basic Income experiment is a great example of design thinking's core mindset, which is that the requirements are not perfect, nor are they fully known. Therefore, constant feedback and adaption are required to deliver a fit solution in a profoundly iterative way.

Similarly, building consensus in the real world is not necessarily about getting everyone to completely agree. Instead, in the spirit of progress and pragmatic compromise, it's about coming to a view that everyone agrees they can live with and support.

Writing a business case is not rocket science; just be really clear to the stakeholders that you understand their problems and how you will solve them. So, maybe it is rather difficult!

Following *PRINCE2*'s seven principles, seven themes, and seven processes, the business case document itself should be a clear and straightforward document that includes the following sections:

- Executive summary
- Introduction
- Analysis
- Options and recommendations
- Key risks and assumptions
- Conclusion

Now, remember to save your finest business case as a template for future use and present it with confidence to your stakeholders!

Keeping the build focused

To keep your team and build focused, you must understand the practical applications of the various methodologies that are used to develop and deliver your software: *PRINCE2, Waterfall, V-Model, Agile,* and *Scrum,* as well as the different world of *ITIL service management.*

Be flexible. Understand and apply the key ideas and practical actions in each methodology when needed and as appropriate. Make sure your team is on board is and part of the methodology selection process.

The **Project Management Office** (**PMO**) is an inescapable stakeholder to satisfy. Yet, they can also be your best friend. You need to make sure you and your team understand how the PMO works and what is required to progress your project, which may well be through a stage-gate process:

- Stage 0: Discovery and ideation
- Stage 1: Scoping
- Stage 2: Build a business case
- Stage 3: Development
- Stage 4: Testing and validation
- Stage 5: Product launch

The world – or more precisely, your stakeholders – does not need another boring project status update. So, use a vivid mix of visuals, KPIs, and colorful narrative, instead of simple, dull, and text-only content-poor emails that can get easily lost among all the other project status updates.

If in doubt, keep things simple. If you can't understand it, then your stakeholders won't either. So, keep things simple and clear, wherever possible. This will help you keep your stakeholders engaged and stay engaged because you're making it easy for them to do so.

As the saying goes: "The definition of insanity is doing the same thing over and over again and expecting a different result."

So, whenever a mistake is made – and there will be many mistakes – you must learn from them. A simple Lessons Log can capture your project's lessons. A review of other projects' Lessons Logs can help you spot and avoid a pattern of common mistakes in your organization!

Launching your product

Software development is a challenging and convoluted process, with many stakeholders and considerations. So, it isn't easy to always be building, never mind shipping a product. It's necessary to recognize and address your techie dev team's, and perhaps even your own, natural tendencies to tweak and tinker the product until it's "perfect" and ready to be launched.

Creating a delivery-focused team ethos, shielding them from scope creep, and maintaining momentum are some of the practical ways to launch your product successfully. Moreover, when times get tough, you need to muck in to support your team and overcome real roadblocks!

You should know the difference between *continuous integration, continuous delivery*, and *continuous deployment*. Implement one, or a combination of them, that best suits your team and project. Understand the difference yourself and explain to your team the importance of time to market. This will all help your team move towards the mindset and practice of always shipping.

User acceptance testing (UAT) is a vital activity in almost all software projects. Your job is to facilitate this activity to make it as smooth and as meaningful as possible. It's not just another tick-in-the-box exercise. Encouraging healthy developer-tester collaboration and a mutual learning mindset can dramatically help progress and complete this critical activity.

The UAT report is a key document to obtain official UAT exit and customer sign-off. Use the model Test Summary Report template to create an interesting and informative report for your stakeholders. Be open and honest, even if the message is not particularly positive.

Whether you realize it, and even whether you like it or not, selling is part of your job as a manager. This could be selling an idea to your own team to influence or motivate them or really selling a product or service to a customer. Adopt a problem-led approach. Understand the customer's real problems before pushing your product as a solution to avoid the awkward and inappropriate hard sell.

Take time and care to educate and train your users. Together with how your team deals with the inevitable support request, you can make your users feel valued and recover from any lost satisfaction, which should be in the forefront of the minds of your customer service-oriented team.

Just the term "project post-mortem" implies a negative connotation. Refrain from playing the destructive blame game. Focus on closing your project formally and constructively by producing and presenting a meaningful End Project Report, which is useful for colleagues and valuable to the organization in the long term.

If you've shipped your software, but no one cares, take a long, hard look at your software product and tackle any shortcomings holistically from the following angles:

- Marketing
- Technical
- Practical

What comes next on your journey?

We've now covered everything I can give you for the journey ahead. The future of organizational management in the 21st century is vastly different from the centuries that came before, of course. Expect to change and adapt. With the modern pressures of time and heightened expectations, some of the challenges you'll face along your journey may be difficult to achieve. So, be kind to yourself, and remember in your days ahead that it's a complete myth that the manager has all the answers.

In your journey ahead, please stay mindful of the different traits, motivations, strengths, and weaknesses of "thinkers" and "doers". And don't forget that leadership and management are not the same thing:

- Large corporations are most frequently over-managed and under-led.
- Small start-ups are most frequently under-managed, especially while they're still in their infancy and bootstrapping days.

To manage others effectively, you know that you must start by managing yourself in any given situation. Start by understanding your role in the team, not as the star player, but as the coach who takes accountability for the losses and praises the team for the wins. To serve your team, you must be present in body and mind. Your team is not getting the best of you if you're busy thinking about something or someone else.

Admitting mistakes and the limits of knowledge is a key skill in a leader. This allows others to share what they know instead. Build trust through honest thoughts and actions. If you don't know something, say you don't know. Don't try to bluff your way out because you'll in all likeliness get caught. No-one truly follows a leader they don't trust, except to see what stupid thing they'll do next. Nudging and habits are powerful ways to positively influence your team.

When you become increasingly managerial, you may be worried about losing your ability to be creative and even code. The truth is creativity is always needed, and yours will be tested, albeit in a different way to before.

There are legitimate reasons for stop coding, but there are also legitimate reasons to keep coding, too! It's yet another aspect of your life as a manager to be flexible and adaptable. Developing others is one of your key responsibilities as a manager. This means sharing your real experiences, whether they are good or bad.

There are no limits to your own unique *Developer-to-Manager* journey. This undefined and convoluted process is every bit as challenging and interesting as the similarly complex software development project, the same one that you now have the responsibility of delivering.

Stay flexible and adaptable. Treat your team, your peers, your boss, your users, and your stakeholders as you'd like to be treated. Learn and enjoy every step of the way to become a *successful software manager*.

Other Books You May Enjoy

If you enjoyed this book, you may be interested in these other books by Packt:

Understanding Software
Max Kanat-Alexander

ISBN: 978-1-78862-881-5

- See how to bring simplicity and success to your programming world
- Clues to complexity - and how to build excellent software
- Simplicity and software design
- Principles for programmers
- The secrets of rockstar programmers
- Max's views and interpretation of the Software industry
- Why Programmers suck and how to suck less as a programmer
- Software design in two sentences
- What is a bug? Go deep into debugging

Skill Up: A Software Developer's Guide to Life and Career
Jordan Hudgens

ISBN: 978-1-78728-703-7

- Improve your soft skills to become a better and happier coder
- Learn to be a better developer
- Grow your freelance development business
- Improve your development career
- Learn the best approaches to breaking down complex topics
- Have the confidence to charge what you're worth as a freelancer
- Succeed in developer job interviews

101 UX Principles
Will Grant

ISBN: 978-1-78883-736-1

- Use typography well to ensure that text is readable
- Design controls to streamline interaction
- Create navigation which makes content make sense
- Convey information with consistent iconography
- Manage user input effectively
- Represent progress to the user
- Provide interfaces that work for users with visual or motion impairments
- Understand and respond to user expectations

Leave a review - let other readers know what you think

Please share your thoughts on this book with others by leaving a review on the site that you bought it from. If you purchased the book from Amazon, please leave us an honest review on this book's Amazon page. This is vital so that other potential readers can see and use your unbiased opinion to make purchasing decisions, we can understand what our customers think about our products, and our authors can see your feedback on the title that they have worked with Packt to create. It will only take a few minutes of your time, but is valuable to other potential customers, our authors, and Packt. Thank you!

Index